Food Preparation and Cookery

AN INTERNATIONAL APPROACH

Clive F Finch

Assisted by
Harry L Cracknell

Addison Wesley Longman

Addison Wesley Longman Limited
Edinburgh Gate
Harlow, Essex CM20 2JE, England
and Associated Companies throughout the world.

First published 1998

ISBN 0 582 30937-9

British Library Cataloguing-in-Publication Data

A catalogue record for this book is
available from the British Library

Set by 35 in 9^1/$_2$/12pt Concorde
Produced through Longman Malaysia, VVP

Contents

Foreword

Today's restaurant menus mix ingredients and styles from continents and countries across the globe. Long gone are the days when all menus and dishes were originated from the styles of French, British and Italian cooking. This text recognises this development and provides a comprehensive reference, including recipes from around the world.

Who better to produce a text such as this than Clive Finch and Harry Cracknell, individually much respected authors of professional cookery books which have been essential references for students of professional cookery. Having used their books in teaching professional cookery, I have come to trust their recipes, which are particularly accurate.

Clive Finch's and Harry Cracknell's lifetime experience of working in professional cookery is reflected in the quality and authoritative approach of this book.

I have no hesitation in recommending this book to students, for professionals as reference, or indeed as a cookery book suitable for the shelves of keen amateurs.

Martyn J Wagner MSc, MHCIMA, DMS, Cert. Ed.
Head of School, Hotel and Catering and Tourism Studies
Westminster College

Authors' Biographies

Clive F Finch M.Phil, MHCIMA, DMS, Cert Ed, Dip WTC, CGLI Adv, ACF

Clive Finch worked for many years as a chef in hotels, restaurants and clubs before entering catering education, where he taught preliminary, intermediate and advanced level craft courses and supervisory and management studies. Formerly Head of School of Hotel, Catering and Tourism Management at Middlesex Polytechnic (now Middlesex University), he is Visiting Professor at the School of Hospitality Management, Thames Valley University. His experience in the fields of catering, catering education, food preparation, recipe formulation, product labelling, consultancy and research is considerable. He is a member of the Hotel and Catering International Management Association and of the Association Culinaire Française de Grande Bretagne. He was author of *Food Preparation*, first published in 1984, which became a standard text for catering students at all levels. He is also co-author of *International Gastronomy* (1997) which provides a unique one-stop reference source to 22 major cuisines of 45 different countries.

Harry L Cracknel FHCIMA, ACF

Harry Cracknell studied at Westminster College and subsequently worked in some of the foremost kitchens in London and abroad, including The Dorchester, the Park Lane Hotel and the Colony Club. As a manager he worked at hotels in Padua and Venice, at the Royal Palace Hotel Kensington and the Hôtel de Paris in Paris. After war service in the Middle East he spent six more years in the kitchens of the Savoy, subsequently being appointed Catering Manager of two London hospitals and also at de Havilland Aircraft factory. Moving from industry to education, Harry Cracknell was appointed Lecturer at Battersea Polytechnic, followed by his appointment as Head of Department at Thanet Technical College, then at the Oxford College of Technology and Food Production Manager at Dorset Institute of Higher Education, now Bournemouth University.

Harry Cracknell is a member of the Association Culinaire Française de Grande Bretagne, was an Examiner for City and Guilds of London Institute and is a Fellow of the Hotel and Catering International Management Association. He is co-author with Clive Finch of *International Gastronomy* (1997).

Preface

This book was first published in 1984 under the title of *Food Preparation*. Since that time there have been major advances in the world of catering and the purpose of this book and its change of title is to take into account the developments which have taken place.

The original book stood the test of its fourteen years' existence and has now been expanded to take account of the intense globalisation of the hospitality industry which has broadened national boundaries. This and other factors such as the unrestricted range of commodities means that the traditional Franco/Italian/Britannic repertoire has had to be expanded and enhanced by dishes from many other cuisines. This expansion is also in response to customers' requirements and their quest for new eating experiences to add to their knowledge of gastronomy.

The aim of this book is to assist all who work in the professional kitchen at all levels from young apprentices to master chefs. It is innovative in its scope but easy to follow. It will appeal to food and beverage managers in the commercial sector and to catering managers in the cost sector, who will find that its contents will have a stimulating effect on their staff. This, in turn, will bring about greater customer satisfaction, which is what the hospitality industry is all about.

To Esther my wife for her encouragement and secretarial support.

Clive Finch

Introduction

The text has been designed for students of catering at supervisory and management levels, GNVQ/GSVQ Level 3, Modern Apprenticeships, City and Guilds (International) Diploma and Advanced Diploma in Culinary Arts, Higher National Diploma (HND), Ordinary and Honours Degree catering courses, Hotel and Catering International Management Association (HCIMA) Certificate and Diploma, and postgraduate Diploma in Management Studies (DMS) hotel and catering courses. The text will also be of particular interest to chefs and people employed in the management of catering operations in both the commercial and cost sectors of the industry.

In 1984, the year this book was first published, it was the forerunner of cookery manuals which grouped recipes around methods of cooking while keeping the chapters in the logical sequence of courses. It was also the first to explain dish assessment and how to rescue items that go wrong during cooking; they are included in this book in the form of examples. All recipes are for 10 portions unless otherwise stated. All the measurements are in metric form, readers who work in Imperial measures will find helpful conversation tables at the end of the book. When spoons are used for small amounts these are level spoonfuls. Recipes written in concise form include weights but as every experienced chef knows, the weights and cooking times can only be approximate because of variations in the function of cooking equipment, customers' tastes and food costs. Standardised recipes ensure that there is no deviation from the formula and that the end-product always attains the required standard.

The scope of this book encompasses several cuisines from around the world, with recipes which give an insight into the eating habits of these nations and, particularly, the wide range of seasonings used. The ever-increasing number of people who are turning to vegetarianism will find a wide range of dishes.

There is no cross-referencing in the main text of this book; if the name of an accompaniment or sauce is given in the recipe and is not included in the instructions, it may be reached in the appropriate chapter or section, via the Index. Capitalisation of a dish, accompaniment or sauce indicates that the recipe is to be found in this book. The culinary glossary covers herbs, nuts, oils, salad greans, seeds, spices, definitions of ingredients and terms used and descriptions of equipment and utensils.

Chefs have to keep up with trends in eating habits, they no longer exclusively produce the time-honoured classics and are keen to express themselves in new dishes and adaptations of ingredients to new uses and presentations. There are no obvious restrictions to these innovative ideas as they move through the culinary world, blending many different concepts. This is exemplified by today's menu titles which have become dish descriptions that give customers a clearer idea of what they can expect than did the old-fashioned approach of reliance upon French terms and names.

It is the authors' hope that the body of knowledge and experience as contained in this book will be of help to those who aspire to a rewarding and fulfilling career in this important industry.

CHAPTER 1 Appetisers

Hors-d'oeuvre

The term appetiser or hors-d'oeuvre generally refers to items served as the opening course of a meal. Hors-d'oeuvre can be made from items of cooked foods such as meat, vegetables and fish. They can also be produced from convenience products in canned, pickled, salted or frozen form. Many fresh items are available in ready-prepared form, e.g. prepacked, washed lettuce, and mayonnaise and vinaigrette-based products.

This does not imply that principles and practices associated with traditionally made products no longer apply. In fact, some of those highlighted in this chapter may be used to augment or complement both freshly made and convenience items.

By contrasting flavours, textures, seasonings and colours and by utilising the convenience product as a base, an almost unlimited range of items may be prepared. Integrating freshly made products with convenience ones and exercising the imagination in the decoration and presentation of completed dishes will ensure a never-ending variety of hors-d'oeuvre which both attract the eye and stimulate the appetite.

HORS-D'OEUVRE VARIÉS

Under this heading, which means a selection of as many as twelve different dishes, creativity and artistic flair should be practised. It must be emphasised, however, that the preparation of hors-d'oeuvre requires understanding of how the selection of dishes all blend together and how their flavour, texture and appearance complement each other. The main principles to be observed are:

- Visual appearance: They must be presented attractively with a range of colours. Each kind is served in a separate ravier (hors-d'oeuvre dish), and may be lightly decorated.
- Texture: There should be a range of textures from soft and tender to firm and crunchy.
- Flavour and seasoning: Each dish in the selection must be well seasoned with salt and pepper and skilfully blended with numerous and varied natural flavours so as to stimulate customer's appetites.

There are five main kinds of assorted hors d'oeuvre:

1. Vegetable and other salads made with *mayonnaise*
2. Vegetables and fish prepared *à la Portugaise*
3. Vegetables and fish prepared *à la Grecque*
4. Vegetables and salads seasoned with a *vinaigrette dressing*
5. Vegetables and fruits with *acidulated cream.*

From these preparations a large number of other dishes may be derived and in addition there are several purchased items which require only a simple garnish as presentation. These include anchovies, rollmops, sardines, tunny fish, gherkins, sweetcorn and olives.

Recipes for mayonnaise and dressings are given later in this chapter.

Hors-d'oeuvre with a mayonnaise dressing

The flavour of this variety of hors-d'oeuvre is influenced by the kind of oil and vinegar used in making the mayonnaise, e.g. olive oil or corn oil, malt or white wine vinegar.

Coleslaw Salad

    250 g shredded white cabbage
     75 g julienne of carrots
     30 g chopped onion
     50 ml French dressing
    200 ml mayonnaise

1. Mix the vegetables with the French dressing.
2. Combine with the mayonnaise and season to taste.

Celeriac Salad (Salade de Céleri-rave)

    250 g celeriac
       1 juice of lemon
    200 ml mayonnaise

1. Peel and cut the celeriac into very fine julienne. Place immediately into cold water to which lemon juice has been added to prevent discolouration.
2. Drain well, season with salt and pepper and combine with the mayonnaise.

Egg Mayonnaise (Mayonnaise d'Oeufs)

5 hard-boiled eggs	5 stoned olives
¼ finely shredded lettuce	5 cucumber slices
200 ml mayonnaise	2 tomatoes, either sliced or in
5 fillets of anchovy	wedges
10 capers	

1. Cut the eggs into halves or quarters lengthways and place round side upwards on the shredded lettuce.
2. Coat with the mayonnaise and decorate with thin strips of anchovies trellis-fashion, capers, olives, cucumber and tomato.

Fish Mayonnaise (Mayonnaise de Poisson)

Prepare in the same way as Egg Mayonnaise, using flaked, cooked fish. The name of the fish used may be included in the title of the hors d'oeuvre.

Potato Salad (Salade de Pommes de Terre)

600 g small potatoes
15 g chopped onion or chives
chopped parsley
25 ml French dressing
200 ml mayonnaise

1. Boil the potatoes in their skins, cool, then peel.
2. Dice or cut into 1 cm slices.
3. Add the onion, parsley and French dressing to the potatoes while still warm and mix in gently.
4. Season to taste, then mix in the mayonnaise.

Vegetable Salad – Russian Salad (Salade Russe)

150 g carrots⎫
150 g turnips⎭ cut into 5 mm dice
150 g peas

150 g French beans, cut into
small diamonds
200 ml mayonnaise

1. Cook the vegetables separately in boiling salted water, keeping them fairly firm.
2. Drain immediately and allow to cool.
3. Season and mix in the mayonnaise.
4. Dress in a ravier.

Waldorf Salad (Salade Waldorf)

200 g prepared celery
200 g eating apples
75 g walnuts
250 ml mayonnaise

1. Cut the celery and apples into julienne and chop the walnuts.
2. Mix together, season to taste and bind with the mayonnaise.
3. Serve either in the hollowed-out apples or on lettuce leaves.

Vegetables or fish Portuguese style

This term means that the vegetables or fish are cooked in a liquid flavoured with tomato, garlic and herbs.

The following vegetables and fish are suitable for this hors d'oeuvre: artichoke bottoms cut into quarters; button onions; celery cut into 3 cm × 1 cm batons; fennel trimmed and cut into quarters; leeks – the white part only, cut into sections after cooking; button mushrooms; cod, herring, mackerel and red mullet, cut into sections on or off the bone.

Cauliflower Portuguese Style (Chou-fleur Portugais)

250 g cauliflower florets, blanched	300 ml dry white wine
100 g finely chopped onion	10 g tomato purée
100 ml olive oil	1 small sprig thyme
1 clove crushed garlic	1 bayleaf
250 g diced, peeled and	chopped parsley
depipped tomatoes	5 g salt

1. Lightly cook the onion and garlic in the oil without colouring them.
2. Add the tomato, wine, tomato purée, thyme, bayleaf and seasoning. Simmer gently for a few minutes.
3. Add the florets and cook gently on top of the stove or in an oven at 120°C, covered with buttered greaseproof paper and a lid, keeping them firm.
4. When cooked, allow to cool and serve barely covered with some of the cooking liquid. Place the bayleaf and thyme on top and sprinkle with chopped parsley.

Note
The prepared vegetables should be blanched for 5 minutes and immediately refreshed in cold water before being cooked in the prepared liquid.

Vegetables or fish Greek style

The term indicates vegetables or fish cooked gently in a prepared court-bouillon flavoured with lemon juice.

Cauliflower Greek Style (Chou-fleur à la Grecque)

250 g cauliflower florets, blanched	1 small sprig thyme
50 g fennel, cut into batons	1 bayleaf
500 ml water	10 coriander seeds
100 ml olive oil	10 peppercorns
1 juice of lemon	5 g salt

1. Simmer the water in a shallow pan with the olive oil, lemon juice, herbs, coriander seeds, peppercorns and salt for 5 minutes.
2. Add the cauliflower florets and batons of fennel and simmer gently until cooked.
3. Allow to cool completely in the liquid before serving.
4. Serve barely covered with some of the cooking liquid, including its ingredients.

Note
The vegetables and fish listed under Portuguese style may be cooked by this method.

Hors d'oeuvre with vinaigrette dressing

The dressings mentioned here can be found later in the chapter.

Beetroot Salad (Salade de Betteraves)

Cut cooked beetroot into batons 2 cm × 0.5 cm. Season with salt and pepper and moisten with French dressing. Garnish with onion rings and chopped parsley.

Beef Salad (Salade de Boeuf)

Cut cooked beef into small dice and add to diced cooked potato and tomato and chopped onion. Season with salt and pepper and moisten with French dressing. Serve sprinkled with chopped parsley.

Cauliflower and Anchovy Salad (Insalata di Rinforzo)

Combine boiled and refreshed cauliflower florets, chopped anchovy fillets, stoned black olives, capers, quartered hard-boiled eggs and chopped fresh mixed herbs, with lemon dressing.

Cauliflower Salad (Salade de Chou-fleur)

Season cooked florets of cauliflower with salt and pepper and moisten with French dressing. Serve sprinkled with chopped parsley.

Cucumber and Yogurt Salad

Place 10 portions of sliced cucumber in a colander, season with salt and retain for 1 hour, then press out the liquid. Combine the cucumber with a dressing made of 600 ml yogurt, 75 ml cream, 1 tsp lemon juice, 2 tsp chopped mint and 2 chopped cloves of garlic.

Mushroom Salad (Insalata di Funghi)

Place sliced raw mushrooms in raviers and moisten with a dressing made of one-third lemon juice and two-thirds olive oil. Sprinkle with chopped cooked egg yolk, parsley, anchovy fillets and clove of garlic.

Niçoise Salade (Salade Niçoise)

Cut cooked French beans into diamond shapes, add quarters of peeled tomatoes and diced potato, season with salt and pepper and mix with French dressing. Dress in a ravier and decorate with strips of anchovy fillets, capers and stoned black olives.

Orange Salad (Insalata di Arance)

Place segments of blood oranges in raviers, sprinkle with chopped shallots and grated and blanched zest of orange. Moisten with olive oil.

Rice Salad (Salade de Riz)

Mix boiled or pilaff rice with diced, peeled and depipped tomatoes and cooked peas. Season with salt and pepper and a little chopped garlic and moisten with French dressing. Dress dome-shaped in a ravier.

Tomato Salad (Salade de Tomates)

Dress peeled sliced tomatoes neatly in a ravier and season with salt and pepper. Sprinkle with finely chopped onion, lightly mask with French dressing and sprinkle with chopped parsley.

Potato Salad (Kartoffelsalat)   GERMANY

Three-quarters steam jacket potatoes, peel and grate, then moisten with hot beef stock. Mix in chopped onion, wine vinegar, olive oil, chopped fresh mixed herbs and seasoning and allow to marinate for 2 hours before serving.

Red Cabbage Salad (Rotkrautsalat)   GERMANY

Combine two-thirds of shredded red cabbage with one-third julienne of dessert apples, a little sliced onion, a few caraway seeds and a little sugar and moisten with French dressing.

Hors-d'oeuvre made with acidulated cream dressing

An acidulated cream dressing may be used on items such as canned sardines, shredded celeriac or peeled and sliced cucumber as well as on a number of salads, as follows.

Florida Salad

Bind segments of grapefruit, diced pineapple, sliced apple and diced celery with acidulated cream. Dress in a ravier slightly dome-shaped and surround with small leaves of lettuce.

Salade Japonaise

Bind diced, peeled and depipped tomatoes, diced pineapple and orange segments with acidulated cream. Dress in a ravier slightly dome-shaped and surround with small leaves of lettuce.

Salade Mimosa

Bind orange segments, depipped grapes and slices of banana with acidulated cream. Dress in a ravier slightly dome-shaped and surround with small leaves of lettuce.

SINGLE HORS-D'OEUVRE

As this title implies, each dish in this category may be looked on as complete in itself. Generally, these items are individually priced à la carte dishes. In terms of appearance, flavour and texture, single hors-d'oeuvre should be high-quality items. Although some may be cooked, in many instances very little preparation is involved because most of the work will have been carried out by the manufacturer, e.g. smoked salmon and pâté de foie gras, while others may be served in their natural state with only a simple decoration, e.g. melon portions and avocado pears. There are many other single hors-d'oeuvre, such as seafood cocktail, Parma ham and dressed crab, which make this course of the menu interesting and varied.

Asparagus Tips with French Dressing (Pointes d'Asperges Vinaigrette)

Prepare and plain boil the asparagus, refresh and drain. Arrange on a folded napkin and decorate with sprigs of parsley. Serve French dressing separately.

Avocado Pear with French Dressing (Avocat Vinaigrette)

Allow half a pear per portion, according to size. Cut the pear lengthways around the middle and towards the centre stone. Divide in two halves and discard the stone. Serve on lettuce leaves with a slice of peeled cucumber, a quarter of tomato and a quarter of lemon, accompanied with French dressing.

Avocado Pear with Prawns (Avocat aux Crevettes)

Cut the pear in half as per the previous recipe, fill with prawns mixed with Cocktail Sauce and arrange on lettuce leaves with sliced cucumber, a quarter of tomato and a quarter of lemon.

Notes
1. Do not prepare avocados too far in advance as the flesh may turn blackish once they are cut into two.
2. Avocado pears may also be served in avocado pear dishes.

Charentais Melon with Port Wine

Using a small melon for a single portion cut a slice from the top to form a lid and remove the seeds. Add a quantity of port, replace the lid, chill and serve.

A large melon can be used for two portions. Cut into half around the middle, remove the seeds, add port, chill and serve.

Honeydew Melon

Cut the melon in half lengthways, remove the seeds, then cut into boat-shaped portions. Serve chilled on crushed ice decorated with sliced orange and cocktail cherries. Ground ginger and castor sugar may be served as accompaniments.

Cold Chicken Mousse (Mousse de Volaille Froid)

500 g cooked chicken	300 ml lightly whipped cream
200 ml chicken velouté	salt, pepper and nutmeg
200 ml melted aspic jelly	100 ml melted aspic jelly

1. Mince the chicken finely and pass through a sieve.
2. Place in a basin and add the cool velouté and melted aspic jelly, stirring with a wooden spatule.
3. Place on ice and continue to stir until the mixture shows signs of beginning to set. Fold in the cream and season to taste.
4. Pour the mixture into a suitable earthenware or glass dish and place into a refrigerator to set.
5. Decorate as desired, e.g. with cooked vegetables cut into neat shapes to form a pattern. Cover with cool melted aspic jelly and allow to set in a refrigerator.

Notes
1. A curdled mixture may be rectified by slowly beating it on to a little velouté or cream, but this is not always entirely successful.
2. The mousse should have an even, fine texture and be just firm enough to set.
3. It should be of a delicate flavour; the flavour of the aspic should not predominate.
4. Decoration should be simple and neat.

Cold Fish Mousse (Mousse Froid de Poisson)

500 g poached fish	300 ml cream
200 ml fish velouté	salt, pepper and nutmeg
200 ml aspic jelly	100 ml melted aspic jelly

Proceed in exactly the same way as for Chicken Mousse.

Note
The name of the fish should be incorporated into the menu title, e.g. Cold Salmon Mousse (Mousse Froid de Saumon).

Ham Mousse (Mousse de Jambon)

This is made in the same way as Chicken Mousse, using ham instead of chicken and veal velouté instead of chicken velouté. As ham mousse is rather pale in colour, a little red colouring or paprika may be added.

Butter Bean Mousse

Cook 250 g soaked butter beans until soft, drain and pass through a sieve. Place in a basin and add 150 ml cool béchamel and 100 ml melted aspic jelly made with vegetable stock and 50 ml lemon juice, stirring with a wooden spatula. Place on ice and continue to stir until it shows signs of beginning to set. Fold in 100 ml lightly whipped cream and season to taste. Pour the mixture into 10 × 100 ml ramekins and place into a refrigerator to set. Decorate as desired, e.g. with cooked vegetables cut into neat shapes to form a pattern. Cover with cool melted aspic jelly made with vegetable stock and allow to set in a refrigerator.

Galantine of Chicken (Galantine de Volaille)

1 × 2.5 kg chicken	1 truffle
100 g pork fat	20 g pistachios
100 g cooked ox tongue	salt, pepper and nutmeg
50 ml brandy	1.5 litres chicken stock
500 g veal	1 litre sauce chaudfroid
250 ml cream	1 litre aspic jelly

1. Remove the skin of the chicken in one piece and soak in cold water to whiten it. Remove all the flesh from the carcass.
2. Cut the fillets of chicken into strips, place into a basin with strips of the truffle, pork fat and ox tongue, sprinkle with the brandy and marinate for 1 hour.
3. Finely mince the rest of the chicken flesh and the veal, then pass through a fine sieve.
4. Place into a basin, season with salt, pepper and nutmeg, stir in the cream and the brandy from the marinade.
5. Place a damp cloth onto a work surface and spread the drained chicken skin on it.
6. Spread one-third of the mixture over the whole skin and arrange half of the strips of chicken, pork fat, tongue, and truffle and a line of pistachios along the length.
7. Spread half of the remainder of the chicken mixture over the top, arrange the rest of the strips along the length, then add the remaining mixture on top and carefully roll to envelop the preparation in the skin. Enclose and tie in the cloth.
8. Poach the galantine in the chicken stock for 1 hour.
9. Remove, drain and place on a tray. Place a tray on top and weigh it down with slight pressure until cool.

10. Coat the galantine with sauce chaudfroid, decorate and glaze with chicken aspic. Present on a dish garnished with crescents of jelly.

Globe Artichoke with French Dressing (Artichaut Vinaigrette)

Prepare and plain boil the artichokes, refresh and drain. Arrange on a folded napkin and decorate with sprigs of parsley. Serve French dressing separately.

Oysters (Huîtres)

Open oysters and release the flesh where it is joined to the bottom shell. Serve on crushed ice, accompanied with brown bread and butter and segments of lemon. Shallot sauce, which consists of chopped shallots, vinegar, pepper from the mill and Tabasco, is sometimes served as an accompaniment.

Pâté de Foie Gras

Serve slices of pâté on a dish with a few lettuce leaves, quartered tomatoes and chopped aspic or portwine jelly. Hot toast is served as an accompaniment.

Pâté Maison

50 ml oil	500 g chicken livers
250 g diced lean pork	150 ml double cream
50 g fat bacon	25 ml brandy
100 g chopped onion	250 g lean bacon with rind
pinch powdered thyme	removed or salt pork fat
1 bayleaf	salt and pepper
1 clove garlic	

1. Heat the oil in a frying pan and fry the pork and bacon quickly. Add the chopped onion, thyme, bayleaf and garlic.
2. Add the prepared livers, and continue to fry very quickly until they are sealed; on no account should the livers be cooked through. Season with salt and pepper.
3. Allow to cool then pass several times through a fine mincer or chop finely in a bowl chopper.
4. Add the cream and brandy and correct the seasoning.
5. Line a 1.5 litre mould or terrine with the lean bacon overlapping at the top.
6. Fill the mould with the mixture, then fold over the bacon slices.
7. Place the mould in a bain-marie of water; cover with either greaseproof paper or a lid and cook in the oven at 175°C for 2 hours.
8. Remove the mould from the bain-marie. Remove the lid or greaseproof paper and place a flat dish on top of the pâté together with a weight to push the pâté down. Allow to get cold so that the fat sets, leaving it for eight hours in a refrigerator before serving.
9. Serve slices garnished with lettuce, tomato and slices of cucumber, accompanied by hot toast.

Notes
1. To obtain a very fine, smooth pâté, pass the liver through a sieve, or use a food processor. For a coarser, peasant-style pâté, use a coarse sieve.
2. When cooked, the juice and fat should be clear and free from all traces of blood.

Quail's Eggs

Present the hard-boiled eggs on a bed of mustard and cress on a plate, garnished with lettuce leaves, tomato, cucumber, segments of lemon and picked parsley. Serve with brown bread and butter.

Note
Gull's eggs, in season, can be presented in the same way.

Smoked Eel

Remove the skin; if the fish is a large whole one, carve into very thin slices, otherwise serve two pieces of fillet. Garnish with lettuce leaves, tomato, cucumber, segments of lemon and picked parsley. Brown bread and butter and horseradish sauce are served separately.

Smoked Salmon

Trim the side of salmon using a thin-bladed carving knife to remove all surface skin and small bones. Carve into very thin slices on the slant, commencing at the tail end. Serve on a dish or plate, garnished with mustard and cress and segments of lemon. Brown bread and butter is served separately.

Smoked Trout

Serve whole, with the skin removed and the head left on. To remove the skin, pierce with the point of a small knife at the tail end, cut along the backbone, then fold back and remove the skin from gills to tail. Repeat for the other side of the fish. Serve garnished with lettuce leaves, tomato, cucumber, segments of lemon and picked parsley. Brown bread and butter and horseradish sauce are served separately.

Fillet of Red Mullet in Vinaigrette Sauce

Shallow fry 20 × 75 g fillets of red mullet without colouring, then marinate for 1 hour in vinaigrette sauce to which 75 g tomato concassée and some chopped basil leaves have been added. Serve the fish fillets coated with the vinaigrette and garnish with segments of lime and basil leaves.

Caviar RUSSIA

Caviar is the salted roe of various kinds of sturgeon. It is generally served in the container in which it was purchased, set in crushed ice or in a special dish called a timbale. It is served accompanied with quarters of lemon, blinis or thinly sliced black bread and butter, soured cream, sieved white and yolk of hard-boiled egg and chopped onion.

Chopped Liver (Gehachte Leber) ISRAEL

```
 75 g sliced onion
 50 ml chicken fat
450 g chicken livers
  2 hard-boiled eggs
    salt and pepper
```

1. Golden fry the sliced onion in the chicken fat. Remove the onion then fry the chicken livers very quickly.
2. Pass the onion and livers through a fine mincer into a basin.
3. Add the sieved eggs, season with salt and pepper and chill in a refrigerator.
4. Serve spoon-moulded portions, sprinkled with sieved egg and chopped parsley, garnished with small lettuce leaves, accompanied by finger toast, challah or matzos.

Note
Calf's or ox liver may be used instead of chicken livers.

Gravlax SCANDINAVIA

2 × 500 g fillets of salmon	25 g caster sugar
50 g dill	50 g crushed black peppercorns
50 g sea salt	25 ml whisky or aquavit

1. Place one fillet, skin side down, in a deep earthenware or stainless steel dish. Sprinkle with the chopped dill, the salt, sugar, crushed peppercorns and alcohol and lay the corresponding fillet on top, skin side up.
2. Cover with clingfilm, place a weight on top and refrigerate for 48–72 hours, turning it every 12 hours and basting with the marinade that accumulates, separating the fillets to baste inside.
3. Remove the fish from the marinade, scrape off the dill and seasonings and dry with kitchen paper.
4. Carve into very thin slices diagonally and serve garnished with lemon wedges and lime, dill and yogurt sauce.

Salmon Sushi (Nigiri-sushi) JAPAN

Cut 20 thin slices on the slant from a 675 g fillet of raw salmon, gravlax or smoked salmon. Encase small balls of Spiced Rice in each slice and coat with 3 tsp wasabi powder mixed with 50 ml water, then decorate with thin strips of cooked leek and prawns. Serve accompanied by Japanese soy sauce.

FISH COCKTAILS

Crab Cocktail (Cocktail de Crabe)

500 g prepared white crabmeat	3 lemons, quartered
200 g shredded lettuce	3 tomatoes, quartered
500 ml Cocktail Sauce	10 g chopped parsley

1. Three-quarters fill cocktail glasses with 20 g shredded lettuce.
2. Place 50 g of crabmeat on top of the lettuce and coat with cocktail sauce.
3. Garnish the glasses with quarters of tomato and lemon and sprinkle with chopped parsley.

Lobster Cocktail (Cocktail de Homard)

This is prepared in the same way as Crab Cocktail, using diced or sliced lobster instead of crab.

Prawn Cocktail (Cocktail de Crevettes)

This is prepared in the same way as Crab Cocktail, using prawns instead of crab.

Seafood Cocktail (Cocktail de Fruits de Mer)

Prepare as for Crab Cocktail, using different kinds of fish and shellfish instead of only crab.

Note
Fish cocktails are also known as seafood cocktails and may consist of a single item of shellfish or a combination of two or more, e.g. crab and mussels or shrimp and lobster and of flaked cooked fish.

FRUIT COCKTAILS

Florida Cocktail

    5 grapefruit
    5 oranges
  10 maraschino cherries

1. Cut off both ends of the fruit and place on a chopping board. Cut downwards, following the contour of the fruit, to remove all peel and pith.

2. Remove the segments by cutting towards the centre, close to the dividing membrane. Retain them in a basin with the juice from the fruit.
3. Serve neatly arranged in a coupe or goblet. Barely cover with the juice from the fruit and place a cherry in the centre as decoration.

Grapefruit Cocktail

Allow 10 grapefruit and proceed as for Florida Cocktail.

Melon Cocktail (Cocktail de Melon)

Cut the melon in half and remove the seeds. Scoop out the flesh with a parisienne cutter and retain the balls in a bowl until required, together with any juice to keep them moist. Place the balls in a coupe or goblet with a maraschino cherry on top and serve slightly chilled. Allow approximately 2 melons for 10 portions.

Miami Cocktail (Cocktail Miami)

Cut 4 grapefruit and 4 oranges into segments, add 150 g small wedges of pineapple and serve with a maraschino cherry in the centre of each.

POTTED ITEMS

Potted Avocado

Blend the flesh of 6 avocado pears with 3 cloves of garlic, 50 g onion, 75 ml lime juice, 150 g tomato flesh, 1 tsp chilli powder, a pinch of fresh herbs and a few drops of Tabasco. Fill into ramekins or glass bowls and serve chilled, garnished with segments of lime.

Potted Char

Shallow fry 10×75 g skinned fillets of char in hot butter. Arrange in layers in a pie dish or oblong ravier, brushing each layer with melted butter and pressing them down. Cover completely with melted butter and keep refrigerated until served.

Note
Fillets of trout or mackerel may be prepared in the same way, changing the title accordingly.

Potted Goose (Confit d'Oie)

Bone out a goose, reserving all the fat; cut the flesh into 5 cm pieces and rub all over in a mixture of 100 g coarse salt and a pinch each of saltpetre, powdered bayleaf, clove and thyme. Cover with clingfilm and leave in the refrigerator for 24 hours. Dry the pieces of goose and cook in the clarified fat from the goose, stirring occasionally and letting it cook gently for 1½ hours. Portion the goose flesh into ramekin dishes, cover completely with the cooking fat and refrigerate for at least 12 hours before serving accompanied by thick slices of toast.

Potted Hough

Bone out a small shin of beef, cut the flesh into pieces, chop the bone small, place it all in a pan and cover with cold water. Bring to the boil and skim, season, cover with a lid and simmer for 3½ hours. Remove the meat, chop it finely or pass through a mincer, replace in the defatted cooking liquor and season well. Pour into a basin or mould and place in the refrigerator to set. Demould and serve cut into slices, garnished with salad greens.

Potted Pigeon and Walnuts

Truss 4 plump pigeons, golden fry in clarified butter, then pot-roast for 1½ hours. Remove the flesh from the pigeons, add half its weight in shelled walnuts and pass through a fine mincer. Add 50 g softened butter, 25 ml brandy and seasoning and fill into ramekin dishes. Cover the top with melted butter and place in the refrigerator. Serve garnished with segments of lemon.

Potted Shrimps

Melt 200 g butter and allow to cool. Mix in 800 g picked grey shrimps, a pinch of each of ground mace, grated nutmeg, white pepper, cayenne pepper and salt. Fill into individual moulds or dishes, cover with melted butter and keep in a refrigerator. To serve, demould or place on a dish with a leaf of lettuce, a segment of lemon and brown bread and butter.

Smoked Salmon Pâté

Finely mince 675 g smoked salmon trimmings and blend with 175 g butter, 10 g chopped fresh herbs and a few drops of Tabasco. Portion into ramekins and chill. Serve garnished with segments of lemon.

Salads

Salads play an important part on most menus. Their popularity stems from a number of factors – they are considered as a health food, they lend themselves particularly to cold buffets, and they blend with and thus complement many types of hot dishes. Traditionally, they are served with main courses such as grills of meat and poultry or with roasts of meat, poultry and game, usually in place of a second vegetable. Many salads can also be served as an hors-d'oeuvre or as a main dish.

There are two main kinds of salad – the simple ones, consisting of a few raw salad vegetables or even a single ingredient such as cucumber, served with an appropriate dressing, then there are the combination ones made with several ingredients, bound with a dressing and served in a composite form. With the addition of small hot items they are referred to as hot salads. Crudités are also a form of salad, being small cuts of crisp salad and vegetable items for dipping in various dips whilst awaiting the arrival of the first course.

Salads may also be made with cooked vegetables flavoured with an appropriate sauce, either when cold or when still warm.

Various types of salad greens, e.g. Chinese leaves, corn salad, lollo rosso, oakleaf lettuce, radicchio, rocket, Webb's Wonder, iceberg and cos lettuce, may be used, also curly and Belgian endives, celery, and watercress. Dandelions and nettle leaves and many herbs may also be added.

Salads may be served in glass or wooden bowls, on side plates or crescent-shaped side dishes.

WARM SALADS

This kind of salad is normally served with an entrée and should be freshly made to order.

Artichokes with Anchovy Filling (Carciofi alla Triestina)

20–30 small artichokes	175 g grated Parmesan cheese
300 g white breadcrumbs	100 g chopped anchovy fillets
10 g chopped parsley	25 ml olive oil
4 chopped cloves of garlic	salt and pepper

1. Cut off the tops of the artichokes and remove the chokes.
2. Combine the remainder of the ingredients into a stuffing.
3. Fill into the centres of the artichokes.
4. Place in a shallow pan, moisten one-third of the way up with salted water and a little olive oil, cover and cook for 40 minutes. Serve hot with some of the cooking liquid.

Spinach and Bacon Salad

Place 1 kg shredded raw spinach in a bowl. Crisp-fry 275 g lardons of bacon in hazelnut oil, add 275 g sliced mushrooms, then sprinkle with 75 ml cider vinegar and add 20 g freshly chopped, mixed herbs and 100 g fried diced bread croûtons. Pour the preparation over the spinach, toss over to mix and serve immediately.

Asparagus Salad with Mustard and Egg Dressing (Asuparagasu Karashi-Ae)

JAPAN

Moisten cooked asparagus tips with warm mustard and egg dressing made by whisking egg yolks, made English mustard and heated soy sauce.

Bean and Potato Salad

USA

Sauté 50 g chopped onion in a little oil, moisten with 125 ml red wine vinegar and reduce by half. Mix into 300 g sliced cooked potatoes and 250 g diamonds of cooked French beans, add 150 g freshly fried lardons of bacon and serve in lettuce leaves.

Bean and Sesame Salad (Sandomame Goma-Miso Ae)

JAPAN

Blend 50 g toasted, ground sesame seeds with 75 g red miso paste, 1 tsp sugar and 50 ml mirin, then mix into 450 g cooked French beans.

Cabbage and Bacon Salad (Weisskrautsalat)

GERMANY

Blanch 1 kg shredded white cabbage for 2 minutes, drain and sprinkle while still hot with 75 ml oil and 75 ml wine vinegar. Crisp fry 275 g lardons of bacon in hot oil, mix into the cabbage and serve sprinkled with chopped, fresh mixed herbs.

Celeriac Salad (Selleriesalat)

GERMANY

Cut 1 kg celeriac into 1 cm batons and cook for 5 minutes in 1 litre beef stock with 75 g chopped onion, 75 ml olive oil, 50 ml wine vinegar, 25 ml lemon juice and 1 tsp sugar. Remove the celeriac and reduce the cooking liquid by two-thirds. Replace the celeriac and serve hot with a little of the cooking liquid and sprinkled with chopped walnuts.

Cucumber Salad (Küri No Sumomi)

JAPAN

Sprinkle 3 peeled and sliced cucumbers with salt, allow to stand for 1 hour, then drain off the liquid. Simmer 125 ml each of dashi and rice vinegar, 4 tbs dark soy sauce and 1 tsp sugar and pour most of it over the cucumber, allow to macerate, then squeeze out all the liquid. Moisten with the rest of the liquid and serve.

Dandelion Salad (Löwenzahnsalat)

GERMANY

Toss 1 kg washed dandelion leaves in a warm dressing of 75 ml sesame oil, 50 ml wine vinegar and a little sugar. Add 350 g diced boiled potato and 275 g freshly fried, crisp lardons of bacon.

Goat's Cheese Salad
USA

Sprinkle 300 g × 1.5 cm cubes of goat's cheese with 50 ml olive oil and retain for 12 hours. Sauté the cheese in the heated oil, add 300 g shredded raw spinach leaves and 50 g crisp-fried lardons of bacon. Toss over and serve accompanied by tarragon dressing.

Warm Potato Salad (Kartoffelsalat)
GERMANY

Steam 1.25 kg jacket potatoes until nearly cooked, peel, slice and marinate for 30 minutes in a hot dressing made of 75 ml of beef stock, 275 ml olive oil and 50 ml wine vinegar, 10 g mixed herbs, 50 ml onion juice, 25 g Dijon mustard and 25 g sugar. Serve surrounded with leaves of lettuce.

COMPOSITE SALADS

Bamboo Shoot and Pork Salad (Yam No Mai Gup Moo)
THAILAND

Blend 25 g chopped shallots and 4 cloves of garlic to a paste, wrap in foil and grill for 1 minute. Combine with 200 g bamboo shoots, 25 g nam pla, the juice of 2 limes, 25 g sugar, 50 g chopped spring onions and 250 g small slices of cooked pork. Serve on a bed of lettuce, sprinkled with dried chilli flakes and chopped mint leaves.

Banana Salad
CARIBBEAN

Boil 5 unripe bananas for 15 minutes, peel, slice and combine with 75 g of strips of tomato flesh, 100 g each of julienne of cucumber, carrot and celery, and sliced avocado. Season and mix with French dressing.

Caesar Salad
USA

Toss roughly torn cos lettuce leaves in a bowl with a dressing made with olive oil, lemon juice, Worcester sauce and anchovy essence. Break into it an egg boiled for 1 minute, sprinkle well with grated Parmesan and garlic-flavoured, diced, fried bread croûtons.

Cracked Wheat Salad (Tabbouleh)
MIDDLE EAST

Soak 150 g cracked wheat in cold water for 10 minutes, drain, sprinkle with 1 tsp salt and the juice of 1 lemon and leave to soften for 1 hour. Mix with 10 g each of chopped mint and parsley, 100 g each of chopped onion and tomato concassée, add 75 ml olive oil, salt and pepper and toss over to mix. Serve surrounded with young vine or cos lettuce leaves.

Cucumber and Yogurt Salad (Khira Raita) INDIA

Peel and slice 3 cucumbers, sprinkle with salt and leave for 1 hour, then drain off the liquid and place the cucumber into raviers. Moisten with a dressing made of 275 ml yogurt, 3 chopped cloves of garlic, 25 g grated root ginger, the juice of 2 lemons and seasoning.

Corn Salad USA

Combine 100 g each of diced green pimento, celery, spring onions, tomato flesh and sweetcorn kernels, then moisten with 250 ml sour cream dressing.

Fruit and Prawn Salad (Yaam Polamai) THAILAND

Combine the segments of 10 oranges, 50 g diced apple, 50 g halves of grapes, 25 g each of sliced lychees and water chestnuts and 25 g prawns. Crisp-fry 4 chopped cloves of garlic, 100 g chopped shallots, 25 g crushed roasted peanuts, then add the juice of 2 limes. Serve the salad sprinkled with the dressing, chopped coriander and fresh red chillies.

Fruit and Vegetable Salad CARIBBEAN

Moisten 100 g each of diced pineapple and firm mango flesh, the segments of 5 oranges, 3 sliced bananas and 1 diced cucumber with a dressing made of 3 chopped cloves of garlic, the juice from the fruits, 25 ml olive oil, 10 g chopped chives and seasoning. Serve surrounded with picked watercress and crisp lettuce leaves.

Grapefruit Salad USA

Sprinkle the segments of 10 grapefruits with julienne of orange peel, garnish with red onion rings then moisten with Orange Dressing.

Orange Salad (Bourekakia Salata) GREECE

Arrange segments of oranges in a ravier. Season with ground cinnamon, garnish with stoned black olives and sliced radishes, and sprinkle with blanched grated zest of orange, olive oil and lemon juice.

Onion, Tomato and Ginger Salad (Kachumbar) INDIA

Sprinkle 675 g sliced spring onions with 50 g salt, retain for 1 hour to extract the liquid, then rinse in cold water and drain. Combine the onion with 25 g tamarind pulp previously soaked in 50 ml hot water, 75 g palm sugar, 225 g strips of tomato flesh, 25 g grated root ginger, 6 sliced fresh green chillies and 75 g chopped coriander leaves.

Spinach and Spiced Yogurt Salad (Palak Raita) INDIA

Golden fry 2 tsp mustard seeds in 25 ml oil or ghee. When they crackle add 1 tsp each of cumin seeds and ground cumin and ½ tsp fenugreek seeds, then remove from the heat. Stir in ¼ tsp chilli powder, cool and combine with 225 ml yogurt and 450 g blanched, chopped spinach and seasoning.

Vegetable and Lime Salad (Ensalada Mixta) MEXICO

Combine 125 g each of diced cooked carrot, beetroot and potato, diamonds of French beans, peas, strips of tomato flesh and sliced cucumber, then mix with lime dressing and serve sprinkled with chopped coriander leaves.

Canapés and Similar Appetisers
COCKTAIL CANAPÉS

Canapés are small savoury titbits served as appetisers before the beginning of a meal. A colourful selection is arranged on a tray to be taken by waiting staff among the guests, who help themselves, usually while drinking an aperitif. Canapés should be small and slight enough to be popped straight into the mouth and devoured with relish in one bite.

The selection usually consists of small pieces of toasted bread or savoury biscuits, spread with butter and covered with a single item, or several in combination, artistically garnished. They are often coated with aspic jelly.

Items used for making canapés include:

1. Fish – smoked eel, mackerel, salmon and trout; anchovy fillets; rollmop herrings; sardines; sild; prawns and shrimps; various kinds of caviar; lobster; crabmeat; mussels and oysters.
2. Meat – roast sirloin; salt brisket; corned beef; pastrami; ox tongue; brawn; salami; mortadella; liver sausage; parma and other dried hams; bierwurst. Poultry – smoked chicken and turkey; roast chicken, turkey and goose; foie gras.
3. Eggs and cheese – hard-boiled eggs; gull's eggs; quail's eggs; grated cheese; slices of all kinds of cheese; cream cheese; cottage cheese; fromage frais; crème fraîche.
4. Vegetables – asparagus; small artichokes; celery; fennel; avocados; pimentos; onion rings; palm hearts; mushrooms.
5. Salads – watercress; tomatoes; cucumber, spring onions; radishes.
6. Fruits – apples; oranges; pineapple; pears; grapes; melon; kiwifruit; pawpaw.
7. Garnishes – gherkins; olives; capers; parsley; pickles; mayonnaise; lemons; horseradish; flavoured butters; hard-boiled eggs.

Other suitable items for cocktail parties include:

Small chipolata sausages; small deep-fried goujons of fish and chicken; bite-sized Chinese spring rolls, Indian vegetable samosas, vegetable, fish and meat pasties; barquettes and tartlets filled with savoury fillings such as prawns, crabmeat and lobster; miniature pizzas; bite-sized bouchées filled with a variety of savoury fillings; ramekins, quichlets; dartois, samosas; crisps; various kinds of shelled nuts; olives; gherkins; small tortillas; cheese straws; dips of various flavours.

Dartois aux Anchois

Combine 200 g chopped anchovy fillets with 50 ml béchamel and season with cayenne pepper. Roll 500 g puff pastry into an oblong 50 cm × 20 cm and cut in half lengthways. Lay one half on a damp baking sheet and spread with the anchovy mixture, leaving the edges clear. Eggwash the edges. Fold the remaining piece of pastry in two lengthways and, using a sharp knife, cut incisions across the fold at 2.5 cm intervals. Unfold and cover the base, seal well together and notch the edge. Allow to rest for 45 minutes, then bake in the oven at 215°C for 20–25 minutes. Remove from the tray and cut into 20 small fingers.

Prawn and Sesame Toasts (Zha Xia Bao) CHINA

Blend 675 g peeled prawns and 25 g grated root ginger to a paste, then add a chilled mixture of 2 tsp cornflour diluted with 2 tsp dry sherry, 1 beaten egg white and salt. Spread on 10 slices of bread, dip the mixture side in sesame seeds and golden fry in oil, drain and cut into neat shapes. Garnish with spring onion flowers and accompany with chilli sauce.

Vegetable Samosas
Cauliflower and Potato Samosa (Gobhi Aloo Samosa) INDIA

Filling	Pastry
10 g ginger	100 g strong flour
50 g ghee	100 g wholemeal flour
4 green chillies	1 tsp salt
1 tsp mustard seeds	50 g ghee
50 g tomato concassée	75 ml warm water
1/4 tsp ground coriander	
1/4 tsp turmeric	
1/4 tsp garam masala	
450 g cauliflower florets	
200 g potatoes, cut in dice	
10 g chopped parsley and coriander leaves	
50 ml lemon juice	

1. Sift the flours and salt into a basin.
2. Add the ghee and water and mix to a smooth dough. Cover with a cloth and allow to rest for 1 hour in a refrigerator.
3. Heat the ghee in a shallow pan, add the grated ginger and chopped chillies, then add mustard seeds and fry until the seeds pop.
4. Add the diced tomato, ground coriander, turmeric and garam masala and cook until it begins to thicken to a pulp.
5. Add the cooked cauliflower, cooked potato, chopped fresh herbs and lemon juice, cook for 3 minutes and allow to cool.
6. Divide dough into 20 pieces and roll them very thinly to 15 cm diameter circles; cut each in half and form two semicircles. Fold cone-shape, brush the edge with water and press securely to seal the seam.
7. Fill each cone three-quarters full with the mixture, dampen the inside of the opening edge with water, then fold over the top to completely seal the seam. Place seam-side down onto a tray; cover with clingfilm and allow to rest in a refrigerator for 2 hours.
8. Deep fry at 190°C for 4 minutes until golden and crisp, drain and serve.

Potato Samosa (Aloo Samosa)   INDIA

Boil 500 g diced potato in salted water, when cooked, drain and cool. Season with $\frac{1}{2}$ tsp chilli powder, $\frac{1}{2}$ tsp panch phora, 1 tsp ground cumin and salt, moisten with 50 ml lemon juice and proceed as for Cauliflower and Potato Samosa.

Vegetable Samosa (Samm-bahr Samosa)   INDIA

Boil 350 g potatoes in salted water, drain, dry and mash them. Season with $\frac{1}{2}$ tsp black pepper, 1 tsp chilli powder, 1 tsp coriander powder, $\frac{1}{2}$ tsp cumin and 25 g dried fenugreek leaves, then add 150 g cooked peas and proceed as for Cauliflower and Potato Samosa.

MEZÉTHES KE ORKTIKÀ (GREECE)

Mezéthes or mezé as they are colloquially known, are a colourful and aromatic display of savoury titbits to be eaten while drinking aperitifs as an appetiser course at any time of the day. A selection would consist of say, 20 different items served well decorated with suitable garnishes, of varying textures – both raw and cooked, served hot with household bread and olive oil. Suitable items include bite-sized pieces of anchovy fillet; pickled eggplant; dolmades; fresh and dried figs; gherkins; melon; olives; radishes; smoked fish; ham and sausages; stuffed vegetables and many salads such as taramasalàta. A popular assortment of appetisers as served in Greek tavernas and restaurants may also include such simple titbits as hot or cold spicy snacks served with various kinds of bread.

SMØRGASBØRD (SCANDINAVIA)

This is an array of open sandwiches and other snack-type small items which are attractively decorated and displayed on a table in the dining room for customers to help themselves, usually as an appetiser for the first course but often as an entire buffet meal. It is the most popular form of meal service in all Scandinavian countries, though each has certain specialities of its own. Basically, it consists of pieces of bread of various kinds, spread with butter and covered with items, either alone or in combination, which can be artistically garnished with appropriate adjuncts to enhance the look and the taste of each smørgasbørd.

Items used for making them can include all the foods listed under Cocktail Canapés.

TAPAS (SPAIN)

Normally associated with tapas bars, these appetisers range from very simple small snacks to very elaborate dishes that have developed into an appetising course to be eaten just before a meal. They comprise any number and variety of small items, their content being a reflection of the imagination of those who make them. They include Ajello – shallow fried prawns with garlic; Calamares Fritos – fried rings of squid; Scoldaditos di Pavia – strips of soaked dried cod fried in batter; Vieiras al Horno – scallops baked in the half shells; Pincho de Morcilla o Chorizo – shallow-fried slices of black pudding or chorizo sausage on toasted French bread, Albondigas – artichokes cooked in oil, montilla wine and garlic. Many kinds of vegetables are also used as well as olives, pieces of omelette, portions of paella, salads and slices of jamón serrano.

ZAKUSKI (RUSSIA)

These are a central characteristic of the traditional Russian table which can take the form of a first course appetiser or hors-d'oeuvre, or as a full buffet in which hot and cold items are featured. Zakuski consist of a selection from a wide range and variety of hot and cold dishes including salted, smoked, marinated and pickled fish, preserved fruits such as plums, cherries and quinces and pickled cucumbers, beetroots and red cabbage. Cold smoked ham, meat and game cut in small slices are accompanied by soured cream, as are sausages and many kinds of poultry in the form of smoked chicken and turkey as well as game pâtés. Several kinds of cheese are a particular feature of zakuski, but the main item is chilled caviar served with soured cream, wedges of lemon, blinis or thinly sliced black bread spread with unsalted butter. Ice-cold vodka is served in liqueur glasses, to be drunk in one gulp between each mouthful of food.

Salad Dressings

There are a large number of different salad dressings in use, the most popular being mayonnaise and French dressing, also known as vinaigrette. Salad cream is a cheaper form of mayonnaise that is only suitable for binding combination salads. Other dressings are variations on mayonnaise and French dressing. Some salads are first treated with French dressing, then bound with mayonnaise.

Acidulated Cream Dressing

Mix 1 part lemon juice into 5 parts lightly whipped cream and season with salt and pepper.

Basil and Wine Dressing (Agliata)

Soak 50 g white breadcrumbs in 25 ml white wine, then squeeze out. Add 2 finely chopped cloves of garlic, 10 g powdered basil leaves and chopped parsley. Gradually blend in 300 ml olive oil and season with salt and pepper.

Black Olive, Tomato and Basil Dressing (Tapenade)

1 kg pitted black olives	225 ml olive oil
175 g capers	50 ml red wine vinegar
100 g anchovy fillets	50 g chopped sun-dried tomatoes
50 g Dijon mustard	75 g chopped parsley
10 g fresh basil	

1. Blend all the ingredients except the parsley and sun-dried tomatoes, to form a smooth paste.
2. Finish by folding in the chopped parsley, dried tomatoes and seasoning.

French Dressing (Vinaigrette)

300 ml vinegar
700 ml oil
  10 g salt
      pepper from the mill
   5 g French mustard (optional)

Put the vinegar, oil, salt and pepper (and mustard if used) into a basin and mix with a whisk until it forms an emulsion.

French Dressing for Calf's Feet and Poultry Salads

Prepare French Dressing, adding 10 g each of finely chopped onion or shallots, capers and anchovy fillets.

Gribiche Dressing (Sauce Gribiche)

Combine 1 tsp French mustard, 125 ml vinegar and 350 ml walnut oil, then add 100 g each of chopped gherkins and capers, 4 sieved hard-boiled eggs, 25 g chopped chives, tarragon and parsley and seasoning.

Mustard Dressing

   20 g made English mustard
500 ml French dressing
300 ml mayonnaise
200 ml cream

Mix all the ingredients together to a smooth consistency.

Roquefort Dressing

Mash 100 g Roquefort cheese with a fork in a basin. Gradually add 300 ml French Dressing, mixing continuously until it is incorporated into the cheese.

Salsa Verde

Combine 275 ml olive oil, 50 ml lemon juice, 25 g each of chopped parsley and basil, 50 g chopped capers, 25 g chopped anchovy fillets, 1 tsp Dijon mustard, and seasoning of salt and pepper.

Stilton Dressing

Combine 100 g mashed Stilton cheese with 225 ml French dressing, 50 ml lemon juice, and seasoning.

Sour Cream Dressing

Flavour crème fraîche, yogurt or cream with lemon juice and seasoning.

Tarragon Dressing

Combine 5 g English mustard, 50 ml vinegar, 100 ml oil and 5 g chopped tarragon.

Lemon Dressing (Epanthicen Latholemono)   GREECE

Combine 275 ml walnut oil with 50 ml lemon juice, 50 g chopped parsley and seasoning.

Lime Dressing (Epanthicen me Fétta Lemonew)   GREECE

Blend 150 ml lime juice with 2 cloves of garlic, 1 chopped fresh green chilli, 275 ml olive oil, 75 g Féta cheese and seasoning. Add the grated zest of 2 limes and 50 g chopped coriander leaves.

Red Chilli Dressing (Greek Rouille)

Blend 3 fresh red chillies, 3 previously soaked dried red chillies, 3 cloves of garlic, 100 g red pimento and 275 ml olive oil, then gradually whisk in 3 pasteurised egg yolks and seasoning.

Orange Dressing

USA

Boil the finely shredded zest of 3 oranges in 50 ml raspberry vinegar, add 25 ml orange juice, 50 ml walnut oil, 5 g chopped tarragon and parsley and seasoning.

Thousand Island Dressing

USA

few drops Tabasco	100 g red pimento ⎱ peeled and
10 g salt	100 g green pimento ⎰ chopped
milled pepper	25 g chopped parsley
200 ml vinegar	3 sieved hard-boiled eggs
800 ml oil	

1. Put the Tabasco, salt, pepper and vinegar into a basin and whisk together.
2. Add the oil and continue to whisk while adding the remaining ingredients.

Dips

Dips may be served as an accompaniment for crudités, which consist of bite-sized pieces of raw vegetables such as carrot, celery, cucumber and pimento. Dips may also be served with a range of savoury snacks such as potato crisps, taco shells, tortillas and small poppadums. They can also be served hot or cold, to accompany hors-d'oeuvre dishes made with fish, shellfish, poultry, meat and vegetables.

Anchovy, Garlic and Truffle Dip (Bagna Cauda)

Heat 200 ml olive oil and 75 g butter in a pan and gently cook 15 large peeled cloves of garlic until soft but not coloured. Add 250 g chopped anchovy fillets and mix to a paste, using a fork to crush the garlic. Finely slice 50 g white truffle, add and mix together. Serve very hot as a dip for crudités.

Avocado and Tomato Dip (Guacamole)

MEXICO

Macerate 150 g diced tomato flesh, 25 g chopped coriander leaves, 100 g chopped onion and 3 chopped fresh green chillies in 75 ml lemon or lime juice for 1 hour. Combine with the puréed flesh of 3 avocados and season with salt and ground black pepper.

Banana and Yogurt Dip (Kela Pachchadi) INDIA

Fry 1 tsp each of mustard and cumin seeds in 25 ml oil or ghee until they crackle. Add to 275 ml yogurt, 450 g sliced banana, 50 ml lemon juice, 75 g grated fresh coconut, 2 tsp sugar, a pinch each of chilli powder and salt, then blend to a smooth paste.

Chickpea and Sesame Dip (Hoummous bi Tahini) MIDDLE EAST

Soak, then boil 275 g chickpeas in salted water for 1 hour; drain and retain the liquid. Blend the chickpeas to a purée with 50 g tahini paste, 150 ml lemon juice, 3 crushed cloves of garlic and salt. Adjust the consistency, if necessary, with some of the cooking liquid to give a smooth, thick paste.

Coriander and Yogurt Dip (Dhania Raita) INDIA

Blend 75 g chopped coriander leaves, 1 chopped fresh green chilli, 25 ml lemon juice and $\frac{1}{4}$ tsp cayenne pepper to a fine paste, then combine with 275 ml yogurt, $\frac{1}{4}$ tsp toasted cumin seeds and seasoning.

Cucumber, Coconut and Yogurt Dip (Khira Raita) INDIA

Combine 350 ml yogurt, 450 g grated and squeezed cucumber, 75 g grated coconut, 2 chopped, fresh green chillies, and salt. Fry 1 tsp each of mustard and cumin seeds in oil or ghee until they crackle, cool and add to the yogurt preparation.

Eggplant and Yogurt Dip (Baigan Raita) INDIA

Fry 1 tsp mustard seeds in 75 ml oil or ghee until they crackle; add 75 g chopped onion, 2 sliced fresh green chillies, and when soft, add 275 g chopped eggplant, 100 g tomato flesh, 1 tsp garam masala and seasoning. Moisten with 50 ml water, cook for 20 minutes and cool. Blend to a purée and add 275 ml yogurt and 25 g chopped coriander leaves.

Pawpaw Dip CARIBBEAN

Place 450 g pawpaw flesh, 75 ml lime juice, $\frac{1}{4}$ tsp ground cloves, 25 g sugar and 300 ml water to cook gently until all the liquid is evaporated. Blend and serve hot or cold.

Spinach and Yogurt Dip (Palak Raita) INDIA

Boil 1 kg spinach in 50 ml salted water, drain and chop. Fry 1 tsp mustard seeds in 50 ml oil or ghee until they crackle, add 1 tsp cumin seeds, 1 tsp ground cumin, $\frac{1}{2}$ tsp fenugreek seeds and a pinch of chilli powder. Allow to cool, then mix into 275 ml yogurt, add the spinach and season well with salt and a pinch of cayenne.

Taramasalàta GREECE

Process 175 g crustless white or brown bread, soaked in water and squeezed out, 275 g smoked cod roe and 75 ml lemon juice, then gradually add 175 ml olive oil. Serve scrolled and garnished with stoned black olives and segments of lemon.

Tentsuyu Dipping Liquid JAPAN

Simmer 250 ml second soup stock with 80 ml soy sauce and 80 ml mirin for 1 minute; cool and use.

Relishes

Relishes are a condiment and as such should have a distinctively piquant flavour to enhance the flavour of the foods (such as plainly cooked fish, shellfish, meats, poultry and vegetables) with which they are served. Their tart and spicy qualities stimulate the appetite.

Cucumber Relish

Soak 500 g cucumber, 250 g onion, 50 g celery and 100 g each of red and green pimentos, all cut into fine brunoise, in salted water for 12 hours. Boil 250 ml vinegar with 125 g sugar, $1/4$ tsp celery seeds, $1/2$ tsp turmeric and $1/2$ tsp salt; add 15 g flour diluted in a little water and boil for 5 minutes. Add the well-drained vegetables and boil for 10 minutes, then pack in jars.

Tomato Relish

Cook 750 g skinned and quartered tomatoes in 150 ml cider vinegar with $1/2$ tsp each of ground nutmeg and cloves, 350 g sugar and half a cinnamon stick until the mixture thickens. Remove the cinnamon, sieve the relish and bottle it.

Cranberry Relish

Cook 400 g cranberries in a little water to a purée and pass through a sieve. Add 350 g sugar, the grated rind of 1 orange and 1 lemon, 1 tbs lemon juice, 45 g chopped walnuts and 85 g diced pineapple; bring to the boil, simmer for 5 minutes and allow to cool.

Chilli Relish (Nam Prik Poa) THAILAND

Fry 20 soaked and dried red chillies, 4 chopped cloves of garlic and 75 g chopped shallot in 75 ml groundnut oil and allow to cool. Blend to a paste with 175 ml lemon juice, 1 tsp sugar and 25 ml nam pla.

Coconut Relish (Narial Pachachadi)

Golden fry 100 g cooked chickpeas, 8 crushed, dried green chillies and 3 curry leaves in 75 ml oil or ghee; allow to cool, then grind to a paste with 350 g grated fresh coconut and salt. Fry a pinch of ground asafoetida and 1 tsp mustard seeds in 25 ml ghee until the seeds crackle, then add to the paste with 50 ml lemon juice. Serve chilled.

Coriander Relish (Dhania Pachachadi)

Blend 225 g coriander leaves and stems, 3 fresh green chillies, 50 g grated coconut, 25 g grated root ginger, the juice of 1 lemon, 1 tsp sugar and salt to a paste. Fry a pinch of ground asafoetida, 1 tsp mustard seeds and 3 crushed dried curry leaves in 25 ml oil or ghee until the seeds crackle, add to the blended mixture and serve chilled.

Eggplant Relish (Sambal Terong)

Fry 75 g chopped onion, 2 chopped cloves of garlic and 4 chopped fresh green chillies in 75 ml olive oil, cool and blend to a paste. Add 275 g chopped eggplant, 1 tsp anchovy paste, 1 tsp ground coriander, the juice of 1 lemon, 1 tsp sugar, 2 tsp chopped mint and salt. Place in a dish and bake in the oven at 170°C for 20 minutes. Serve hot or chilled.

Horseradish and Beetroot Relish (Chrain)

Combine 350 g grated cooked beetroot, 225 g grated horseradish, 75 ml vinegar and 50 g castor sugar.

Hot Red Chilli Relish

Place 225 g chopped fresh red chillies, 225 g chopped onion, 25 ml water and 1 tsp salt in a pan, cover with a lid and simmer very gently for 30 minutes; allow to cool.

Mango Relish

Boil 300 ml vinegar and 350 g soft brown sugar until reduced by half, then stir in 75 ml tamarind juice. Add 2 chopped fresh red chillies, 1/2 tsp ground cloves, 1/4 tsp allspice, 75 g seedless raisins, 50 g grated root ginger, 50 ml lime juice and 450 g diced mango flesh and simmer for 20 minutes; season with salt and ground black peppercorns.

CHAPTER 2 # Soups

INTRODUCTION

Soup is a general term that includes every kind of flavoured liquid, whether thick, thin, clear, hot or chilled. In French the word for soup is 'potage', but this usually applies to thick soups rather than to clear soups.

Although usually served hot as the first course of a meal, some soups can be served chilled, clear soups in particular being popular in semi-set jellied form.

Soups are made from a very wide range of ingredients and it is possible to put both a clear and a thick soup on the menu for every meal, every day of the year without having to repeat a recipe once.

It is possible to classify soups under nine main headings as follows:

- **Consommés** – clarified stocks with the flavour of the basic ingredient; may be served plain or garnished, hot or chilled
- **Bouillons** – unclarified, clear stocks served plain or with a garnish
- **Potages** – very good quality white stocks thickened with cream and egg yolks and finished with a garnish
- **Purées** – smooth, passed soups made from dried pulses or fresh vegetables
- **Creams** – passed soups made with vegetables, dried pulses or chicken and béchamel and always finished with cream; may be served hot or chilled
- **Veloutés** – silky-smooth soups made from second stage roux and appropriate stocks and always finished with egg yolks and cream; may be served hot or chilled
- **Fawn roux-based** – made with second stage roux and white stocks and finished with cream; may be served hot or chilled
- **Brown roux-based** – thick passed meat soups such as oxtail and kidney, garnished with meat; always served hot
- **Fish and Shellfish (Bisques)** – thick passed fish or shellfish soups finished with cream; may be served hot or chilled.

Thickenings for soups

1. Using a second or third stage roux
2. Adding diluted arrowroot or cornflour
3. Adding ground or whole rice
4. Adding cream and butter, e.g. Cream of Chicken Soup
5. Adding a combination of egg yolks, cream and butter, e.g. Velouté Dame Blanche
6. Some Asian soups are thickened with coconut milk
7. Adding equal quantities of soured cream and plain yogurt.

If a finished soup is found to be too thick, its consistency can be corrected without depleting its flavour by adding some well-flavoured stock or liquid cream or yogurt. If it is too thin, its consistency can be adjusted by adding sufficient cornflour diluted in cold stock or milk or by whisking in some potato powder or cream of rice powder. Extra liaison of egg yolk, butter or cream can be used. In all these cases, the soup must be heated through after adjustment.

If, for some reason, the desired colour of a soup has not been attained, it is permissible to restore the eye-appeal by using the appropriate natural food colour, very sparingly, to obtain the right colour.

CONSOMMÉS

Consommé is a clarified meat or chicken stock (or a combination of both) either brown or white; it should be amber in colour and transparent in appearance. It is completed at the point of service with a garnish that can consist of cut vegetables, savoury egg custards, farinaceous or cereal foods, small meat or fish quenelles, shredded savoury pancakes, and many other items. Some consommés are served cold or jellied.

Consommé

2 egg whites	10 peppercorns
500 g coarsely minced shin of beef	1 bayleaf
100 g carrots ⎫	1 sprig thyme
100 g onion ⎪ coarsely cut	salt
100 g leek ⎪	3 litres cold beef stock, brown or white
100 g celery ⎭	

1. Whisk the egg whites with a little of the stock in the pan in which the consommé is to be cooked.
2. Add the minced beef, vegetables and herbs, salt and peppercorns.
3. Add the cold stock and mix well together.
4. Bring slowly to the boil, stirring at intervals with a wooden or metal spatule to prevent it sticking to the bottom of the pan and burning.
5. When it comes to the boil turn down the heat, remove the spatule and allow to simmer very gently for $1^{1}/_{2}$–2 hours.
6. Strain through a fine muslin without disturbing the crust that settled on the surface during cooking.
7. Reboil, remove all traces of fat, correct the seasoning and, if necessary, the colour.
8. Serve in a consommé cup, soup bowl or soup plate.

Notes
1. If white stock or light-coloured brown stock is used, the onions – cut in halves – may be coloured on top of the stove before being added to the consommé during the initial stages.

2. The crust that forms must not be disturbed. The soup therefore should not be skimmed during cooking as this may cause it to become cloudy.
3. Do not adjust the seasoning or colour until the consommé is completed.

Cold Consommé

This is a single or double consommé that has been cooled to a temperature of 4°C before serving.

Double Consommé

This is made with very strong stock or the gentle reduction of a normal consommé to about half its quantity. It is advisable not to season this type of consommé until the completion stage as it is likely to be naturally salty as a result of the concentration of mineral salts from the raw ingredients. When cold, double consommé will have a natural capacity to form a light jelly without the addition of gelatine.

Jellied Consommé (Consommé en Gelée)

This is consommé with the addition of 5 g gelatine per litre, added at the point where the consommé is ready for straining. It is advisable to test a small quantity in the refrigerator to see if it sets, so that adjustments can be made as necessary.

Note
Extensions to consommés are produced by the addition of a range of garnishes. Generally 100 g of garnish is sufficient for 10 standard portions and ideally it should be cooked separately and added at the point of service.

Consommé Brunoise

Consommé garnished with 100 g cooked brunoise of vegetables.

Consommé Celestine

Consommé garnished with savoury pancakes made by adding finely chopped parsley, tarragon and chervil to ordinary pancake batter, making the pancakes in the usual way then cutting them into 4 cm × 5 mm strips.

Consommé Julienne

Proceed as for consommé and serve garnished with 100 g cooked julienne of vegetables.

Consommé Madrilène

Prepare a consommé with the addition of 300 g chopped celery, 200 g tomatoes and 100 g pimento and 100 g tomato purée added at stage 2. Garnish with 50 g cooked vermicelli; 30 g shredded sorrel, cooked in a little butter; 30 g peeled and depipped tomatoes, cut into strips and 30 g skinned red pimento, cut into small diamonds.

Consommé Royale

Proceed as for consommé and garnish with 100 g of Savoury Egg Custard, cut into small diamond shapes.

Consommé Xavier

Pour 3 well-beaten and seasoned eggs through a conical strainer into the simmering consommé and cook for a few moments until the egg is slightly set.

Zuppa alla Pavese

Place sliced fried bread croûtons in the bottom of individual soup bowls, crack a small egg into each, sprinkle with grated Parmesan cheese, pour over boiling beef consommé and serve.

BOUILLONS

A bouillon is an unclarified meat or chicken stock, or a stock made with beef and chicken. It is trade practice to serve consommé as a bouillon soup. It should be amber in colour and clear in appearance and is usually garnished with small shaped pieces of beef, and chicken and vegetables, added at successive stages during the cooking process. In classical cookery a bouillon was cooked in an earthenware container, known as a marmite. Nowadays it is served in individual or multi-sized marmites.

Petite Marmite

2.5 litres consommé
  200 g carrots ⎱ turned 2 cm
  200 g turnips ⎰ barrel-shape
  150 g celery ⎱
   75 g cabbage ⎬ cut paysanne
  100 g leek ⎰ shape

200 g lean beef
10 chicken winglets
10 slices bone marrow
30 bread croûtes
50 g grated Parmesan cheese

1. Bring the consommé to the boil, add the blanched piece of beef and simmer gently for 45 minutes until tender.
2. Blanch the winglets, remove the bones, cut each in half and add to the consommé.
3. Add the vegetables in the listed order, allowing 3 minutes cooking time between each.

4. Remove the beef, cut into 1 cm dice and return to the soup.
5. Portion the very hot soup and all its ingredients between 10 individual marmite pots, add a thin slice of bone marrow and cover with the lids.
6. Serve accompanied with the toasted thin slices of French bread and the grated Parmesan cheese.

Croûte-au-pot

This is made in the same way as Petite Marmite, omitting the beef, winglets and bone marrow.

Leek, Caraway and Chicken Soup

Sweat 675 g strips of white of leek in 50 ml oil, add 2 litres chicken stock, $\frac{1}{2}$ tsp saffron, $\frac{1}{2}$ tsp caraway seeds and a bouquet garni. Simmer for 30 minutes then add 125 g vermicelli and complete the cooking. Garnish with 200 g strips of cooked chicken breast.

Potages

A further subdivision of unclarified bouillon soups is potages, thickened with a liaison of cream, or egg yolks and cream, one of the most popular in this category being Potage Germiny.

Potage Germiny

1.5 litres chicken or veal stock	100 g butter
12 egg yolks	200 g sorrel
300 ml cream	30 cheese straws

1. Whisk the yolks of egg with the cream.
2. Add one-third of the hot stock, whisking well, then pour it into the rest of the stock.
3. Stir the soup continuously over moderate heat until it thickens but do not allow it to get too close to boiling point as that will cause it to curdle.
4. Add the shredded sorrel, previously cooked in half the butter, then finish the soup by adding seasoning and the rest of the butter in small pieces.
5. Serve accompanied with the cheese straws.

Note
The stock may be thickened first with 25 g diluted cornflour, then with only 8 yolks and the cream. This will be advantageous if the soup has to be held for a period of time.

Rice and Chicken Liver Soup (Minestra di Riso e Fegatini)

Cook 275 g of long-grain rice and 100 g finely chopped and fried chicken livers in 2 litres chicken and beef stock. Finish with chopped parsley and serve sprinkled with grated Parmesan cheese.

Chicken and Egg Soup (Dahn Tong) CHINA

2 litres chicken stock	100 ml soy sauce
100 g dried mushrooms	100 ml vinegar
275 g cooked breast of chicken	25 ml chilli oil
550 g tofu	6 eggs

1. Boil the stock in a saucepan with the sliced mushrooms and chicken.
2. In a second saucepan heat the soy sauce, vinegar and chilli oil, then add the strips of tofu.
3. Add to the simmering stock and complete with the beaten eggs to form threads; season and serve.

Chicken and Galingale Soup with Coconut Milk (Kai Tom Ka) THAILAND

2 litres chicken stock	250 g strips of shiitake or oyster
25 g sliced galingale	mushrooms
2 stems lemon grass	250 ml coconut milk
2 kaffir lime leaves	2 juice of lemons
2 dried red chillies	chopped basil
50 g nam pla	seasoning
250 g strips of cooked chicken	

1. Bring the stock to the boil in a saucepan.
2. Add the lemon grass, kaffir lime leaves, sliced galingale, chillies, nam pla and mushrooms and simmer for 5 minutes. Remove and discard the lemon grass, kaffir lime leaves and chillies.
3. Season and garnish with the strips of chicken and chopped basil; finish with the coconut milk and lemon juice and serve.

Chicken Soup with Kreplach (Marak Kreplach) ISRAEL

Boil 2 litres chicken stock in a saucepan and season well. Add 30 kreplach, simmer for 8 minutes and serve.

Lokshen Soup ISRAEL

To 2 litres seasoned chicken stock add 250 g lokshen, simmer for 5 minutes and serve.

Chicken and Sweetcorn Soup (Tiansuan Gai Tong)   CHINA

2 litres chicken stock
275 ml saké
  550 g sliced mushrooms
175 ml soy sauce
  25 g chopped coriander leaves
175 ml white wine vinegar

500 g sliced cooked chicken
250 g sliced spring onions
  20 sliced, cooked baby
      sweetcorn
      seasoning

1. Boil the saké until it has reduced by one-third, then add to the hot chicken stock.
2. Add the sliced mushrooms, soy sauce, chopped coriander leaves, white wine vinegar, sliced cooked chicken, spring onion and the baby corn and simmer for 5 minutes. Season to taste and serve.

Chicken, Prawn and Noodle Soup (Mah Mee)   CHINA

2 litres chicken stock
  25 ml sesame oil
  10 g grated ginger
    2 chopped cloves of garlic
275 g bean sprouts
500 g egg noodles
  2 tsp five spice powder

100 g diced cooked chicken
250 g peeled prawns
200 g lardons of bacon, fried and
      drained
250 g crabmeat
  75 g coarsely grated cucumber
  75 g sliced spring onions

1. Heat the sesame oil in a saucepan and lightly fry the ginger and garlic, then drain off the surplus fat.
2. Add the stock and bring to the boil.
3. Add the bean sprouts and egg noodles, flavour with the five spice powder, season and simmer for 3 minutes.
4. Garnish with the chicken, prawns, lardons and crabmeat and serve accompanied by the grated cucumber and sliced spring onions.

Clear Egg Soup (Suimono)   JAPAN

Bring 2 litres dashi to the boil and thicken with 25 g diluted cornflour. Serve garnished with 50 g chopped spring onions and complete by pouring in 2 beaten eggs to form threads as it is poured into the simmering soup.

Clear Egg Soup (Consommé Con Huevos)   SPAIN

Prepare 2 litres rich chicken, veal and ham stock. Place a lightly poached egg in individual marmite bowls on a toasted round bread croûton and cover with the very hot stock.

Noodle Soup (Kakejiru) JAPAN

Simmer 2 litres second soup stock, 275 ml light soy sauce and 275 ml mirin or dry sherry. Season with salt and monosodium glutamate, add 500 g fine noodles, cook for 3 minutes and serve.

CLEAR VEGETABLE SOUPS

The vegetables for this kind of soup are cut into very neatly cut brunoise, julienne or paysanne. If potatoes are included in the recipe, they should be added last after any peas, beans or farinaceous products. Clear vegetable soups may be served either in a soup tureen or a soup plate.

Cockieleekie

1 kg chicken	60 g butter
2 litres white chicken stock	10 soaked prunes
6 leeks	salt and pepper
1 bouquet garni	

1. Blanch the chicken and place in the stock together with 4 of the leeks cut in half, seasoning and the bouquet garni; allow to simmer for 40 minutes.
2. Meanwhile, cut the other leeks into coarse julienne and sweat in the butter without coloration.
3. Remove the chicken, leeks and bouquet garni.
4. Add the sweated leek and prunes, cook for 15 minutes, remove the prunes and skim the stock.
5. Cut 200 g of julienne of the white of the chicken, stone the prunes and cut into coarse strips and add both to the soup which is now ready to serve.

Leek and Potato Soup (Potage Poireaux et Pommes)

75 g butter	2.5 litres white chicken stock
450 g white of leek ⎱ cut into	1 bouquet garni
450 g potatoes ⎰ paysanne	salt and pepper

1. Melt the butter in a pan, add the leek, cover with a lid and sweat without coloration.
2. Add the stock, bring to the boil and skim.
3. Add the bouquet garni, potatoes and seasoning.
4. Simmer gently for 15 minutes until the vegetables are cooked.
5. Remove the bouquet garni, skim all traces of fat from the surface and serve.

Minestrone

50 g butter		50 g peas
50 g carrots		50 g French beans, cut into diamonds
50 g turnips		
50 g leek	cut into paysanne	50 g tomato concassée
50 g celery		50 g fat bacon
50 g onion		2 cloves garlic
2 litres white stock		chopped parsley
25 g tomato purée		salt and pepper
50 g potatoes cut into paysanne		50 g grated Parmesan cheese
1 bouquet garni		30 croûtes de flûte
50 g spaghetti, broken into 2 cm lengths		

1. Melt the butter in a pan, add the vegetables, cover with a lid and sweat without coloration.
2. Add the stock, bring to the boil and skim.
3. Add the tomato purée, potatoes, bouquet garni and seasoning.
4. Simmer gently for 20 minutes.
5. Add the French beans, peas, tomato concassée and the spaghetti and simmer for a further 15 minutes until they are cooked.
6. Remove the bouquet garni and skim.
7. Chop the bacon, garlic and parsley into a fine paste, add to the simmering soup in small pieces and cook until it has completely disintegrated.
8. Serve the grated Parmesan cheese and croûtes de flûte separately as accompaniments.

Potage Bonne Femme

Proceed as for Leek and Potato Soup and finish with 100 ml cream and 25 g butter.

Potage Paysanne

75 g butter		1 bouquet garni
150 g carrots		50 g French beans, cut into diamonds
75 g turnips		
75 g leek	cut into paysanne	50 g peas
75 g celery		chopped parsley
75 g onion		salt and pepper
2 litres white stock		

1. Melt the butter in a pan, add the paysanne of vegetables, cover with a lid and sweat without coloration.
2. Add the stock, bring to the boil and skim.
3. Add the bouquet garni and seasoning.

4. Simmer gently until the vegetables are cooked, then add the French beans and peas, simmer for a further 10 minutes until they are cooked.
5. Remove the bouquet garni, skim off all traces of fat from the surface and add the chopped parsley.

Soupe au Chou

Sweat 350 g lardons of bacon in 50 ml oil with a paysanne of 50 g onion, 100 g leek, 175 g carrot, 450 g cabbage and 2 chopped cloves of garlic. Add 2 litres chicken stock, and bring to the boil. Add 225 g paysanne of potato and cook for 20 minutes until all the vegetables are cooked. Finish with a liaison of 4 egg yolks and 225 ml cream and serve.

Nettle Soup (Zuppa di Ortiche)

Lightly fry 100 g lardons of unsmoked streaky bacon or pancetta and 100 g chopped onion in 50 ml olive oil. Add 225 g tomato concassée and 1.5 kg chopped young nettle leaves; moisten with 2 litres chicken stock, simmer for 30 minutes. Liquidise, reboil, season and serve.

Red Bean Paste Soup (Akadashi) JAPAN

2 litres dashi
  125 g red bean paste
  125 g finely diced tofu
   50 g spring onions

1. Bring the dashi to simmering point in a saucepan.
2. Pass the bean paste through a fine sieve and add to the dashi, then add the tofu and simmer for 2 minutes.
3. Serve garnished with the chopped spring onions.

BROTH SOUPS

Broth soups are made by cooking various cuts of several kinds of vegetables in a white chicken, game or mutton stock, with the addition of a cereal and diced meat or poultry, according to the name of the broth.

A cereal such as pearl barley or rice may be cooked separately and added at the completion stage but is best cooked in the soup.

Chicken Broth

2.5 litres white chicken stock		1 bouquet garni
75 g carrots		40 g long-grain rice
75 g turnips	cut into brunoise	150 g chicken
75 g leek		salt and pepper
75 g celery		chopped parsley

1. Boil the stock and add the vegetables, bouquet garni and seasoning.
2. Simmer gently for 15 minutes, then add the washed rice, bring to the boil and skim.
3. When the vegetables and rice are cooked, remove the bouquet garni and all traces of fat.
4. Add the chicken cut into small dice, finish with chopped parsley and serve.

French Onion Soup (Soupe à l'Oignon Gratinée)

50 g butter	20 croûtes de flûte
800 g sliced onions	100 g grated Parmesan and
25 g flour	Gruyère cheese
2 litres brown stock	salt and pepper

1. Melt the butter in a deep pan. Add the onions, cover with a lid and sweat, then allow to colour lightly by removing the lid.
2. Stir in the flour with a wooden spatule and allow to cool.
3. Add the hot stock a little at a time, season and allow to simmer gently for 30 minutes until the onion is cooked.
4. Ladle the soup into earthenware soup bowls (petites marmites) and cover the surface with overlapping croûtes de flûte. Sprinkle with the grated cheeses and place under a salamander grill until golden.

Mutton Broth

2.5 litres white mutton stock	150 g scrag end of mutton
75 g carrots	1 bouquet garni
75 g turnips cut into brunoise	40 g pearl barley
75 g leek	salt and pepper
75 g celery	chopped parsley

1. Cook the scrag end of mutton and the barley in the mutton stock for 1 hour, then remove the meat and retain.
2. Add the vegetables, bouquet garni and seasoning to the stock.
3. Simmer gently for 15 minutes and skim.
4. When the vegetables are cooked, remove the bouquet garni, add the mutton cut into small dice and skim off any traces of fat. Serve sprinkled with chopped parsley.

Scotch Broth

2.5 litres white stock	1 bouquet garni
75 g carrots	40 g pearl barley
75 g turnips cut into brunoise	salt and pepper
75 g leek	chopped parsley
75 g celery	

1. Cook the barley in the stock for 1 hour.
2. Add the vegetables, bouquet garni and seasoning.
3. Simmer gently for 15 minutes and skim.
4. When the vegetables are cooked, remove the bouquet garni.
5. Season and remove any traces of fat. Serve sprinkled with chopped parsley.

Bortsch

400 g cooked beetroot, cut into batons	2 litres white stock
225 g carrots, cut into strips	250 g finely shredded cabbage
100 g sliced onion	100 g leek, cut into strips
50 ml oil	4 chopped cloves of garlic
1 juice of lemon	1 bouquet garni
100 g tomato concassée	250 g diced potatoes
25 g tomato purée	250 g diced cooked beef
10 g sugar	250 ml smetana
50 ml white wine vinegar	salt and pepper

1. Heat the oil in a saucepan, add the beetroot, carrot and onion, cover with a lid and allow to sweat without coloration.
2. Add the lemon juice, tomato concassée, tomato purée, sugar, vinegar and stock, bring to the boil and skim.
3. Add the cabbage, leek, potato, garlic, bouquet garni and seasoning.
4. Simmer gently for 20 minutes until the vegetables are cooked.
5. Remove the bouquet garni and garlic and skim all traces of fat from the surface.
6. Add the diced beef, reboil and serve accompanied with the smetana.

Cabbage Soup (Shchi)

Sweat 50 g chopped onion and 50 g each of diced parsnip and celery in 50 ml oil. Add 2 litres white stock and simmer, adding 450 g shredded cabbage; 75 g tomato concassée; 100 g julienne of carrot; a bouquet garni including some dill; 3 chopped cloves of garlic and seasoning. Simmer for 20 minutes. Add 100 g diced potato and, when cooked, serve sprinkled with chopped dill on a swirl of smetana or yogurt.

Corn Chowder

1 litre chicken stock	225 g lardons of bacon
500 g sweetcorn kernels	10 g chopped parsley
350 g sliced onion	125 ml milk
25 ml oil	150 ml cream
225 g diced potatoes	seasoning

1. Liquidise the sweetcorn kernels with the seasoned stock.
2. Sweat the onion in the oil, drain off the surplus and add the liquidised corn.
3. Bring to the boil, add the potatoes and simmer for 10 minutes.
4. Add the milk, the fried lardons and chopped parsley.
5. Finish with the cream and serve.

Garlic and Coriander Soup (Sopa a Alentejana)   PORTUGAL

Blend 3 cloves of garlic and 25 g coriander leaves to a paste. Spread 20 croûtons with the paste and place into soup bowls. Moisten with 1.5 litres water boiled with 300 ml olive oil and seasoning; break an egg into each bowl, allow to simmer until poached and serve.

Green Bortsch (Zelyony Borscht)   RUSSIA

Sweat 350 g shredded sorrel in 25 ml oil, add 225 g cooked, finely chopped spinach, 2 litres veal velouté and seasoning and simmer for 20 minutes. Finish with 175 ml soured cream and garnish each serving with half a hard-boiled egg. Sprinkle with chopped dill, parsley and coriander leaves and serve accompanied with yogurt.

Gulyàs   HUNGARY

50 ml oil	25 g tomato purée
75 g carrots	1 litre white beef stock
75 g turnips	1 litre chicken stock
75 g leek } cut into small dice	1 bouquet garni
75 g celery	1 tsp caraway seeds
2 cloves of chopped garlic	200 g tomato concassée
20 g flour	150 g diced cooked beef
30 g paprika	salt and pepper

1. Heat the oil in a pan, add the diced vegetables and the garlic, cover with a lid and sweat without coloration.
2. Stir in the flour and paprika, then add the tomato purée.
3. Add the stocks, bring to the boil, season and skim.
4. Add the bouquet garni, caraway seeds, tomato concassée and seasoning.
5. Simmer gently for 20 minutes until the vegetables are cooked.
6. Remove the bouquet garni and skim off any fat.
7. Add the diced beef, bring to the boil and serve.

Haricot Bean Soup (Fassoulatha)   GREECE

Cook 350 g soaked small haricot beans with 50 g chopped onion, 2 chopped cloves of garlic, 50 g tomato purée, 100 g each of diced celery, carrot and tomato concassée, 50 ml olive oil and $1/4$ tsp sugar in 2 litres of white stock until tender. Sprinkle with chopped parsley and serve.

Mutton and Dill Soup (Harcho) HUNGARY

Sweat 100 g chopped onion, 1 chopped clove of garlic and 100 g chopped celery in 25 ml oil. Add 50 g tomato purée and 2 litres mutton stock. Rain in 100 g rice, add 75 g chopped pickled plums and simmer for 20 minutes, then season. Garnish with diced cooked mutton and chopped dill and serve.

Peas and Kleis ISRAEL

1 kg boiled peas	*Kleis batter*:
2 litres milk	1 egg
50 g butter	200 ml milk
50 g chopped mint	175 g fine matzo meal
seasoning	salt

1. Boil the milk in a saucepan, season, add the peas, butter and chopped mint and gently simmer.
2. Make the Kleis batter. Whisk together the egg, milk and matzo meal and season with salt.
3. Drop teaspoonfuls of Kleis batter into the soup and poach for 4 minutes.

Spring Green Soup (Caldo Verde) PORTUGAL

Sweat 250 g sliced onion in 50 ml olive oil. Moisten with 2 litres chicken stock, add 150 g roughly cut potatoes, season and cook for 30 minutes. Liquidise, reboil and add 100 g each of shredded, boiled spring greens and diced chorizo sausage.

Vegetable Broth with Dumplings (Frische suppe) GERMANY

Cut 100 g each of carrot, turnip and celery into 5 mm dice and sweat in 50 ml oil. Add 2 litres vegetable stock, 75 g peas, 75 g French beans, cut diamond shape, and cook for 15 minutes until all the vegetables are tender.

To make the dumplings boil 150 ml salted water with 25 g butter. Mix in 100 g flour to a firm paste, allow to cool then beat in 1 egg and 2 egg yolks. Form into small balls and cook about 20 in the soup until they are firm.

PURÉE SOUPS

Purée soups are made from dried pulses or fresh vegetables, processed in a liquidiser then, if necessary, passed through a sieve. Vegetables which contain a high level of starch should thicken the soup by themselves; those with a low level will require an additional thickening agent such as potatoes, potato flour or powder, or rice. No garnish is added but they are usually served with toasted bread sippets or diced, fried bread croûtons as the accompaniment.

Purée soups based on dried pulses

Dried pulses which have an outer shell require soaking in cold water for twelve hours before cooking; they are then washed in cold water. Pulses such as green split peas and lentils which do not have an outer shell do not require soaking.

Purée of Green Split Pea Soup (Purée St Germain)

600 g green split peas	150 g bacon trimmings or ham bone
3 litres vegetable stock	1 bouquet garni
1 whole carrot	salt and pepper
1 whole onion	100 g diced fried bread croûtons

1. Place the split peas in a deep pan, cover with the stock, bring to the boil and skim.
2. Add the carrot, onion, bacon trimmings and bouquet garni and allow to simmer until the peas are soft.
3. When cooked, remove the carrot, onion, bouquet garni and bacon trimmings.
4. Pass the soup through a soup machine or process in a blender, return to a clean saucepan and reboil.
5. Correct the consistency and seasoning as necessary.
6. Serve accompanied by the croûtons.

Notes
1. Salt should not be added until the pulse is cooked.
2. To test if cooked remove some of the pulse with a perforated spoon and rub between the fingers to a smooth paste. If still slightly gritty it requires further cooking.

Potage Esaü

Proceed as for Purée of Green Split Pea Soup, using lentils instead of green split peas. Serve garnished with 100 g boiled long grain rice.

Purée of Haricot Bean Soup (Potage Bretonne)

Soak 600 g haricot beans for 12 hours. Proceed as for Purée of Green Split Pea Soup, adding 75 g tomato purée after the soup has been passed.

Purée of Yellow Split Pea Soup (Purée Egyptienne)

Proceed as for Purée of Green Split Pea Soup, using yellow split peas instead of green split peas.

Purée soups based on fresh vegetables

The name of a soup is determined by the main vegetable used, e.g. Purée of Carrot Soup, Purée of Turnip Soup, Purée of Mixed Vegetable Soup. This kind of soup tastes better if the vegetables are sweated in butter, before adding the stock. The vegetables must be completely cooked before puréeing, or the soup will have a coarse texture. This can be corrected by passing it through a very fine strainer, though this will reduce the finished quantity. When making a purée soup with cauliflower, Jerusalem artichokes or haricot beans the result will be grey or off-white if it is cooked in an aluminium pan. Purée of vegetable soups should be made with vegetable rather than meat stock.

Potage Solférino

This soup consists of equal quantities of Purée of Potato and Leek Soup and Tomato Soup. Garnish with small balls of carrot and potato.

Purée of Carrot Soup (Purée Crécy)

100 g butter	1 bouquet garni
1 kg carrots	salt and pepper
2.5 litres vegetable stock	100 g diced fried bread croûtons

1. Melt the butter in a deep saucepan, add the chopped carrots; cover with a lid and sweat without coloration.
2. Add the stock, bring to the boil and skim.
3. Add the bouquet garni and seasoning and allow to simmer until the carrots are cooked.
4. Remove the bouquet garni, pass the soup through a soup machine or process in a blender, return to a clean saucepan and reboil.
5. Serve accompanied by the croûtons.

Purée of Potato and Leek Soup (Potage Parmentier)

75 g butter	750 g potatoes
150 g white of leek	1 bouquet garni
100 g onions	100 g diced fried bread croûtons
2.5 litres vegetable stock	salt and pepper

1. Melt the butter in a deep pan.
2. Add the sliced leek and onion; cover with a lid and sweat without coloration.
3. Add the stock, bring to the boil and skim.
4. Add the roughly cut potatoes, bouquet garni and seasoning and allow to simmer until cooked.

5. Remove the bouquet garni, pass the soup through a soup machine or process in a blender, return to a clean pan and reboil.
6. Serve accompanied by the croûtons.

Purée of Vegetable Soup
(Purée de Légumes or Potage Garbure)

100 g butter	600 ml vegetable stock
200 g carrots	400 g potatoes
200 g celery	1 bouquet garni
200 g white of leek	100 g bread sippets
100 g turnip	salt and pepper
150 g onion	

1. Melt the butter in a deep pan.
2. Add the roughly cut vegetables, cover with a lid and sweat without coloration.
3. Add the stock, bring to the boil and skim.
4. Add the potatoes, bouquet garni and seasoning and allow to simmer until the vegetables are cooked.
5. Remove the bouquet garni, then pass the soup through a soup machine or process in a blender, return to a clean pan and reboil.
6. Serve accompanied by the bread sippets.

Purée of Turnip Soup (Potage Freneuse)

Proceed as for Purée of Vegetable Soup, using 1 kg turnips.

Purée of Cabbage and Nettle Soup (Zelonyeshchi)   RUSSIA

To 2 litres boiling stock add 450 g each of roughly cut potatoes and cabbage. Cook for 15 minutes, then add 450 g young nettle leaves. Complete the cooking then liquidise, strain, reboil and season with salt and pepper. Add cooked diced beef and serve garnished with 1 small soft-boiled egg for each portion, accompanied by smetana or yogurt.

Purée of Pumpkin Soup   USA

Sweat 100 g sliced onion in 25 ml oil, add 1 litre stock and 300 ml milk, 1 kg diced pumpkin flesh, 50 ml lemon juice, seasoning and 1 tsp grated nutmeg or mace. Cook for 20 minutes, then liquidise, strain, reboil and serve.

CREAM AND VELOUTÉ SOUPS

There are four ways of making these soups, each using a traditional cooking method, but all being finished with cream.

They are:

1. Vegetables are sweated in butter to which flour is added to form a roux. White stock is added and the soup is cooked, puréed, then finished with cream or a liaison.
2. A purée-type soup is prepared with the addition of one-third each of béchamel and white stock. It is finished with cream or a liaison.
3. A second stage roux is prepared to which a white stock is added to make a velouté. This is then finished with a liaison or cream.
4. The basic ingredients are cooked in a prepared velouté, then passed and finished with a liaison or cream.

The cream soups listed first in this section may also be served as velouté soups by finishing them with a liaison of 4 yolks of egg, 100 ml cream and 50 g butter instead of only cream, taking care not to let them boil after adding the liaison. Garnished cream and velouté soups were traditionally served only for dinner but now are appropriate at any meal time.

Cream of Asparagus Soup
(Crème d'Asperges or Crème Argenteuil)

125 g butter	200 ml cream
125 g flour	50 g butter
2 litres vegetable stock	100 g asparagus tips
800 g asparagus stalks	salt and pepper

1. Melt the butter in a deep pan.
2. Mix in the flour with a wooden spatule, cook to a second stage roux and allow to cool.
3. Add the hot stock, season, add the blanched asparagus stalks and simmer gently for 1 hour.
4. Pass through a fine conical strainer or liquidise in a blender and return to a clean pan.
5. Reboil and finish with the cream and knobs of butter. Garnish with the cooked asparagus tips.

Cream of Cauliflower Soup (Crème Dubarry)

125 g butter	1 bouquet garni
125 g flour	200 ml cream
2.5 litres vegetable stock	50 g butter
1 kg cauliflower	salt and pepper

1. Melt the butter in a deep pan, stir in the flour to form a white roux and allow to cool.
2. Pick 100 g small florets from the cauliflower, cook until slightly tender, drain and reserve.

3. Add the hot stock to the roux, add the remainder of the cauliflower, the bouquet garni and seasoning and allow to cook for 1 hour.
4. Pass the soup through a fine sieve, soup machine or in a blender.
5. Reboil, correct the seasoning, and consistency, then add the cooked cauliflower florets.
6. Finish the soup with the cream and butter and serve.

Cream of Celery Soup (Crème de Céleris)

Proceed as for Cream of Asparagus Soup, using 1 kg celery and serve garnished with 100 g cooked julienne of celery.

Cream of Chicken Soup (Crème de Volaille)

125 g butter	50 g butter
125 g flour	100 g cooked breast of chicken
2 litres white chicken stock	salt and pepper
200 ml cream	

1. Melt the butter in a deep pan.
2. Mix in the flour with a wooden spatule, cook to a second stage roux and allow to cool.
3. Add the hot stock and simmer gently for 1 hour.
4. Pass through a fine conical strainer or liquidise in a blender and return to a clean saucepan.
5. Reboil, remove from the heat and finish with the cream and knobs of butter and garnish with strips of chicken.

Cream of Pea Soup (Crème de Pois Frais)

75 g butter	200 ml cream
150 g white of leek	50 g butter
2 lettuces	100 g boiled peas
1.5 litres vegetable stock	pluches of chervil
1 kg peas	salt and pepper
500 ml béchamel	

1. Melt the butter in a deep saucepan.
2. Add the roughly shredded lettuce and leek, cover with a lid and sweat without coloration.
3. Add the stock, bring to the boil and skim.
4. Add the fresh peas and seasoning and allow to simmer until cooked; add the béchamel and mix in well.
5. Pass through a soup machine or blender, then through a fine conical strainer and return to a clean saucepan.
6. Reboil and finish with the cream and knobs of butter and garnish with cooked peas and pluches of chervil.

Crème Camelia

Prepare 2 litres Cream of Pea Soup and add a garnish of 75 g each of julienne of breast of chicken and white of leek, both cooked in butter.

Note
To serve as Velouté Camelia, finish with a liaison of 4 egg yolks, 100 ml cream and 50 g butter.

Crème Fontanges

Garnish 2 litres Cream of Pea Soup with 75 g shredded sorrel cooked in butter and 25 g pluches of chervil.

Cream of Jerusalem Artichoke Soup (Crème Palestine)

Proceed as for Cream of Asparagus Soup, using 1.5 kg Jerusalem artichokes.

Crème Lamballe

Prepare 2 litres Cream of Pea Soup and garnish with 100 g cooked seed tapioca.

Crème Longchamps

Prepare 2 litres Cream of Pea Soup and garnish with 75 g cooked broken vermicelli, 50 g shredded sorrel cooked in butter and 25 g pluches of chervil.

Cream of Mushroom Soup (Crème de Champignons)

125 g butter	200 ml cream
125 g flour	50 g butter
2 litres vegetable stock	100 g button mushrooms
800 g sieved mushrooms	salt and pepper

1. Melt the butter in a deep pan.
2. Mix in the flour with a wooden spatule, cook to a second stage roux and allow to cool.
3. Add the hot stock, the sieved mushrooms and seasoning and simmer gently for 1 hour.
4. Pass through a fine conical strainer into a clean saucepan.
5. Reboil and finish with the cream and knobs of butter and garnish with julienne strips of cooked mushrooms.

Cream of Sweetcorn Soup (Crème Washington)

Proceed as for Cream of Asparagus Soup, using 800 g raw or canned sweetcorn kernels and serve garnished with 100 g sweetcorn kernels.

Cream of Watercress Soup (Crème Cressonière)

100 g sliced white of leek
100 g sliced onion
25 g butter
2 litres vegetable stock
225 g potatoes, roughly cut

1 bouquet garni
225 g watercress
200 ml cream
seasoning

1. Melt the butter in a deep saucepan, add the sliced leek and onion, cover with a lid and sweat without coloration.
2. Add the stock, bring to the boil and skim.
3. Add the potatoes, bouquet garni and seasoning.
4. Simmer gently for 20 minutes until the vegetables are cooked.
5. Remove the bouquet garni, add the watercress, boil for 2 minutes, then pass through a soup machine, sieve or blender; strain and reboil.
6. Finish with the cream and serve garnished with blanched watercress leaves.

Note
To serve as Velouté Cressonière, finish with a liaison of 4 egg yolks, 100 ml cream and 50 g butter.

Crème Reine

Prepare 2 litres Cream of Chicken Soup and garnish with 125 g cooked rice and 75 g breast of chicken cut into small dice.

Velouté Agnes Sorel

Prepare 2 litres Cream of Chicken Soup and garnish with 75 g each of julienne cooked button mushrooms, ox tongue and breast of chicken. Complete with a liaison of 4 egg yolks, 100 ml cream and 50 g butter.

Velouté Dame Blanche

Prepare 2 litres Cream of Chicken Soup and garnish with 75 g breast of chicken cut into small dice. Complete with a liaison of 4 egg yolks, 100 ml cream and 50 g butter.

Cream of Haricot Bean Soup (Palòc Soup)   HUNGARY

Lightly fry 2 chopped cloves of garlic, 100 g chopped onion and 100 g lardons of bacon in 25 ml oil. Sprinkle with 1 tbs paprika and 50 g flour to form a roux. Add 2 litres mutton stock, a bouquet garni, 1 tsp caraway seeds and 450 g previously soaked small haricot beans; simmer for 30 minutes. Add 450 g diced potatoes and 225 g French beans cut into diamond shapes, 150 g diced cooked lamb and 10 g finely chopped parsley and simmer for a further

20 minutes. Season the soup and finish with 225 ml yogurt, crème fraîche or soured cream.

Cream of Peanut Soup CARIBBEAN

2 litres chicken stock
100 g chopped onion
25 ml groundnut oil
225 g roasted peanuts
2 dried red or green chillies

50 g chopped chives
2 tsp angostura bitters
225 ml cream
seasoning

1. Sweat the chopped onion in the groundnut oil.
2. Blend it with the peanuts, chillies and 500 ml of the chicken stock to form a fine paste.
3. Boil the remainder of the stock in a saucepan, season, add the blended ingredients and simmer for a few minutes.
4. Add the chives, angostura bitters and cream and serve.

Cream of Potato Soup (Kartoffelsuppe) GERMANY

Sweat 100 g each of roughly cut carrot, celery and leek in 50 ml oil. Moisten with 2 litres chicken stock and add 1 kg cut potatoes and seasoning. Simmer for 30 minutes, liquidise, strain and reboil. Season with nutmeg, garnish with strips of boiled potatoes, sautéd diced onions and chopped chives, finish with 250 ml cream and serve.

Cream of Spinach Soup (Spinatsuppe) SCANDINAVIA

Boil 2 litres chicken velouté, add 350 g purée of spinach and season with salt, pepper and nutmeg. Finish with 225 ml yogurt, crème fraîche or cream and serve garnished with sliced hard-boiled egg.

Cream of Summer Vegetable Soup with Prawns (Kesäkeitto) SCANDINAVIA

Add 1 kg roughly cut carrots, cauliflower, French beans and radishes to 2 litres vegetable stock and cook for 30 minutes; when almost cooked, add 175 g peas, 450 g shredded spinach and cook again. Liquidise, reboil and season. Finish with 225 ml yogurt, crème fraîche or cream and serve garnished with 350 g peeled prawns and sprinkle with chopped dill.

Egg and Lemon Soup (Avgolemono Soupa) GREECE

Cook 275 g long-grain rice or short egg noodles in 2 litres white chicken stock and thicken with a liaison of 8 yolks of egg mixed with 50 ml lemon juice.

Lemon Soup (Citronsuppe)

Flavour 2 litres chicken velouté with the grated zest of 4 lemons and finish with a liaison of 4 egg yolks, 100 g sugar and 125 ml lemon juice. Cook gently until it thickens, then adjust the seasoning and serve accompanied by croûtons and yogurt, crème fraîche or whipped cream.

ROUX-BASED SOUPS

Oxtail Soup (Potage Queue de Boeuf Lié)

100 g dripping	1.5 kg oxtail ends
125 g flour	50 g small balls of carrot
25 g tomato purée	50 g small balls of turnip
2.5 litres brown stock	100 ml dry sherry
200 g carrots ⎫	salt and pepper
200 g onions ⎬ roughly cut	
100 g celery ⎭	

1. Heat the dripping in a deep pan, add the flour and stir with a wooden spatule to a third stage roux; add the tomato purée and allow to cool.
2. Add the hot stock a little at a time, mixing well to prevent lumps forming.
3. Lightly fry the oxtail and vegetables to colour them, drain and add to the soup, season and simmer gently for 2 hours, skimming as necessary.
4. When the oxtail is cooked, remove from the soup, cool, remove the flesh and cut into small dice. Retain in stock until required for garnishing.
5. Pass the soup through a strainer; reboil, skim and add the diced oxtail and the carrot and turnip balls; finish with the sherry.

Brown Windsor Soup

Proceed as for Oxtail Soup, omitting the oxtail. Finish the soup with 100 ml dry sherry and serve garnished with 120 g boiled long grain rice and 300 g diced carrot and turnip, peas and diamonds of French beans.

Mock Turtle Soup (Potage Fausse Tortue)

Proceed as for Oxtail Soup, replacing the oxtail with 4 boned calf's feet. Add an infusion of turtle herbs and 100 ml dry sherry during the last stages of cooking. Serve garnished with diced calf's feet, accompanied by cheese straws.

Note
This soup was traditionally made with calf's head and served garnished with diced calf's cheek.

Cream of Tomato Soup (Crème de Tomate)

100 g butter	125 g flour
100 g carrots ⎫	150 g tomato purée
100 g onions ⎬ roughly cut	2.5 litres vegetable stock
75 g celery ⎭	100 ml vinegar ⎫ reduction
75 g bacon trimmings	30 g sugar ⎭
1 clove garlic	200 ml cream
1 sprig thyme	salt and pepper
1 bayleaf	

1. Melt the butter in a saucepan.
2. Add the vegetables, herbs, bacon and garlic and fry gently to a light golden colour.
3. Add the flour and stir with a wooden spatule to a second stage roux.
4. Add the tomato purée; allow to cool slightly and gradually add the boiling stock. Season with salt and pepper and simmer for 1 hour.
5. Cook the vinegar and sugar until slightly evaporated.
6. When cooked, taste the soup, add the required amount of the reduction to give the correct degree of tartness then pass through a conical strainer and reboil.
7. Finish the soup at the last moment with the cream and serve.

Crème Malakoff

Mix together equal quantities of Cream of Tomato Soup and Potato and Leek Soup and garnish with shredded spinach or sorrel cooked in butter.

Crème Portugaise

Garnish Cream of Tomato Soup with 50 g tomato concassée and 100 g plain boiled long-grain rice.

Mulligatawny Soup

100 g butter	1 clove garlic
400 g onions	50 g chopped chutney
50 g curry powder	50 g chopped apple
25 g flour	50 g cooked long grain rice
25 g tomato purée	salt and pepper
2.5 litres vegetable stock	

1. Melt the butter in a deep pan, add the sliced onion and cook until light golden in colour.
2. Stir in the flour and curry powder with a wooden spatule and cook to a second stage roux, add the tomato purée and allow to cool slightly.

3. Add the hot stock, bring to the boil and skim, then add the garlic, chutney, apple and seasoning. Allow to simmer gently for 45 minutes, skimming as necessary.
4. Pass the soup through a conical strainer, sieve or process in a blender.
5. Reboil and finish with the plain boiled rice.

Kidney Soup (Soupe aux Rognons)

Proceed as for Oxtail Soup, substituting 500 g minced and fried ox kidney for the oxtail. Once the soup has cooked and been passed, garnish with 150 g ox kidney cut into dice, lightly fried and drained. Finish with 100 ml dry sherry.

FISH AND SHELLFISH SOUPS

Fish soups are made in the same way as broth-type soups, Clam Chowder and Cream of Mussel Soup being good examples. Pieces of fish and shellfish are cooked in fish stock, water or wine with vegetables, herbs and flavourings, the liquid being served as a soup with slices of crusty bread, followed by the fish in the remains of the soup as a main course.

Shellfish soups, known as Bisques, are very popular because of their richness of flavour, colour and consistency which puts them in the category of high-class soups even though they can be made from the shells only of crustaceans. They are, of course, better when made from raw crustacea; molluscs are not suitable for making bisques.

Mussel Soup, also called Billy-Bye Soup

Cook 2 kg mussels with 100 g chopped shallots, 50 g chopped parsley and ½ tsp saffron in 600 ml dry white wine and 1 litre fish stock for 10 minutes. Strain the cooking liquor through muslin, reboil and thicken with 50 g diluted arrowroot. Garnish with the shelled and bearded mussels and finish with a liaison of 4 egg yolks and 250 ml crème fraîche or cream.

Lobster Soup (Bisque de Homard)

100 ml oil	1 litre fish stock
100 g carrots ⎫	50 g tomato purée
100 g onions ⎬ roughly cut	1.5 litre fish velouté
50 g celery ⎭	50 g butter
few parsley stalks	100 ml cream
1 sprig thyme	50 ml brandy
1 bayleaf	100 g diced cooked lobster
2 kg lobster shells	salt and pepper

1. Heat the oil in a shallow pan, add the vegetables and herbs and lightly colour them.
2. Add the crushed lobster shells and cook.
3. Add the fish stock and tomato purée and allow to simmer gently to extract the flavour, for 1 hour.
4. Strain the liquid into another saucepan and boil to reduce by half.
5. Whisk in the velouté and continue cooking for a further 10 minutes.
6. Pass the soup through a fine strainer, reboil, remove from the heat and finish with the cream, knobs of butter and brandy and add the diced lobster.

Note

If the soup appears pale in colour after the cream is added, extra tomato purée may be added to give the required pink lobster colour.

Soupe de Poisson

Lightly fry 100 g each of chopped onion, sliced white of leek, sliced carrot, sliced celery and 3 crushed cloves of garlic in 50 ml olive oil. Add 350 g tomato concassée, 2 litres fish stock and a bouquet garni. Add 1 kg goujons of assorted fish, e.g. monkfish, mackerel, red mullet, bream, whiting, cod and haddock. Simmer for 30 minutes and when the fish is cooked remove and keep warm. Liquidise the cooking liquor, strain and reboil. Add $1/2$ tsp saffron and 225 g vermicelli and cook for 5 minutes. Replace the fish and serve accompanied by sliced fried bread croûtons rubbed with garlic, Parmesan cheese and rouille.

Note

To make rouille, cut a 7 cm piece of French bread in dice and soak in a little of the fish soup then press to a paste. Blend 4 cloves of garlic, a pinch of saffron, 1 yolk of egg and the bread to a purée then gradually add 75 ml olive oil to give the consistency of mayonnaise.

Fish Chowder   USA

Lightly fry 175 g lardons of bacon or salt pork and 1 kg sliced onions in 50 ml oil. Add 50 g flour to form a roux, then moisten with 1 litre fish stock, simmer and add 1 kg sliced potatoes and a bouquet garni and cook for 15 minutes. Add 850 ml milk, 1 kg goujons of white fish and seasoning and simmer for another 25 minutes. Serve sprinkled with chopped parsley, accompanied by broken cream cracker biscuits.

Psarosoupa   GREECE

Simmer 2 litres fish stock with 450 g of tomato flesh and 50 ml olive oil. Rain in 100 g rice or tapioca and simmer for 20 minutes. Season, finish with 50 ml lemon juice and serve sprinkled with chopped parsley.

Prawn Soup (Kung Tom Yam)   THAILAND

1 kg prawns	25 g nam pla
25 ml groundnut oil	2 juice of lemons
2 litres water	30 g coriander leaves
2 stems lemon grass	50 g spring onions
3 fresh green chillies	seasoning

1. Heat the oil in a saucepan; add the heads and shells of the prawns and fry for 4 minutes.
2. Moisten with the water and bring to the boil; add the lemon grass, sliced chillies and simmer for 20 minutes, then strain into a clean saucepan.
3. Add the nam pla and lemon juice, season and garnish with the peeled prawns, chopped coriander leaves and spring onions and serve.

Sour Soup with Prawns (Tom Yam Koong)   THAILAND

2 litres chicken stock	100 g sliced oyster mushrooms
6 slices of tamarind	50 g chopped coriander leaves
6 dried red chillies	50 g nam pla
4 kaffir lime leaves	2 juice of lemons
75 g grated ginger	200 g peeled prawns
1 stem lemon grass	seasoning
1 bunch watercress	

1. Simmer the seasoned chicken stock in a saucepan with the tamarind, chillies, kaffir lime leaves, ginger and lemon grass for 15 minutes, then strain into a clean saucepan.
2. Reboil, add the watercress leaves, oyster mushrooms, coriander leaves and nam pla and simmer for 15 minutes. Finish with the lemon juice, garnish with the peeled prawns, and serve.

CHILLED SOUPS

Vichyssoise

Prepare 2 litres of Potato and Leek Soup and garnish with 100 g chopped chives. Finish with 200 ml cream and serve chilled.

Chilled Almond and Grape Soup (Sopa Blanca Al Uvas)   SPAIN

To 450 g finely ground almonds and 3 chopped cloves of garlic, slowly whisk in 125 ml olive oil, 125 ml wine vinegar and 1.5 litres water to form an emulsion. Chill, garnish with 450 g peeled, deseeded and halved white grapes and serve.

Chilled Rosehip Soup (Nyponsoppa)

Soak 1 kg rosehips in 2 litres water for 48 hours. Cook together with the grated zest of 2 lemons for 20 minutes. Liquidise and reboil, then thicken with 25 g diluted arrowroot and season. Finish with 75 ml lemon juice, chill and garnish with toasted shredded almonds. Serve accompanied by yogurt, crème fraîche or cream.

Chilled Spinach, Sorrel and Cider Soup (Botvinya)

Sweat 350 g shredded sorrel in 25 ml oil, then blend with 125 g purée of cooked spinach, 1 tsp sugar, seasoning and 25 g English mustard. Add 2 litres dry cider or kvas, and boil. Chill and garnish with 175 g sliced pickled cucumber, 75 g chopped chives and 50 g chopped dill. Divide 275 g flaked, cooked pike or perch and 50 g grated horseradish into 10 soup bowls, ladle in the chilled soup and serve.

Chilled Elderberry, Plum and Apple Soup (Fliederbeersuppe)

Poach 1 kg elderberries in 1.5 litres water with 50 g sugar for 15 minutes. Liquidise, strain and reboil, then thicken with 75 g diluted arrowroot. Add 450 g diced dessert apples, 450 g halved stoned plums and complete the cooking. Serve chilled.

Gazpacho

Liquidise 225 g bread previously soaked in 200 ml white wine with 6 cloves of garlic, 150 ml wine vinegar, 125 ml olive oil, 350 g tomato flesh, 175 g chopped green pimento, 10 g crushed cumin seeds and 1 litre water. Chill and serve accompanied by a dish each of chopped parsley, onion, cucumber, red pimento and hard-boiled egg, and fried bread croûtons.

CHAPTER 3 Egg and Cheese Dishes

Egg Dishes

The factor which differentiates the cooking of eggs from most other commodities is the short space of time between the point when the eggs are cooked to the peak of perfection and the point when they become inedible due to overcooking. The decision as to whether they are cooked to the required degree must be taken in a matter of seconds rather than minutes. The holding time – the period between when the dish is cooked and when it is consumed – must always be taken into consideration. Unlike most other foods, eggs continue to cook after removal from the heat and are affected by even a low level of heat such as a warm plate.

There are four main methods of cooking eggs:

- **Poaching** – This is cooking eggs without their shells in water so as to set the white around the yolk, which should remain soft. The term also covers oeufs en cocotte which are eggs cooked in special porcelain dishes with various garnishes.
- **Boiling** – This is cooking eggs in their shells for varying lengths of time: 2–3 minutes for soft-boiled served in the shell; 5–7 minutes for soft-centred eggs to be shelled for further use; and 10 minutes for hard-boiled eggs. These times apply to medium-sized eggs, large ones require an additional minute.
- **Shallow frying** – This is cooking eggs in a small amount of fat. The term also covers the making of omelettes.
- **Scrambled eggs** – This is cooking beaten eggs until almost set, with the addition of butter and/or cream.

Always use eggs kept at room temperature rather than straight from the refrigerator and do not leave cooked eggs in contact with any metal dish for more than a few moments or the underside will start to discolour.

POACHED EGGS

Poached eggs are cooked by gentle simmering completely submerged in water containing a little vinegar. Alternatively, they can be cooked in a special pan with indentations for each egg, which works by steaming on the bain-marie system.

Eggs en cocotte are cooked by breaking each egg into an individual oven-to-table porcelain dish placed in a pan of hot water, covered with a lid.

Poached Egg – Oeuf Poché

Bring a shallow pan of water to the boil, add 1 part vinegar to 10 parts water, then let it simmer gently. Crack the eggs into the water one at a time, allowing one second between each; the white should envelop the yolk. Poach for about four minutes and when the white is firm but not hard, remove from the water with a perforated spoon. Trim off the loose edges and place on the prepared dish or plate; if for future use or for serving cold, keep them in a basin of cold water in a refrigerator.

Notes
1. Use a shallow pan of sufficient size three-quarters full of water so that there is ample room for the eggs to remain apart.
2. If poaching is done in batches the water may be used several times over.

Poached Eggs, using an egg-poacher

Bring the water in the bottom of the pan to the boil. Lightly butter the moulds and break in the eggs; replace in the pan. Cover with the lid until the whites are set but the yolks still soft. Remove from the moulds and serve according to the recipe.

Poached Egg with Asparagus (Oeuf Poché Argenteuil)

Half fill tartlets with hot, diced asparagus tips; place a poached egg on top, coat with Sauce Suprême and garnish with a tiny bouquet of asparagus tips.

Poached Egg Benedictine (Oeuf Poché Bénédictine)

Place a poached egg on a toasted, buttered muffin or slice of toast covered with a warmed slice of ox tongue; coat with Sauce Hollandaise and decorate with a slice of truffle.

Poached Egg with Chicken (Oeuf Poché à la Reine)

Place a poached egg on some finely diced breast of chicken lightly bound with Sauce Suprême and coat with the same sauce.

Poached Egg Mornay (Oeuf Poché Mornay)

Place a little Mornay Sauce in the bottom of an egg dish, place a poached egg on top, then coat with the same sauce; sprinkle with grated Parmesan cheese and melted butter and glaze under a salamander grill.

Poached Egg Washington (Oeuf Poché Washington)

Place a poached egg on hot sweetcorn kernels previously heated in a little butter and coat with Cream Sauce.

Poached Egg with Spinach (Oeuf Poché Florentine)

Place a poached egg on a bed of leaf spinach heated in butter and seasoned with salt and pepper from the mill. Coat with Sauce Mornay, sprinkle with grated Parmesan cheese and melted butter and glaze under a salamander grill.

EGGS EN COCOTTE

Egg en Cocotte (Oeuf en Cocotte)

Butter and season an egg cocotte and place in a shallow pan. Break the egg into the mould. Add boiling water to the pan until it comes half way up, cover with a lid and simmer gently on top of the stove until the white is set and the yolk still soft. Take the cocotte out of the pan, wipe with a cloth and serve on an underdish with a dish paper.

Extensions of Egg en Cocotte

All garnishes should be hot when added; they may be placed in the cocotte before adding the egg, or on top of the cooked egg before serving.

Egg en Cocotte with Cream (Oeuf en Cocotte à la Crème)

Add warmed cream to the cooked egg just before serving.

Egg en Cocotte with Tomato (Oeuf en Cocotte Portugaise)

Place some cooked tomato concassée in the cocotte and pour a little tomato sauce around the egg when cooked.

Egg en Cocotte with Chicken (Oeuf en Cocotte à la Reine)

Place some finely diced chicken bound with Sauce Suprême in the bottom of the cocotte, cook in the usual way and finish by pouring a little warmed cream on top.

BOILED EGGS

Boiled eggs are a versatile product, whether served in the shell for breakfast, soft-boiled with a garnish and sauce as a lunchtime snack or hard-boiled and used in dozens of different ways, e.g. egg mayonnaise as an appetiser; hard-boiled eggs covered with sausage meat and deep fried; hard-boiled eggs, opened, stuffed and coated with sauce.

Boiling times for medium-sized eggs are as follows.

Soft boiled in the shell (Oeuf à la Cocque):   4 minutes
Soft boiled out of the shell (Oeuf Mollet):   5 minutes
Hard boiled (Oeuf Dur): 10 minutes

To serve soft-boiled eggs out of their shells, plunge into cold water for a few seconds and remove the shells carefully, then reheat in hot water for a few seconds and serve whole with the same garnishes and sauces as poached eggs, e.g. Oeuf Mollet Florentine.

Hard-boiled eggs should be drained and placed under running cold water until cold. To remove the shells, roll the eggs on a hard surface to crack the shells, then peel and retain in a basin of cold water. To serve hot, dip into hot water for one minute.

Eggs in Curry Sauce and Rice (Oeufs Durs à l'Indienne)

Halve or quarter hot hard-boiled eggs, place on a bed of boiled rice and coat with Curry Sauce finished with cream.

Stuffed Hard-Boiled Eggs with Cheese Sauce (Oeufs Farcis Chimay)

10 hard-boiled eggs	500 ml Sauce Mornay
100 g purée of mushrooms (duxelles)	50 g melted butter
	50 g grated Parmesan cheese

1. Cut the eggs in half lengthways, remove the yolks and pass them through a sieve.
2. Mix with the mushrooms and place the mixture in the empty whites either by piping with a star tube or using a spoon.
3. Place in a previously buttered porcelain egg dish.
4. Coat with Sauce Mornay and sprinkle with grated cheese and melted butter.
5. Gratinate under a salamander grill and serve on an underdish with a dish paper.

Scotch Eggs

10 hard-boiled eggs	breadcrumbs
800 g sausage meat	sprigs of parsley
75 g flour	500 ml tomato sauce
2 eggs	

1. Divide the sausage meat into 10 even portions.
2. Enclose each egg in sausage meat and mould in the shape of a large egg.
3. Coat with flour, eggwash and breadcrumbs.
4. Deep fry at 175°C for 5 minutes until golden and cooked.
5. Drain on absorbent kitchen paper.
6. Serve whole or cut in half on a dish lined with a dish paper, garnish with sprigs of parsley and serve accompanied by a sauceboat of tomato sauce, or serve cold with a mixed salad.

Eggs with Sweet and Sour Sauce
(Saure Eier mit Specksauce)

Lightly fry 25 g each of finely chopped onion and lardons of bacon in oil. Drain off the oil, moisten with 25 ml vinegar, add 25 g sugar and boil until reduced by half. Moisten with 50 ml jus lié and finish with a little crème fraîche, yogurt or cream. Place 2 soft-boiled eggs per portion on a blinis, coat with the sauce and serve.

Stuffed Eggs with Shrimps
(Huevos Rellenos de Gambas)

Combine the sieved yolks of 10 hard-boiled eggs with 100 g chopped shrimps and 50 g lightly sautéed chopped onion. Fill the whites with the mixture and place into a buttered dish. Coat with chicken velouté and sprinkle with melted butter and chopped fresh herbs.

SHALLOW-FRIED EGGS

There are three ways of shallow-frying eggs:

1. in fat in a frying pan or on a griddle plate;
2. in butter in a shallow oeuf sur le plat dish;
3. as an omelette.

For large-scale catering use an egg-frying tray which has slight indentations into which each egg is broken and fried. For ordinary work use an egg ring into which an egg is broken in the frying pan, thus giving it a good shape.

When serving fried eggs, remove from the fat with an egg slice and allow excess fat to drain back into the pan. It is advisable to serve directly onto a plate as contact with metal will turn the eggs black or grey underneath. Always serve immediately as they dry out quickly. The cooked egg should have the yolk in the centre of the white, indicating that it is fresh and the white and yolk should be just set.

Fried Eggs (Oeufs Frits)

Heat the fat into a suitable frying pan, break the eggs into it and shallow fry, basting with some of the fat until just cooked but not crisp. Eggs fried on a hot, greased griddle plate are best done in an egg ring, which is similar to but much smaller than a flan ring.

Deep Fried Eggs, also known as French Fried Eggs

These are used mainly as a garnish, e.g. Poulet Sauté Marengo. To cook, break an egg into a small frying pan two-thirds full of hot oil at 175°C, turn it over with a well-oiled spoon so that the white envelops the yolk. Remove and drain as soon as the outside is crisp.

Fried Quail's Eggs (Huevos de Codorniz a la Plancha) SPAIN

Fry quail's eggs in a pan two-thirds full of hot olive oil so that the whites envelop the yolks, until the outsides become light golden and the yolks remain soft inside. Drain on a cloth and serve on fried bread croûtons.

Fried Eggs with Garlic and Paprika SPAIN
(Huevos Fritos al Ajillo)

Shallow fry eggs in butter, transfer to plates and garnish with sautéed strips of red pimento. Golden fry sliced garlic in oil, moisten with a little vinegar, add paprika, then pour over the eggs and serve with slices of fried bread.

OEUFS SUR LE PLAT (SHIRRED EGGS)

Eggs cooked in Butter (Oeufs sur le Plat)

Heat a little butter in shallow, fireproof egg dishes and lightly season with salt and pepper. Break in the eggs, allowing one or two per portion. Cook on the side of the stove until the white has set, then flash finish under a salamander grill for a few seconds until the yolk is almost set. Serve at once in the cooking dish. Eggs cooked this way are also known as shirred or baked eggs.

Oeufs sur le Plat Bercy

Garnish with grilled chipolatas and surround with tomato sauce.

Oeufs sur le Plat au Lard

Garnish with grilled rashers of bacon.

OMELETTES

An omelette is a versatile item because it can be made so quickly. It is suitable as a breakfast dish, snack, starter, main course for lunch, dinner or supper, and as a vegetarian meal.

There are two kinds of savoury omelette:

1. oval;
2. flat and round.

Use three medium eggs for a standard-sized omelette, or two eggs for a table d'hôte meal. Season the eggs with salt and pepper and use a fork to beat the eggs vigorously in a china or plastic basin; using a whisk will change the characteristic of the omelette by incorporating too much air. Beat until completely free of streaks of egg whites. If omelettes are a main feature it is helpful to use canned liquid egg or crack a lot of eggs and have them mixed in readiness. Keep a 20 cm and a 25 cm black or cast-iron frying pan solely for making omelettes and clean them after use with kitchen paper rather than washing them. The patina of fat left in the pan prevents sticking, as does a non-stick omelette pan.

The filling for an oval omelette may be added:

(a) cold to the raw mixture
(b) hot when folding over
(c) after the omelette is cooked and turned out by cutting a slit along the top and placing the hot filling in it.

Plain Oval Omelette (Omelette Nature)

> 3 beaten and seasoned eggs
> 15 g/ml butter or oil
> melted butter

1. Heat the omelette pan.
2. Add the butter or oil and when hot – but before it begins to change colour – add the eggs.
3. Distribute the mixture around the base of the pan with the back of a fork. Bring in the mixture as it sets around the edge.
4. Continue to distribute the mixture with the fork, at the same time shaking the pan backward and forward whilst keeping it over the heat.
5. When set remove from the heat, tilt the pan slightly and fold the omelette with the inside of the fork away from the handle to the leading edge of the pan. Bring in the extreme ends with the fork to form an oval shape, bringing the join to the centre by hitting the handle of the pan with the side of the hand. Return to the heat to set, adding a little butter to the leading edge of the pan.
6. Turn out onto a dish by resting the omelette pan on the leading edge and bringing up the handle until the omelette is turned over into the centre of the dish, preferably a stainless steel one.

Tomato Omelette (Omelette aux Tomates)

Make a plain omelette. Add a filling of tomato concassée, either at Stage 5, when folding the omelette, or at Stage 6, once the omelette has been turned out, by cutting a slit in the centre 5 cm long and spooning in the hot filling. Sprinkle with chopped parsley. Place a small amount of filling at each end of the omelette, brush with melted butter and if desired pour a small amount of Tomato Sauce around the edge of the dish or plate before serving.

Carrot and Herb Omelette (Omelette Crécy)

Add 25 g sliced, cooked small carrots and chopped fresh herbs to the beaten eggs. Prepare the omelette, place on a plate and serve with sliced cooked carrots on top.

Cheese Omelette (Omelette au Fromage)

Add grated cheese to the beaten eggs and make in the usual way.

Ham Omelette (Omelette au Jambon)

Add diced ham to the beaten eggs and decorate the finished omelette with warmed diamonds of ham.

Herb Omelette (Omelette aux Fines Herbs)

Add chopped parsley, tarragon, chervil and chives to the beaten eggs and make in the usual way.

Mushroom Omelette (Omelette aux Champignons)

Add sliced, cooked, button mushrooms to the beaten eggs and put a whole cooked one on top as a garnish.

Sorrel Omelette (Omelette à l'Oseille)

Add 25 g finely shredded sorrel sweated in a little butter, a pinch of chopped chervil and a little finely chopped garlic to the beaten eggs and make the omelette in the usual way.

Omelette Arnold Bennett

Add a filling of 500 g flaked, cooked smoked haddock bound with hot cream when folding the omelette over and turn out onto a serving dish. Coat with Mornay Sauce; sprinkle with grated Parmesan and gratinate briefly under a salamander grill.

Flat Garnished Omelette

3	beaten and seasoned eggs
60 g	garnish according to recipe
15 g/ml	butter or oil melted butter

1. Add the prepared garnish, as per the recipe, to the eggs.
2. Heat the omelette pan, add the butter or oil and when hot – but before it begins to change colour – add the eggs.
3. Distribute the mixture around the base of the pan using the back of a fork. Bring in the mixture as it sets around the edge.
4. Continue to distribute the mixture with the fork, keeping the pan over the heat.
5. When the omelette is set and fairly firm, toss like a pancake and cook the other side, then turn out onto a warm buttered dish. (As an alternative to turning it over, set it briefly under a salamander grill.)
6. Brush the top of the omelette with the melted butter.

Eggplant Omelette (Omelette Niçoise)

Add 50 g thinly sliced small eggplant lightly fried in oil, 1 tsp each of grated Parmesan cheese, chopped parsley and chopped chervil to the beaten eggs. Make the omelette, slide onto a plate and serve.

Globe Artichoke Omelette (Frittata di Carciofi)

Golden fry 1/2 clove chopped garlic in a little olive oil, add 25 g thinly sliced cooked artichoke bottom, toss, season, then drain off the oil. Add the artichoke to the beaten eggs with 1 tsp grated Parmesan cheese, then make the omelette, slide onto a plate and serve.

Spanish Omelette (Omelette Espagnole)

Add 1 tbs each of tomato concassée, short julienne of skinned pimento and shredded onion, all previously cooked, to the beaten eggs, together with seasoning, and make the omelette in the usual way. Decorate with 4 small diamonds of cooked red pimento.

Omelette Fermière

Add diced ham and chopped parsley to the eggs and serve garnished with four diamond-shaped pieces of ham.

Omelette Paysanne

Add diced ham, small dice of shallow-fried potatoes, shredded sorrel previously stewed in butter, a little chopped chervil and parsley to the eggs and make the omelette in the usual way.

Spanish Potato Omelette (Tortilla Espagñola) SPAIN

Lightly fry 50 g diced potato and 20 g chopped onion in a little oil, drain and season. Add to the beaten eggs and make into a flat omelette, slide onto a plate and serve.

Spanish Vegetable Omelette (Tortilla a la Payesa) SPAIN

Golden fry 25 g diced potato in 50 ml olive oil, drain, season and retain. Lightly fry 100 g chopped onion, ¼ clove chopped garlic, 10 g chopped green pimento and 10 g diced tomato flesh in the same pan. Add to the beaten eggs and make into a flat omelette, slide onto a plate and serve.

SCRAMBLED EGGS

Ideally, scrambled eggs should be cooked and served to order but as this is not always possible, they may be cooked in advance and kept warm in a bain-marie, each portion being mixed again when serving. The addition of a little Cream Sauce will help to keep them from solidifying. To prevent streaks of white in scrambled egg, beat the eggs vigorously with a fork or whisk while adding the salt and pepper but do not make the mixture frothy.

Scrambled Eggs (Oeufs Brouillés)

2 medium beaten and seasoned eggs
  15 g butter
  15 ml double cream

1. Warm the butter in a shallow pan.
2. Add the eggs and stir gently with a wooden spoon, starting to bring in the egg that starts to coagulate around the bottom of the pan.
3. When lightly coagulated, add the cream and mix in.
4. Serve on buttered toast on a plate or in an oval or round white porcelain dish on an underdish with a dish paper.

Scrambled Eggs with Chicken Livers (Oeufs Brouillés aux Foies de Volaille)

Serve scrambled egg on a round of buttered toast and garnish at the side with shallow-fried chicken livers bound with a little Madeira Sauce.

Scrambled Eggs with Lobster (Oeufs Brouillés aux Lames de Homard)

Cook the eggs in the normal way and serve garnished with small slices of lobster tossed in butter.

Scrambled Eggs with Mushrooms (Oeufs Brouillés aux Champignons)

Serve scrambled egg on buttered toast with cooked sliced and button mushrooms in the centre.

Scrambled Eggs with Saffron (Oeufs Brouillés au Safran)

Infuse a few strands of saffron in 1 tsp warm milk, add to the beaten eggs and cook in the usual manner.

Scrambled Eggs with Tomatoes (Oeufs Brouillés aux Tomates)

Serve scrambled eggs on buttered toast with cooked tomato concassée in the centre, sprinkled with chopped parsley.

SAVOURY SOUFFLÉS

Cheese Soufflé – Soufflé au Fromage

For 4 portions brush a 14 cm diameter soufflé mould with oil or melted butter, then line with grated Parmesan cheese. Whisk 2 egg yolks into 150 ml warm béchamel, add 50 g grated Parmesan cheese and season with salt and a little cayenne pepper. Fold in 3 stiffly beaten egg whites in two stages, then pour the mixture into the mould. Cook at 200°C for 20 minutes and serve immediately.

Chicken Soufflé (Soufflé de Volaille)

Proceed as for Cheese Soufflé, adding 175 g purée of cooked chicken in place of cheese.

Courgette Soufflé (Soufflé de Courgette)

Proceed as for Cheese Soufflé, adding 175 g stiff purée of cooked baby marrow in place of cheese.

Crab Soufflé (Soufflé au Crabe)

Proceed as for Cheese Soufflé, adding 175 g purée of cooked crabmeat in place of cheese, together with a pinch of paprika pepper and a few drops of Tabasco sauce.

Spinach Soufflé (Soufflé d'Epinards)

Proceed as for Cheese Soufflé, adding 50 g firm spinach purée in place of cheese, with the addition of a pinch of grated nutmeg.

Cheese Dishes

Buck Rarebit

Make a Welsh Rarebit and serve with a well-drained poached egg on top.

Calgore

Roll out pizza dough and stamp out 8 cm rounds, lay half rounds of Bel Paese cheese and ham on each, fold over to seal well. Allow to prove and bake in the oven at 210°C.

Camembert Fritters (Beignets de Camembert)

Cut the rind off a Camembert and divide into eight pieces; dip into flour then into yeast batter and golden deep fry for 5 minutes.

Note
Brie can also be treated in this way and these two cheeses can also be served warm and runny by keeping them in a hotplate.

Cheese Fritters (Beignets au Fromage)

Bring 600 ml water, 100 g butter and a pinch of salt to the boil, add 350 g flour, mix well over heat till it leaves the pan clean, then allow to cool. Add 6 eggs one by one, mixing thoroughly, 50 g Parmesan and 150 g diced Gruyère cheese. Mould into 50 pieces using two tablespoons and golden deep fry at 190°C for 5 minutes.

Cheese Kebabs (Attereaux au Parmesan)

Bring 1 litre milk to the boil, rain in 200 g semolina and cook gently for 5 minutes, stirring continuously. Add a pinch of nutmeg, 150 g Parmesan, 2 yolks of egg, 50 g butter and seasoning. Spread 0.5 cm thick on a buttered tray, butter the surface and allow to cool. Cut out 2.5 cm rounds and thread on skewers alternating with 2.5 cm round slices of Gruyère cheese. Coat with egg and breadcrumbs and deep fry.

Croque Monsieur

Spread 20 thin slices of bread with butter and sandwich with 10 slices each of Gruyère cheese and ham. Seal well, cut off the crusts and golden shallow fry in vegetable oil or clarified butter.

Galettes au Fromage

Mix together 100 g flour, 150 g grated Emmenthal, 100 ml vegetable oil or butter and 3 eggs to make a firm dough. Roll out, cut into 5 cm circles, brush with eggwash and bake in the oven at 220°C for 10 minutes.

Mozzarella in Carozza

Sandwich a slice of Mozzarella cheese between two buttered slices of bread, trim the crusts, dip into beaten egg and golden shallow fry in oil or clarified butter.

Welsh Rarebit

Mix 400 g grated Cheddar cheese into 200 ml hot Béchamel Sauce and, when melted, add 2 yolks of egg, a few drops of Worcester sauce, 1 tsp made English mustard, a small pinch of cayenne and 25 ml reduced ale. Spread on slices of buttered toast, trim and colour under a salamander grill.

Beurrecks   TURKEY

Cut 250 g Gruyère cheese into small dice and mix with 125 ml cold Béchamel Sauce. Roll out noodle pastry very thinly, cut into 8 cm squares and roll a cigar-shaped piece of the cheese filling in each, sealing the ends well. Coat in egg and breadcrumbs and golden deep fry.

Cheese Blintzes   ISRAEL

Whisk together 4 eggs, 300 ml milk, 225 g flour and ½ tsp salt to form a batter and make into blintzes (pancakes). Combine 225 g cottage cheese, 1 beaten egg yolk, 50 g sugar, 50 g raisins and the grated zest and juice of 1 lemon. Spread on the blintzes, roll up to seal then lightly fry in butter. Serve accompanied by soured cream mixed with sugar and cinnamon.

Note
Fruit such as stoned cherries, segments of mandarin or small slices of peach may be added to the cheese filling.

Cheese Dumplings (Glumskeilchen)   GERMANY

Combine 450 g cottage cheese, 75 g sugar, ¼ tsp salt and 2 beaten eggs, stir in 50 g each of flour and cornflour, then mix in 275 g dry mashed potato and 100 g currants. Mould the mixture into small wedge-shapes, then drop into simmering salted water and cook for 10 minutes. Drain the dumplings and serve sprinkled with sugar mixed with cinnamon.

Cheese Fondue (Fondue Suisse) SWITZERLAND

Rub the interior of a fondue pan with crushed garlic and add 400 g Emmenthal and 800 g Gruyère cheese, both cut into 0.5 cm dice and dusted with cornflour. Place over heat and gradually add 600 ml dry white wine, the juice of ½ lemon, 125 ml kirsch, grated nutmeg and a very small pinch of cayenne. Place the pot on a table heater so as to keep it gently simmering while guests dip their pieces of bread in it.

Cheese Pancake Fritters (Nalesnikis) RUSSIA

Mix together 250 g each of pressed curd cheese and butter with 1 beaten egg and seasoning; mould into 25 g squares, wrap each in a small pancake, forming them square, dip into yeast batter and deep fry until crisp and golden.

Curd Cheese Dumplings (Galushki) RUSSIA

Combine 300 g curd cheese, 25 g butter, 100 g flour and ¼ teaspoon each of salt and sugar, then fold in 3 stiffly beaten egg whites. Drop teaspoonsful of the mixture into simmering salted water, and when they rise to the surface, remove, drain and serve coated with a sauce of soured cream and chopped mixed herbs.

Note
Fruit such as stoned cherries, segments of mandarins, or slices of peaches may be served to accompany them.

Fried Cheese (Saganaki) GREECE

Pass slices of Féta, Kefalotiri or Kasseri cheese through flour, then golden shallow fry in olive oil. Serve sprinkled with lemon juice and chopped fresh herbs.

Fried Cheese Crescents (Piroguis) RUSSIA

Mix 100 ml jus lié with 250 g breadcrumbs and 50 g butter and heat until it becomes quite stiff. Spread on a tray to cool, then cut out crescents and sandwich two together with twarogue. Shallow fry in oil or clarified butter.

Note
To make twarogue, mix together 225 g each of cream cheese and butter with 1 egg and seasoning.

Fried Cheese Puffs (Tirakia Tiganita) GREECE

To 3 stiffly beaten egg whites fold in 225 g finely grated Kefalotiri cheese and season with milled pepper. Drop teaspoonsful of the mixture into hot olive oil and deep fry until golden.

Poached Cheese Kreplach

Roll out 1 kg noodle pastry very thinly to 90 cm × 36 cm and cut into 6 cm squares. Mix 250 g cottage cheese with 1 egg and 50 g sugar, place a little in the centre of each piece of pastry, fold over as triangles and seal well. Allow the kreplachs to dry, then simmer in boiling water for 15 minutes, drain well and serve sprinkled with melted butter and sugar.

CHAPTER 4 # Farinaceous Dishes and Dumplings

ITALIAN PASTAS

Italian pastas are made from noodle paste in a wide range of shapes and sizes. There are three main sorts:

1. Pasta alimentare, available in a wide variety of shapes, usually served with a sauce or garnish. They include cappellini, farfalle, farfallini, fiochetti, lasagne, macaroni, spaghetti, tagliatelle and vermicelli.
2. Stuffed pastas (pasta ripieni), usually associated with freshly-made products such as ravioli, tortellini and cappelletti.
3. Pastas for stuffing (pasta ripiena) such as cannelloni, conchiglione, lasagne.

Pastas are available as dried, factory made and as fresh, known as pasta all'uovo. The shapes in general use include:

Cannelloni – cylinders for filling with a savoury stuffing
Lasagne – normally 8 cm wide × 16 cm long
Linguine – narrow flat strips
Macaroni – thin cylinders available in long and short cuts and as elbow shapes
Tagiatelli – flat strips approximately 8 mm wide × 1 mm thick in various
(Noodles) lengths and in the form of nests
Penne – small cylindrical shapes
Rigatoni – spirals
Fettuccine – small ribbon noodles 5 mm wide
Ravioli – small squares or rounds containing a savoury stuffing
Spaghetti – thin rods, usually 21 cm in length
Vermicelli – very thin long strands

General rules for cooking and serving pasta

Allow 25 g dried pasta per person as a garnish and 60 g dried pasta for a main course. Use 35 g and 85 g fresh pasta respectively.

All pastas are cooked in boiling salted water. Cooking times are 5 minutes for very fine types, 9–12 minutes for those of medium size, 12–15 minutes for thick and filled types. Some products are labelled as quick-cooking pastas and need a minute or so less cooking time.

Baking or full gratination is the term applied to pastas which are placed in a serving dish and barely covered with a sauce, sprinkled with grated Parmesan cheese and melted butter and placed in an oven at 170°C until the cheese melts and forms a soft crust. Light gratination is the term applied to pastas mixed with Sauce Mornay, sprinkled with grated Parmesan cheese and melted butter and placed under a salamander grill until an even golden colour. Another way of serving freshly cooked pastas to order in quick time is to put individual packets of frozen cooked pastas into a machine that regenerates them in just 60 seconds; filled pastas such as ravioli, require half a minute longer. Adjuncts of butter, cheese and sauce are kept ready at hand.

Most pastas are boiled before being baked and should be put into a pan of plenty of boiling salted water, without overfilling it. Stir from time to time to prevent the pasta from sticking together or to the pan. Boil steadily until it is soft but still retains a degree of chewiness, then drain, wash under hot water and continue according to the particular recipe.

Using a shallow pan helps prevent ravioli from breaking during the finishing process. The addition of oil to the water when cooking prevents all kinds of pasta from sticking together. Ravioli may also be served with any of the sauces and garnishes associated with spaghetti dishes.

Pastas, especially those mixed with a sauce or pesto, can be reheated in a microwave oven but must be covered with clingfilm.

Pasta may be served directly into a soup plate or entrée dish. Parmesan cheese is generally served separately, grated or shaved or it can be sprinkled over in the kitchen. It may be served with the sauce in the centre, mixed into it or in a sauceboat to be added at table. Cannelloni and lasagne should be served in the dish in which they were baked.

Noodle Paste (Pâte à Nouilles)

Makes 1kg

650 g strong or durum flour	3 yolks of eggs ⎤
10 g salt	3 eggs ⎥ mixed
5 g nutmeg	1 tbs oil ⎥ together
	125 ml water ⎦

1. Sift the flour, salt and nutmeg into a basin. Make a bay in the centre and add the mixed eggs, oil and water.
2. Mix together and work it to form a smooth dough.
3. Cover with a damp cloth and allow to rest for 45 minutes before using.
4. The paste may either be rolled by machine or with a rolling pin to the required thickness and cut into the appropriate shapes.

Pasta Verde

Add 125 g finely sieved cooked spinach to the flour at the same time as the liquid.

Pasta Rossa

Add 125 g concentrated tomato purée to the flour at the same time as the liquid.

Wholemeal Pasta

Use 500 g wholemeal flour sieved with 150 g ordinary white flour and proceed as for Noodle Paste.

Ravioli au Jus

1 kg noodle pastry	100 g butter
500 g filling	50 g grated Parmesan cheese
50 ml oil	500 ml jus lié
10 g salt	salt and milled pepper
2 cloves of garlic	

1. Roll out the pastry into an oblong 80 cm × 40 cm and not more than 2 mm in thickness.
2. Cut into two equal parts.
3. Place the filling into a piping bag with a 1 cm plain tube and pipe 100 × 5 g pieces 4 cm apart on one of the sheets of pastry.
4. Eggwash between each piece of filling and lay the second piece of pastry over the top.
5. Press down between the fillings, then cut into rounds with a small fancy round cutter or into squares with a serrated pastry wheel.
6. Spread out the ravioli on a tray previously sprinkled with fine semolina and allow to dry for 10 minutes.
7. Heat 5 litres water, add the salt and oil and, when simmering, place in the ravioli.
8. Gently move the ravioli around while cooking to prevent them from sticking and simmer for 8–10 minutes.
9. Melt the butter in a shallow pan but do not let it colour; add the crushed garlic and cook for a few moments in order to flavour the butter, then remove it.
10. Add the drained ravioli and gently toss without breaking them up and season with salt and black pepper from the mill.
11. Place a little of the jus lié in the bottom of a suitable shallow dish, add the ravioli then mask with the remainder of the sauce.
12. Sprinkle with the grated Parmesan cheese and melted butter and gratinate under a salamander grill.

Cannelloni al Sugo

1 kg noodle pastry	500 ml jus lié
1 kg filling	100 g butter
50 ml oil	50 g grated Parmesan cheese
10 g salt	seasoning

1. Roll the pastry out into a square 80 cm × 80 cm, 2 mm thick and cut into 8 cm × 8 cm squares.

2. Lay the pieces on a tray previously sprinkled with fine semolina and allow to dry for 25 minutes.
3. Heat 5 litres water in a saucepan, add the oil and salt and, when simmering, place in the cannelloni.
4. Move the pieces around very gently while cooking to prevent them sticking and simmer for 8–10 minutes until cooked.
5. Refresh under running water until perfectly cold.
6. Lay out a clean cloth on a work surface and arrange the drained and dried pieces of pasta in rows along the cloth.
7. Place the filling into a piping bag with a 1 cm plain tube and pipe 10 g along the leading edge of each piece.
8. Roll up to enclose the filling.
9. Butter a shallow ovenproof dish and place a little of the jus lié at the bottom.
10. Arrange the cannelloni neatly in the dish with the join underneath.
11. Cover with the rest of the hot jus lié.
12. Sprinkle with the grated Parmesan cheese and melted butter and bake in the oven at 180°C until fully gratinated.

Note
Cannelloni may be served with any of the sauces and garnishes associated with spaghetti dishes.

Fillings for pasta dishes

Meat Filling

Sweat 75 g chopped onion and 2 crushed cloves of garlic in 50 ml olive oil, add and fry 350 g diced raw meat, moisten with 150 ml dry white wine, cover with a lid and cook for 1 hour until almost dry. Pass through a fine mincer and season well.

Cheese, Ham and Mushroom Filling

Combine 200 g cooked chopped mushrooms, 100 g short julienne of prosciutto crudo and 75 g grated Gruyère cheese with 300 ml Béchamel Sauce.

Chicken and Ham Filling

Fry 75 g chopped onion, 50 g each of diced carrot and celery in 50 ml olive oil until lightly coloured. Add 300 g finely diced chicken breast, 50 g chopped prosciutto crudo, 100 g chopped mushrooms, 100 g tomato concassée and 50 g chopped basil. Add 125 ml dry white wine, reduce, then add 225 ml jus lié, season well and add a little grated nutmeg.

Florentine Filling

Heat 50 g butter and cook 75 g chopped onion and 2 chopped cloves of garlic without coloration. Add 500 g spinach purée, 1 yolk of egg and 50 ml jus lié. Stir while cooking to a firm consistency.

Fontina Cheese and Chive Filling

Combine 450 g grated Fontina cheese with 50 g chopped chives and seasoning.

Spinach and Ricotta Cheese Filling

Mix together 225 g finely chopped spinach, 175 g Ricotta cheese, salt and nutmeg and combine with 100 g diced Mozzarella cheese.

Pasticcia di Lasagne Bolognaise

1 kg noodle pastry	500 ml Bolognaise Sauce
50 ml oil	50 g grated Parmesan cheese
10 g salt	50 g butter

1. Roll the pastry out into an oblong 80 cm × 32 cm and cut into 20 cm × 16 cm oblongs.
2. Lay the pieces on a tray previously sprinkled with fine semolina and allow to dry for 25 minutes.
3. Heat 5 litres water in a saucepan, add the oil and salt and, when simmering, place in the lasagne.
4. Move the pieces around very gently to prevent them sticking and simmer for 10 minutes.
5. Refresh under running water until perfectly cold, then drain and dry on a cloth.
6. Butter the bottom of a shallow ovenproof dish and cover with a layer of the pasta.
7. Pour a layer of thick Bolognaise Sauce on the lasagne, add a further layer of lasagne and repeat the process, alternating layers of lasagne and sauce and finishing with sauce.
8. Sprinkle with the grated Parmesan cheese and melted butter and bake in the oven at 180°C until fully gratinated.

Spaghetti Bolognaise

600 g spaghetti	500 ml Bolognaise Sauce
10 g salt	75 g grated Parmesan cheese
50 g butter	salt and milled pepper

1. Place the spaghetti into plenty of simmering salted water and move it around gently to prevent it sticking; cook for 8–10 minutes, then drain in a colander.
2. Melt the butter in a shallow pan, add the hot spaghetti and stir with a fork. Season with salt and black pepper.
3. Place in a serving dish accompanied by a sauceboat of the sauce and grated Parmesan cheese.

Spaghetti à l'Italienne

600 g spaghetti
50 g butter
75 g grated Parmesan cheese
    salt and pepper from the mill

1. Place the spaghetti into plenty of simmering salted water and move it around gently to prevent it sticking; cook for 8–10 minutes, then drain in a colander.
2. Melt the butter in a shallow pan, add the hot spaghetti, stir with a fork and season with salt and pepper.
3. Place in a serving dish accompanied with grated Parmesan cheese.

Spaghetti alla Crema

600 g spaghetti	50 g butter
300 ml cream } beaten together	75 g grated Parmesan cheese
2 yolks of egg	salt and pepper

1. Place the spaghetti into plenty of simmering salted water and move it around to prevent it sticking; cook for 8–10 minutes, then drain in a colander.
2. Melt the butter in a shallow pan, add the spaghetti and stir with a fork.
3. Add the beaten yolks and cream, mixing them in with a fork. Season with salt and pepper and allow to thicken.
4. Place the spaghetti in a serving dish, accompanied by grated Parmesan cheese.

Spaghetti al Pesto

Toss 600 g cooked spaghetti in 50 g melted butter and mix in 200 ml of pesto. It is not necessary to serve grated Parmesan with this dish.

Spaghetti al Fuoco

Lightly fry 3 crushed cloves of garlic and 3 fresh red chillies in 150 ml olive oil. Cool, liquidise and retain. Lightly fry 2 crushed cloves of garlic in 125 ml olive oil, remove the garlic and add the liquidised mixture. Toss the cooked spaghetti in this sauce and serve very hot.

Spaghetti alla Carbonara

Lightly fry 2 cloves of garlic in 50 ml olive oil, then remove the garlic. Add 275 g lardons of bacon and crisp fry, then add the drained pasta and a liaison of 6 egg yolks and 450 ml cream; heat gently but do not boil. Serve with grated Parmesan cheese.

Spaghetti alla Tarantina

Lightly fry 6 chopped cloves of garlic in 125 ml olive oil and add 50 g chopped parsley. Toss cooked spaghetti in the same pan, together with 40 cooked mussels and serve.

Spaghetti au Gratin

Proceed as for Spaghetti alla Crema, omitting the yolks of egg and mixing in 250 ml hot Béchamel Sauce. Pour into a shallow dish, sprinkle with 75 g grated Parmesan cheese and 50 g melted butter and gratinate under a salamander grill or at the top of a hot oven.

Spaghetti con Aglio, Olio e Peperoncino

Lightly fry 6 crushed cloves of garlic and 3 whole dried red chillies in 125 ml olive oil, then remove and discard the garlic and chillies. Toss the cooked spaghetti in the same pan and serve.

Spaghetti con Cacio e Pepe

Season cooked spaghetti with coarsely ground black pepper and mix with 225 g grated Pecorino cheese and a little cooking liquid from the pasta to melt the cheese.

Spaghetti con Guanciale e Cipolla

Crisp fry 225 g lardons of unsmoked bacon in 125 ml olive oil, remove and retain. Add and sweat 225 g sliced onion, then return the lardons. Mix the spaghetti into this mixture with 225 g grated Pecorino cheese and serve each portion sprinkled with a little chilli powder.

Spaghetti con Piselli

Sweat 75 g chopped onion and 100 g lardons of bacon in 50 ml olive oil. Add 125 ml chicken stock, 25 g tomato purée, 275 g peas and seasoning. Cover with a lid and cook for 10 minutes. Toss the cooked spaghetti in this mixture and finish with chopped parsley.

Spaghetti con Pomodoro

Golden fry 4 chopped cloves of garlic in 125 ml olive oil, add 275 g strips of tomato flesh, season and cook for 5 minutes. Toss 600 g cooked and drained spaghetti in the same pan and serve accompanied by grated Parmesan cheese.

Spaghetti con Pomodoro e Basilico

Proceed as above with the addition of chopped fresh basil.

Spaghetti con Prosciutto e Funghi

Gently fry 275 g sliced mushrooms in 50 ml olive oil and add 275 g lardons of prosciutto crudo and 2 tsp chopped basil. Mix in 600 g cooked and drained spaghetti, add grated Parmesan cheese, season and serve.

Spaghetti con Zucchine

Sweat and lightly colour 50 g chopped shallot, 50 g chopped onion, 3 chopped cloves of garlic, 50 g each of brunoise of carrot and celery and 150 g diced courgettes in 50 ml olive oil. Add 100 g tomato concassée and 300 ml tomato sauce; cover with a lid and cook for 10 minutes. Mix in 600 g cooked and drained spaghetti, place in a serving dish and cover the surface with rondels of crisp deep-fried baby marrow. Serve accompanied by grated Parmesan cheese.

Spaghetti Milanaise

600 g spaghetti	50 g cooked ham ⎫
50 g butter	50 g cooked tongue ⎬ cut into
500 ml Tomato Sauce	50 g cooked button ⎭ julienne
250 g tomato concassée	mushrooms
75 g grated Parmesan cheese	
salt and pepper	

1. Place the spaghetti into plenty of simmering salted water and stir gently to prevent it sticking; cook for 8–10 minutes, then drain in a colander.
2. Melt the butter in a shallow pan, add the spaghetti and stir with a fork.
3. Mix in the Tomato Sauce and tomato concassée with a fork and season with salt and milled pepper.
4. Gently incorporate the julienne of ham, tongue and mushrooms and place in a serving dish.
5. Serve accompanied with a sauceboat of grated Parmesan cheese.

Spaghetti Napolitaine

600 g spaghetti
50 g butter
500 ml Tomato Sauce

250 g tomato concassée
75 g grated Parmesan cheese
salt and pepper

1. Place the spaghetti into plenty of simmering salted water and stir to prevent it sticking; cook for 8–10 minutes, then drain in a colander.
2. Melt the butter in a shallow pan, add the spaghetti and mix with a fork.
3. Stir in the Tomato Sauce and tomato concassée and season with salt and pepper.
4. Serve the spaghetti in a suitable dish, accompanied with a sauceboat of grated Parmesan cheese.

Macaroni au Gratin

Using 600 g cooked and drained macaroni proceed as for Spaghetti alla Crema, omitting the yolks of egg and mixing in 250 ml hot Béchamel Sauce. Pour into a shallow dish, sprinkle with 75 g grated Parmesan cheese and 50 g melted butter and gratinate under a salamander grill or at the top of a hot oven.

ASIAN AND OTHER NOODLE DISHES

Farfel   ISRAEL

Mix 700 g fine matzo meal, 5 beaten eggs, 75 ml water and salt to form a stiff paste. Form into 30 small balls and lay on a cloth to dry for 1 hour. Coarsely grate and leave again to dry on a cloth. Cook by sprinkling into boiling chicken stock or salted water, allow to simmer for 5 minutes, drain and serve as a farinaceous dish.

Kreplach   ISRAEL

450 g noodle pastry
50 g finely chopped onion
10 ml oil
1 egg

250 g finely minced, cooked
beef or veal
seasoning

1. Cook the onion in oil without colouring.
2. Combine the onion, minced meat, seasoning and eggs to make a filling, adding white breadcrumbs if necessary.
3. Roll out the pastry to form an oblong 40 cm × 25 cm and 2 mm thick and cut into 5 cm squares.
4. Place a little of the filling in the centre of each square, brush the edges with eggwash, then fold over as a triangle and press and seal the edges.

5. Spread out on a tray previously sprinkled with fine semolina and allow to dry out, then cook in simmering chicken soup for 8 minutes.

Lokshen
ISRAEL

Roll out 250 g noodle pastry into a 35 cm square 2 mm thick, then cut into 1 cm × 1.5 cm strips. Spread out on a tray previously sprinkled with fine semolina and allow to dry out, then cook in simmering chicken soup for 5 minutes.

Cellophane or Bean Starch Noodles

Soak in hot water for 20 minutes, drain, then cook in boiling water for 15 minutes; drain and serve.

Egg Noodles

Soak noodles in hot water for 10 minutes, drain well, then plunge into boiling water to which a little oil has been added and cook for 3 minutes. Drain and serve.

Rice Noodles

Soak noodles in cold water for 45 minutes, drain well, then plunge into boiling water for 8 minutes. Drain and use as required.

Rice Vermicelli

Place the vermicelli into boiling water and cook for 3 minutes, drain and use as required.

Buckwheat Noodles

Place the noodles into boiling salted water, cook for 3 minutes, drain and serve.

Buckwheat Noodles with Chicken (Torinanban)
JAPAN

Boil 550 g buckwheat noodles, drain well and divide into 10 bowls. Marinate 250 g strips of cooked chicken in 100 ml soy sauce. Boil 250 g spinach, drain, then refresh and squeeze out excess water, place onto a cloth, roll Swiss-roll fashion and cut into ½ cm slices. Simmer the strips of chicken for a few minutes in the marinade, together with 50 ml mirin and 10 sliced spring onions, then place the slices of spinach on top of the noodles in the bowls. Fill with the hot marinade combined with 100 ml hot second soup stock and serve accompanied by a dish of seven-flavour spice or grated root ginger.

Cellophane Noodles with Pork (Yook Nup Fun See) CHINA

Heat 75 ml oil in a wok and stir-fry 250 g strips of pork and 100 g sliced Chinese mushrooms; add 80 g sliced spring onions, 10 g grated ginger, 50 ml bean sauce, 3 chopped fresh red chillies and cook for a few moments. Add 100 ml stock, lightly thicken with diluted cornflour and continue to simmer until the sauce has reduced by two-thirds. Stir in 550 g cooked noodles, season and serve in bowls, sprinkled with chopped coriander leaves.

Chow Min CHINA

Golden deep fry 550 g cooked egg noodles in groundnut oil, drain well and retain. Fry 3 chopped cloves of garlic, and 2 tsp grated root ginger in a wok in 175 ml oil, then add and stir-fry 100 g each of strips of fillet of pork and breast of chicken, 175 g sliced abalone, 125 g each of shredded Chinese cabbage and bean sprouts, 200 g bamboo shoots, and 150 g chopped spring onions. Moisten with 725 ml boiling chicken stock previously thickened with a little arrowroot and cook for 3 minutes. Place the noodles in a serving dish, cover with the meat and vegetables and serve immediately.

Fried Rice Vermicelli (Pad Thai) THAILAND

Fry 6 chopped cloves of garlic in 350 ml oil, add 550 g shrimps, 25 g sugar, 25 g nam pla and 125 ml tomato ketchup and stir until the sugar has dissolved. Pour in 5 beaten eggs and stir until they begin to set. Add 800 g rice vermicelli and 75 g bean sprouts and stir until the bean sprouts are just cooked. Place in a serving dish and garnish with segments of lime and serve sprinkled with chopped raw bean sprouts, shrimp powder, peanuts, chilli flakes and chopped spring onions and coriander leaves.

Rice Vermicelli with Prawns CHINA
(Choy Yuen Har Kau Chow Mi Fun)

Stir-fry 250 g prawns in 25 ml groundnut oil, remove and retain. Add 200 g shredded Chinese cabbage to the pan and fry for 2 minutes. Moisten with 300 ml stock, 100 ml saké and 25 ml light soy sauce, then add 4 chopped cloves of garlic, 50 g grated ginger and seasoning and cook for a further 2 minutes. Mix in 550 g cooked rice vermicelli, add the prawns and serve.

DUMPLINGS AND GNOCCHI

There are four main types of small dumplings apart from those made of suet pastry:

1. Gnocchi Romaine made from semolina, egg yolks and cheese
2. Gnocchi Parisienne, which are small pieces of choux paste

3. Gnocchi Piedmontaise made from potatoes, flour and egg yolk
4. Polenta made from maize flour and water.

Gnocchi Romaine and Gnocchi Piedmontaise are generally served as first course dishes on their own, whereas Gnocchi Parisienne are mainly served as a garnish with Hungarian Goulash. Polenta is a very popular dish in Italy, usually served as a garnish with meat or fish rather than on its own.

Gnocchi Romaine

1 litre milk or white stock	75 g butter
200 g semolina	75 g grated Parmesan cheese
salt, nutmeg and pepper	200 ml Tomato Sauce
2 egg yolks	

1. Place the selected liquid to boil, then rain in the semolina, whisking well.
2. Cook gently for 8 minutes, stirring all the time.
3. Mix in the yolks, butter, cheese and seasoning, then spread on a buttered tray to a thickness of 1 cm. Cover with buttered greaseproof paper and allow to go cold.
4. Cut into rounds or crescents with a 5 cm pastry cutter.
5. Place the trimmings in buttered ovenproof dishes, and arrange the pieces neatly overlapping on top.
6. Sprinkle with more grated Parmesan cheese and melted butter and gratinate under a salamander grill or at the top of a hot oven.
7. Pour the Tomato Sauce around the edge, or serve it in a sauceboat separately.

Gnocchi Parisienne (Gnocchi Mornay)

1 litre choux paste
75 g butter
500 ml cream sauce
salt and pepper
50 g grated Parmesan cheese

1. Fill a shallow sided pan three-quarters full with water, add salt and heat until gently simmering.
2. Place the choux paste into a piping bag with a 1 cm plain tube and pipe it into the water in 2 cm lengths. Rest the tube on the side of the pan as the paste leaves the bag and cut off the lengths with a knife or against a piece of string tied across the pan.
3. Poach until cooked, then drain in a colander or remove with a spider.
4. Melt the butter in a shallow pan, add the gnocchi, season and incorporate the cream sauce by a tossing and shaking motion.
5. Place in an earthenware dish, sprinkle with grated Parmesan cheese and melted butter and lightly gratinate under a salamander grill.

1. When piping the paste into the simmering water it is necessary to dip the knife into the hot water from time to time to prevent it from sticking.
2. The gnocchi will swell in size during cooking and become lighter in colour. They are cooked when firm to the touch.
3. Instead of tossing the gnocchi in butter they may be placed directly in a buttered earthenware dish, coated with the sauce then gratinated.

Gnocchi Piédmontaise

600 g purée of boiled potatoes made very dry	120 g potato flour or cornflour (for moulding)
5 egg yolks	75 g butter
150 g strong flour	75 g grated Parmesan cheese
salt, pepper and nutmeg	

1. Place the freshly mashed potato in a saucepan on the stove.
2. Add the egg yolks, flour and seasoning and mix thoroughly with a wooden spatule.
3. Divide the mixture into 100 small pieces.
4. Roll them into small balls or walnut-shaped pieces, place on a sieve, press lightly with a fork and roll against the wires of the sieve so as to make slight indentations.
5. Poach in a shallow pan of simmering salted water, then drain using a spider and place into a buttered earthenware dish.
6. Sprinkle with the grated Parmesan cheese and melted butter and gratinate under a salamander grill.

Notes
1. If the mixture begins to break up, add a little more flour.
2. A little Tomato Sauce may be poured around the gnocchi to complete the dish.

Polenta

1 litre	boiling water
200 g	maize flour
2	egg yolks
75 g	grated Parmesan cheese
100 g	melted butter

1. Sprinkle the maize flour into a pan of boiling water, mixing with a whisk to prevent lumps from forming. Stir slowly with a wooden spatule for 8 minutes.
2. Remove from the heat and add the egg yolks, cheese and seasoning.
3. Spread in a buttered tray to a thickness of 1.5 cm. Cover the polenta with buttered greaseproof paper and allow to cool until firm and easy to handle.

4. Cut the polenta into 7 cm square or round shapes.
5. Shallow fry in the hot butter until a light golden colour on both sides.

Notes
1. The mixture will become very thick while cooking and a crust will form on the bottom and sides of the pan. This should not be disturbed when turning out the soft polenta.
2. As a garnish with meat, place the pieces in an earthenware dish, sprinkle with grated cheese and nut brown butter and gratinate under a salamander grill.

Gnocchi di Ricotta

Combine 350 g spinach purée with 350 g Ricotta cheese, 125 g grated Parmesan cheese, 5 eggs, salt, pepper, nutmeg and sufficient flour to make a soft mixture. Form into croquette shapes and cook in simmering salted water for 5 minutes. Place in an earthenware dish, sprinkle with oil and grated Gruyère or Parmesan cheese and gratinate under a salamander grill.

Polenta con Funghi

Proceed as for Polenta and serve coated with a sauce made by sweating 50 g chopped onion and 3 chopped cloves of garlic in 50 ml olive oil, adding 1 kg quartered mushrooms and 50 g chopped parsley and simmering until all the liquid has been absorbed.

Buckwheat Dumplings (Pampushki)   RUSSIA

Make a yeast dough using 800 g buckwheat flour, 25 g yeast, 275 ml warm water and salt. Mould into 20 balls, poach in simmering salted water, then drain and lightly golden fry in sunflower oil with a crushed clove of garlic. A smaller version of these may be served to accompany Bortsch Soup.

Caraway Dumplings (Galushki)   RUSSIA

Combine 550 g flour, 2 eggs, 100 g melted butter, 250 ml milk, 50 g chopped cooked onion and ¼ tsp caraway seeds. Mould into 20 balls and poach in simmering salted water for 5 minutes. Remove, drain and serve accompanied by crisp, fried bacon rashers.

Dim Sum Savoury Dumplings (Wonton)   CHINA

Combine 175 g chopped, blanched bamboo shoots, 225 g chopped raw prawns, 50 g chopped spring onions, 450 g minced pork, 50 ml light soy sauce, 2 tsp sesame oil, 12 dried Chinese mushroom caps, reconstituted and chopped, and seasoning. Envelop 25 g pieces of this mixture in 40 wonton wrappers (small squares of fresh noodle dough), to form triangular shapes. Deep fry in groundnut oil until golden and serve with a sweet and sour-type sauce.

Dim Sum Steamed Pork and Prawn Dumplings (Shiumai)

Combine 12 chopped water chestnuts, 175 g chopped bamboo shoots, 50 g chopped spring onions, 450 g minced pork, 50 ml light soy sauce, 50 ml saké or dry sherry, 2 tsp sesame oil, 2 egg whites, 12 dried Chinese mushroom caps, reconstituted and chopped, 675 g chopped raw prawns and seasoning. Envelop 25 g pieces of this mixture in 50 wonton wrappers to form purses. Place a whole prawn on top of each purse and place onto a lightly oiled steamer tray. Steam over hot water for 20 minutes and serve with a dipping sauce such as Soy Sauce with Ginger.

Knaidlach or Matzo Ball Dumplings

Mix together 125 g matzo meal, 2 beaten eggs, 50 g rendered chicken fat or 2 tbs oil, 2 tbs chicken stock and seasoning, then allow to stand for 20 minutes. Form into 30 walnut-sized balls and cook in simmering chicken stock for 5 minutes.

Potato Dumplings (Buabaspätze)

Boil 675 g potatoes, drain, dry and pass through a sieve. Add 75 g butter, 125 g flour, 4 egg yolks, seasoning and nutmeg. Mould into 40 cigar-shaped pieces and poach in simmering salted water for 5 minutes. Remove, drain and serve with Sauerkraut.

CHAPTER 5 # Pizzas, Rice and Grain

Pizzas

Pizza Dough

800 g strong flour
10 g salt
40 g yeast

375 ml water at 40°C
10 g sugar
75 ml olive oil

1. Sift the flour and salt into a warmed bowl.
2. Dissolve the yeast and sugar in the water and mix into the flour to form a soft dough.
3. Knead thoroughly, replace in the bowl, cover with a cloth and allow to prove in a warm place for 1 hour.
4. Knead the oil into the dough and allow to prove slowly before rolling out for use.

Garlic Bread Pizzas

Mix the pizza dough, omitting the oil. Add a purée made by processing 6 cloves of garlic, 2 tsp each of oregano and parsley, 75 ml olive oil and mix well. Allow to prove and mould into long baton loaves. Lightly bake, cut in half lengthways and cover with any of the pizza garnishes before baking again.

Pizza Topping (Passata)

100 g chopped onion
100 g chopped cloves of garlic
50 ml olive oil
1 kg tomato concassée
75 g tomato purée

2 tsp chopped fresh oregano
2 tsp chopped basil
1 bayleaf
1 tsp demerara sugar
salt and pepper

1. Sweat the chopped onion and garlic in olive oil.
2. Add the remainder of the ingredients and simmer for 1 hour until a smooth consistency is obtained, then season to taste.

Notes
1. When cooked the passata may be liquidised to obtain a smooth consistency.
2. Allow 1 kg of topping per 10 standard-sized pizzas; this topping (Passata) is not an essential ingredient for all pizzas.

Pizza – Preparation and Cooking

1 kg pizza dough
1 kg passata
50 ml olive oil

1. Divide the dough into ten, roll out each piece into a circle 15 cm in diameter and place onto an oiled baking sheet.
2. Spread each base with 100 g passata, leaving 1.5 cm space around the edges, then top with the pizza ingredients.
3. Sprinkle with olive oil and bake in the oven at 240°C for 10 minutes until crisp but not dry. Serve hot.

Pizzas with tomato and cheese topping

Pizza ai Funghi

Spread bases with passata and add sliced mushrooms, chopped Mozzarella cheese, dried oregano and seasoning. Sprinkle with olive oil and bake.

Pizza ai Quattro Formaggi

Spread bases with passata and add chopped Mozzarella and Gorgonzola cheeses and grated Pecorino and Parmesan cheeses. Sprinkle with dried oregano, seasoning and olive oil and bake.

Pizza ai Sardine

Spread bases with passata and add chopped Mozzarella and chopped onion; arrange sardines on top and sprinkle with dried oregano, seasoning and olive oil and bake.

Pizza al Tonno

Spread bases with passata and add chopped Mozzarella cheese and chopped canned tuna fish; sprinkle with dried oregano, seasoning and olive oil and bake.

Pizza alla Gorgonzola

Spread bases with passata and add chopped Mozzarella and Gorgonzola cheeses; sprinkle with dried oregano, seasoning and olive oil and bake.

Pizza Capriccioso

Spread bases with passata and add sliced mushrooms, diced ham and chopped Mozzarella cheese; sprinkle with dried oregano, seasoning and olive oil and bake.

Pizza con Salami

Spread bases with passata and add chopped Mozzarella cheese; season and cover with slices of salami, then sprinkle with olive oil and bake.

Pizza Lazio

Spread bases with passata and add chopped Mozzarella cheese, julienne of pimento and onion; sprinkle with seasoning and olive oil and bake.

Pizza Marinara

Spread bases with passata and add mussels, shrimps and chopped Mozzarella cheese; sprinkle with dried oregano, seasoning and olive oil and bake.

Pizza Margherita

Spread bases with passata and add chopped Mozzarella cheese; sprinkle with dried oregano and fresh basil leaves, seasoning and olive oil and bake.

Pizza Napoletana

Spread bases with passata and add chopped Mozzarella cheese and anchovy fillets; sprinkle with seasoning and olive oil and bake.

Pizza Piccola Roma

Spread bases with passata and add chopped Mozzarella cheese and ham and diced pineapple; sprinkle with oregano, seasoning and olive oil and bake.

Pizza Quattro Stagioni

Spread the bases with passata, sprinkle one quarter with diced ham, the second with sautéed sliced button mushrooms, the third with sautéed quartered artichoke bottoms and the fourth quarter with sliced black olives and anchovies. Sprinkle with chopped mozzarella cheese, a few drops of olive oil and oregano and bake.

Pizza Romana

Spread bases with passata and add diced artichoke bottoms and chopped Mozzarella cheese; sprinkle with dried oregano, seasoning and olive oil and bake.

Pizza Tropicale

Spread bases with passata and add chopped Mozzarella cheese and ham, diced pineapple, sliced banana and oregano. Season, sprinkle with olive oil and bake.

Pizzas without tomato and cheese

Pizza Andréa

Spread bases with stewed sliced onion, chopped anchovy and sliced olives. Sprinkle with a few drops of olive oil and bake.

Pizza Cinquemila

Spread bases with deep-fried whitebait and chopped garlic, sprinkle with oregano and olive oil and bake.

Pizza Calabrese

Spread bases with anchovy fillets, flaked canned tuna, capers and olives. Sprinkle with olive oil and bake.

Pizza Francesco

Spread bases with small slices of ham and tongue and stewed mushrooms. Sprinkle with olive oil and bake.

Pizza Giardiniera

Spread bases with blanched slices of carrot, eggplant, courgette and pimento. Sprinkle with olive oil and bake.

Pizza Religioso

Spread bases with stewed sliced ceps, anchovy fillets and flaked smoked mackerel. Sprinkle with olive oil and bake.

Pizza Vesuvio

Spread bases with stewed sliced mushrooms, small pieces of salami and red pimento. Sprinkle with olive oil and bake.

Savoury Rice Dishes

There are three basic ways of cooking rice: boiling, braising and stewing.

1. Boiled rice is used as an accompaniment for curries and as a garnish in soup.
2. Braised rice (referred to as savoury rice, pilau or pilaff) is cooked in an oven with white stock. It is used as a garnish with a variety of first course dishes, stuffed vegetable and poultry dishes and main meal entrées.

3. Stewed rice (referred to as risotto) is cooked in white stock on top of the stove. It is generally served as the first course of a meal, but with garnishes also forms main course dishes.

There are many types of rice:

Arborio – ideal for making risotto
Basmati – has a pronounced flavour; used with curries
Brown – unpolished, with the germ intact, much appreciated by health food enthusiasts
Patna – long-grain, for use with curries and pilaffs
Short-grain or *Carolina* – for puddings and pilaffs
Wild – actually an aquatic grass with black grains, mixes well with all other kinds, needs twice the normal cooking time of rice
Jasmine – soft-grain, from Thailand with a fragrant flavour
Easy-cook – blanched to remove the starch, yields loose grains.

The amount of uncooked rice per portion is 30 g for a garnish or accompaniment, 45 g as a supplementary with a main item and 60 g as a dish in its own right. These weights also apply to easy-cook rice. According to kind, rice increases in volume fivefold in cooking.

BOILED RICE

Plain Boiled Rice (Riz Poché)

500 g long-grain rice
5 litres water
25 g salt

1. Bring the water to the boil in a deep pan and add the salt.
2. Rain in the rice and stir occasionally with a wooden spoon until it reboils, then simmer gently for 18 minutes until the grains are soft but still compact.
3. Refresh under cold running water and drain in a colander.
4. To reheat for service place in a colander under running hot water until hot, then drain thoroughly. Spread on a cloth in a tray, cover with a damp cloth and place in a hotplate or oven at 60°C. From time to time redistribute the rice with a fork.

Boiled Rice (Dry or Conservative Method)

500 g rice
1.5 litres water
15 g salt

1. Wash the rice well.
2. Place into a deep pan with the cold water and salt; bring to the boil, cook rapidly for 1 minute, then cover with a lid and simmer very gently for 20 minutes. Do not remove the lid while it is cooking.
3. Remove from the heat, stand for a further 10 minutes still covered with a lid, then lightly stir with a fork to fluff the grains.

Boiled Rice (Simiao Bia Fan)   CHINA

550 g long-grain rice
400 ml water
5 g salt

1. Wash the rice until clean.
2. Place into a saucepan, add the measured water and salt, bring to the boil and boil rapidly for 1 minute. Cover with the lid and simmer for 12 minutes until cooked.
3. Remove from the heat, stand for 10 minutes still covered with the lid, then stir with a fork to fluff the grains of rice.

Crusty Steamed Rice (Chelou Ta Dig)   MIDDLE EAST

550 g basmati rice
1 egg yolk
30 ml yogurt

1. Wash the rice until clean.
2. Add to plenty of boiling salted water, boil for 5 minutes, then drain.
3. Add the mixed egg yolk and yogurt to half the rice.
4. Spread it in the bottom of a pan in the form of a mound and cover with the remainder of the rice.
5. Cover with a cloth and lid and cook for 15 minutes over low heat, then for a further 30 minutes over a glimmer of heat. When cooked, loosen the golden crust from the lower part of the pan, turn out and serve.

Fried Rice (Chao Fan)   CHINA

30 ml groundnut oil
500 g boiled rice
200 g diced cooked chicken
100 g chopped spring onions

3 beaten eggs ⎫
10 ml sesame oil ⎬ combined
125 g bean sprouts ⎭
seasoning

1. Heat the groundnut oil in a wok, add the rice and stir-fry for a few moments, then add the diced chicken, spring onions and seasoning.
2. Continue to cook, adding the egg and oil mixture, and stir until the eggs begin to set. Add the bean sprouts, cook for a further 2 minutes and serve.

Glutinous Rice and Pork (Nuoc Lèo) CHINA

550 g glutinous rice (pulot)
500 ml water
20 ml oil
   2 cloves of garlic
200 g minced pork
125 ml Chinese bean sauce

250 ml chicken stock
50 g sugar
25 g nuoc nam
10 ml chilli sauce
100 g ground roasted peanuts
   seasoning

1. Place the rice and water into a saucepan, bring to the boil, cover with a lid and simmer for 20 minutes. Remove the lid and cook until all the liquid has been absorbed.
2. Heat the oil in a wok, fry the chopped garlic, then add the pork and cook for 10 minutes. Add the bean sauce, moisten with the stock, add the sugar and nuoc nam, then boil to reduce the cooking liquor; season to taste.
3. Stir the pork mixture into the rice, then remove from the heat. Stir in the chilli sauce and ground roasted peanuts and serve at room temperature.

Namkin Chawal INDIA

550 g long-grain rice
80 g ghee
1.5 litres water
5 g salt

1. Wash the rice until clean, then drain in a colander.
2. Heat the ghee in a deep pan, add the rice, stirring with a wooden spatule to incorporate the ghee.
3. Add the cold water and salt, bring to the boil and cook rapidly for 1 minute, then cover with the lid and simmer for 20 minutes. Do not remove the lid whilst cooking. Remove from the heat, stand for a further 10 minutes still covered with the lid, then stir gently with a fork to fluff the grains of rice. If desired, 125 g ghee or butter may then be added.

Rice with Dried Seaweed (Sushi) JAPAN

550 g Japanese short-grain rice
1 litre water
8 cm kelp seaweed
100 ml mirin

20 g castor sugar
5 g salt
5 g monosodium glutamate

1. Wash the rice until clean and place into a colander to drain.
2. Place the rice, salt and kelp into a saucepan with the cold water, bring to the boil, when just on boiling point, remove and discard the kelp.
3. Cover with a lid, reduce the heat and cook for 20 minutes. Remove from the heat and allow to stand with the lid on for a further 10 minutes, then stir with a fork to fluff the grains.

4. Combine the mirin, sugar and monosodium glutamate and pour over the rice, mixing it in with a fork.

Rice with Lemon and Saffron (Kesar Pilau)

8 crushed cardamom pods	600 ml water
6 cloves	2 juice of lemons
1 cinnamon stick	20 g sugar
25 g ghee	few strands saffron
550 g long-grain rice	5 g salt

1. Wash the rice until clean, then drain well in a colander.
2. Heat the ghee in a deep pan, add and lightly fry the crushed cardamom pods, cloves and cinnamon stick, add the rice and cook for 3 minutes.
3. Add the water, lemon juice, sugar and salt. Cover with a lid, bring to the boil and cook for 10 minutes, then add the saffron without stirring the rice. Cook for a further 10 minutes, discard the spices, then fluff the rice with a fork to separate the grains.

Rice with Spices (Parsi Pilau) INDIA

Proceed as for Rice with Lemon and Saffron but omit the saffron. When almost cooked, remove the spices, add 50 g sultanas and garnish with shredded almonds and pistachio nuts.

BRAISED RICE OR PILAFF

Braised Rice (Riz Pilaff)

75 g butter	1 bayleaf
75 g chopped onion	1 clove crushed garlic
500 g long-grain rice	salt and pepper
1 litre chicken stock	

1. Melt the butter in a shallow pan, add the onion and cook without coloration.
2. Add the rice, and mix it into the butter and onion; lightly fry but do not allow to colour.
3. Add the hot stock, seasoning, bayleaf and garlic.
4. Bring to the boil, stirring with a wooden spoon, then cover with buttered greaseproof paper and a lid and place in the oven at 200°C and cook for 15 minutes until the rice is cooked but firm.
5. Remove the bayleaf and garlic, add 50 g butter and separate the grains of rice with a fork.
6. Transfer to a clean receptacle, and keep covered with a clean piece of greaseproof paper until required.

Notes
1. Use two parts of stock to one part rice.
2. To test if cooked, squeeze a grain of rice between the fingers; it should be firm but not hard, with each grain being separate and whole.

Saffron Rice (Riz Pilaff Safrané)

Proceed as for Braised Rice, with the addition of 1g saffron infused in the stock before it is added to the rice.

Pilaff with Orange (Zarda Palau) TURKEY

Boil basmati rice in salted water for 10 minutes and drain. Golden fry chopped onion and slivered almonds in ghee with a julienne of orange peel previously cooked in syrup; moisten with saffron-flavoured stock, season and cook in the oven at 150°C for 40 minutes.

RISOTTO

Risotto

75 g butter	1.5 litres chicken stock
75 g chopped onion	1 small bayleaf
500 g Italian rice	salt and pepper

1. Melt the butter in a deep pan, add the onion and cook without coloration.
2. Add the rice and cook for a few moments.
3. Moisten with the boiling stock, adding in several stages as it is absorbed; add the seasoning and bayleaf and cover with a lid.
4. Cook for 20 minutes altogether, stirring occasionally with a wooden spoon until the rice is soft but unbroken.
5. Remove the bayleaf, transfer the risotto to a clean receptacle and retain in a bain-marie, covered with a lid.

Risotto alla Milanese

Proceed as for Risotto, infusing 1 g saffron in the stock before adding it to the rice. When cooked, add 50 g each of julienne of ham and ox tongue and 50 g sliced button mushrooms cooked in a little butter and lemon juice. Serve accompanied by a sauceboat each of Tomato Sauce and grated Parmesan cheese.

Risotto with Fennel (Risotto al Finocchio)

Sweat 100 g chopped onion and 2 chopped cloves of garlic in 125 ml olive oil and add and lightly fry 100 g lardons of unsmoked bacon or pancetta.

Add 400 g sliced fennel, cover with a lid and allow to stew for 10 minutes. Add 500 g Arborio rice, ladle in 1.5 litres boiling chicken stock a little at a time and proceed as for Risotto.

Risotto Italienne

Proceed as for Risotto, forking in 50 g each of butter and grated Parmesan cheese when cooked.

Risotto with Saffron and Almonds (Timman Zaffaran)   MIDDLE EAST

Proceed as for Risotto, with the addition of saffron infused in rose-water. Garnish with fried diced lamb, slivered almonds and sultanas.

Risotto with Lentils and Pine-nuts (Mejedrah)   TURKEY

Proceed as for Risotto, with the addition of 225 g cooked whole brown lentils. Garnish with 100 g fried pine-nuts.

Risotto with Pistachio Nuts (Dugun Pilav)   TURKEY

Proceed as for Risotto, using beef stock, and finish with 75 g pistachio nuts.

Risotto with Spinach (Spanakorizo)   GREECE

Proceed as for Risotto, adding 125 ml lemon juice, 2 tsp chopped dill and 1 kg shredded spinach previously sweated in vegetable oil or butter.

Risotto with Tomato (Pilaff me Domates Glace)   GREECE

Proceed as for Risotto and serve moulded and masked with cooked tomato concassée.

Cracked wheat

Cracked Wheat Pilaff (Pourgouri Pilafi)   GREECE

Sweat 75 g chopped onion in 50 ml olive oil. Moisten with 1 litre boiling chicken stock, then rain in 450 g cracked wheat, season and stir to the boil. Cover with a lid and simmer for 20 minutes until cooked and the liquid absorbed. Remove from the heat, cover with a cloth and lid and allow to stand for 15 minutes before serving.

Cracked Wheat Pilaff (Burghal Pilaff)

Sweat 100 g chopped onion in 50 g samneh, add 300 g cracked wheat, moisten with 450 ml chicken stock, bring to the boil and simmer for 10 minutes until the stock has been absorbed. Cover with a cloth and allow to stand for 15 minutes before serving.

Couscous

Heat 50 ml oil in a pan and colour 100 g each of diced onion, carrot and celery, 4 crushed cloves of garlic, 12 g ground ginger and 1 tsp cumin, then add 2 litres water. Place 1 kg coarsely ground millet in a basin and gradually work in 100 ml water. Line a steamer inset with a damp cloth, add the millet and cover with the cloth. Fit over the pan containing the boiling vegetables and flavourings and steam for 45 minutes, stirring occasionally with a fork. Transfer it to a basin, add 100 g butter, season with ground ginger, cumin, cayenne and paprika, forking it in. Place back over the boiling liquid and steam for a further 15 minutes, toss over and serve in dishes, sprinkled with melted samneh.

CHAPTER 6 Fish

INTRODUCTION

The range of fish available is extensive and is in no way limited to those included in this chapter. The types of fish selected are those most commonly used in the catering industry and are aligned to specific principles, methods and dishes.

Fish may be classified in several different ways, e.g. marine or fresh water, or according to their shape, whether tapering, arrow-shaped, flat or round. The two main headings for shellfish are crustaceans and molluscs.

Some kinds of fish are more suitable for a particular method of cooking than others. White fish is ideally suited to the wet methods of cookery, whereas oily fish are best cooked by the dry methods. White fish are good for deep frying but oily fish are not.

PREPARATION

Preparation of whole round fish

To skin a round fish
Examples of whole round fish are herring, salmon and trout.

1. Remove the scales by scraping with a knife from tail to head.
2. Remove all fins, using scissors.
3. Cut an opening from the vent and remove the gut, using the fingers or the handle of a fork or spoon.
4. If the head is to be left on, remove the gills with a small knife and the eyes with the pointed end of a peeler. Care should be taken not to break the connective tissue joining the underpart of the head to the body.
5. If the head is to be removed, cut an inverted V-shaped incision each side of the head just below the gills.
6. Make two or more – according to the size of the fish – very shallow incisions on each side of the fish, just penetrating the skin at the thickest part – this is to speed up cooking and is known as 'ciseler'.

To fillet a round fish
1. Cut a deep incision along the backbone.
2. Cut from the head end along the top of the backbone until the fillet comes free. Repeat for the other side.
3. Place the fillet on a work surface skin side down with the tail end facing. Cut and lift the skinned fillet from the tail, pulling back the skin with the fingers.

Preparation of whole flat fish

To skin Dover sole
Dover sole cannot be skinned in the same way as other flat fish, so this method must be followed.

1. Remove the fins, using scissors.
2. Remove the dark skin, commencing at the tail end by making a slight incision across it; scrape backwards and forwards until the skin begins to lift, then take it between the fingers and a cloth and pull it upwards and away. It is usual to leave the white skin on.
3. Remove the head by cutting at an angle following its natural shape.
4. Remove the gut and roe by pushing with the fingers along the external area, or use a knife.

To skin turbot, plaice, etc
Flat fish such as turbot and plaice are prepared as follows.

1. Remove the fins by cutting close to the body against the natural formation.
2. Remove the head by cutting along the natural line, following its shape.
3. Remove the gut and roe by cutting an opening just below the head; scrape clean and remove all traces of blood and gut that adheres to the bone.

To fillet a flat fish
1. Make an incision along the line of the backbone, from head to tail.
2. Cut down against the bone structure, allowing it to direct the knife in a clean sweeping action from the centre of the fish to the fins. Remove the fillet and repeat with the other three fillets.
3. Place the fillet on a work surface skin side down with the tail end facing. Cut and lift the skinned fillet from the tail, pulling back the skin with the fingers.

CUTS OF FISH

Fillet – The flesh of the fish is completely cut from the bone in its natural form. Flat fish yield four fillets. Round fish yield two fillets. Fillets are suitable for poaching, shallow and deep frying, grilling and baking. They may be lightly flattened for use and a few shallow incisions made at the thick end to prevent curling.

Suprême – This term applies to large fillets of fish cut into portions on the slant. Supremes are suitable for poaching, shallow and deep frying, grilling and baking. They may be lightly flattened for use.

Goujons and Goujonettes – Goujons are cut from thin fillets of fish on the slant into strips 8 cm × 1 cm. Goujonettes are a smaller version of goujons cut into 4 cm × 5 mm strips. Both goujons and goujonettes are suitable for deep and shallow frying and can also be poached.

Tronçon – This is a slice weighing 180–250 g cut on the bone from the half side of a large flat fish. They are suitable for boiling and grilling.

Darne – This is a slice weighing 180–250 g cut on the bone from a large round fish. It is sometimes referred to as a steak and is suitable for boiling, grilling and shallow frying.

Délice – A menu term for a fillet of small flat fish with the two ends folded underneath, skin side inwards. It is suitable for poaching.

Paupiette – This is a fillet of small flat fish which is spread with a fish farce or stuffing and rolled up, skin side inwards. It is suitable for shallow poaching.

En Tresse – This is a plaited fillet of flat fish made by cutting it into three or four strips 1 cm from the head end then entwining to reform the fillet. It is mainly suitable for shallow poaching.

BAKING

Baking is a suitable method for cooking a whole fish previously stuffed with a bread, mushroom or fish forcemeat, basting it with butter or oil to prevent it drying out. The sediment in the pan can be utilised in the accompanying sauce.

Baked fish also refers to the gratination of fish cooked with the addition of duxelles so that the surface of the sauce coating is evenly coloured and lightly crisped. This method may be applied to whole sole, supremes of halibut, turbot, cod and haddock and fillets of whiting.

Sole au Gratin

10 × 250 g whole soles	300 ml dry white wine
250 g butter	100 g white breadcrumbs
100 g chopped shallots	100 g butter
1 litre Sauce Gratin	2 juice of lemons
250 g sliced button mushrooms	10 g chopped parsley
	seasoning

1. Remove the dark skin from the fish. Cut along the backbone from below the head to the tail and lay back the top fillets, cut through and remove the backbone. Place a small knob of butter under each and lay back the fillets.
2. Butter a shallow oven-to-table dish, season and sprinkle with the chopped shallots and add a little of the sauce to cover the bottom of the dish.
3. Place the soles on top and surround with the sliced or whole mushrooms.
4. Add the white wine and barely cover with the sauce.

5. Sprinkle the surface with the white breadcrumbs and melted butter and cook in the oven at 175°C for 15 minutes.
6. To serve, clean the dish, sprinkle with lemon juice and chopped parsley and serve on an underdish with a dish paper.

Salmon Parcels

2 kg fillet of salmon	650 g short pastry
150 g preserved ginger	eggwash
200 g butter	seasoning

1. Skin the salmon, remove the thin bones with a salmon tweezer and cut the fish into 10 pieces.
2. Chop the ginger and mix with the softened butter.
3. Roll out the pastry into an oblong 70 cm × 28 cm and cut into 10 × 14 cm pieces.
4. Season the pieces of salmon, spread each with 35 g of the ginger butter and place one on one side of each square of pastry.
5. Brush the edges with eggwash and fold the pastry to enclose the salmon, mitring the ends.
6. Turn over onto a greased baking sheet, brush with eggwash and bake at 180°C for 35 minutes. Serve with Sauce au Beurre Blanc.

Baked Carp in Cider (Pechionyi Karp v Pive)   RUSSIA

Place a carp into a shallow dish, sprinkle with sweated diced carrot and onion, moisten with 200 ml cider and bake. Reduce the cooking liquor by two thirds and finish with cream. Mask the fish with this sauce and serve.

Baked Fillets of Bream and Cod   PORTUGAL
(Caldeirada Estilo Nazaré)

Fry chopped onion in oil then add diced tomato flesh and red pimento and chopped garlic, moisten with white wine and add a bayleaf and a few strands of saffron. Place a fillet each of cod and bream per person in a shallow dish, moisten with the prepared liquid and bake, basting occasionally at 180°C for 15 minutes.

Baked Supreme of Cod with Sauerkraut   GERMANY
(Fisch mit Sauerkraut)

Place Sauerkraut into a shallow dish, arrange supremes of cod on top and moisten with milk; sprinkle with butter and bake.

Baked Fillet of Haddock USA

Pass small fillets of haddock through flour, milk and breadcrumbs mixed with chopped fresh herbs, then shallow fry to colour. Place in a dish, sprinkle with red wine vinegar and bake at 180°C for 20 minutes.

Baked Herring in Cream (Forshmak) RUSSIA

Combine finely minced, raw fillets of herring with lightly sautéed chopped onion, breadcrumbs soaked in milk and squeezed out, grated apple, cream and seasoning. Place into a shallow dish, sprinkle with breadcrumbs, grated nutmeg, zest of lemon and butter and bake for 30 minutes.

Baked Salt Codfish with Tomato and Pimento PORTUGAL
(Bacalhau Dourado)

Sweat chopped onion in olive oil, add diced red pimento and tomato flesh, chopped parsley and garlic, then moisten with white wine. Shallow fry the previously soaked slices of codfish in olive oil, flake, then place it into a shallow dish. Mask with the prepared liquid, sprinkle with sieved hard-boiled egg and bake.

Baked Sardines (Psari Riyànato) GREECE

Place sardines in a shallow dish, moisten with lemon juice and olive oil, add chopped oregano and salt, then bake at 200°C for 5 minutes, basting once.

Baked Skate with Sauerkraut GERMANY
(Rochen mit Sauerkraut)

Poach skate portions in milk flavoured with cloves, bayleaf and peppercorns. Drain, pass through butter and flour, then wrap in foil and bake. Serve with braised sauerkraut.

Baked Stuffed Bream (Farshirovanyi Lieshch) RUSSIA

Stuff a whole bream with cooked buckwheat combined with golden-fried chopped onion, chopped hard-boiled eggs and a raw egg to bind. Place in a shallow dish, moisten with soured cream and bake.

Baked Supreme of Swordfish with Tomato and Herbs SPAIN
(Sarde a Beccafico)

Shallow fry 10×175 g supremes of swordfish, remove and retain. Sweat 100 g chopped shallots, 3 chopped cloves of garlic, 100 g diced celery and 50 g diced white of leek in 50 ml olive oil, then add 250 g tomato concassée, 1 bayleaf, 50 g pine-nuts, 25 g capers and 20 stoned green olives; season and simmer for 10 minutes. Add the fish, cover with foil and bake in an oven at 200°C for 20 minutes. Remove the bayleaf and just before serving add 50 g peeled seedless white grapes and sprinkle with chopped fresh herbs.

Coulibiac of Salmon (Kulibiaka) RUSSIA

Lightly shallow fry 750 g thin supremes of salmon, then add 75 g cooked, chopped vésiga. Roll 675 g puff pastry into a strip 45 cm × 25 cm, spread 175 g cooked rice down the centre then cover with alternate layers of 400 g sautéd chopped mushrooms, 6 chopped hard-boiled eggs, the fish and the vésiga. Encase with the pastry, eggwash the edges and seal, allow to rest for 30 minutes and bake in the oven at 200°C for 15 minutes to colour, then reduce the temperature to 150°C and cook for a further 30 minutes. While hot, pour 50 ml melted butter through a hole in the top and serve cut into 3 cm slices accompanied by Beurre Blanc as a sauce.

Note
Vésiga is the tasteless spinal column of the sturgeon, available in dry form to be soaked before use as an essential ingredient of this dish.

BOILING

Boiling, which is really deep poaching, is a suitable method for cooking all kinds and cuts of fish as indicated below.

Oily fish

Oily fish may be cooked in a court-bouillon of water, vinegar, vegetables, seasoning and herbs.

Mackerel – whole fillets
Salmon – whole, darnes, supremes
Salmon trout – whole, fillets
Skate – wings
Trout – whole live

White round and flat fish

White round and flat fish may be cooked in water, lemon juice and salt.

Cod and haddock – darnes and supremes
Brill, halibut and turbot – troncons and supremes

Smoked fish

Smoked fish may be cooked in milk or milk and water.

Finnan haddock – whole, supremes
Smoked cod – supremes

Kippers, whole or filleted, are cooked in water.

The cooking of fish

Cooking times vary according to the size of the fish being deep poached. A 180 g cod or salmon steak takes 10 minutes; a whole salmon weighing 4 kg served cold should be brought to the boil then poached at just below boiling point for 10 minutes before being left in the fish kettle until cold. Once it has cooled it should be kept under refrigeration.

1. Adhere to the time and temperature given in the recipe.
2. The centre bone of a tronçon comes out easily with the point of a small knife.
3. The flesh should not yield to pressure and should have lost its glassy look.

Serving boiled fish

1. The dark skin and centre bone of darnes and tronçons should be removed just before being served, or by waiting staff in front of the customer.
2. A whole sole can be boned by waiting staff in front of the customer by cutting along the backbone and pushing back the bones around the edges. This allows the backbone to be removed whole and the four fillets to be replaced in the sole's original form.
3. Some of the court-bouillon cooking liquid and its vegetables can be poured over boiled fish.
4. It is usual to serve small boiled potatoes, lemon slices and picked parsley with poached white fish. In the case of salmon and salmon trout sliced cucumber is also served.

Fish Court-bouillon

5 litres water	150 g onions cut into rings
500 ml vinegar	150 g grooved and sliced carrots
10 white peppercorns	5 g salt
10 g parsley stalks	

1. Place all the ingredients in a saucepan and boil steadily for 20 minutes. Skim and use.
2. When boiling a whole fish, prepare a cold court-bouillon by placing all the ingredients in the fish kettle. Immerse the fish in it, bring to the boil and cook for 20 minutes, according to type and cut. Serve hot with some of the court-bouillon, boiled new potatoes, lemon slices and the accompanying sauce.

Blue Trout (Truite au Bleu)

Makes 1 portion

750 ml court-bouillon
1 live trout
25 ml vinegar
5 potatoes
100 ml Hollandaise Sauce

1. Remove a trout from the fish tank.
2. Stun it by hitting the back of the head with the butt end of a heavy knife.
3. Make a small incision in the belly of the fish and pull out the gut.
4. Place the trout into a shallow dish containing the vinegar and let it soak for a few moments, then turn it over so that it becomes completely blue.
5. Remove from the vinegar, place in the special fish kettle and poach gently in the hot court-bouillon for 8 minutes.
6. Serve either in the fish kettle in which it has been poached on the drainer or on a table napkin, garnished with picked parsley and accompanied by a dish of small boiled potatoes and a sauceboat of Hollandaise Sauce.

Note
The trout should be handled quickly and carefully because there is a risk of removing the natural outer mucus which makes it go blue when it contacts the vinegar.

Poached Fillet of Mackerel with Parsley Sauce
(Filet de Maquereau Sauce Persil)

```
10 × 100 g  mackerel fillets
    500 ml  court-bouillon
    600 ml  parsley sauce
        30  plain boiled potatoes
            picked parsley
```

1. Place the prepared fillets into the simmering court-bouillon and allow to cook for 6 minutes.
2. Remove from the cooking liquid, drain and remove the skin.
3. Dress on a serving dish with a little of the cooking liquid and garnish with the plain boiled potatoes and picked parsley.
4. Serve the parsley sauce in a sauceboat separately.

Poached Salmon Steak with Hollandaise Sauce
(Darne de Saumon Pochée Sauce Hollandaise)

```
10 × 150 g  salmon steaks            1/2  picked parsley
 2 litres  court-bouillon             2  lemons
       30  plain boiled potatoes    600 ml  Hollandaise Sauce
      1/2  cucumber
```

1. Place the prepared salmon steaks into the simmering court-bouillon and allow to cook for 7 minutes.
2. Remove from the cooking liquid, drain and remove the skin and centre bone.

3. Dress on a serving dish with a little of the cooking liquid. Garnish with slices of the lemon, picked parsley and plain boiled potatoes.
4. Serve with a dish of the sliced, peeled cucumber and the Hollandaise Sauce in a sauceboat.

Skate with Black Butter (Raie au Beurre Noir)

10 × 150 g skate wings	150 g butter
2 litres court-bouillon	50 ml vinegar
100 g capers	5 g chopped parsley

1. Place the prepared pieces of skate into the simmering court-bouillon and allow to cook for 10 minutes.
2. Remove from the cooking liquid and skin.
3. Dress in an earthenware dish and sprinkle with the capers.
4. Place the butter into a pre-heated pan and cook until light brown in colour. Remove to the side of the stove, add the vinegar and chopped parsley, pour over the skate and serve immediately.

Poached Brill Steak with Melted Butter
(Tronçon de Barbue Poché, Beurre Fondu)

2 litres water ⎫	150 g beurre fondu
2 lemons ⎬ court-bouillon	3 lemons
5 g salt ⎭	picked parsley
10 × 175 g brill steaks	30 plain boiled potatoes

1. Boil the water, lemon juice and salt; add the steaks, bring back to boiling point, skim and simmer gently for 10 minutes until cooked.
2. Remove the tronçons, drain and remove the skin and centre bone.
3. Dress the fish on a serving dish with a little of the cooking liquid, garnish with slices of lemon, picked parsley and the plain boiled potatoes.
4. Serve the beurre fondu separately in a sauceboat.

Notes
The other ways of serving fish prepared in this way are:

1. In an earthenware dish on an underdish and dish paper
2. On an oval silver or stainless steel flat dish with special in built-in drainer
3. On a folded table napkin on a silver or stainless steel dish.

Poached Cod Steak with Egg Sauce
(Darne de Cabillaud Pochée, Sauce aux Oeufs)

Prepare 10 × 175 g cod steaks, proceed as for Poached Brill Steak and serve accompanied by 600 ml Egg Sauce.

Poached Supreme of Haddock with Anchovy Sauce
(Suprême d'Aiglefin Pochée, Sauce Anchois)

Prepare 10 × 100 g haddock supremes, proceed as for Poached Brill Steak and serve accompanied by 600 ml Anchovy Sauce.

Poached Halibut Steak with Parsley Sauce
(Tronçon de Fletin Poché, Sauce Persil)

Prepare 10 × 175 g halibut steaks, proceed as for Poached Brill Steak and serve accompanied by 600 ml Parsley Sauce.

Poached Supreme of Turbot with Chantilly Sauce
(Suprême de Turbot Pochée, Sauce Chantilly)

Prepare 10 × 175 g turbot supremes, proceed as for Poached Brill and serve accompanied by 600 ml Sauce Chantilly.

Smoked fish boiled in milk or water

Poached Finnan Haddock

10 × 200 g smoked haddocks
   2 litres milk/milk and water

1. Cut off the fins and tails of the haddocks, place into a shallow pan and cover with the milk.
2. Bring to the boil and simmer gently for 10 minutes.
3. Dress in an earthenware dish, remove the centre bone and coat with a little of the milk.

Haddock Monte Carlo

10 × 200 g smoked haddocks   1.5 litres cream
   400 g tomato concassée   10 poached eggs
    75 g butter   chopped parsley

1. Cut off the fins and tails and place the haddocks in a buttered tray.
2. Add the tomato concassée and the cream.
3. Cover with a buttered piece of greaseproof paper and poach in the oven at 185°C for 10–12 minutes.
4. Remove the haddocks and place in an earthenware dish, remove the centre bones and keep the fish warm.
5. Reduce the cooking liquid to a light coating consistency and pour over the fish.
6. Sprinkle with chopped parsley, place a hot poached egg on each fish and serve.

Kedgeree

750 g smoked haddock	600 ml Curry Sauce
600 g braised saffron rice	10 g chopped parsley
5 hard-boiled eggs	seasoning
100 g butter	

1. Cut off the fins and tails of the haddocks, place in a shallow pan and cover with water.
2. Bring to the boil and simmer gently for 12 minutes.
3. Drain the fish, discard the skin and bone and break it into flakes.
4. Heat the butter in a shallow pan, add the rice, fish and seasoning and mix together gently.
5. Fill a savarin mould with the mixture and turn it out onto a shallow dish, decorate with quarters of hard-boiled egg, sprinkle with chopped parsley and serve accompanied by sauceboats of Curry Sauce.

Gefillte Fish ISRAEL

450 g fillet of hake ⎤	50 g chopped parsley
250 g fillet of haddock ⎱ coarsely	600 ml fish stock
225 g fillet of cod ⎰ minced	75 g sliced carrot
50 g onion ⎦	50 g sliced onion
2 eggs	25 g sugar
25 g ground almonds (optional)	salt
50 g medium matzo meal	

1. Place the mixed minced fish into a basin, add the eggs, ground almonds, matzo meal, chopped parsley and seasoning, mix well and place in the refrigerator to chill. Mould the mixture into 20 balls.
2. Boil the fish stock and add the sliced carrot and onion, sugar and salt.
3. Place the fish balls into the stock and simmer, covered with a lid for 30 minutes.
4. Remove the lid and simmer to reduce the liquor.
5. Place the balls into a dish, cover with some of the strained liquor, garnish with the carrot and chill. Serve with the jellied liquor, accompanied by chollah or matzo.

Marinated Mackerel Steak (Caballa en Escabeche) SPAIN

Shallow fry 10 × 150 g mackerel steaks in olive oil, then transfer to an earthenware dish. Sweat 75 g chopped onion and 2 chopped cloves of garlic in oil, add 75 g carrots, cut into small dice, 1 bayleaf, 10 crushed peppercorns, chopped parsley and oregano, 2 tsp chilli powder, 225 ml dry sherry or wine vinegar and 125 ml water. Simmer for 5 minutes then pour over the fish, cover with clingfilm and marinate for 24 hours.

Poached Darne of Carp in Brandy and Fruit Sauce (Schwarzfisch)

GERMANY

Shallow poach 10 × 125 g darnes of carp in 600 ml fish stock for 10 minutes, remove and retain. Caramelise 75 g sugar and 50 g butter, then add 50 g chopped almonds, 25 g chopped walnuts, 50 g sultanas and 50 g chopped fresh figs. Flambé with 25 ml brandy, then add some of the cooking liquid, boil and reduce to sauce consistency. Thicken with white breadcrumbs and finish with 25 ml each of lemon and orange juices. Serve the fish coated with the sauce.

Blue Eel (Blauer Aal)

GERMANY

Season an unskinned eel with salt then marinate in hot tarragon vinegar for 1 hour. Cut into 5 cm sections and poach in court-bouillon made with the vinegar. Serve accompanied by melted butter.

Poached Cuttlefish (Chocos com Tinta)

PORTUGAL

Golden fry chopped garlic in olive oil, then add breadcrumbs and colour slightly. Add pieces of cuttlefish, moisten with a little water and the ink from the cuttlefish, sprinkle with paprika, then poach. Serve accompanied by boiled potatoes.

Poached Eel in Dill Sauce (Aal in Grüner Sosse)

GERMANY

Cut skinned and cleaned eels into 5 cm sections, rub with salt, then marinate in hot wine vinegar. Poach the eel in court-bouillon made with the vinegar and serve accompanied by a sauceboat of white wine sauce containing chopped dill.

Poached Fillet of Perch (Zander Balaton)

HUNGARY

Sprinkle fillets of perch with salt and lemon juice and allow to marinate for 30 minutes. Place a layer of duxelles of mushrooms in a shallow dish, lay the fillets on top, cover with white wine and fish stock and poach in the oven at 180°C for 10 minutes. Remove the fillets and retain. Reduce the strained cooking liquor, add soured cream and seasoning. Garnish with sliced boiled potatoes, coat with the sauce and serve.

Poached Halibut Steak with Saffron Rice (Plov)

RUSSIA

Poach halibut steaks in water with diced onion, carrot and parsnip, peppercorns, bayleaf and salt for 10 minutes. Transfer the fish to a buttered earthenware dish, sprinkle with chopped onion, chopped dill, crushed fennel seeds and a little saffron or turmeric, moisten with cream and steam for 10 minutes. Make a risotto with the fish cooking liquor with the addition of a little saffron. Serve the fish accompanied by the rice, sprinkled with grated zest of lemon.

DEEP FRYING

Deep frying is the cooking of small whole and cuts of fish in dripping or vegetable oil at a high temperature with the fish totally immersed, having previously been coated with flour, batter or eggwash and breadcrumbs.

Fried fish should be cooked and served to order. If it must be cooked in advance it should be placed on kitchen paper and retained in a hot cupboard, but if the temperature is too high or the fish is kept too long it will lose its crispness, and if held at a moderately hot temperature the fish will weep and become soft. Deep-fried items must not be covered once cooked as the steam will condense and fall back onto the fish, causing it to become damp and soft. Serve deep-fried fish on an oval flat dish on a dish paper.

Fried Fillet of Dover Sole in Batter (Filet de Sole à l'Orly)

10 × 85 g fillets of sole	350 ml yeast batter
50 g flour	3 lemons
1 juice of lemon ⎫	picked parsley
5 g chopped parsley ⎬ marinade	600 ml Tomato Sauce
100 ml oil ⎭	salt

1. Place the fish in the marinade for 30 minutes.
2. Pass through flour, shaking off the surplus, then through the batter, draining off all excess by pulling through the fingers before immersing in the fat at 180°C.
3. Fry until crisp and golden, turning the fillets during cooking to ensure even cooking and coloration; when cooked they will float on the surface.
4. Drain on absorbent kitchen paper and season with salt.
5. Dress on a dish paper on a flat dish. Garnish with lemon wedges and picked or fried parsley and serve accompanied by a sauceboat of Tomato Sauce.

Note
Fillets of other kinds of fish can be cooked by this method.

Deep-fried fish in breadcrumbs

This is fish with a coating of flour, eggwash and breadcrumbs, either fresh white, dried brown, manufactured breadcrumbs in many shapes and sizes, or matzo meal.

Fried Fillet of Plaice, Tartare Sauce
(Filet de Plie à l'Anglaise, Sauce Tartare)

10 × 85 g fillets of plaice	picked parsley
flour, eggwash and	600 ml Tartare Sauce
breadcrumbs	salt
3 lemons	

1. Dry the fillets in a cloth or absorbent kitchen paper and season with salt.
2. Coat with the flour, eggwash and breadcrumbs, reshape and place into hot fat.
3. Fry for 3 minutes until crisp and golden, turning the fillets during cooking to ensure even cooking and coloration.
4. Drain on absorbent kitchen paper and season with salt.
5. Dress on a dish paper on a flat dish. Garnish with lemon wedges and picked parsley and serve accompanied by a sauceboat of Tartare Sauce.

Fried Curled Whiting (Merlan en Colère)

Remove the skin, gills, eyes and entrails from 10 × 220 g whitings. Curl the fish by placing the tail between the teeth and secure with a cocktail stick. Pass the fish through flour, eggwash and breadcrumbs and proceed as for Fried Fillet of Plaice.

Fried Goujons of Sole, Sauce Tartare (Goujons de Sole Frits)

Cut 750 g fillets of sole into 6 cm × 1 cm goujons and proceed as for Fried Fillet of Plaice.

Sole Colbert

10 × 300 g Dover soles	3 lemons
flour, eggwash and	picked parsley
breadcrumbs	salt
175 g parsley butter	

1. Remove the black skin and trim off the fins; make an incision down the centre of the skinned side from the head to the tail and lay back the two fillets in a filleting motion to the edge of the fish. Cut through the backbone in three places.
2. Dry the fish in a cloth or absorbent kitchen paper.
3. Season and coat with flour, eggwash and breadcrumbs, keeping the top fillets turned back.
4. Place the fish between two frying grills and deep fry for 5 minutes until crisp and golden.
5. Drain on absorbent kitchen paper.

6. Remove the backbones and dress the fish on a dish paper on a flat dish. Place 2 slices of parsley butter in the centre of each and garnish with lemon wedges and picked parsley and serve.

Note
Other small flat fish may be cooked by this method.

Fried fish in milk and flour

This is fish coated with milk then with flour and deep fried at 180°C until lightly golden in colour and crisp on the outside. It is a method of cooking that is only really suitable for immediate consumption such as à la carte service. This method is only suitable for thin, small cuts of fish such as fillets and goujons. There is a danger of damaging larger pieces as there is no thick protective coating. This method contributes to rapid breakdown of the frying fat when surplus flour falls off.

Fried Fillet of Sole, French Style (Filet de Sole Frit à la Française)

10 × 85 g fillets of sole	3 lemons
150 ml milk	picked parsley
100 g flour	salt

1. Dip the fillets one at a time in milk, drain and coat with flour. Shake off any surplus and place one by one into hot fat.
2. Fry for 3 minutes until crisp and lightly golden, turning during cooking to ensure even coloration.
3. Drain on absorbent kitchen paper and season with salt.
4. Dress on a dish paper on a flat dish with lemon wedges and picked parsley.

Note
Fillets of other small fish can be cooked by this method.

Fried Whitebait (Blanchailles Frites)

1 kg whitebait	3 lemons
200 ml milk	picked parsley
150 g flour	salt

1. Pass the washed and drained whitebait through the milk, drain well, then pass through the flour. Place into a frying basket and shake well to remove surplus flour.

2. Place into hot deep fat at 190°C and fry for 3 minutes until crisp and lightly golden, shaking the basket from time to time to prevent the fish from sticking together.
3. Drain on absorbent kitchen paper and season with salt.
4. Dress in a pile on a flat dish on a dish paper and garnish with lemon wedges and picked parsley.

Fried Devilled Whitebait (Blanchailles Diablées)

Prepare as for Fried Whitebait and when cooked season with salt and cayenne pepper.

Accra   CARIBBEAN

1.25 kg salt cod	25 g curry powder
450 g flour	250 ml water
50 g chives	5 lemons
50 g onion	picked parsley
4 fresh red chillies	seasoning
6 cloves of garlic	

1. Soak the salt cod in water for 12 hours, then drain and plunge into simmering water, remove from the stove and allow to cool completely. Remove the skin and bones and flake the flesh.
2. Combine the fish with the flour, chopped chives, chopped onion, chopped chillies and garlic and curry powder, add sufficient water to form a thick paste.
3. Drop tablespoonfuls of the mixture into hot oil and deep fry until golden. Drain, season with salt and sprinkle with lemon juice. Serve garnished with wedges of lemon and deep-fried parsley.

Assortment of Fried Fish (Fritura de Pescado)   SPAIN

Cut 450 g each of fillet of red mullet and halibut into goujons and cut 450 g squid into rings. Pass through flour, golden deep-fry in olive oil and drain. Garnish with picked parsley and segments of lemon.

Fried Sardines (Sardinhas Fritas)   PORTUGAL

Split open, remove the backbones and heads then pass the sardines through flour, eggwash and breadcrumbs containing finely chopped garlic. Deep fry in olive oil.

Fried Salt Codfish Balls   USA

Combine 600 g flaked, poached salt cod, 600 g mashed potatoes, 3 egg yolks, 50 g butter and 100 ml cream. Mould into small balls, flatten to form round cakes, and mark criss-cross fashion. Place into frying baskets and deep fry at 190°C until golden brown. Serve garnished with lemon wedges and picked parsley.

Fried Stuffed Fillet of Plaice (Riga Tel'noe)   RUSSIA

Marinate fillets of plaice in oil, lemon juice, chopped dill and parsley for 1 hour. Spread with duxelles of mushrooms, then roll up and secure with a cocktail stick. Pass through flour, eggwash and breadcrumbs, deep fry in oil and serve garnished with picked parsley.

Golden-Fried Baby Squid (Kalamarakia)   GREECE

Season 1.5 kg whole baby squid, pass through flour then golden deep fry in olive oil. Drain, season with salt and sprinkle with lemon juice. Serve garnished with wedges of lemon and deep-fried parsley.

GRILLING

Grilling is the cooking of fish under or over direct heat, brushed with oil to prevent sticking. When cooked, garnish with lemon wedges, parsley butter and picked parsley.

Fish for grilling must be dried and passed through flour at the last moment and any surplus shaken off. Fish may also be grilled by coating with butter and breadcrumbs in the Saint-Germain style.

Types and cuts of fish suitable for grilling are:

1. Small whole fish such as Dover sole, lemon sole, herring, trout and whiting
2. Fillets of sole, plaice and whiting
3. Cuts of large fish such as halibut, salmon and cod and supremes of haddock.

Fillet of Sole Saint-Germain (Filet de Sole Saint-Germain)

10 × 85 g fillets of sole	40 noisette potatoes
100 g flour	500 ml Béarnaise Sauce
250 g butter	picked parsley
250 g white breadcrumbs	seasoning

1. Dry the fish, season and pass through the flour, melted butter and breadcrumbs.
2. Lightly flatten and mark the skinned side trellis-fashion with the back of a knife.
3. Place on a well-buttered grilling tray and sprinkle the surface with melted butter.
4. Grill gently under a salamander grill for 6 minutes to a light golden colour and a firm texture.

5. Arrange on an oval flat dish, garnish with the noisette potatoes and picked parsley and serve the Béarnaise Sauce separately in a sauceboat.

Fillet of Sole Caprice (Filet de Sole Caprice)

Prepare fillets of sole as for Fillet of Sole Saint-Germain and serve with a garnish of halves of banana cut on the slant, passed through flour and butter and grilled. Serve with a sauceboat of Sauce Robert separately.

Grilled Dover Sole (Sole de Douvre Grillée)

10×350 g Dover soles	100 g parsley butter
100 g flour	picked parsley
200 ml oil	seasoning
3 lemons	

1. Season and pass the fish through the flour and shake off the surplus.
2. Brush all over with oil and place on an oiled grilling tray or in a hinged fish grill.
3. Grill for 10 minutes, brushing occasionally until cooked.
4. Dress on a dish, place a slice of lemon and a slice of parsley butter on each and garnish with picked parsley.

Notes
1. When cooked, the soles may be brushed with melted butter; the parsley butter may be served separately in a sauceboat.
2. The skin side of the fish should be placed face downwards on the grilling tray so that when turned to cook the other side it is the right side up for serving.

Grilled Herring with Mustard Sauce (Hareng Grillé)

Using 10×200 g cleaned ciselled herrings, proceed as for Grilled Dover Sole and serve accompanied by 500 ml mustard sauce.

Grilled Cod Steak with Parsley Butter
(Darne de Cabillaud Grillée)

Using 10×100 g cod steaks, proceed as for Grilled Dover Sole.

Grilled Fillet of Plaice with Parsley Butter (Filet de Plie Grillé)

Using 10×85 g plaice fillets, proceed as for Grilled Dover Sole.

Grilled Tuna Fish Steak (Costolette di Tonno)

Marinate 10×200 g tuna steaks for 1 hour with 3 crushed cloves of garlic, 50 g chopped rosemary, 600 ml dry white wine and seasoning. Remove and dry the fish, brush with olive oil and grill until cooked and golden, basting with the marinade. Transfer the fish to a dish, coat with 100 g breadcrumbs combined with 50 g chopped fresh herbs, the juice and grated zest of 2 lemons and seasoning, then sprinkle with olive oil and return to the grill to gratinate. Serve with wedges of lemon.

Grilled Fillet of Carp (Saramura)   HUNGARY

Coat fillets of carp with chopped fresh herbs, oil and salt and leave for 30 minutes, then grill until golden brown. Reduce some fish stock with chopped chillies to a coating consistency, then add butter to make a light sauce. Serve the fillets on a slice of shallow-fried polenta, coated with the sauce.

SHALLOW POACHING

The shallow poaching of fish is done by barely covering it with either fish stock, wine or acidulated water. It is seasoned, covered with a buttered piece of greaseproof paper, brought to boil on the stove, then cooked in the oven at 175°C for 10 minutes or so until firm to the touch. In some recipes it is cooked together with its garnish and the cooking liquid is used to make the sauce which is an inherent feature of the dish. Some dishes are glazed at the moment of service, others not.

Small whole fillets and supremes of most kinds of fish are suited to this method of cookery.

Poached Fillet of Sole Bercy (Filet de Sole Bercy)

10 × 85 g fillets of sole	600 ml fish velouté
50 g shallots	100 ml cream
10 g chopped parsley	2 egg yolks for sabayon
100 ml dry white wine	75g butter
200 ml fish stock	

1. Butter and season a shallow tray, sprinkle with the finely chopped shallots and parsley and lay the prepared fillets in the tray in a single layer.
2. Add the wine and stock to barely cover the fish, cover with a buttered piece of greaseproof paper and poach in the oven at 175°C for 10 minutes.
3. Remove the fillets and place in a serving dish, cover and keep warm.
4. Strain the cooking liquor into a shallow pan, adding the garnish to the fish. Add the velouté and cream and reduce to a coating consistency.
5. Add the sabayon and pass through a fine strainer.
6. Whisk in the butter a little at a time, away from the stove, and season with salt and cayenne.
7. Coat the fish evenly with the sauce and glaze under a very hot salamander grill.

Poached Fillet of Sole Bonne Femme
(Filet de Sole Bonne Femme)

This is prepared in the same way as Poached Fillet of Sole Bercy with the addition of 250 g sliced button mushrooms.

Poached Fillet of Sole Bréval (Filet de Sole Bréval)

This is prepared in the same way as Poached Fillet of Sole Bercy with the addition of 200 g sliced button mushrooms and 200 g tomato concassée.

Poached Fillet of Sole Dugléré (Filet de Sole Dugléré)

Proceed as for Poached Fillet of Sole Bercy with the addition of 200 g tomato concassée. This dish is not glazed.

Poached Fillet of Sole D'Antin (Filet de Sole D'Antin)

Proceed as for Fillets of Sole Dugléré. When serving, sprinkle with 200 g diced fried bread croûtons.

Poached Fillet of Sole Palace (Filet de Sole Palace)

Proceed as for Fillet of Sole Bréval with the addition of chopped tarragon. Complete the sauce with 25 ml brandy.

Poached Fillet of Sole in White Wine Sauce
(Filet de Sole au Vin Blanc)

10 × 85 g fillets of sole	100 ml cream
50 g shallots	75 g butter
100 ml dry white wine	seasoning
200 ml fish stock	10 fleurons
600 ml fish velouté	

1. Butter and season a shallow tray and sprinkle with the finely chopped shallots.
2. Lay the prepared fillets in the tray in a single layer, add the wine and stock to barely cover the fish.
3. Cover with buttered greaseproof paper and poach in the oven at 175°C for 10 minutes.
4. Remove the fillets and place in a serving dish, cover and keep them warm.
5. Strain the cooking liquor into a shallow pan, add the velouté and the cream, reduce to a coating consistency, then pass through a fine strainer.
6. Whisk in the butter a little at a time, away from the stove, and season with salt and cayenne.
7. Coat the fish evenly with the sauce, garnish with the fleurons and serve.

Poached Fillet of Sole Dieppoise (Filet de Sole Dieppoise)

Proceed as for Poached Fillet of Sole in White Wine Sauce and add a garnish of 20 cooked button mushrooms, 100 g prawns and 50 g cooked mussels; coat the fish evenly with the sauce and serve.

Poached Fillet of Sole Suchet (Filet de Sole Suchet)

Add blanched julienne of 75 g each of carrot, turnip, leek and celery and 50 g truffle then proceed as for Poached Fillet of Sole in White Wine Sauce.

Poached Fillet of Sole Glazed in White Wine Sauce (Filet de Sole Vin Blanc Glacé)

10 × 85 g fillets of sole	100 ml cream
50 g shallots	2 egg yolks for sabayon
100 ml dry white wine	75 g butter
200 ml fish stock	seasoning
600 ml fish velouté	10 fleurons

1. Butter and season a shallow tray, sprinkle with the finely chopped shallots and lay the prepared fillets in the tray in a single layer.
2. Add the wine and stock to barely cover the fish, cover with buttered greaseproof paper and poach in the oven at 175°C for 10 minutes.
3. Remove the fillets and place in a serving dish, cover and keep them warm.
4. Strain the cooking liquor into a shallow pan, add the velouté and cream and reduce to a coating consistency.
5. Add the sabayon and pass through a fine strainer.
6. Whisk in the butter a little at a time, away from the stove, and season with salt and cayenne.
7. Coat the fish evenly with the sauce and glaze under a very hot salamander. Garnish with the fleurons and serve.

Poached Fillet of Sole Véronique (Filet de Sole Véronique)

Proceed as for Poached Fillet of Sole glazed in White Wine Sauce, garnish with 250 g skinned and depipped white grapes, coat with the sauce, glaze and serve. Alternatively, the grapes may be chilled and placed on the dish after it has been glazed.

Poached Fillet of Sole Mornay (Filet de Sole Mornay)

10 × 85 g fillets of sole	2 egg yolks for sabayon
200 ml fish stock	75 g grated Parmesan cheese
600 ml béchamel	75 g butter
100 ml cream	seasoning

1. Butter and season a shallow tray and arrange the prepared fillets in a single layer.
2. Add the stock to barely cover the fish, cover with buttered greaseproof paper and poach in the oven at 175°C for 8 minutes.
3. Remove and place the fillets in a serving dish, cover and keep them warm.
4. Strain the cooking liquor into a shallow pan, add the béchamel and cream and reduce to a coating consistency.
5. Add the sabayon away from the heat, then pass through a fine strainer.
6. Whisk in the butter a little at a time, then add 50 g of the cheese and season with salt and cayenne.
7. Coat the fish evenly with the sauce, sprinkle with the rest of the grated Parmesan, glaze under a salamander grill and serve.

Poached Fillet of Sole Cubat (Filet de Sole Cubat)

This is prepared in the same way as Fillet of Sole Mornay, placing the poached fillets on a base of 250 g duxelles of mushrooms.

Poached Fillet of Sole Florentine (Filet de Sole Florentine)

This is prepared in the same way as Fillet of Sole Mornay, placing the fillets on a base of 250 g buttered leaf spinach.

Fillet of Sole Walewska (Filet de Sole Walewska)

This is prepared in the same way as Fillet of Sole Mornay, placing a slice of cooked lobster on each of the fillets before coating with the sauce, and a slice of truffle on top.

Poached Fillet of Sole in Red Wine Sauce (Filet de Sole au Vin Rouge)

10 × 85 g fillets of sole	2 tbs anchovy essence
50 g shallots	75 g butter
300 ml red wine	seasoning
200 ml fish stock	10 fleurons
600 ml jus lié or demi-glace	

1. Butter and season a shallow tray, sprinkle with the finely chopped shallots and lay the prepared fillets in the tray in a single layer.
2. Add the wine and stock to barely cover the fish, cover with buttered greaseproof paper and poach in the oven at 175°C for 10 minutes.
3. Remove the fillets and place in a serving dish, cover and keep them warm.
4. Strain the cooking liquor into a shallow pan and reduce by half.
5. Add the brown sauce, reduce to a coating consistency, then add the anchovy essence and pass through a fine strainer.

6. Whisk in the butter a little at a time, away from the stove, and season with salt and cayenne.
7. Coat the fish evenly with the sauce, garnish with the fleurons and serve.

Poached Eels in Tomato and Basil Sauce (Anguilla alla Comacchiese)

Cut 1.5 kg skinned eels into 2.5 cm sections and shallow fry in 75 ml olive oil; remove and retain. Lightly fry 100 g chopped shallots or onion and 3 chopped cloves of garlic in the same pan, add 450 g tomato concassée, 50 g tomato purée, 50 g chopped basil, 300 ml dry white wine, 150 ml fish stock and seasoning. Replace the eels and simmer for 20 minutes. Serve the eel coated with the sauce, accompanied by a dish of Polenta.

Fish forcemeat, mousses and quenelles

Hot Fish Mousseline (Mousseline Chaud de Poisson)

500 g raw firm fish	300 ml cream
200 g frangipane panada	300 ml White Wine Fish Sauce
2 egg whites	salt, pepper and nutmeg

1. Mince the fish finely and pass through a sieve.
2. Add the warm panada, then gradually add the egg whites, working hard with a wooden spatule.
3. Allow the mixture to rest in a refrigerator or in a basin of ice and water, for 30 minutes.
4. Gradually add the cream, working it well with a spatule and add the seasonings.
5. Place into buttered dariole moulds and cook in a bain-marie in the oven at a temperature of 200°C for 20 minutes, or mould with tablespoons into a buttered tray, add fish stock and poach for 15 minutes until firm.
6. When cooked, allow to cool for a few moments, then turn out of the moulds or drain and place into a porcelain or earthenware dish and coat with the sauce. Serve on an underdish with a dish paper.

Fish Soufflé with Lobster Sauce (Soufflé de Poisson, Sauce Homard)

Proceed as for Fish Mousseline, using a buttered soufflé mould in which it is cooked and served, accompanied by Lobster Sauce.

Note
The name of the fish used should be included in the menu title, e.g. Hot Salmon Soufflé.

Mousseline of Fish with Lobster Sauce
(Mousseline de Poisson, Sauce Homard)

Proceed as for Hot Fish Mousseline, moulding the mixture into 20 oval or cigar shapes, using two serving spoons. Place in a serving dish and coat with Lobster Sauce.

Fish Quenelles (Quenelles de Poisson)

These are made in the same way as Hot Fish Mousseline, moulding the mixture into 20 × 50 g oval shapes, using two serving spoons, and cooking and serving in the same way. The same mixture may be piped out as small fancy shapes for garnishing consommés, or moulded with coffee or tea spoons for bouchée and vol-au-vent fillings.

ROASTING

Roast Salmon (Mitan de Saumon Rôti)

750 g middle cut of salmon	¹/₂ tsp ground cloves
50 ml oil	120 ml Hollandaise Sauce
2 bayleaves	picked parsley
¹/₂ tsp ground mace	seasoning

1. Scrape off the scales. Wash, then open up the salmon to remove the backbone; place the fish on a piece of foil.
2. Season with salt and pepper, sprinkle with the mace and cloves, add the bayleaves and brush with oil.
3. Reform the piece of salmon, enclose in the foil and refrigerate for 1 hour.
4. Heat a little of the oil in a roasting tray, add the salmon in the foil and roast at 180°C for 10 minutes, then open the foil, baste the fish and roast for a further 10 minutes.
5. Serve for 2 people, garnished with picked parsley and accompanied by a sauceboat of Hollandaise Sauce.

Peppered Salmon Roulade (Roulade de Saumon Poivrée)

1.5 kg fillets of salmon, middle cut	750 g leeks
250 g fish forcemeat	75 g butter
50 ml oil	500 ml tomato coulis
15 g black peppercorns	seasoning

1. Select a thick fillet, skin, remove the small bones with a salmon tweezer and cut through the thick part to 1cm from the edge.
2. Lay back the slice and flatten the fish gently with a moist cutlet bat to give an even thickness and dimensions of 22 cm × 18 cm.

3. Season the salmon, spread with the forcemeat, and roll tightly into a 20 cm long cylinder. Wrap securely in foil and refrigerate for 1 hour.
4. Unwrap the salmon. Brush the foil with oil and spread with the finely crushed peppercorns; reroll tightly and refrigerate again.
5. Shred the white and pale green ends of leeks, blanch, drain and stew in the heated butter for 5 minutes.
6. Heat a little of the oil in a roasting tray, add the cylinder of salmon and roast at 180°C for 20 minutes.
7. Unwrap and cut into 2 cm rounds, arrange on a bed of the leeks and surround with the coulis of tomato; serve the rest separately.

SHALLOW FRYING

Shallow frying or meunière is a method for cooking all kinds of fish in a small amount of fat in a frying pan on top of the stove. The fish is finished with lemon rounds and juice, chopped parsley and nut brown butter.

Fillet of Sole Meunière (Filet de Sole Meunière)

10 × 85 g fillets of sole	3 lemons
50 g flour	150 g nut brown butter
100 ml oil	chopped parsley

1. Heat the oil in a frying pan. Pass the fillets through the flour and shake off the surplus.
2. Place into the pan presentation side down. Fry until coloured, then turn and continue to fry until nicely coloured and firm to the touch.
3. Dress on a serving dish, place a slice of peeled lemon on each portion, squeeze lemon juice over the fish and sprinkle with the chopped parsley.
4. Just before serving, pour the hot nut brown butter over the fish.

Goujons of Sole Murat (Goujons de Sole Murat)

750 g fillets of sole	10 cooked artichoke bottoms
50 g flour	2 juice of lemons
100 ml oil	150 g butter
30 olivette potatoes	chopped parsley

1. Cut the fillets into strips 6 cm × 1 cm, pass the goujons through the flour and shake off the surplus.
2. Heat the oil in a frying pan, place the fish into the hot oil and fry quickly until golden, then drain. Add the artichokes cut into 1 cm strips and the cooked potatoes and toss to heat and mix.
3. Heat the butter in another frying pan, add the goujon mixture, sprinkle with the chopped parsley and lemon juice and toss over, without breaking the pieces.
4. Serve dome-shaped in a dish.

Shallow-Fried Trout with Almonds (Truite Meunière aux Amandes)

Using 10 × 200 g prepared trout, proceed as for Fillet of Sole Meunière. Fry 150 g slivered almonds in the nut brown butter, pour over the trout with the lemon juice and parsley and serve.

Fillet of Plaice Belle Meunière (Filet de Plie Belle Meunière)

Using 10 × 85 g fillets of plaice, proceed as for Fillet of Sole Meunière. Place a cooked half of a peeled tomato, a fried soft herring roe and one cooked button mushroom on top of each fillet, add the lemon juice and parsley and finish with hot nut brown butter.

Shallow-Fried Supreme of Cod Bretonne (Suprême de Cabillaud Bretonne)

Using 10 × 100 g cod supremes, proceed as for Fillet of Sole Meunière, sprinkling 200 g prawns and 200 g sliced cooked button mushrooms over the fish.

Shallow-Fried Supreme of Halibut with Capers (Suprême de Fletin aux Capres)

Using 10 × 100 g supremes of halibut, proceed as for Fillet of Sole Meunière, sprinkling 150 g capers over the fish.

Shallow-Fried Salmon Steak Doria (Darne de Saumon Doria)

Using 10 × 150 g salmon steaks, proceed as for Fillet of Sole Meunière, sprinkling 250 g small diamond-shapes of peeled and blanched cucumber over the fish.

Shallow-Fried Fillet of Sole Grenobloise (Filet de Sole Grenobloise)

Using 10 × 85 g fillets of sole, proceed as for Fillet of Sole Meunière, sprinkling peeled segments of lemon and 150g capers over the fish.

Shallow-Fried Supreme of Turbot Niçoise (Suprême de Turbot Niçoise)

Using 10 × 100 g supremes of turbot, proceed as for Fillet of Sole Meunière, adding a garnish of cooked tomato concassée, fillets of anchovy and stoned black olives.

Shallow-Fried Supreme of Salt Cod Florentine Style (Baccalà alla Firenziana)

Soak 1.25 kg salt cod in water for 12 hours, then drain, remove the skin and cut on the slant into 100 g supremes. Pass through flour and golden shallow fry in 75 ml olive oil; remove and retain. In the same pan, lightly fry 100 g chopped shallots or onion, 3 chopped cloves of garlic, 1 crumpled bayleaf and ¼ tsp powdered thyme; add 450 g tomato concassée and seasoning. Simmer for 5 minutes, then replace the fish and cook for a few more minutes; serve sprinkled with chopped basil.

Shallow-Fried Fish Fans (Boquerones Fritos) SPAIN

Pass 1.25 kg prepared small fish such as anchovies, sardines, sprats and whitebait through flour, press their tails together to form fan-shapes and carefully shallow fry in olive oil. Garnish with segments of lemon on serving.

Shallow-Fried Gefillte Fish ISRAEL

Mould the basic Gefillte Fish mixture into 20 balls, pass through fine matzo meal, form into fish cakes and golden fry in oil. Remove and drain on kitchen paper. Allow to cool and serve accompanied by green olives, pickled cucumber and chollah bread or matzo.

Shallow-Fried Supreme of Turbot in Lemon Sauce GREECE
(Psari me Selino Avgolemono)

Shallow fry 10 × 200 g supremes of turbot in a pan in a little olive oil, then add 300 ml dry white wine, 300 ml fish stock, 50 g chopped dill and seasoning. Cover with greaseproof paper and a lid and cook for 5 minutes. Transfer the fish to a serving dish and reduce the cooking liquid by half, lightly thicken with 20 g diluted arrowroot and a liaison of 4 egg yolks, the grated zest and juice of 2 lemons and 225 ml cream. Cook gently until it thickens, then pour over the fish and serve garnished with sprigs of dill.

Soused Red Snapper Escovitch CARIBBEAN

Boil 600 ml water, 100 ml white wine vinegar, 50 ml olive oil, 175 g julienne of green pimento, 100 g strips of carrot, 75 g sliced onion, 25 g chopped chives, 1 bayleaf, 10 peppercorns and salt for 30 minutes. Shallow fry 1.25 kg supremes of red snapper in olive oil, place into an earthenware dish and moisten with the court-bouillon with the addition of 25 ml lime juice. Serve hot or chilled.

STEAMING

Steamed fish, as recommended for special diets, is usually done between two plates over a pan of boiling water and this is really the extent of this practice. A better result is obtained by shallow or deep-poaching, which has the advantage of providing a serving liquid or the basis of an accompanying sauce.

STEWING

Fish stews are very popular dishes, Bouillabaisse being a good example. Pieces of fish and shellfish are cooked in fish stock, water or wine with vegetables, herbs and flavourings, the liquid being served as soup with crusty bread, followed by the fish in the remains of the stock as a main course.

The principle of staggered cookery is sometimes applied, whereby the more delicate types of fish, shellfish and those liable to break up during cooking should be added at a later stage. Shellfish such as oysters and prawns will become rubbery and tough if permitted to overboil or overcook.

Marseillaise Fish Stew (Bouillabaisse)

450 g each of brill, conger eel, mackerel, John Dory, red mullet, whiting and squid	2 cloves finely chopped garlic
	pinch fennel seeds
	2 bayleaves
1 kg mussels	pinch saffron
250 g scampi	5 g chopped parsley
200 ml olive oil	500 g tomato concassée
250 g white of leek, cut into julienne	500 ml dry white wine
	seasoning
200 g sliced onion	

1. Clean all the fish and cut into 5 cm sections on the bone; scrape and wash the mussels.
2. Heat the oil in a large shallow pan, add the vegetables, herbs, garlic and all the fish. Cover with a lid and sweat for 5 minutes, shaking occasionally.
3. Add the remainder of the ingredients, cover and allow to cook gently for 15 minutes.
4. Check the seasoning and the balance between the fish and the liquid. Remove one shell and the beards from the mussels.
5. Serve in a soup tureen, accompanied by slices of French bread. It is the tradition to sup most of the liquid as a soup and follow it with the fish as main course, eaten from the same soup plate.

Note
An authentic bouillabaisse is made using Mediterranean fish; the above recipe closely approximates to it using North Sea fish.

Fish Stew Italian Style (Brodetto all'Anconatana)

Heat 275 ml olive oil in a pan and sweat 225 g sliced onion, 2 whole cloves of garlic, 2 bayleaves and 250 g diced red pimento, then add 250 g tomato concassée and cook for 5 minutes. Discard the garlic and add 2 kg mixed fish cut into 5 cm sections on the bone, such as red and grey mullet, sea bass, sole and halibut. Cover with a lid and sweat for 5 minutes, then add 1 kg of shellfish such as shrimps, clams or mussels; moisten with 600 ml dry white wine and cook for a further 5 minutes. Serve on slices of toast in a soup plate or tureen.

Stewed Octopus in Tomato Sauce and Basil (Polpi in Umido)

Heat 300 ml olive oil in a pan, then add and lightly fry 1.5 kg octopus cut into 2.5 cm pieces. Add 600 ml dry white wine. Boil and reduce by half, then add 250 g tomato concassée and seasoning; cover with a lid and simmer for 45 minutes. Serve sprinkled with 50 g chopped basil combined with 2 cloves of chopped garlic.

Paella   SPAIN

Simmer the following fish in chicken stock with ¼ tsp saffron and seasoning until cooked: 450 g mussels, 350 g monkfish cut into small cubes and 2 small squid, the tentacles cut into short lengths and the bag into rings. Cut 1 × 1.5 kg chicken into 16 pieces. Heat 50 ml olive oil in a paellera or shallow pan, add the chicken pieces and shallow fry until golden on all sides, then add 4 crushed cloves of garlic and 450 g red and green pimentos cut into strips and cook until they are soft. Stir in 550 g short-grain rice then add 450 g strips of tomato flesh and seasoning. Ladle in 1.5 litres boiling chicken stock in several stages, allowing each addition to become absorbed before adding more and stirring constantly until the rice is cooked and all the stock completely absorbed. Just before serving add the bearded and shelled mussels, the monkfish and squid, plus 450 g cooked prawns and 225 g cooked lobster cut into small pieces. Serve garnished with wedges of lemon.

Stewed Squid in Red Wine (Kalamarakia Krassata)   GREECE

Lightly fry 500 g chopped shallots or onion, 2 chopped cloves of garlic and 100 g diced green pimento in 125 ml olive oil, then add 1.5 kg small squid cut into 2.5 cm strips and continue to fry until any liquid has reduced. Moisten with 250 ml red wine and 250 ml fish stock, adding 1 bayleaf, 1 sprig of thyme, 225 g tomato concassée and seasoning. Cover with a lid and simmer for 25 minutes. Serve on a base of boiled rice, sprinkled with 50 g chopped fresh basil.

Stewed Shark Steaks Creole Style   CARIBBEAN

2 juice of lemons		10 × 150 g shark steaks
75 ml rum		75 ml oil
50 ml water		100 g chopped onion
6 crushed cloves of garlic	marinade	250 g diced tomato flesh
50 g chopped chives		seasoning
4 chopped red chillies		

1. Place the shark steaks in a shallow dish, season with salt and pepper, cover with the marinade and leave for 2 hours.
2. Remove the fish from the marinade, dry in a cloth and golden shallow fry in oil, remove and retain.
3. In the same pan, sauté the chopped onion and tomato flesh, add the marinade and cook for a few moments. Replace the fish and simmer gently for 15 minutes. Serve accompanied by rice cooked in the Caribbean style.

Stewed Supreme of Halibut with Cabbage and Caraway (Fische mit Kümmelkraut) GERMANY

Sweat shredded cabbage in oil, then add potatoes cut into paysanne and moisten with fish stock and water; add caraway seeds and stew until nearly cooked. Place supremes of halibut on top, cover with buttered greaseproof paper and stew in the oven until the cabbage and halibut are cooked.

Stewed Tuna Steaks Caribbean Style CARIBBEAN

10 × 150 g	tuna steaks	1 litre	fish stock
4	juice of limes	6	cloves
4	fresh red chillies	2	bayleaves
75 ml	oil	1 sprig	thyme
100 g	chopped onions	15 g	chopped parsley
350 g	diced tomato flesh		seasoning

1. Marinate the tuna steaks for 4 hours in the lime juice with the chopped chillies and seasoning.
2. Remove the fish from the marinade, dry in a cloth and golden shallow fry in oil.
3. Add the chopped onion to the pan and cook, then drain off any surplus fat; moisten with the fish stock, add the diced tomato flesh, cloves, bayleaves, thyme and chopped parsley and cook for 5 minutes.
4. Add the fish, cover with a lid and stew for a further 20 minutes.

SHELLFISH

The two types of shellfish are:

1. Molluscs, of which there are two types:
   (a) Bivalves, which have two shells joined by a hinge, the most common being oysters, scallops and mussels;
   (b) Univalves, which have one shell, the most common being whelks and winkles.
2. Crustaceans, which have a single shell and legs, the most common being crab, lobster, scampi, prawns and shrimps.

When purchasing any kind of shellfish it is very important to ensure that it is fresh and alive and lively. Bivalves must be tightly closed and crustaceans must be animated.

Crab

To boil a crab wash it in cold water, then plunge it into sufficient boiling court-bouillon to cover. Allow to simmer for 20 minutes, according to weight, then leave to cool completely in the liquid.

Crab Meat, Bean Curd and Rice (Hai Yook Par Dau Fu)   CHINA

Lightly sauté 100 g chopped spring onions and 25 g grated ginger in 50 ml oil. Moisten with 300 ml fish stock, add 1 kg crab meat, then thicken to a light sauce consistency with 25 g cornflour diluted in a little water. Remove from the heat and add 10 × 1 cm cubes of bean curd, season to taste and serve on a bed of boiled rice.

Lobster

To boil a lobster plunge it live into plenty of boiling court-bouillon, boil for 20 minutes then leave to cool in the liquid. Lobsters that appear lifeless must be rejected because they will have become waterlogged and lost most of their flesh and flavour. The flesh of a freshly cooked lobster should be white, moist and flavourful. To serve it as half lobster, either cold or hot, first remove the claws by twisting them from the carapace and crack them open with a heavy knife so as to take out the flesh whole. Remove the small legs, then lay the lobster on the work surface and cut into two halves along the natural line on the head, turning it and continuing through the body to the end of the tail. Discard the sac from the head and the black trail through the body. It is now ready to serve cold or for further hot processing according to recipe. To cut a live lobster from raw see the recipe for Lobster Americaine.

The thin legs and shells of a cooked lobster should be kept for making soup and sauces.

Lobster Cardinal (Homard Cardinal)

100 g butter	2 egg yolks ⎱ liaison
5 × 750 g boiled lobsters	50 ml cream ⎰
150 g button mushrooms	50 g grated Parmesan cheese
65 ml brandy	10 g slices of truffle
600 ml lobster sauce	picked parsley

1. Cut the lobsters into halves lengthways and remove the flesh.
2. Cut the flesh into thick slices on the slant, leaving the claws whole. Wash and dry the shells.

3. Melt half of the butter in a shallow pan, add the sliced mushrooms and cook, then add the lobster pieces and gently reheat. Add 50 ml of the brandy and flambé.
4. Add sufficient of the lobster sauce to bind the lobster and mushroom together.
5. Boil the remaining lobster sauce, remove from the heat, add the liaison and cook to thicken.
6. Place a little of the sauce in the warmed shells, place the lobster and mushrooms in the tail ends and the reheated claws at the head end, then coat all over with the rest of the sauce. Sprinkle with the cheese and the rest of the melted butter and gratinate in the oven or under a salamander grill until lightly golden.
7. Heat the slices of truffle in the rest of the brandy and arrange on the lobsters.
8. Dress on an oval flat dish lined with a dish paper, decorated with sprigs of parsley.

Lobster Mornay (Homard Mornay)

    100 g butter
5 × 750 g boiled lobsters
  600 ml Mornay Sauce
      50 g grated Parmesan cheese
          picked parsley

1. Cut the lobsters in halves lengthways and remove the flesh.
2. Cut the flesh into thick slices on the slant, leaving the claws whole. Wash and dry the shells.
3. Melt half of the butter in a shallow pan, add the lobster and reheat.
4. Place a little of the hot sauce in the warmed shells, arrange the flesh in the tail ends with the claws at the head end.
5. Coat with the sauce, sprinkle with grated Parmesan cheese and the rest of the melted butter and gratinate in the oven or under a salamander grill to a light golden colour.
6. Dress on an oval flat dish lined with a dish paper and decorate with sprigs of parsley.

Lobster Thermidor (Homard Thermidor)

50 g butter	30 g English mustard
5 × 750 g boiled lobsters	200 g butter
300 ml Sauce Bercy	50 g grated Parmesan cheese
600 ml Mornay Sauce	picked parsley

1. Cut the lobsters in halves lengthways and remove the flesh.
2. Cut the flesh into thick slices on the slant, leaving the claws whole. Wash and dry the shells.

3. Melt the butter in a shallow pan, add the lobster and reheat.
4. Place a little of the Sauce Bercy, previously flavoured with a little of the made mustard, in the warmed shells; arrange the flesh in the tail end with the claws at the head end.
5. Coat with the Mornay Sauce, also flavoured with the mustard. Sprinkle with grated Parmesan cheese and gratinate in the oven or under a salamander grill until lightly golden.
6. Dress on an oval flat dish lined with a dish paper and decorate with sprigs of parsley.

Lobster Newburg (Homard Newburg)

100 g butter	6 egg yolks
5 × 750 g boiled lobsters	700 ml cream
50 ml brandy	500 g cooked pilaff of rice
80 ml Marsala or Madeira	seasoning

1. Cut the lobsters in half lengthways and remove the flesh.
2. Cut the flesh into thick slices on the slant, leaving the claws whole.
3. Melt the butter in a shallow pan, add the lobster and reheat.
4. Add the brandy and flambé, then the wine and reduce by half.
5. Add the cream, boil, then add the yolks and cook gently to thicken without boiling; season to taste.
6. Neatly arrange in a warmed timbale and serve accompanied with another timbale of the rice pilaff.

Lobster Americaine (Homard à l'Américaine)

50 ml oil	15 g tomato purée
1 × 750 g live lobster	100 g tomato concassée
50 g brunoise of carrots,	25 g butter
shallots and celery	5 g parsley and tarragon
1 clove crushed garlic	50 g long-grain rice for
25 ml brandy	pilaff (optional)
100 ml dry white wine	seasoning
200 ml fish stock	

1. Wash the lobster in cold water.
2. Pierce the head with the pointed end of a knife so as to kill the lobster, then cut the tail from the head. Remove the claws from the body and crack them so that the flesh can be easily removed when cooked.
3. Cut the tail into its natural sections and divide the head lengthways.
4. Discard the sac from the head end; remove the coral and creamy parts and mix with the butter to make the lobster butter.
5. Heat the oil in a shallow pan, add the pieces of lobster and cook until it turns red. Add the brunoise of vegetables and crushed garlic, cover with a lid and allow to sweat until the vegetables are soft.

6. Add the brandy and flambé. Add the white wine, fish stock, tomato purée, tomato concassée and seasoning. Bring to the boil, skim, cover with a lid and cook gently for 15 minutes; do not overcook.
7. Remove the lobster, take out the flesh from the shell and place it into a timbale, keeping it hot.
8. Reduce the cooking liquid by half, remove from the heat and add the lobster butter, using a shaking action to form a light coating consistency.
9. Coat the lobster with the sauce and decorate with the tips of the lobster head and the tail, spread to give a butterfly effect. Sprinkle with the freshly chopped parsley and tarragon and serve the timbale on a round flat dish with a dish paper, optionally accompanied with a timbale of pilaff rice.

Mussels

Moules Marinière

2.5 kg mussels, washed and scraped	1 juice of lemon
	100 ml cream
75 g chopped shallots or onion	50 g butter
250 ml dry white wine	5 g chopped parsley
250 ml fish stock	cayenne pepper

1. Place the mussels into a deep pan with the shallots or onion, white wine, fish stock and lemon juice.
2. Cover with a lid and bring to the boil, then cook rapidly for 3 minutes until the shells have opened.
3. Remove the mussels from the cooking liquid.
4. Decant the liquid into a basin and allow it to stand so that any sand falls to the bottom.
5. Remove the mussels from the shells and beard them.
6. Replace each mussel in a half shell, arrange in a serving dish and cover to keep warm and prevent drying out.
7. Decant the liquid into a shallow pan, bring to the boil, add the cream and thicken with the butter away from the heat. Add the chopped parsley and a point of cayenne, then test for seasoning and consistency.
8. Pour over the mussels and serve immediately.

Oysters

Poached Oysters (Hûitres Pochées)

Open oysters and remove them from their shells. Strain the oyster juice into a saucepan and bring to the boil. Add the oysters and simmer for a few seconds, remove from the heat and leave covered for a few minutes. Overcooked oysters are rubbery.

Prawns

Prawns are generally purchased ready-cooked or in frozen cooked form. When defrosted they can be used either as an hors-d'oeuvre item, a fish dish, a main course, as a garnish or savoury dish.

Curried Prawns

    75 g butter
   700 g prawns
   600 ml Curry Sauce
   500 g boiled rice
          chopped parsley

1. Melt the butter in a shallow pan, add the prawns and toss gently to heat them through.
2. Add the curry sauce and incorporate the prawns.
3. Serve the prawns and the rice in two separate entrée dishes, sprinkled with chopped parsley.

Fried Prawns   USA

Pass prawns through garlic-flavoured mayonnaise thinned with milk, then through breadcrumbs mixed with chopped fresh herbs. Deep fry until golden and serve garnished with wedges of lemon and picked parsley.

Grilled Skewered Prawns and Scallops with Mango Sauce   USA

Marinate 20 scallops and 600 g prawns in a liquidised blend of 200 g mango flesh, 50 ml olive oil and 50 ml lime juice. Skewer cooked snow peas with the prawns and scallops and grill. Boil the strained marinade, thicken with diluted arrowroot to a sauce consistency, season and serve in sauceboats.

Prawn Butterflies (Woo Dip Har)   CHINA

Shell and devein 20 king prawns, make an incision along the back and marinate for 15 minutes in 50 ml saké or dry sherry, 50 ml light soy sauce, 1 crushed clove of garlic, 1 tsp grated root ginger, and salt. Pass the prawns through cornflour, eggwash and breadcrumbs and golden deep fry in groundnut oil. Garnish with segments of lemon and accompany with chilli sauce.

Prawns and Vegetables in Batter (Tempura)   JAPAN

Golden fry 270 g goujons of sole, 10 shelled king prawns, 10 scallops, 275 g sliced squid, 10 slices eggplant, 10 mushrooms, 125 g square pieces of green pimento and 10 small squares of dried lava seaweed, all dipped in tempura batter at 175°C. Do not let the items get too crisp. Serve accompanied by tempura dip.

Prawns in Beer Batter (Gambas con Gabardina)   SPAIN

Pass 1.25 kg peeled king prawns through beer batter, golden deep fry and drain. Garnish with segments of lemon.

Shallow-Fried Prawns with Garlic (Gambas al Ajillo)   SPAIN

Fry 3 chopped cloves of garlic and a little salt in 75 ml olive oil, add 1.25 kg cooked and peeled king prawns and toss over to reheat. Garnish with segments of lemon.

Scallops

There are several ways in which scallops may be featured on the menu: shallow-fried, plain or breadcrumbed; for breakfast with bacon; as part of a shellfish cocktail or a vol-au-vent filling; in a border of duchesse potato, coated with a sauce and gratinated. All the sauces associated with shallow-poached fish may be used either glazed or unglazed.

Scallop shells are also used for presenting other dishes, with or without the scallops. The dish should then be worded on the menu as 'en Coquille', together with the name denoting the main item and sauce used, e.g. Scallop Shell of Cod in White Wine Sauce – Coquille de Cabillaud, Sauce Vin Blanc Glacée. It is necessary to wedge the filled shells together on a tray to stop them rolling around.

To cook Scallops

To open, place the scallops on the side of a hot stove, or on a heated hot-plate, where they will soon open of their own accord. Remove from the bottom shells and discard the frill, leaving the white centre and red tongue. Wash under cold water, then cook by simmering in a little milk with sliced onion, herbs and seasoning, or in a white wine court-bouillon for 5 minutes. Keep the lower shells for presenting the shellfish. If overcooked scallops become firm and rubbery.

Scallops in Cheese Sauce (Coquilles Saint-Jacques Mornay)

   1 kg duchesse potato mixture
  75 g butter
600 ml Sauce Mornay
    20 cooked scallops
  50 g grated Parmesan cheese

1. Pipe the edges of buttered large scallop shells with the duchesse potato using a fancy tube, sprinkle with melted butter and dry lightly under a salamander grill without coloration.

2. Pour a little of the Mornay Sauce in the bottom of the shells, place the hot sliced scallops and tongues on top and coat with more Mornay Sauce.
3. Sprinkle with grated Parmesan cheese and melted butter and glaze the sauce and potato under a salamander grill.
4. Serve on a flat dish on a dish paper with picked parsley.

Glazed Shells of Cod in White Wine Sauce
(Coquille de Cabillaud Glacée au Vin Blanc)

1 kg duchesse potato mixture	600 ml White Wine Fish Sauce
75 g butter	seasoning
750 g poached fillet of cod	picked parsley

1. Pipe the edges of the buttered scallop shells with the duchesse potato, sprinkle with melted butter and dry under the salamander grill without coloration.
2. Melt the butter in a shallow pan, add the flaked fish, season and toss to reheat.
3. Pour a little of the sauce in the bottom of the shells, add the hot fish and coat with the same sauce.
4. Glaze under a salamander grill and serve on a flat dish on a dish paper with picked parsley.

Shallow Fried Scallops in Tarragon Sauce USA

Lightly sauté 40 scallops in garlic-flavoured butter and retain. Swill the pan with 50 ml white wine and 25 ml lemon juice; add 300 ml fish velouté, seasoning and 100 ml cream; simmer for 5 minutes, then strain. Add chopped tarragon and the scallops and serve.

Spring Scallop Rolls (Dai Tze Guen) CHINA

Combine 225 g scallops cut into small slices, 4 chopped Chinese dried mushrooms, previously soaked, 8 chopped water chestnuts, 3 chopped spring onions, 1 tsp grated root ginger, 1 tsp light soy sauce, 1 tsp sesame oil and seasoning. Cut 5 spring roll wrappers into 4, envelop 2 tsp of the filling in each and seal with eggwash made with the addition of 25 g flour. Golden deep fry in groundnut oil for 5 minutes.

Scampi/Dublin Bay prawns/Langoustines

This species of shellfish is very popular, mainly because it is more easily digestible than other crustacea, but also because of its delicate, sweetish taste. They are available in several forms: whole, fresh in the shells; fresh tails; frozen tails in iced glaze; reformed and breaded. In size, scampi range from jumbo, at about 56 to the kilogram, to selected, at double that number per kilo.

Fried Scampi (Scampi Frits)

850 g scampi	3 lemons
flour, eggwash and	seasoning
breadcrumbs	picked parsley
	600 ml Tartare Sauce

1. Season the scampi and coat with flour, eggwash and breadcrumbs, then reshape by rolling them in the hands.
2. Place into a frying basket, then into hot deep fat at 185°C. Fry for 3 minutes, according to size, until crisp and golden, shaking the frying basket to ensure even coloration.
3. Drain on kitchen paper and sprinkle with salt.
4. Dress on a dish paper on a flat dish, garnish with lemon wedges and picked parsley and serve accompanied by a sauceboat of Tartare Sauce.

Scampi Meunière

850 g scampi	150 g butter
100 g flour	seasoning
300 ml oil	chopped parsley
3 lemons	

1. Heat the oil in a frying pan, season and pass the scampi through the flour, shaking off the surplus.
2. Place the scampi in the very hot oil and fry to a golden-brown colour.
3. Dress dome-shaped in a service dish and arrange 20 slices of peeled lemon on top.
4. Squeeze a little lemon juice over the scampi and sprinkle with chopped parsley.
5. Just before serving, cook the butter until it is nut brown and pour over the scampi.

Scampi Provençale

850 g scampi	500 ml Tomato Sauce
100 g flour	chopped parsley
75 g butter	seasoning
500 g tomato concassée	

1. Heat the butter in a shallow pan, season and pass the scampi through the flour, shaking off the surplus.
2. Add to the pan and fry without much coloration. Drain off any surplus butter.
3. Add the tomato concassée and Tomato Sauce and gently mix into the scampi.
4. Fill into a serving dish and sprinkle with the chopped parsley.

Plain Boiled Crayfish (Ecrevisses à la Nage)

1 litre fish stock
500 ml white wine
  250 g carrots, grooved ⎤ cut into
  250 g button onions ⎦ thin slices

   1 bouquet garni
  15 g fresh thyme
  80 crayfish
    seasoning

1. Make a court-bouillon with the stock, wine, vegetables, herbs and seasoning and simmer for 30 minutes.
2. Gut each crayfish by taking hold of the centre of the tail flap, twisting and pulling out the gut. If desired, truss them by turning the tails over the heads and secure by sticking the points of the claws into the shell under the tails.
3. Wash the crayfish, place in the court-bouillon and simmer gently for 15 minutes. Serve them in a timbale, covered with the cooking liquid.

Fish and Shellfish Vol-au-Vent (Vol-au-Vent de Fruits de Mer)

10 × 8 cm vol-au-vent cases
  250 g turbot (cut into
      goujonettes)
  250 g scampi (cut into pieces)
  200 g butter
    10 slices of lobster
    20 button mushrooms

     5 poached scallops
  100 ml Pernod
few drops Tabasco
  300 ml cream
     seasoning
     picked parsley

1. Season and lightly fry the turbot and scampi separately in the butter.
2. Combine them with the lobster and button mushrooms and heat through for a few minutes, then keep warm.
3. Place the Pernod, Tabasco and cream in a pan, boil and reduce to a coating consistency.
4. Add the fish and mushrooms, together with the sliced scallops, and season to taste.
5. Place the warm pastry cases on an oval flat dish, fill to overflowing with the mixture, replace the pastry lids and serve hot garnished with picked parsley.

CHAPTER 7 Meats

Beef

QUALITY POINTS

1. The flesh should be moist and firm, light red in colour with a fine even grain.
2. Marbling, or flecks of fat should be visible in the prime joints such as sirloin and fillet.
3. Fat should be creamy white in colour and evenly distributed over the outside of the carcass.
4. The bones should be pale pink in colour.

MAIN JOINTS

The following weights include the bones, where applicable.

Hindquarter of beef – Contains nearly all the prime joints and weighs, according to breed, from 63–90 kg.

Shin (7 kg) – Stewing and for minced beef. Contains a lot of sinews which cannot all be trimmed.

Silverside (11 kg) – Roasting, stewing, pickling in brine, boiling. Needs hardly any trimming.

Topside (9 kg) – Braising, roasting and stewing. Usually divided into small joints, as steak for braising and diced for stewing; no trimming is needed.

Rump (11 kg) – Grilling and shallow frying. Bone out and trim excess fat and membrane; includes the thick end of the fillet.

Sirloin (14 kg including the fillet (2¹⁄₂ kg)) – Roasting and pot-roasting as steaks. Remove the bones and back sinews, then tie or cut.

Forequarter of beef – Has only one prime joint, the rib, the remaining joints being suitable for braising and stewing only. Weighs 60–85 kg according to breed.

Forerib (7 kg), also called Wing Rib – Roasting on the bone. The ends are trimmed of fat, the chine bones semi-released and tied back on, the sinew along the backbone cut out and the covering fat folded back. Can also be boned, rolled and tied.

Middle ribs (11 kg) – Braising, stewing. Cut through the shoulder blade and 2nd and 3rd rib bones; bone out and trim of all sinew.

Brisket (11 kg) – Stewing, braising, boiling, either plain or pickled. Bone out and trim excess fat; can also be rolled and tied.

Steakmeat (17 kg) – Braising, stewing. Cut and tie as joints or cut into braising steaks or cubes for stewing. Includes the leg of mutton cut and the chuck.

Clod and Stickling (16 kg) – Stewing and for minced beef. Bone out and remove sinew and fat. This joint includes the ball joint of the shoulder and six neck bones.

Shank (6 kg) – Stewing and for minced beef. Bone out and remove the sinew; the shin bone can be split to yield bone marrow.

PRIME CUTS FOR GRILLING AND SHALLOW FRYING

Chateaubriand (240 g per person multiplied by the number of customers) – Cut from the thick end of the fillet and slightly flatten.

Fillet steak (200 g) – Cut from the thick end of the fillet in slices 5 cm thick.

Minute steak (200 g) – Cut a steak from a boned sirloin and flatten with a meat bat to 3 mm thickness.

Sirloin steak (200 g) – Cut from a boned sirloin 1.5 cm thick.

Porterhouse Steak or 'T' Bone Steak (350–450 g) – Cut from the whole sirloin 4–5 cm thick to include the fillet and the bone.

Tournedos (200 g) – Cut from the centre of the fillet in sections, 3 cm thick; tie with string.

Point steak (200 g) – Cut as 2 cm thick slices from the point end of a boned rump.

Rump steak (200 g) – Cut from the boned rump. Cut a 2 cm thick slice the length of the joint and cut into pieces or grill whole then cut into portions.

BAKING

Beef Wellington

1 kg larded fillet of beef	500 g duxelles
100 ml oil	1.5 kg puff pastry
seasoning	eggwash

1. Heat the oil in a frying pan.
2. Add the seasoned fillet and fry until a light golden brown all over. Remove from the pan and allow to cool completely and drain by standing it on a wire grid.
3. Roll out the pastry 3 mm thick, a little longer than the fillet, to allow for sealing the ends, and wide enough to surround the fillet with a little overlap for sealing.
4. Place some of the duxelles in the centre of the pastry. Place the fillet on top and cover the surface area with the remainder of the duxelles.
5. Enclose the meat in the pastry, overlapping the top at least 1cm, brush with eggwash and seal. Seal the ends in a similar fashion. (Generally the end pieces are discarded when serving.)
6. Turn it over onto a baking sheet which has been greased or sprinkled with water.
7. If desired, decorate with leaves or shapes of pastry.
8. Allow to rest for at least 1 hour in a refrigerator.
9. Bake in the oven at 200°C for the first 15 minutes, reducing the temperature to 150°C for a further 30 minutes.

10. Remove from the oven and allow to settle for a few moments before cutting and serving. Serve in a shallow dish or on a plate, accompanied with an appropriate sauce such as Madeira Sauce.

Notes
1. The dish may be presented whole or cut into portions. The portioning must be left to the last moment to prevent drying out.
2. This dish is generally produced in multiples of 2 to 6 portions.
3. Foie gras may be added to the duxelles in equal proportions.
4. The meat should be medium-done, that is, rare in the centre, be moist, tender and fresh-looking when sliced and evenly surrounded with the filling. The pastry should be an even golden colour and, where it comes into contact with the filling, be slightly moist.

Cottage Pie

1.5 kg raw minced beef	1 kg mashed potato or Duchesse
100 g dripping	Potato
250 g chopped onion	100 g melted butter
25 g tomato purée	seasoning
500 ml jus lié or demi-glace	

1. Heat the dripping in a deep pan, add the meat and fry until slightly coloured. Add the chopped onion and cook until it is soft but not too brown.
2. Drain off any surplus fat, add the tomato purée and brown sauce, bring to the boil and season. Simmer gently for 30 minutes until the meat is cooked. Skim if necessary to remove all traces of fat that may surface.
3. Transfer the meat into shallow dishes to a depth of 5 cm.
4. Spread the surface with either mashed or Duchesse Potato mixture and mark with a palette knife. Alternatively pipe the potato to form a scroll design, using a star tube.
5. Sprinkle the surface with the melted butter.
6. Place in the oven and bake at 180°C for 30 minutes until the surface is crisp and golden. Brush with melted butter and serve. Originally, this pie was made with cooked beef, finely chopped or minced and reheated in brown sauce for 15 minutes before being covered with potato and baked for 30 minutes.

Steak, Kidney and Mushroom Pie (pre-cooked filling)

1 kg stewing steak cut into 2.5 cm cubes	1 litre water
	seasoning
400 g ox kidney cut into small cubes	50 g flour or arrowroot
	25 g chopped parsley
250 g sliced or quartered mushrooms	few drops Worcester sauce
	650 g Puff Pastry
250 g sliced or chopped onion	eggwash

1. Place the meat and kidney into a deep pan and cover with cold water. Bring to the boil and skim.
2. Add the mushrooms, onion and seasoning and simmer gently for 1½ hours.
3. Thicken with the flour or arrowroot mixed in cold water and continue to simmer until thick. Finish with a few drops of Worcester sauce and the chopped parsley, then pour into a pie dish and allow to cool.
4. Roll out the pastry 3 mm thick and line the edge of the pie dish with thin strips of pastry and brush with eggwash.
5. Cover with the sheet of pastry, seal firmly, trim off excess pastry and crimp the edges; decorate with leaves of pastry and make a small hole in the centre to allow the steam to escape. Allow to rest for 1 hour, then eggwash the surface.
6. Place onto a baking tray and bake at 215°C for 15 minutes until the pastry has risen, then reduce the temperature to 190°C and cook for a further 45 minutes.
7. Remove from the oven and place a pie collar around the pie.

Steak and Kidney Pie (raw filling)

Cut 1 kg topside of beef into 2.5 cm cubes and combine with 300 g diced ox kidney, 225 g chopped onion, 25 g chopped parsley, 400 ml cold brown stock, a few drops of Worcester sauce and seasoning. Place into a pie dish and cover with 650 g Puff Pastry rolled 3 mm thick; decorate the top, eggwash and make a small hole in the centre to allow steam to escape, then allow to rest for 1 hour. Bake in the oven at 210°C for 15 minutes then at 150°C for a total of 2½ hours. If necessary, cover with foil to prevent over-colouring. Serve on a dish paper on an underdish.

Notes
1. The pastry should be an even golden colour, light, flaky and moist but not soggy underneath.
2. The filling should be hot, tender and moist, firm yet soft when eaten, and the surrounding liquid full of aroma and flavour, with a slight undertone from the Worcester sauce.

Toad in the Hole

20 × 50 g beef sausages
   100 g dripping
   1 litre Yorkshire Pudding batter
   500 ml jus lié

1. Heat the dripping in a shallow roasting dish or tray. Add the sausages and shallow fry until brown on all sides.

2. Arrange neatly and pour in the batter mixture.
3. Place in the oven to bake at 220°C for 45 minutes until the sausages are cooked and the batter is crisp and golden.
4. Cut into portion sizes, arrange in an entrée dish and serve accompanied by the sauce.

Meat Loaf, American Style   USA

Sweat 100 g chopped onion in 50 ml oil and combine with 1 kg minced beef, 450 g minced pork or veal, 75 g breadcrumbs, 10 g chopped parsley, 3 beaten eggs, 2 tsp Worcester sauce and seasoning. Mould in a loaf tin, cover with 275 g rashers of bacon and cook in the oven at 200°C for 1 hour. Serve cut into 0.5 cm slices accompanied by jus lié.

Moussaka (Moussaká)   GREECE

1.5 kg raw minced beef	$^1/_2$ tsp oregano
250 g chopped onion	1 cinnamon stick
3 chopped cloves of garlic	100 ml jus lié
75 ml olive oil	600 ml Cheese Sauce
200 g diced tomato flesh	100 g grated Kefalotiri cheese
75 g tomato purée	100 g fresh breadcrumbs
450 g eggplant	seasoning

1. Peel and cut the eggplant into long slices 2.5 cm thick. Place in a colander, sprinkle with salt and allow to stand for 30 minutes. Drain and dry, then lightly fry in some of the oil and reserve.
2. Lightly fry the beef, onion and garlic in the rest of the oil, add the tomato flesh, tomato purée, cinnamon, oregano and seasoning and jus lié. Cover with a lid and cook for 30 minutes until the meat is cooked and appears dry. Remove the cinnamon.
3. Line an oiled and seasoned shallow dish with the eggplant, add the meat and cover with a layer of the eggplant.
4. Mask with the cheese sauce made using Kefalotiri cheese instead of Parmesan, sprinkle with the cheese, breadcrumbs and oil and bake at 200°C for 1 hour until golden brown.
5. When cooked, cut into square or oblong shapes and serve.

Pomey's Head   USA

Combine 600 g minced beef, 600 g minced veal, 300 g pork sausage meat, 100 g chopped shallots, 10 g Dijon mustard, 2 tsp each of rubbed thyme and sage, 4 beaten eggs and a little water. Form into 10 round dome shapes, making 2.5 cm holes in the centre. Sprinkle with flour and butter and bake at 180°C for 30 minutes.

BOILING

Boiled Beef and Dumplings

1.5 kg salted silverside of beef	300 g button onions
1 onion studded with	400 g carrots (barrel-shaped)
a bayleaf and clove	300 g turnips (barrel-shaped)
1 bouquet garni	500 g suet pastry

1. Soak the salt beef in cold water for 2–3 hours.
2. Place in a deep pan and cover with fresh cold water, bring to the boil and skim thoroughly.
3. Add the studded onion and bouquet garni and simmer gently for a total time of 2 hours, adding the vegetables according to the time they take to cook: first the button onions, followed by the carrots and then the turnips.
4. When cooked, transfer the meat to one saucepan and the vegetables to another, moistening with a little of the cooking liquid. Discard the bouquet garni and studded onion.
5. Divide the suet pastry into 20 pieces and mould into round balls. Place into the cooking liquor and simmer gently for 20 minutes.
6. Carve the meat into slices 3–4 mm thick across the grain at an angle of 45°.
7. Neatly arrange on a dish and garnish with the vegetables and dumplings. Moisten with some of the strained cooking liquid.

Note
To test if cooked, pierce the meat with a trussing needle or skewer. If it penetrates without having to use pressure, the meat is cooked.

Boiled Beef, French Style (Boeuf Bouilli à la Française)

1.5 kg thick flank or brisket	5 leeks
12 peppercorns	500 g cabbage (tied)
1 bayleaf	200 g turnips (barrel-shaped)
1 sprig thyme } tied in a piece of muslin	salt
4 cloves	gherkins
4 juniper berries	sea salt or
2 celery, tied in bundles	coarse salt } accompaniments
250 g button onions	French
250 g carrots (barrel-shaped)	mustard

1. Place the prepared meat in a deep pan of boiling salted water. Bring back to the boil and skim thoroughly.
2. Add the bag of flavourings and salt and simmer gently for 2 hours.
3. Add the vegetables according to the time they take to cook: first the celery, then button onions, carrots, leeks, cabbage and turnips.

4. When cooked, transfer the meat to one saucepan and the vegetables to another with a little of the cooking liquid. Discard the bag of flavourings.
5. Carve the meat into slices 3–4 mm thick across the grain at an angle of 45°. Arrange on a dish, garnish with the vegetables and moisten with cooking liquid.
6. Serve with dishes of gherkins, coarse salt and French mustard.

Boiled Ox Tongue

1 × 2 kg salted ox tongue

1. Soak the tongue in cold water for 3 hours.
2. Place in a deep pan and cover with fresh cold water, bring to the boil, skim and allow to simmer for 3 hours. When cooked, remove the skin and trim off the root end; keep the tongue hot in the cooking liquor.
3. Serve cut into 4 mm thick slices with an appropriate sauce, e.g. Madeira Sauce, or allow to cool in a press for service as a buffet item, glazed with reddish-brown aspic jelly.

Tripe and Onions

  1.5 kg tripe
  450 g sliced onions
1 litre Parsley Sauce
        seasoning

1. Place the tripe, cut into 5 cm squares, into a saucepan, cover with water, bring to the boil and skim.
2. Add the sliced onions, season and simmer until tender.
3. Drain the tripe and mix in the Parsley Sauce; reheat and serve.

Boiled Beef, Chicken and Pork with Vegetables (Cozido à Portuguesa) PORTUGAL

Boil 1.5 kg diced beef, pork and chicken in water in that order, with 125 g each of turned carrots, turnips and potatoes and quarters of cabbage, also in that order. Serve the meats with the vegetables in an earthenware marmite moistened with the cooking liquor and garnished with sliced chorizo sausage, accompanied by boiled rice.

Boiled Beef, Pork and Lamb and Chicken with Vegetables (Burgoo) USA

Place 225 g shin of beef, 450 g hand of pork, 225 g breast of lamb and 1 × 1.5 kg chicken in a pan, cover with water, season and simmer until tender. Remove all the flesh from the bones and cut it into large dice. Simmer 350 g each of chopped onion, sliced carrot and diced potato, 125 g each of sliced okra and lima beans and 1 fresh red chilli in the cooking liquid from the meat, then add 675 g tomato concassée, the diced meats, Worcester sauce, Tabasco sauce and cayenne pepper. Cook until it is reduced to a thickish consistency and serve.

BRAISING

Braised Beef (Pièce de Boeuf Braisée)

1.5 kg topside or thick flank, larded	1 sprig thyme
100 g dripping	1 crushed clove garlic
200 g carrots ⎤	1 litre brown stock
200 g onion ⎬ roughly cut	1 litre jus lié or Espagnole
150 g celery ⎦	1 bouquet garni
1 bayleaf	seasoning

1. Heat the dripping in a frying pan.
2. Add the seasoned joint and fry until brown on all sides, then place in a braising pan.
3. Fry the vegetables in the frying pan, drain and add to the meat.
4. Add the stock, brown sauce and seasoning. Bring to the boil and skim. Add the bouquet garni.
5. Cover with a lid and braise in the oven at 180°C for 2 hours.
6. Remove the meat from the cooking liquid and retain in a covered dish to keep warm.
7. Discard the bouquet garni. Boil the cooking liquid and skim any traces of fat.
8. Correct the consistency using diluted arrowroot; taste and colour to produce a rich sauce.
9. Pass through a fine strainer and reboil. Skim if necessary.
10. Remove the string and carve the joint into slices 3 mm thick across the grain of the joint.
11. Arrange on a dish, coat with the sauce and serve.

Note
Vegetable garnishes are usually cooked separately and added at the point of service; buttered noodles may also be served as a garnish.

Braised Beef, Burgundian Style
(Pièce de Boeuf Braisée Bourguignonne)

Place a 1.5 kg larded joint in a Red Wine Marinade for 5–6 hours then proceed as for Braised Beef, cooking it with the marinade. Just before serving add a garnish of 250 g fried lardons of bacon, 20 glazed button onions and 30 cooked button mushrooms.

Braised Beef with Noodles
(Pièce de Boeuf Braisée aux Nouilles)

Proceed as for Braised Beef and serve garnished with 300 g buttered noodles.

Braised Beef with Vegetables (Pièce de Boeuf Braisée Jardinière)

Proceed as for Braised Beef and serve garnished with 250 g jardinière of vegetables.

Braised Steaks (Bifteck Braisé)

10 × 150 g braising steaks, 1 cm thick	50 g tomato purée
200 g dripping	1.5 litres brown stock
250 g onions ⎱ roughly cut	1 bouquet garni
250 g carrots ⎰	chopped parsley
2 cloves garlic, crushed	seasoning

1. Heat the dripping in a frying pan.
2. Season the steaks, pass through flour and fry until brown on both sides.
3. Transfer to a shallow pan or braising pan.
4. In the same frying pan fry the onion, carrot and garlic to a light brown colour, drain and add to the steaks.
5. Mix in the tomato purée and moisten with the stock to barely cover.
6. Bring to the boil and skim. Season, add the bouquet garni, cover with a lid and braise in the oven at 180°C for 1 hour.
7. Place the steaks in a clean pan and strain the cooking liquid into a clean saucepan.
8. Boil and skim to remove any trace of fat, thicken with diluted arrow-root and, if necessary, adjust the colour and pour over the steaks.
9. Serve in a suitable dish, sprinkled with chopped parsley.

Braised Steaks with Beer and Onions (Carbonnade de Boeuf Flamande)

BELGIUM

10 × 150 g braising steaks, 1 cm thick	100 g butter
200 g dripping	500 ml beer
750 g sliced onions	1 litre brown stock
	seasoning

1. Heat the dripping in a frying pan.
2. Season the steaks, pass through flour and fry until golden brown on both sides.
3. Transfer the steaks to a shallow pan or a braising pan.

4. Fry the onions in dripping, add to the steaks, together with the beer and sufficient stock to cover them.
5. Bring to the boil and skim. Season, cover with a lid and braise in the oven at 180°C for 1 hour.
6. Skim off any fat and serve in a dish, sprinkled with chopped parsley.

Braised Oxtail (Queue de Boeuf Braisée)

Prepare 2.5 kg sections of oxtail, allowing 2 pieces per portion, and proceed as for Braised Steaks, cooking the oxtail for 3 hours at 175°C. When cooked the flesh should begin to come away from the centre bone.

Braised Oxtail with Vegetables
(Queue de Boeuf Braisée aux Légumes)

Prepare 2.5 kg sections of oxtail and proceed as for Braised Steaks. Just before serving add 250 g jardinière of vegetables.

Haricot Oxtail (Queue de Boeuf Braisée aux Haricots Blancs)

Prepare 2.5 kg sections of oxtail and proceed as for Braised Steaks. Just before serving add 200 g cooked haricot beans.

Beef Olives (Paupiettes de Boeuf)

10 × 150 g braising steaks, 1 cm thick	150 g sliced onion	
350 g beef sausage meat	150 g sliced carrot	
200 g dripping	50 g sliced celery	bed of roots
25 g butter	75 g bacon trimmings	
1.5 litres brown stock	1 crushed clove garlic	
seasoning	1 sprig thyme	
	1 bayleaf	

1. Flatten the steaks with a cutlet bat to 10 cm × 8 cm in size and season.
2. Place 35 g sausage meat on each piece, roll up and secure with string.
3. Butter the bottom of a braising pan and cover with the bed of roots.
4. Heat the dripping in a frying pan.
5. Season the beef olives, pass through flour and fry until golden brown on all sides.
6. Transfer to the prepared braising pan and pour in sufficient stock just to cover.
7. Bring to the boil and skim. Season, cover with a lid and braise in the oven at 180°C for 1½ hours.
8. Take out the olives, remove the string and place them in a clean pan.
9. Boil the sauce and skim to remove all traces of fat.
10. Correct the consistency so that it just coats the olives and, if necessary, adjust the colour.

11. Add the olives to the sauce and serve neatly arranged in an entrée dish, coated with the sauce.

Braised Beef Olives with Veal Forcemeat

Roll up 10×150 g thin beef steaks with 350 g veal forcemeat, tie with string and proceed as for Beef Olives.

Braised Beef Olives Spanish Style (Matambre)   SPAIN

Combine 150 g each of chopped onion and finely shredded and blanched spinach, 2 cloves chopped garlic, $\frac{1}{4}$ tsp oregano and seasoning to form a stuffing. Spread 10×150 g thin beef steaks with it; roll up and tie and proceed as for Beef Olives.

Braised Beef Olives with Gherkins (Rindsrouladen)   GERMANY

Spread 10×150 g thin beef steaks with English mustard, then place a pickled gherkin wrapped in a rasher of bacon in each. Roll up and tie and proceed as for Beef Olives.

Braised Paprika Steaks with Soured Cream   HUNGARY
(Alföldi Felàl)

Pass 10×150 g larded and seasoned braising steaks through a mixture of 1 part flour to 3 parts paprika and shallow fry in oil until brown, then place in a braising pan. Sauté 200 g sliced onion in the first pan, add 1 litre beef stock, thyme, bayleaf and seasoning; bring to the boil and pour over the steaks. Cover and braise at 180°C for 1 hour. Strain the cooking liquid, thicken with 25 g diluted cornflour and 225 ml soured cream. Strain over the steaks and onion, reheat and serve garnished with braised green pimentos.

Braised Soured Beef   USA

Place a 1.5 kg larded joint of beef in a marinade of 500 ml wine vinegar, 100 ml lemon juice, 200 ml water, 2 crushed cloves of garlic, 200 g each of chopped celery, carrot and onion, parsley stalks, 1 bayleaf, 1 sprig of thyme, 6 cloves and 25 ml Worcester sauce for 5–6 hours, then proceed as for Braised Beef, using the marinade as the braising liquid.

Braised Steaks in Beer (Ochsenfleisch in Bier)   GERMANY

Proceed as for Braised Steaks but using 500 ml each of brown stock and beer, 25 ml vinegar and 25 ml corn syrup. Garnish with fried lardons of bacon, sautéed onion and glazed turned carrots and serve sprinkled with chopped fresh herbs.

GRILLING

Grilled Double Sirloin Steak (Entrecôte Double Grillée)

10 × 400 g sirloin steaks	150 g parsley butter ⎫
oil	200 g Straw Potatoes ⎬ garnish
salt and pepper	1 bunch watercress ⎭

1. Season and brush the steaks all over with oil.
2. Brush the grill bars with oil, place the meat on the hottest part of the grill, moving the steaks so that a criss-cross effect is marked on both sides. Then move them to a heat zone that will enable them to cook to the desired degree without burning.
3. Serve neatly arranged on a dish. Garnish with the straw potatoes and watercress and serve the sliced parsley butter separately in a sauceboat on a little crushed ice.

Grilled Chateaubriand (Chateaubriand Grillé Sauce Béarnaise)

This steak is cut from the thick end of a fillet of beef for 2–4 portions, allowing not less than 250 g meat per portion. It is flattened slightly to enable the heat to penetrate more quickly and is served whole for the waiter to cut into portions on the slant, in front of the customers. It can be served with the ordinary grilled meat garnishes but sauce Béarnaise is obligatory.

The other kinds of steaks are cooked and served in the same way as Grilled Double Sirloin Steak, the following being examples of menu terms:

Grilled Sirloin Steak with Tomatoes and Mushrooms (Entrecôte Grillée Garnie)
Grilled Minute Steak with Straw Potatoes, parsley butter and watercress (Entrecôte Minute Grillée Vert-Pré)
Grilled Fillet Steak with Devilled Sauce (Filet Grillé, Sauce Diable)
Grilled Tournedos Steak with Herb Butter (Tournedos Grillé, Beurre aux Fines Herbes)
Grilled Porterhouse Steak garnished with Watercress
Grilled Point Steak with Piquante Sauce
Grilled Rump Steak with Straw Potatoes
Grilled T-Bone Steak with Garlic Butter

Beef Satés (Satay Daging)   THAILAND

Marinate 1.25 kg cubes of tail-end of fillet of beef in 2 tsp ground turmeric, 1 tsp curry powder, 1 tsp ground cumin, 2 tsp sambal ulek, 50 ml lemon juice, 50 g brown sugar, 175 ml thick coconut milk and salt, for 1 hour. Soak 10 bamboo skewers in water for 1 hour and skewer the cubes of beef, then grill for 5 minutes. Serve accompanied with peanut sauce.

Grilled Meat Balls (Koftah)

Combine 1.5 kg minced beef, 3 cloves chopped garlic, 10 g fenugreek, 25 g chopped coriander leaves and dried mint and 3 beaten eggs, then season with baharat and salt. Form into balls, then grill and serve with boiled rice.

POT-ROASTING

Pot-Roasted Fillet of Beef (Filet de Boeuf Poêlé)

200 g sliced carrot		1.5 kg larded fillet of beef
200 g sliced onion		75 g dripping
150 g sliced celery		100 g melted butter
1 bayleaf	bed of root	1 litre jus lié
1 sprig thyme	vegetables	seasoning
parsley stalks		
1 crushed clove of garlic		

1. Butter and season the bottom of a braising pan or other deep pan large enough to afford room for basting and with a lid that does not touch the meat.
2. Sear the meat quickly in hot dripping until browned on all sides.
3. Place the bed of roots in the pan. Season the meat, place on top and coat with the melted butter.
4. Cover with the lid and pot-roast in the oven at 220°C for 45 minutes, basting the meat from time to time.
5. When the meat is nearly cooked, remove the lid to allow the meat to colour for the last 10 minutes. Remove and keep hot.
6. Place the braising pan on top of the stove without allowing the vegetables to burn. Drain off the fat, add the jus lié and simmer until the flavour from the juices and butter has been absorbed into the sauce.
7. Pass through a fine strainer without pressure. Reboil and skim all traces of fat. Season and correct the consistency so that it just coats the meat.
8. Carve the fillet into 5 mm slices and arrange overlapping on a dish. Coat with the sauce and serve with a sauceboat of the sauce.

Notes
1. The meat should look shiny and brown and taste succulent and full of flavour.
2. The sauce should be medium-brown in colour, fairly thin in consistency so as to coat the meat, be mellow in flavour from the meat, vegetables and herbs, and transparent so that the meat is clearly visible under it.
3. Any garnishes should be sufficient for the number of portions and be neatly and evenly prepared.

Filet de Boeuf Poêlé Bouquetière

This is prepared in the same way as Pot-Roasted Fillet of Beef, garnished with bouquets of glazed turned carrots, minted peas, French beans, Pommes Château and cauliflower coated with Hollandaise Sauce. Coat with the sauce flavoured with Madeira.

Filet de Boeuf Poêlé Dubarry

This is prepared in the same way as Pot-Roasted Fillet of Beef, garnished with Pommes Château and small bouquets of Cauliflower Mornay.

Contrefilet de Boeuf Richelieu

This is prepared in the same way as Pot-Roasted Fillet of Beef, using a boned sirloin garnished with stuffed tomatoes, stuffed mushrooms, braised lettuce and pommes château.

Pot-Roasted Sirloin of Beef in Garlic Sauce   SPAIN
(Solomillo All-I-Pebre)

This is prepared in the same way as Pot-Roasted Fillet of Beef, using a boned sirloin and substituting sliced onion and chopped garlic for the bed of root vegetables. Carve the sirloin and serve on a bed of the sliced onion, lightly coated with the sauce.

ROASTING

To roast a joint of beef, season it with salt just before putting it in the oven, place in a roasting tray resting on its bones, or, if boned out, on a trivet or some chopped bones. Coat with a little melted dripping and roast at 220°C for 20 minutes to seal and colour the outside, then reduce the heat to 180°C. Baste the joint occasionally and turn once or twice. To calculate the cooking time for medium done, allow 30 minutes per kilogram weight plus 15 minutes, e.g. a 2 kg rib of beef will need 2¼ hours in a normal oven. Allow 225 g raw beef on the bone or 165 g off the bone per person.

Carving joints of beef

When cooked, the meat should be allowed to stand for 20 minutes before carving commences. Any string should be removed and the item placed on a firm surface to prevent any movement during carving. To avoid wastage and give greater accuracy when carving, select the correct thin-bladed, sharp carving knife; sirloin and ribs are carved thinly across the grain, fillets are carved slightly thicker on the slant.

Roast Sirloin of Beef (Aloyau de Boeuf Rôti)

2.25 kg sirloin on the bone	1 litre brown stock
100 ml melted dripping or oil	1 bunch watercress
salt	100 ml Horseradish Sauce

1. Season the joint and place bone side downwards in a roasting tray. Coat with the dripping and place into the oven at 220°C, reducing the temperature after 20 minutes to 180°C. Baste at regular intervals.
2. When cooked, remove from the roasting tray and retain in a tray, preferably standing on a wire grid, for 20 minutes. Any juices collected should be used for making the gravy.
3. Place the roasting tray on the stove and heat gently, allowing the sediment to settle.
4. Drain off all fat, leaving the sediment in the tray, add the brown stock and simmer gently for a few minutes.
5. Strain through a fine conical strainer into a saucepan. Reboil, skim all traces of fat and season to taste.
6. Arrange the slices of meat slightly overlapping on an oval flat dish, coat with some of the roast gravy and serve garnished with picked watercress.
7. Serve the remainder of the gravy and the Horseradish Sauce in sauceboats.

Roast Fillet of Beef with Vegetables
(Filet de Boeuf Rôti Bouquetière)

Prepare 1.5 kg fillet of beef and proceed as for Roast Sirloin of Beef, allowing a cooking time of 45 minutes. Serve garnished with bouquets of glazed carrots, glazed turnips, minted peas, buttered French beans, Château Potatoes and florets of cauliflower coated with Hollandaise Sauce, accompanied by a sauceboat of roast gravy.

Roast Rib of Beef with Yorkshire Pudding

Prepare a 2.25 kg rib of beef and proceed as for Roast Sirloin of Beef. Serve with sections of or individual Yorkshire puddings, accompanied by a sauceboat each of gravy and Horseradish Sauce.

SHALLOW FRYING

Shallow-Fried Sirloin Steak (Entrecôte Sautée au Beurre)

10 × 200 g sirloin steaks
100 g butter
    salt and pepper
150 g butter

1. Heat the butter in a sauté pan.
2. Season the steaks, place in the pan and fry to the required degree and to a golden brown on both sides.
3. Arrange on an oval dish, mask with the butter cooked to the nut-brown stage and serve.

Entrecôte au Poivre

10 × 200 g sirloin steaks	100 g butter
100 g butter	chopped parsley
30 g peppercorns, crushed	salt
100 ml brown stock	

1. Season the steaks with salt and coat well with the peppercorns, pressing them in.
2. Heat the butter in a sauté pan.
3. Place the steaks in the pan and fry to the required degree and to a golden brown on both sides.
4. Arrange on an oval dish.
5. Drain the fat from the pan, add the stock and reduce by half.
6. Incorporate knobs of butter off the heat to form a light sauce and season to taste.
7. Coat the steaks with the sauce, sprinkle with chopped parsley and serve.

Entrecôte Bordelaise

10 × 200 g sirloin steaks	20 × 5 mm slices bone marrow
100 g butter	chopped parsley
100 ml red wine	salt and pepper
600 ml Sauce Bordelaise	

1. Heat the butter in a sauté pan.
2. Season the steaks, place into the pan and fry to the required degree and to a golden brown on both sides.
3. Arrange the steaks on a dish.
4. Drain the fat from the pan, add the wine and reduce by half.
5. Add the sauce, simmer and season to taste.
6. Lightly poach the marrow in a little stock and place two pieces on each steak.
7. Coat with the sauce, sprinkle with chopped parsley and serve.

Entrecôte Chasseur

10 × 200 g sirloin steaks	600 ml Sauce Chasseur
100 g butter	15 g chopped tarragon
100 ml dry white wine	salt and pepper

1. Heat the butter in a sauté pan.
2. Season the steaks, place into the pan and fry to the required degree and to a golden brown on both sides.
3. Arrange on an oval dish.
4. Drain the fat from the pan, add the wine and reduce by half.
5. Add the sauce, simmer and season to taste.
6. Coat the steaks with the sauce, sprinkle with chopped tarragon and serve.

Tournedos Rossini

10 × 200 g tournedos	200 ml jus lié or demi-glace
100 g butter	10 slices of truffle
10 croûtons, round	50 g butter
10 slices foie gras	salt and pepper
100 ml Madeira	

1. Heat the butter in a sauté pan.
2. Season the tournedos, place in the pan and fry to the required degree and to a golden brown on both sides.
3. Remove the strings from the tournedos and place on the croûtons on an oval dish.
4. Drain the fat from the pan, add the Madeira and reduce by half, add the sauce, reheat, correct the consistency and season. Pass through a fine strainer, reheat and add knobs of butter off the heat.
5. Place a sautéd slice of foie gras and a thin slice of truffle on each tournedos, mask with the sauce and serve.

Beef Rissoles Florentine Style (Polpette alla Florentina)

Combine 450 g cooked minced beef, 450 g dry mashed potatoes, 2 chopped cloves garlic, 20 g chopped parsley, 100 g grated Parmesan cheese, 150 g bread soaked in milk and squeezed dry, 3 beaten eggs to bind, and seasoning. Shape into cutlet shapes and shallow fry in olive oil, drain and serve.

Sirloin Steaks Pizzaiola (Costata alla Pizzaiola)

Lightly fry 4 chopped cloves of garlic in 75 ml olive oil, moisten with 1 litre Passata, then add 15 g chopped parsley, 25 g chopped basil and seasoning. Shallow fry 10 × 200 g sirloin steaks to the required degree in garlic-flavoured olive oil and transfer to the sauce for 2 minutes but do not allow to boil. Serve the steaks coated with the sauce and sprinkled with chopped fresh basil.

Beef Rissoles (Keftethes)   GREECE

Combine 1.5 kg finely minced beef, 100 g finely chopped onion, 175 g breadcrumbs, 25 g chopped parsley, 2 tsp chopped mint, $1/2$ tsp oregano, 2 chopped cloves of garlic, 2 beaten eggs, 50 ml olive oil, 25 ml vinegar, 50 ml hot water and seasoning. Mould into 20 balls and golden shallow fry in olive oil, drain and serve.

Beef Steak in Cream Sauce (Bifé à Marrare) PORTUGAL

Rub tender beef steaks with garlic and shallow fry in butter. Swill the pan with cream, replace the steaks and serve.

Beef Stroganoff (Bef Stroganoff) RUSSIA

1.5 kg tail end of fillet of beef	1 juice of lemon
100 g butter	tarragon, chopped
50 g shallots, chopped	seasoning
300 ml soured cream	

1. Cut the meat into 5 cm × 1 cm strips.
2. Heat the butter in a sauté pan.
3. Season and add the beef, quickly shallow fry, tossing continuously, keeping it underdone. Remove and retain in a warm place.
4. Add the shallots to the pan and cook without colouring. Drain off any excess fat.
5. Add the cream, boil and reduce by half. Add the drained meat and incorporate by gently tossing. Do not boil.
6. Add the lemon juice, season and serve in dishes, sprinkled with chopped tarragon.

Corned Beef Hash USA

Combine 200 g chopped corned beef, 120 g cooked diced potato and seasoning. Heat 50 g butter in an omelette pan, place in the mixture, press down and fry until golden and crisp on both sides.

Sautéed Fillet Steak with Blue Cheese SPAIN
(Filetes con Cabrales)

Cut 1.5 kg fillet of beef into 3 mm slices and marinate in 100 ml olive oil, 4 crushed cloves of garlic and seasoning for 30 minutes. Shallow fry the steaks in oil to the desired degree and serve on fried round croûtons with slices of blue cheese on top of the steaks.

STEAMING

Steak and Kidney Pudding

1½ kg Steak and Kidney Pie Filling (p. 149)
  1 kg suet pastry

1. Line 3 greased medium-sized pudding basins with suet pastry rolled out 3 mm thick.

2. Add the raw filling. Dampen the rim of the pastry with water, place round layers of pastry on top and seal well.
3. Cover with greaseproof paper and a cloth and tie with string, or cover with kitchen foil and fold under the rims of the basins.
4. Steam the puddings in a pressure steamer for the required length of time.
5. Serve in the basins in which cooked, cleaned of all cooking stains and surround with a clean napkin on a flat dish with a dish paper.

STIR-FRYING

Stir-Fried Beef, or Beef Bowl (Gyudon) JAPAN

Heat 50 ml oil in a wok and stir-fry 100 g sliced onion and 1.5 kg thin strips of beef. Moisten with 300 ml water, 50 ml dark soy sauce, 25 ml mirin and 25 ml ginger juice and cook for 2 minutes. Serve in donburi bowls on a bed of boiled rice.

Stir-Fried Beef in Black Bean Sauce (See Jup Ngau Yook) CHINA

Combine 100 ml black bean sauce, 75 ml soy sauce, a little water and sugar. Heat 50 ml garlic-flavoured oil in a wok, add 1.5 kg strips of beef, stir-fry for 2 minutes, remove and retain. Add the bean mixture to the pan, thicken with 25 g diluted cornflour to form a light sauce and simmer for 2 minutes. Replace the meat, cook for 1 minute and serve with boiled rice.

Stir-Fried Beef with Ginger (Xin Jiang Chao Niu Rou) CHINA

Marinate 1.5 kg strips of beef in 75 ml soy sauce, 25 ml saké, 25 ml sesame oil, 10 g sugar, 25 g cornflour and seasoning for 5 minutes. Heat 50 ml sesame oil in a wok, add the strips of beef and stir-fry for 2 minutes, remove and retain. Add 50 g grated ginger, 3 chopped cloves of garlic, then moisten with a little stock, 50 ml oyster sauce and the marinade and simmer for 2 minutes. Replace the meat and serve garnished with chopped spring onions.

Stir-Fried Beef in Green Curry (Khiaw Waan Nuea) THAILAND

Heat 25 ml groundnut oil in a wok, add 100 g green curry paste, cook for a few moments then add 1.5 kg thin slices of beef and stir-fry. Moisten with 100 ml thick coconut milk, a little sugar, 25 g nam pla and 25 ml soy sauce. Finish with chopped basil, coriander and fresh green chillies.

Stir-Fried Beef with Peanuts THAILAND
(Dendeng Belado Dan Katjang)

Marinate 1.5 kg strips of beef in 50 ml lime juice. Heat 50 ml oil in a wok, then add the beef and stir-fry for a few moments, remove and retain. Blend 100 g onion, 4 cloves of garlic, 25 g sambal ulek and 75 g peanut butter to a paste; add the mixture to the pan and stir in 100 ml coconut milk and 50 g roasted peanuts. Cook the sauce, then add the meat and serve garnished with sliced cucumber and chillies.

Note
Strips of lamb, pork, poultry and veal can be cooked in the same way.

STEWING

Brown Beef Stew (Ragoût de Boeuf)

1.5 kg stewing beef cut into 2.5 cm cubes	75 g flour
200 g dripping	50 g tomato purée
200 g carrots	1.5 litres brown stock
200 g onions } roughly cut	1 bouquet garni
150 g celery	seasoning

1. Season the meat and fry in hot dripping until golden in colour on all sides; drain in a colander and place in a stewing pan.
2. Fry the vegetables in the same fat until golden, drain in a colander and add to the meat.
3. Singe the meat and vegetables by sprinkling with flour and placing in a hot oven until the flour turns brown.
4. Add the tomato purée and stir in the stock. Bring to the boil, skim, season and add the bouquet garni.
5. Cook covered in an oven at 180°C or simmer on top of the stove for 1½ hours.
6. When cooked, transfer the meat to another saucepan and discard the vegetables and bouquet garni. Strain the sauce through a conical strainer over the meat.
7. Bring to the boil and skim to remove all traces of fat. Correct the consistency so that it just coats the meat and, if necessary, adjust the colour.

Note
It is preferable to cook stews in an oven because it gives more even cooking.

Beef Stew, Burgundian Style (Ragoût de Boeuf Bourguignonne)

Proceed as for Brown Beef Stew and just before serving add 250 g fried lardons of bacon, 20 glazed button onions and 30 cooked button mushrooms.

Beef Stew with Vegetables (Ragoût de Boeuf Jardinière)

Proceed as for Brown Beef Stew and serve garnished with 250 g jardinière of vegetables.

Beef and Onions in Red Wine (Stiffàto) GREECE

1.5 kg stewing steak, cut into 2.5 cm cubes	125 ml red wine
1 kg blanched button onions	750 ml beef stock
2 crushed cloves of garlic	50 ml vinegar
250 g diced tomato flesh	50 ml olive oil
1 bayleaf	seasoning
1 cinnamon stick	chopped parsley

1. Place all the ingredients into a fireproof dish, cover with the lid and cook in the oven at 180°C for 1½ hours.
2. Remove the meat and onions and strain the cooking liquid, skim off any fat and thicken with diluted cornflour.
3. Pour back over the meat and onions and serve sprinkled with chopped parsley.

Beef Stew Spanish Style (Estofado à la Catalana) SPAIN

Cut 1.5 kg stewing beef into 2.5 cm cubes, season and pass through flour and fry until brown in 75 ml oil, then add 400 g chopped onion and 3 chopped cloves of garlic. Moisten with 1.5 litres stock, 100 ml white wine, add a bouquet garni with oregano, 120 g lardons of bacon and seasoning and simmer for 1 hour until almost cooked. Mix in 50 g grated bitter chocolate, add 20 small potatoes and continue cooking. Serve garnished with sautéed slices of butifarra white sausage.

Couscous NORTH AFRICA AND THE MIDDLE EAST

550 g couscous	200 g carrots, turned
150 g chickpeas	1 × 1.25 kg chicken
450 g shin of beef	350 g cabbage
275 g scrag end of lamb	350 g courgettes
35 ml oil	75 g raisins
300 g onion	25 g coriander leaves
¼ tsp saffron	50 g butter
10 g cinnamon stick	seasoning
200 g tomato concassée	

1. Soak the couscous in warm water for 15 minutes and the chickpeas in cold water for 30 minutes.
2. Cut the beef and lamb into 2 cm cubes and fry in the oil. Slice the onions and cook with the meat.
3. Barely cover the meat with water, bring to the boil and skim. Add the drained chickpeas, saffron, cinnamon and tomatoes, the turned carrots and seasoning; bring to the boil and simmer for 30 minutes.
4. Remove the fat, add the chicken, whole or cut into pieces, and cook for a further 30 minutes.

5. Place the drained couscous in the top container or in a colander lined with muslin. Cover and allow to steam over the meat, stirring from time to time.
6. Add the shredded cabbage, 1 cm dice of courgettes, the raisins and chopped coriander leaves to the stew in the bottom pan and simmer until cooked.
7. To serve, place the couscous in a dish, fork in the butter and arrange the meat, chicken and vegetables on top. Moisten with some of the cooking liquor.

Note

A special pot known as a couscousier is used to make couscous. It has two parts: the bottom pan in which the stew is cooked and an upper container in which the couscous is cooked in the steam generated from the bottom pan (see p. 476).

Goulash of Beef (Porkolt)   HUNGARY

1.5 kg stewing beef cut into 2.5 cm cubes	300 ml wine vinegar
100 ml oil	600 ml beef stock
400 g chopped onion	2 tsp caraway seeds
3 chopped cloves of garlic	1 tsp marjoram
50 g paprika	200 ml soured cream
	salt and pepper

1. Season the meat and fry in the oil until brown on all sides. Drain in a colander and place in a pan for stewing.
2. Fry the onion and garlic in the same oil until golden, drain in a colander and add to the meat.
3. Sprinkle the meat and onions with paprika and moisten with the wine vinegar, stock and salt and pepper. Bring to the boil and skim; add the marjoram and caraway seeds and cover with a lid.
4. Simmer gently, either in the oven at 180°C or on top of the stove, for 1½ hours.
5. When cooked remove all traces of fat and mix in the soured cream, or serve the cream in a sauceboat.
6. Serve accompanied by Sauerkraut.

Pepperpot   CARIBBEAN

Cut 1 kg stewing beef and 450 g salt beef into 2.5 cm cubes, 1 boiling fowl into 10 pieces and 1 kg oxtail and 3 pigs' trotters into sections. Blanch the meats, then place into a clean pan, cover with cold water, bring to the boil and simmer for 1 hour. Add 150 ml cassareep, cook for another 30 minutes then flavour with 6 chopped fresh red chillies, 10 cloves, 3 bayleaves, the juice of 2 lemons, 50 ml vinegar, 25 g brown sugar, 2 cinnamon sticks and salt and pepper. Continue to simmer for 1 hour until all is cooked and serve with plain boiled rice.

Lamb

QUALITY POINTS

Lamb is derived from sheep of either sex under 12 months old when slaughtered.

1. The flesh should be 'sappy' or moist and have a fine grain.
2. The fat should be creamy white in colour and be evenly distributed over the saddle.
3. The bones should be soft and porous.

MAIN JOINTS

Leg (2–2.5 kg) – Boiling, roasting and pot-roasting. Remove the pelvic bone and trim off surplus fat. Saw the leg bone off at the first knuckle joint and cut off the flesh and membrane, if necessary tie at the thick end.

Shoulder (1.5–2 kg) – Roasting, pot-roasting and stewing. Either saw off the knuckle bone and neatly trim the flesh and membrane or bone out completely, remove surplus fat and gristle, roll and tie, or stuff, roll and tie. For stewing, cut into 2.5 cm pieces free of excess fat and gristle.

Saddle (3.5 kg) – Roasting and pot-roasting. Remove the outer skin and trim excess fat covering. Remove the hip bones and cut away the flank parallel to the joint. Tie, keeping its original shape. For roasting as a presentation dish the kidney and kidney fat should be removed, the tail left intact and curled above the chump end. Can also be boned out completely and tied.

Loin (1.5 kg) – Roasting and pot-roasting. Split the saddle through the centre bone into two loins. Remove the outer skin and bone out completely. Cut the flank parallel to the joint, roll and tie; the inside fillet can be left inside or removed for other uses. A boned loin and best end is known as a Cannon of Lamb. A Baron of Lamb is a hindquarter joint including the two legs attached to the whole saddle.

Best End (3 kg) – Roasting. Chine by splitting lengthways through the backbone and remove the outer skin. Remove the breast, leaving the joint twice as long as the eye of the centre meat. Remove the sinew which runs along the back just under the outer fat. Remove the flesh from the end of each cutlet bone. The fat may be scored in a criss-cross pattern. This joint is also called a Rack of Lamb. A Crown of Lamb is an inverted whole best end of lamb trussed into a circle with the trimmed cutlet bones on the outside.

Breast (2.5 kg) – Roasting and stewing. Remove outer skin, sinew and excess fat. Either roll as a joint and tie, or stuff, roll and tie. For stewing cut into 2.5 cm cubes or into sections on the bone.

Middle Neck (1.5 kg) – Grilling, shallow frying and stewing. Split through the middle lengthways. Cut into pieces between the bones or remove all bone and cut into dice. This cut is usually sold in one piece with the neck.

Neck (2.5 kg) – Stewing. Bone out completely, remove any sinew and cut into 2.5 cm cubes or cut down the centre and cut each piece into sections on the bone. This joint usually includes the middle neck.

PRIME CUTS FOR GRILLING AND SHALLOW FRYING

Loin Chop (200 g) – Cut from the prepared loin into 4 cm thick chops, the flank end being skewered in to keep its shape. For grilling, a lamb kidney may be skewered into it.

Crown Chop (400 g) – Cut across a prepared short saddle, into a 4 cm chop joined at the centre bone. Trim to remove excess fat. This is also called a Barnsley Chop.

Fillet of Saddle (120 g) – Remove the fillets from the underside of the saddle. Trim off the outer membrane, fat and sinew. Cut open lengthways and lightly flatten.

Noisette (2 × 75 g) – Cut from a boned prepared loin on the slant at 45° into 3 cm thick slices. Lightly flatten and trim to a pear shape. Noisettes may also be cut from a boned out best end. A Valentine Steak is prepared by cutting open a thick-cut noisette and flattening it slightly to give a heart-shaped cut.

Rosette (2 × 75 g) – Cut from boned prepared loin rolled into a joint, including the fillet. Trim excess fat and tie at regular intervals along the length. Cut between the strings to give 4 cm thick pieces.

Lamb Cutlet (2 × 75 g) – Cut from a prepared unscored best end between the bones. Trim excess fat and flatten slightly, leaving 15 mm of trimmed end bone cut at an angle. A Butterfly Cutlet is cut across the whole best end.

Double Lamb Cutlet (150 g) – Cut from the prepared best end between every other bone, flatten slightly and trim as for single cutlets.

Chump Chop (150 g) – Cut from the chump end of the saddle slantwise on the bone.

Mutton, also known as *hogget*, is maiden ewe or wether (castrated male sheep) showing not more than two permanent incisor teeth when slaughtered. It is not readily obtainable in this country. The joints and cuts are identical to those from a lamb.

BAKING

Cornish Pasties

250 g finely diced raw potato		500 g short pastry
250 g finely diced raw lamb	filling	salt and pepper
100 g chopped onion		25 g chopped parsley
100 g finely diced raw turnip or swede		eggwash

1. Roll out the pastry 3 mm thick and cut out ten circles 14 cm in diameter.
2. Place the filling in a basin, season, add the parsley and mix together with a little water.
3. Place 70 g of the filling in the centre of each piece of pastry, eggwash the edges, fold over into a semi-circular shape and crimp the edges to form a rope effect.
4. Place onto a lightly greased baking sheet and brush with eggwash.
5. Bake at 200°C for 10 minutes, reducing the heat to 170° for a further 35 minutes.
6. Remove from the oven and serve accompanied by Tomato Sauce.

Note
Cornish pasties may also be made with puff pastry and with the join top centre instead of as a turnover.

Lancashire Hot Pot

2.5 kg middle neck of lamb	1 litre white stock
200 g dripping	50 g melted butter
500 g sliced onion	seasoning
1.5 kg sliced potatoes	

1. Cut the meat into sections on the bone and trim.
2. Heat the dripping in a frying pan and brown the seasoned meat on both sides, drain and retain.
3. Fry the onion in the same pan, adding more dripping if necessary.
4. Season the thinly sliced potatoes and place a layer of them in a shallow ovenproof dish, add a layer of the onion, then the meat, then more onions and finish with neatly overlapping potatoes, seasoning each layer.
5. Moisten with sufficient stock to just cover and bake at 180°C for 1½ hours.
6. Clean the sides of the dish, brush with the melted butter and serve sprinkled with chopped parsley.

Notes
1. During the cooking it is important to press down the surface layer of potatoes with a palette knife to prevent curling and burning.

2. When cooked, the contents of the dish should be moist and most of the stock should have been absorbed by the potatoes.

Chop Champvallon

Substituting 10×150 g chump chops for middle neck of lamb and adding a layer of 200 g diced tomatoes, proceed as for Lancashire Hot Pot with the same ingredients and using the same method.

Shepherd's Pie

1.5 kg cooked minced lamb	1 kg mashed potato or
75 g dripping	duchesse mixture
250 g chopped onion	100 g melted butter
25 g tomato purée	seasoning
500 ml jus lié or demi-glace	

1. Heat the dripping in a pan, add the onion and fry until slightly coloured.
2. Add the cooked minced lamb, the tomato purée and brown sauce and bring to the boil. Season and gently simmer for 15 minutes until fairly stiff.
3. Transfer to a shallow dish to a depth of 5 cm.
4. Cover the surface with either mashed potato or Duchesse Potato mixture and mark with a palette knife. Alternatively, pipe it in a scroll design using a star tube.
5. Sprinkle the surface with melted butter and place in the oven at 180°C until the surface is crisp and golden.
6. Clean the sides of the dish, brush the surface with melted butter and serve on a dish paper on a flat underdish.

Note
This recipe is the traditional one used in small-scale production; the recipe for Cottage Pie in the section on Beef gives the method for using raw meat.

BOILING

Blanquette of Lamb (Blanquette d'Agneau)

1.5 kg shoulder or	75 g butter
middle neck of lamb	50 g flour
2 litres white stock	200 ml cream
1 whole carrot	¼ juice of lemon
1 studded onion with a	seasoning
bayleaf and clove	chopped parsley
1 bouquet garni	

1. Cut the meat into 2.5 cm cubes, place in a saucepan and blanch by covering it with cold water, bringing to the boil for 5 minutes, then running hot

water onto it to remove scum and grease. Refresh under cold water and drain in a colander.

2. Place the meat into a saucepan, add the stock, bring to the boil and skim.
3. Add the onion, carrot, bouquet garni and seasoning. Allow to simmer gently for 1½ hours until cooked, then remove the onion, carrot and bouquet garni.
4. Make a second stage roux with the butter and flour and allow to cool.
5. Strain most of the cooking liquid, keeping the meat moist in the remainder. Add to the roux to make a velouté sauce, cook for 20 minutes and add the cream and lemon juice.
6. Strain over the drained meat and simmer or a few minutes, then serve sprinkled with chopped parsley.

Blanquette of Lamb with Mushrooms and Onions (Blanquette d'Agneau à l'Ancienne)

Proceed as for Blanquette of Lamb with the addition of 30 each cooked button mushrooms and cooked button onions.

Boiled Leg of Lamb with Caper Sauce (Gigot d'Agneau Bouilli)

1 × 2 kg leg of lamb	1 bouquet garni
2 carrots	seasoning
1 studded onion with a bayleaf and clove	600 ml Caper Sauce

1. Place the meat into a deep pan and cover with cold water. Bring to the boil and skim.
2. Add the studded onion, carrots, bouquet garni and seasoning and simmer gently for 1½ hours.
3. Carve the meat into slices and arrange on an oval dish, moisten with some of the strained cooking liquid and serve the caper sauce separately.

Note
To test if cooked pierce with a trussing needle or skewer. If the juice that runs out is clear the leg is cooked.

Boiled Leg of Lamb with Dill Sauce (Kokt Lamm i Dill Soas)   SCANDINAVIA

Proceed as for Boiled Leg of Lamb with Caper Sauce with the addition of sprigs of dill to the cooking liquid. Serve the carved meat coated with the cooking liquid, accompanied by dill sauce.

Boiled Shoulder of Lamb with Cabbage and   HUNGARY
Caraway (Ürühús Édes Kàposztàval)

Boil 1 × 2 kg boned and rolled shoulder of lamb in salted water with 1 tsp caraway seeds, 3 green pimentos, 250 g quarters of cabbage and 20 small turned potatoes. Serve the sliced meat with the cabbage and boiled potatoes, moistened with the liquor and accompanied by 300 ml paprika-flavoured lamb velouté made from the cooking liquor finished with 225 ml soured cream.

BRAISING

Braised Lamb Chop with Vegetables (Chop d'Agneau Braisé aux Légumes)

10 × 150 g lamb chops	1.5 litres brown stock
200 g dripping	1 bouquet garni
150 g onions ⎱ roughly cut	chopped parsley
150 g carrots ⎰	seasoning
2 cloves garlic, crushed	250 g mixed vegetables cut into
50 g tomato purée	baton shapes

1. Heat the dripping in a frying pan.
2. Pass the seasoned chops through flour and fry until brown on both sides.
3. Transfer to a shallow pan or braising pan.
4. Add the onion, carrot and garlic to the pan and fry to a light brown colour, drain and add to the chops.
5. Mix in the tomato purée and moisten with the stock.
6. Bring to the boil and skim. Season, add the bouquet garni, cover with a lid and braise in the oven at 180°C for 1 hour until cooked.
7. Place the chops in a clean pan. Strain the cooking liquid into another pan, bring to the boil and skim to remove all traces of fat, thicken with diluted cornflour if necessary and pour over the chops.
8. Serve in an entrée or earthenware dish, sprinkled with the mixed vegetables and chopped parsley.

Braised Lamb's Heart with Vegetables (Coeur d'Agneau Braisé aux Légumes)

Substitute 10 × 150 g lamb's hearts for lamb chops and proceed as for Braised Lamb Chop with Vegetables.

Note
To test if cooked pierce with a trussing needle or fork; the point should penetrate to the centre without undue pressure.

Braised Lamb's Tongue (Langue d'Agneau Braisée)

10 lambs' tongues
1 litre jus lié

1. Place the tongues in a saucepan, cover with cold water, bring to the boil and cook for 5 minutes. Place under hot water to remove scum and grease, then refresh under cold water. Drain and remove the root from the tongues.

2. Place the tongues in a shallow pan, cover with the jus lié and bring to the boil. Cover with a lid and braise in the oven at 180°C for 1½ hours until cooked.
3. Remove the tongues from the cooking liquid, remove the skins using a small knife and retain in a dish to keep warm.
4. Strain the cooking liquid into a clean saucepan, boil and skim.
5. Slice the tongues lengthways 3 mm thick and arrange on a flat oval dish. Coat with the sauce and serve.

Braised Lamb's Tongues with Madeira Wine and Spinach (Langue d'Agneau Braisées aux Epinards)

Proceed as for Braised Lamb's Tongue. When serving lightly sprinkle the carved tongues with Madeira wine, coat with Madeira Sauce and garnish with 250 g purée of spinach.

GRILLING

Grilled Lamb's Kidneys (Rognons Grillés)

20 lambs' kidneys	200 g Straw Potatoes ⎫
50 ml oil	100 g parsley butter ⎬ garnish
seasoning	1 bunch watercress ⎭

1. Cut the kidneys almost in half from the rounded side, pull off the skin, trim the root end and place on skewers. Season and brush all over with oil.
2. Brush the grill bars with some of the oil and place the kidneys in the centre, cut side downward, to seal quickly, then turn them over and grill more slowly, keeping them slightly under cooked.
3. Remove the skewers and neatly arrange the kidneys on an oval flat dish. Place a piece of parsley butter in the centre of each and garnish with the Straw Potatoes and picked watercress; serve the remainder of the parsley butter in a sauceboat on crushed ice.

Grilled Lamb Cutlets (Côtelettes d'Agneau Grillées Vert-Pré)

20 × 75 g lamb cutlets	100 g parsley butter ⎫
50 ml oil	200 g Straw Potatoes ⎬ garnish
seasoning	1 bunch watercress ⎭

1. Season the cutlets and brush all over with oil.
2. Brush the grill bars with oil, place the cutlets in the centre of the grill so that a criss-cross effect is marked on both sides, then move to a heat zone where they will cook to the desired degree without burning, brushing with the oil from time to time; cooking time is 5–6 minutes.
3. Serve arranged on an oval flat dish with a cutlet frill on each. Garnish with the Straw Potatoes and picked watercress and serve the parsley butter separately on a little crushed ice in a sauceboat.

Mixed Grill

10 × 75 g lamb cutlets
   10 lamb's kidneys
   10 chipolata sausages
   10 open mushrooms
   10 tomatoes
   10 rashers of bacon

100 ml oil
    seasoning
150 g parsley butter ⎫
200 g Straw Potatoes ⎬ garnish
1 bunch watercress ⎭

1. Season and brush the cutlets with the oil.
2. Brush the grill bars with oil, place the cutlets on the grill so that a criss-cross effect is marked on both sides, then move to the side to cook to the desired degree without burning.
3. Cut almost through the kidneys, open out and thread on skewers, brush with oil and grill at the same time as the cutlets and sausages, keeping the kidneys slightly underdone.
4. Place the tomatoes cut in halves or with a cross incision on top and the washed mushrooms on an oiled tray. Season, brush with some of the oil and cook under a salamander grill or in an oven.
5. Arrange all the grilled items on an oval dish with a small piece of parsley butter in the centre of each kidney. Garnish with the Straw Potatoes and watercress and serve. If desired, place a cutlet frill on each cutlet.

Grilled Butterfly Lamb   USA

Bone out a leg of lamb, open it up and marinate for 12 hours in 250 ml yogurt, 2 crushed cloves of garlic and 50g chopped mint, then grill on a barbecue and serve carved into slices.

Kebabs   MIDDLE EAST

1.5 kg fillets of lamb
   2 juice of lemons
pinch powdered thyme
  30 bayleaves
250 g onions, cut into
    2 cm squares

100 ml oil
    seasoning
500 g savoury rice
500 ml jus lié

1. Cut the fillets into 3 cm × 1 cm pieces, place in a tray, add the lemon juice, seasoning, 50 ml of the oil, thyme, bayleaves and onion and allow to marinate for 2–3 hours.
2. Arrange the pieces of lamb, bayleaves and pieces of onion on skewers in that order, each skewer containing 8–10 pieces of lamb.
3. Brush all over with oil. Brush the grill bars with oil, place the kebabs on the hottest part of the grill, then move to a heat zone that will enable the food to cook to the desired degree without burning, brushing occasionally with the oil.
4. Arrange the skewered kebabs on a bed of savoury rice on an entrée dish and serve the sauce separately.

Note

The kebabs are placed on the bed of rice on the plate, the waiter holds the ring end of the skewer with a fork and pulls the food off the skewer using another fork.

Lamb Kebabs, Armenian Style (Shashlik Kebab)   RUSSIA

Cut 1.5 kg fillet of lamb into 2.5 cm cubes and marinate in 50 ml olive oil, 1 tsp ground cumin, 1 tsp crushed cassia bark, 50ml red wine, the juice of 1 lemon, 25 g tomato purée and 2 chopped cloves of garlic for 1 hour. Arrange the pieces of lamb, bayleaves and square pieces of onion, fresh red chillies and squares of green pimento on skewers in that order, each skewer containing 8 pieces of lamb. Brush all over with oil, place on the hottest part of the grill, then move to a heat zone that will enable the food to cook to the desired degree without burning, basting with the marinade. Arrange the skewered kebabs on a bed of savoury rice on an entrée dish and serve.

Lamb Kebabs (Arni Souvláki)   GREECE

Cut 1.5 kg fillet of lamb into 2.5 cm pieces, then marinate for 6 hours in 100 ml olive oil, 100 ml dry white wine, 50 ml lemon juice, 2 tsp chopped oregano, 3 crushed cloves of garlic, 4 crushed bayleaves and seasoning. Arrange the pieces of lamb between bayleaves on a skewer, each skewer containing 8 pieces of lamb. Brush with oil and grill, basting them with the marinade and cook to the required degree. Serve the kebabs on their skewers on a bed of savoury rice and garnish with lemon wedges and picked parsley.

Lamb Kebabs with Yogurt Sauce (Yogurtlu Kebabs)   TURKEY

Cut 1.5 kg fillet of lamb into 2.5 cm pieces and marinate for 6 hours in 100 ml olive oil, 75 ml lemon juice, 4 crushed cloves of garlic and seasoning. Arrange on skewers and grill, basting them with the marinade, and cook to the required degree. Serve the kebabs on their skewers on a base of toasted strips of pitta bread topped with 275 g strips of tomato flesh sautéed in a little olive oil. Mask with Yogurt Sauce made of 600ml heated plain yogurt seasoned with cayenne pepper and salt.

Lamb Tikka Kebab (Tikka Kebab)   INDIA

1.5 kg lamb cut into 2.5 cm cubes	10 g paprika
250 g onion cubes	10 g grated ginger
4 cloves of garlic	1 bayleaf
80 ml lemon juice	3 lemons
125 ml vinegar	500 g rice pilaff
850 ml yogurt	salt
30 g garam masala	

1. Blend the garlic, spices, salt, lemon juice, vinegar and yogurt and use it to marinate the lamb for 24 hours.

2. Skewer the lamb between pieces of onion and bayleaves and grill the kebabs, basting with the marinade.
3. Serve the kebabs on their skewers on a base of the rice, garnished with lemon wedges.

POT-ROASTING

Pot-Roasted Loin of Lamb (Longe d'Agneau Poêlée)

200 g sliced carrot		1.5 kg loins of lamb	
200 g sliced onion		75 g dripping	
150 g sliced celery		100 g melted butter	
1 bayleaf	bed of root	500 ml jus lié	
1 sprig thyme	vegetables	seasoning	
parsley stalks			
1 crushed			
clove garlic			

1. Butter and season the bottom of a braising pan or other suitable deep receptacle sufficiently large to afford room for basting and which can be covered with a lid that does not touch the meat.
2. Sear the meat quickly in hot dripping until brown on all sides.
3. Place the bed of root vegetables in the bottom of the pan. Season the meat, place on top and coat with the melted butter.
4. Cover with the lid and pot-roast in the oven at 200°C for 45 minutes, basting from time to time.
5. When the meat is nearly cooked, remove the lid and allow it to colour slightly for the last 10 minutes.
6. When cooked, remove the meat and keep it warm. Place the pan on top of the stove but do not allow the vegetables to burn. Add the jus lié and allow to simmer until the flavour from the juices and butter has been absorbed into the sauce.
7. Pass through a fine strainer, reboil and skim. Season to taste and correct the consistency so that it just coats the meat.
8. Carve the loins into 5mm slices and arrange on a dish slightly overlapping, lightly coat with some of the sauce and serve the rest in a sauceboat.

Pot-Roasted Loin of Lamb Dubarry (Longe d'Agneau Poêlée Dubarry)

Pot-roast a boned and rolled loin of lamb as for Pot-Roasted Loin of Lamb. Serve garnished with cauliflower coated with Cheese Sauce and glazed and Château Potatoes.

ROASTING

Carving joints of lamb

A *leg* is carved into slices 3–4 mm thick from above the knuckle, working backwards to the thick end, at an angle of 45°. As the slices increase in size due to the shape of the joint, change the direction of carving and carve from alternate sides to give two smaller slices. Continue turning the joint to carve all the meat from the leg.

A *boned and rolled shoulder* is carved across the joint in 5 mm slices.

A *saddle* of lamb can be carved lengthways into long thin slices or crosswise by first making a cut along each side of the backbone then carving into slices across the width of each side. For a party the two sides should be removed whole, cut into slices and replaced on the bone. The fillet under the saddle is removed, carved and laid on top of the joint.

A *best end* of lamb may be carved into single cutlets between each bone or as double cutlets, in which case the end rib bone is discarded and the joints carved between each second rib bone.

Roast Best End of Lamb Persillé (Carré d'Agneau Persillé)

4 best ends of lamb	10 g chopped parsley
200 g butter	seasoning
50 g chopped shallots	500 ml brown stock
250 g white breadcrumbs	1 bunch watercress

1. Place the seasoned best ends in a roasting tray and coat with melted dripping. Roast at 220°C for 10 minutes, baste and cook at 200°C for a total time of 40 minutes, keeping slightly underdone.
2. Melt the butter in a shallow pan, add the shallots and cook without colouring. Add the breadcrumbs, seasoning and parsley and combine.
3. Cover the fat side of the joints with the mixture, pressing it firmly.
4. Return the best ends to the oven to colour light brown; make the gravy in the usual way with the sediment and the stock.
5. Arrange the best ends on a flat oval dish, garnish with the picked watercress and serve the gravy in a sauceboat.

Roast Best End of Lamb with Savoury Potatoes (Carré d'Agneau Boulangère)

4 best ends of lamb	
10 portions Boulangère Potatoes	
500 ml brown stock for gravy	

1. Roast the best ends as for Roast Best End Persillé, turning them over to cook evenly.

2. For the last 10 minutes of cooking, place the meat on top of the almost cooked dish of potatoes.
3. Serve the best ends on the savoury potatoes on an underdish, accompanied by a sauceboat of roast gravy.

Note
The lamb and the savoury potatoes are usually cooked separately, the best ends are carved and arranged overlapping on top of the potatoes.

Roast Leg of Lamb with Mint Sauce (Gigot d'Agneau Rôti, Sauce Menthe)

2.25 kg leg of lamb	500 ml brown stock
200 g dripping	1 bunch watercress
salt	75 ml mint sauce

1. Season the meat and place in a roasting tray, fat side uppermost. Coat with the dripping and place in the oven at 220°C. Reduce the temperature to 180°C after 20 minutes, allowing a total time of 1½ hours and basting at regular intervals.
2. When cooked, remove the meat from the tray and stand it on a wire grid for 20 minutes. Any juices collected should be used in making the gravy.
3. Place the roasting tray on the stove and heat gently, allowing the sediment to settle.
4. Drain off surplus fat, leaving the sediment in the tray.
5. Add the brown stock and simmer gently for a few minutes.
6. Strain through a fine conical strainer into a pan, reboil, skim all traces of fat and season to taste.
7. Carve the joint across the grain, allowing either one thick or two thin slices per portion.
8. Arrange the slices of meat slightly overlapping on an oval flat dish, coat with some of the gravy and serve with the picked watercress.
9. Serve the remainder of the gravy and the mint sauce in sauceboats.

Roast Leg of Lamb with Rosemary Sauce

Bone out a 2.25 kg leg of lamb and rub powdered rosemary and seasoning into the flesh; tie into shape with string and proceed as for Roast Leg of Lamb. Serve accompanied by the lightly thickened roast gravy containing chopped rosemary and finished with 100ml cream and 50 ml brandy.

Roast Leg of Lamb with Savoury Potatoes (Gigot d'Agneau Boulangère)

Proceed as for Roast Leg of Lamb. Carve into slices, arrange neatly on top of the Boulangère Potatoes and serve accompanied by a sauceboat of roast gravy.

Roast Leg of Lamb Roman Style (Abbacchio Arosto alla Romana)

Proceed as for Roast Leg of Lamb adding 10 lambs' kidneys during the last 20 minutes of cooking. Liquidise 600 ml red wine vinegar, 5 g rosemary, 25 g anchovy fillets, 3 cloves of garlic and seasoning. About 10 minutes before the leg is done pour the mixture over the meat and finish cooking. Remove the meat from the roasting tray, strain the cooking liquor, thicken with a little diluted arrowroot and season to taste. Serve carved slices of lamb garnished with watercress and accompanied by the cooking liquor made into a sauce.

Roast Stuffed Shoulder of Lamb (Epaule d'Agneau Rôtie Farcie)

Bone out a 2 kg shoulder of lamb, envelop 500 g thyme, parsley and lemon stuffing shaped into a long roll in the centre and tie securely. Season and roast as for Roast Leg of Lamb. Serve carved into 5 mm thick slices garnished with picked watercress, roast gravy and mint sauce.

Roast Leg of Lamb with Buttermilk and Rosemary   USA

Make incisions in a 2.25 kg leg of lamb and insert a quarter clove of garlic in each incision. Combine 2 crushed cloves of garlic and rosemary, 200 ml Dijon mustard, 200 ml buttermilk, 50 ml oil and seasoning, spread it over the leg and leave for 8 hours. Proceed as for Roast Leg of Lamb with Mint Sauce. Swill the pan with 500 ml brown stock and simmer gently for a few minutes. Strain through a fine strainer into a pan, reboil, skim all traces of fat and season to taste. Carve across the grain of the joint, allowing one thick or two thin slices per portion. Arrange overlapping on a flat dish. Lightly coat with some of the gravy and serve the remainder in sauceboats.

Roast Leg of Lamb with Savoury Potatoes (Arni Psito)   GREECE

Proceed as for Roast Leg of Lamb. When it is half cooked, add 1 kg sliced potatoes mixed with 250 g sliced onion, 200 g tomato concassée, 10 g chopped parsley and seasoning to the roasting tray with the meat and moisten with 250 ml white stock and 50 ml lemon juice. Brush the potato mixture with olive oil and continue to roast until it is cooked. Serve slices of the joint with the savoury potatoes, sprinkled with chopped fresh herbs.

Roast Leg of Lamb with Tarragon and Orange (Bàrànycomb Frascati Módra)   HUNGARY

Score a 2.5 kg leg of lamb, rub with salt and fill the slots with strips of bacon, lamb's liver and ham. Roast the joint in the oven at 180°C for 2 hours. When almost cooked drain off the fat, add 50 g chopped tarragon, 50 g sliced mushrooms, the grated zest and juice of 2 oranges and 200 ml white wine and finish to cook. Remove the joint, swill the pan with 300 ml stock and finish with a liaison of 2 egg yolks and 125 ml cream to make a sauce.

SHALLOW FRYING

Breaded Lamb Cutlets (Côtelettes d'Agneau Panées)

20 × 75 g lamb cutlets		200 ml butter or oil
flour	⎫	300 ml jus lié
eggwash	⎬ for coating	100 g butter
breadcrumbs	⎭	

1. Flatten the cutlets slightly, season and pass through the flour, eggwash and breadcrumbs, then mark trellis-fashion.
2. Heat the butter in a plat à sauter.
3. Place in the cutlets and shallow fry until golden brown. Turn and fry the other side.
4. Arrange the cutlets on a dish, surround with a thread of the jus lié, heat the butter until it turns golden brown and pour over the cutlets. Serve the remainder of the jus lié separately.

Lamb Cutlets Milanaise (Côtelettes d'Agneau Milanaise)

Proceed as for Breaded Lamb Cutlets and garnish with 500 g Spaghetti Milanaise.

Lamb Cutlets Napolitaine (Côtelettes d'Agneau Napolitaine)

Proceed as for Breaded Lamb Cutlets and garnish with 500 g Spaghetti Napolitaine.

Lamb Cutlets with Reform Sauce (Côtelettes d'Agneau Réforme)

flour	⎫	20 × 75 g lamb cutlets
eggwash	⎬ for	200 g butter
breadcrumbs	coating	300 ml Sauce Réforme
25 g chopped parsley	⎭	150 g butter

1. Flatten the cutlets slightly, season and pass through the flour, eggwash and breadcrumbs mixed with the chopped parsley, then mark trellis-fashion.
2. Heat the butter in a plat à sauter, add the cutlets and shallow fry until golden brown, then turn and fry the other side.
3. Arrange the cutlets on a dish, heat the butter until it turns golden brown and pour over the cutlets. Serve accompanied by a sauceboat of Reform Sauce.

Note

Cutlets can be shallow fried without being breadcrumbed and may be served with the same garnishes as the breadcrumbed ones. It is necessary to colour the edge of plain cutlets by standing them up in the pan.

Noisettes d'Agneau Niçoise

20 × 75 g noisettes of lamb	300 g French beans ⎤
100 g butter	40 Château Potatoes ⎬ garnish
20 croûtons	10 small tomatoes ⎦
400 ml jus lié	100 ml white wine
seasoning	

1. Heat the butter in a plat à sauter, season the noisettes and shallow fry on both sides until coloured and cooked, time 7 minutes.
2. Arrange each noisette on a heart-shaped croûton on a serving dish.
3. Arrange 10 small bundles of French beans and 10 of the Château Potatoes together with the skinned and cooked tomatoes around the dish; keep it warm.
4. Discard the fat from the sauté pan, swill with the wine and reduce by half, add the jus lié, boil and strain.
5. Mask the noisettes with a little of the sauce and serve the rest in a sauce boat.

Noisettes d'Agneau Dubarry

Shallow fry the noisettes as for Noisettes d'Agneau Niçoise and arrange on heart-shaped croûtons. Garnish with small pieces of Cauliflower Mornay and Château Potatoes.

Noisettes d'Agneau Clamart

Shallow fry the noisettes as for Noisettes d'Agneau Niçoise and arrange on heart-shaped croûtons. Coat with madeira sauce and garnish with artichoke bottoms filled with minted peas and Château Potatoes.

Noisette d'Agneau Crécy

Shallow fry the noisettes as for Noisette d'Agneau Niçoise and arrange on heart-shaped croûtons. Coat with Madeira Sauce and garnish with turned glazed carrots.

Sautéed Kidneys (Rognons Sautés)

20 lambs' kidneys
100 g butter
200 ml jus lié
seasoning

1. Heat the butter in a shallow pan.
2. Season and add the kidneys previously cut in half and shallow fry quickly, keeping them underdone. Drain and retain in a warm place.
3. Add the jus lié to the pan and allow to boil for a few moments. Take off the boil, add the drained kidneys, mix in and season to taste.
4. Pour into an earthenware dish and serve.

Sautéed Kidneys with Madeira Wine (Rognons Sautés au Madère)

Proceed as for Sautéed Kidney, using Madeira Sauce instead of jus-lié.

Sautéed Kidneys Turbigo (Rognons Sautés Turbigo)

Proceed as in Sautéed Kidneys, using Madeira Sauce. Garnish with 10 grilled chipolata sausages and 450 g button mushrooms cooked in butter. When serving, place the kidneys onto small oblong fried bread croûtons and surround with the chipolatas, mushrooms and sauce.

Sautéed Fillet of Lamb with Peas (Arnaki me Araka)   GREECE

Shallow fry slices of fillet of lamb in olive oil as for Noisette d'Agneau Niçoise, remove and retain. Add 100 g chopped spring onions to the pan and cook for a few moments, moisten with 50 ml lemon juice and 500 ml brown stock and season, then add 250 g peas and 25 g chopped dill; simmer until the peas are cooked. Coat the meat with the gravy and the peas and serve.

Sautéd Lamb's Kidneys with Sherry (Riñones al Jerez)   SPAIN

Soak 20 halved lamb's kidneys in vinegar and water for 1 hour, remove, drain and dry. Fry 100 g chopped onion and 3 chopped cloves of garlic in 80 ml olive oil, add and sauté the kidneys, then stir in 30 g paprika, 75 g breadcrumbs and 1 tsp marjoram; when cooked, transfer the kidneys to a serving dish. Add 100 ml dry sherry and 500 ml brown stock to the pan, reduce to a sauce consistency and season. Replace the kidneys in the sauce and serve sprinkled with chopped fresh herbs.

STEWING

Lamb stews

The term 'Navarin' is used on the menu to refer to a brown stew made from lamb. The meat should be trimmed of excess fat, sinew and gristle and cut into 2.5 cm cubes; various cuts of vegetables can be used as garnishes.

Fricassée of Lamb (Fricassée d'Agneau)

1.5 kg shoulder of lamb	200 ml cream ⎫
100 g butter	3 egg yolks ⎬ liaison
75 g flour	10 heart-shaped croûtons
1.5 litres white stock	12 g chopped parsley
1 bouquet garni	salt and pepper

1. Cut the boned meat into 2.5 cm cubes.
2. Heat the butter in a shallow pan, season the meat, add to the butter and cover with a lid. Allow to set without much coloration.
3. Sprinkle with the flour and stir gently with a wooden spatule to form a roux. Cook to a second stage roux and allow to cool.
4. Add the hot stock a little at a time until a light sauce consistency is reached.
5. Bring to the boil, skim, add the bouquet garni and seasoning, cover with a lid and place in the oven at 180°C for 1 hour until cooked.
6. Discard the bouquet garni, place the meat in a clean saucepan and keep it warm.
7. Whisk the liaison into the sauce and cook until it thickens but do not allow it to boil. Strain onto the meat and mix in gently.
8. Serve in an entrée dish, dip the tips of the croûtons in some of the sauce and then into chopped parsley, place upright around the meat and serve.

Note
Fricassée may be finished with cream, crème fraîche or yogurt and egg yolk.

Fricassèe of Lamb with Vegetables (Fricassèe d'Agneau aux Légumes)

Proceed as for Fricassée of Lamb and serve garnished with 250 g mixed vegetables cut into jardinière.

Irish Stew   IRELAND

200 g celery ⎫	1.5 kg middle neck and
200 g white of leek ⎪	breast of lamb
150 g white cabbage ⎬ sliced	1 bouquet garni
(optional) ⎪	12 g chopped parsley
150 g onion ⎪	seasoning
1 kg potatoes ⎭	20 small plain boiled potatoes
	20 white glazed button onions

1. Cut the lamb into 2.5 cm pieces on or off the bone.
2. Place into a saucepan, cover with cold water, bring to the boil and cook for 5 minutes. Place under hot running water to remove scum and grease then refresh under cold water. Drain in a colander.

3. Place the meat into a saucepan, cover with cold water, bring to the boil and skim.
4. Add the sliced vegetables, reboil and skim. Add the bouquet garni and seasoning. Allow to cook gently for 45 minutes, then discard the bouquet garni and remove any fat.
5. Pass the vegetables through a sieve or purée in a blender; adjust the consistency if necessary, then pour over the meat, button onions and potatoes.
6. Reheat gently and serve sprinkled with chopped parsley; offer Worcester sauce separately.

Notes
1. Irish Stew may be finished in either of two ways. The vegetables may be cut into paysanne and left intact, or be cut into pieces and puréed when cooked.
2. The raw onions may be added to the stew at the commencement of cooking and the blanched small potatoes 15 minutes before completion.

Navarin of Lamb (Navarin d'Agneau)

1.5 kg middle neck and breast of lamb	50 g tomato purée
100 g dripping	1.5 litres brown stock
200 g carrots ⎫	1 bouquet garni
200 g onions ⎬ roughly cut	20 small barrel-shaped potatoes
150 g celery ⎭	20 button onions
2 crushed cloves of garlic	seasoning
50 g flour	

1. Season the meat and fry in hot dripping to a light golden brown colour on all sides. Drain in a colander and transfer to a suitable stewing pan.
2. Fry the vegetables and garlic in the same pan until golden, drain and add to the meat.
3. Singe the meat and vegetables by sprinkling with flour and placing in a hot oven until the flour takes on a brown colour.
4. Stir in tomato purée and add the stock gently. Bring to the boil, skim, season and add the bouquet garni.
5. Either cook in an oven at 180°C with a tight-fitting lid, or gently simmer on top of the stove, for 1 hour.
6. When almost cooked, transfer the meat to another saucepan and discard the vegetables and bouquet garni. Strain the sauce through a conical strainer onto the meat and bring to the boil.
7. Sauté the button onions and potatoes in a little oil until lightly golden in colour, add to the stew and continue cooking.
8. Skim as necessary to remove all traces of fat and serve in earthenware dishes, sprinkled with chopped parsley.

Note
It is advisable to cook stews in the oven because of the evenness of heat.

Haricot de Mouton

Proceed as for Navarin of Lamb to stage 7. Add 500 g cooked haricot beans, 75 g golden-fried lardons of bacon and 20 brown glazed button onions and serve in an entrée dish, sprinkled with chopped parsley.

Lamb Stew with Vegetables (Navarin d'Agneau Jardinière)

Proceed as for Navarin of Lamb and serve garnished with 250 g mixed vegetables cut into batons for jardinière.

Curried Mutton (Mutton K'ari)   INDIA

1.5 kg mutton cut into 2.5 cm cubes	175 g tomato concassée
75 ml ghee	2 chopped fresh green chillies
225 g chopped onion	75 g chopped mint
4 chopped cloves of garlic	275 ml white stock
25 g grated root ginger	1 tsp garam masala
50 g curry powder	50 g chopped coriander leaves
50 ml wine vinegar or lemon juice	seasoning

1. Heat the ghee in a deep pan and golden fry the chopped onion, garlic and ginger.
2. Sprinkle with the curry powder, then moisten with the wine vinegar or lemon juice.
3. Stir in the meat until well coated, then add the tomato concassée, chillies and mint.
4. Moisten with the stock, season and simmer for 1½ hours.
5. Finish with the garam masala and coriander leaves.
6. Serve accompanied by boiled rice and Sambals (optional).

Sambals

The following are suitable accompaniments for curried dishes, serving not more than six in individual dishes:

poppadoms – grilled or deep fried	chopped apple with lemon juice
grilled Bombay ducks	sliced banana
mango chutney	peeled and sliced cucumber
lime pickle	peeled, depipped and diced tomato
grated coconut	combined with natural yogurt
chopped onion	nan bread.

Grecian Lamb (Arni Fricassée)   GREECE

Pass 1.5 kg cubes of stewing lamb through flour and lightly fry in 75 ml olive oil. Add 225 g chopped spring onions, 5 sliced Belgian endives, 225 g young broad beans in their pods and 225 g shredded cos lettuce and moisten with 2 litres white stock; add a bouquet garni, 25 g chopped dill and seasoning and simmer for 1 hour. When cooked, discard the bouquet garni and finish the stew with a liaison of 225 ml cream combined with 4 egg yolks and 50 ml lemon juice. Serve sprinkled with chopped fresh herbs.

Lamb Biryani (Moglai Biriani)   INDIA

350 g sliced onion	2 dried red chillies
6 chopped cloves of garlic	75 g chopped mint
20 g grated ginger	75 g tomato concassée
125 ml ghee	15 g chopped coriander leaves
100 g curry powder	500 g Kesar Pilau
75 ml lemon juice	1 g saffron
1.5 kg lamb cut into 2.5 cm cubes	50 ml milk
1 tsp garam masala	50 g pistachio nuts
1 tsp ground cardamom	seasoning

1. Golden fry the onion, garlic and ginger in the ghee.
2. Sprinkle with the curry powder and moisten with the lemon juice.
3. Stir in the lamb, completely coating with the curry mixture then add the garam masala, chillies, mint, cardamom, tomato concassée and seasoning.
4. Cover with a lid and cook in the oven at 180°C for 1 hour.
5. Layer a dish with Kesar Pilau, add the meat and its sauce, sprinkle with chopped coriander and finish with the rest of the pilau.
6. Sprinkle with the milk flavoured and coloured with the saffron, and return to the oven for 30 minutes.
7. Serve sprinkled with pistachio nuts.

Note
A Biryani is basically a curry-flavoured rice dish with more rice than other ingredients; it is a festive dish of Pakistan and the north-west provinces of India. Partially cooked rice is arranged in layers with cooked meat, poultry, fish or vegetables. Saffron milk is sprinkled over the surface, leaving some areas white, others saffron yellow. It is then baked in a slow oven and served accompanied by a yogurt dish and Indian breads. It can also be accompanied by Sambals (see p. 186).

Lamb Casserole with Fruit (Koresh or Korak)   MIDDLE EAST

Sauté 150 g chopped onion in 50 ml oil, then add 2 tsp turmeric, 1 tsp cinnamon, 6 cloves and a pinch of pepper. Mix in 1.5 kg cubes of lamb and 125 g each of dried apricots and prunes, 100 g sour cherries and 25 g sliced limes, then place in a casserole, moisten with 1 litre stock and stew for 1½ hours until tender.

Lamb Korma (Korma)

25 g chopped ginger
2 cloves of garlic
50 g blanched almonds
2 of each dried, deseeded red and green chillies
25 g ginger
2 tsp coriander (ground)
1 tsp cumin (ground)
½ tsp cinnamon (ground)
½ tsp cardamom (ground)
¼ tsp cloves (ground)
50 ml water

} blended to a fine paste

1.5 kg lamb cut into 2.5 cm cubes
50 g sliced onion
25 g ghee
100 g sliced onion
few strands saffron
50 ml yogurt
20 g chopped coriander leaves
seasoning

1. Heat the ghee in a deep pan, add the sliced onion and shallow fry until golden brown, add the blended spice paste and cook for a few minutes until the oil begins to separate from the mixture.
2. Stir in the cubes of lamb, infused saffron, the yogurt and, if necessary, a little water. Cover with a lid and simmer for 1 hour until the meat is cooked.
3. Serve sprinkled with chopped coriander, accompanied by boiled rice.

Pork

QUALITY POINTS

The flesh should be moist and light pink in colour with a fine, even grain. The skin should be shiny and very smooth. The fat should be evenly distributed over the carcass.

MAIN JOINTS

A *carcass* or *side* of pork usually includes the head and trotters, both are classed as offal.

Leg (6.5 kg) – Roasting. Remove the pelvic bone and trotter. Saw off the leg bone and trim the flesh and membrane around it, leaving 4 cm of bare bone. Score the skin to a depth of 4 mm, 1 cm apart. Tie the thick end with string.

Loin (5.5 kg) – Roasting. Either cut into two joints, score the skin to a depth of 4 mm at 1 cm intervals; or cut into two joints, bone out and remove the skin. Score it at 1 cm intervals, replace, roll and tie.

Sparerib (2 kg) – Roasting, stewing and barbecuing. Either score the skin to a depth of 4 mm at 1 cm intervals; or bone out and remove the skin.

Hand (3 kg) – Roasting, boiling and stewing. Either score the skin to a depth of 4 mm at 1 cm intervals; or bone out and remove the skin.

Belly (3 kg) – Roasting and boiling. Remove the bones and skin, trim excess fat and roll and tie.

Blade Bone (1.5 kg) – Stewing. Bone out and cut into dice.

Neck End, also known as *Fore-end* (4.5 kg) – Cut into chops or bone out and cut into dice.

SMALL CUTS

Pork Chops (200 g) – Grilling and shallow frying. Remove the skin and excess fat from the long loin of pork and cut into even-sized chops 2.5 cm thick on the bone. Because of their fairly large size, pork cutlets are also referred to as chops.

Pork Fillet (2 × 100 g) – Grilling and shallow frying. Trim off excess fat and sinew, cut lengthways and lightly flatten with a butcher's bat.

Pork Escalope (120 g) – Shallow frying. Trim off excess fat and sinew from the fillet, cut lengthways and lightly flatten with a butcher's bat 2 mm thick. Can also be cut from the trimmed top part of the leg.

Noisette of Pork (2 × 60 g or 1 × 125 g) – Shallow frying. Cut on the slant from a skinned and boned loin, flatten slightly and trim heart-shape.

BOILING

Boiled Leg of Pork with Broad Beans

Cook a 1.5 kg salted leg of pork as for Boiled Hand of Pork with Beer, along with 250 g each of turned carrots, turnips and sliced onion and a bouquet garni. When almost cooked, add 150 g broad beans and cook until tender. Serve slices of the meat with the vegetables, moistened with the cooking liquor and accompanied by Parsley Sauce.

Boiled Hand of Pork with Beer (Schweinshaxe)   GERMANY

1.5 kg hand of pork	50 g honey
2 small whole carrots	200 ml beer
1 studded onion	seasoning
1 bouquet garni	1 kg sauerkraut

1. Place the meat into a saucepan and cover with cold water, bring to the boil and skim thoroughly.
2. Add the onion, carrots and bouquet garni, season and gently simmer for 1 hour.
3. Place the joint into a shallow dish, spread with honey, moisten with the beer and glaze in the top of an oven at 220°C.

4. Carve into 3 mm slices and arrange on a flat dish, moisten with some of the strained cooking liquid and serve accompanied by the braised Sauerkraut.

Boiled Knuckle of Pork (Eisbein) GERMANY

Cook 1.5 kg fresh or salted knuckles of pork as for Boiled Hand of Pork, omitting the beer. Remove the bones from the knuckles and serve with some of the strained cooking liquor, accompanied by purée of green peas.

GRILLING

Grilled Pork Chop with Parsley Butter
(Côte de Porc Grillée Vert-Pré)

10 × 200 g pork chops	150 g parsley butter ⎫
100 ml oil	200 g Straw Potatoes ⎬ garnish
seasoning	1 bunch watercress ⎭

1. Season and brush the chops with oil.
2. Brush the grill bars with oil, place the meat on the hottest part of the grill so that a criss-cross effect is marked on both sides of the chops, then move to a heat zone that will enable them to cook to the desired degree without burning.
3. Serve arranged on an oval dish, garnished with the Straw Potatoes and picked watercress with the parsley butter separately in a sauceboat on crushed ice.

Barbecued Spare Ribs (Siu Pai Gwut) CHINA

Cut 2 kg spare ribs of pork into 20 × 100 g pieces and marinate in 300 ml hoisin sauce with 4 chopped cloves of garlic and seasoning for 2 hours. Brush with vegetable oil, then grill for 15 minutes. Serve accompanied by lemon wedges.

ROASTING

Roast Leg of Pork (Cuissot de Porc Rôti)

2 kg leg of pork	500 ml brown stock
100 ml oil	1 bunch watercress
salt	300 ml Apple Sauce

1. Season the scored joint and place onto some bones or on a trivet in a roasting tray. Coat with the oil, rubbing it into the skin, and place in the

oven at 220°C, reducing the temperature after 20 minutes to 180°C. Roast for 1¹/₂ hours, basting occasionally, ensuring that it is well done and the juice runs clear.

2. Remove from the roasting tray and retain, preferably standing on a wire grid for 20 minutes before carving. Any juices collected should be used in making the gravy.
3. Place the roasting tray on the stove and heat gently, allowing the sediment to settle.
4. Drain off the fat, leaving the sediment in the tray.
5. Add the brown stock and allow to simmer gently for a few minutes.
6. Strain through a fine conical strainer into a saucepan, reboil, skim off all traces of fat and season to taste.
7. Remove the crackling and cut into pieces. Carve the leg across the grain, allowing one thick or two thin slices per portion, together with a piece of crackling.
8. Arrange slightly overlapping on an oval flat dish, coat with some of the roast gravy and serve garnished with the picked watercress.
9. Serve the remainder of the roast gravy and the Apple Sauce in sauceboats.

Roast Loin of Pork with Apple Sauce (Longe de Porc Rôti à l'Anglaise)

2 kg loin of pork	500 ml brown stock
100 ml oil	1 bunch watercress
salt	300 ml Apple Sauce

1. Season the scored joint and place onto some bones or on a trivet in a roasting tray, fat side uppermost. Coat with the oil, rubbing it into the skin and place in the oven at 220°C, reducing the temperature after 20 minutes to 180°C. Baste at regular intervals.
2. Proceed as for Roast Leg of Pork, serving the gravy and Apple Sauce separately in sauceboats.

Roast Stuffed Shoulder of Pork with Apple Sauce (Epaule de Porc Rôtie Farcie)

2 kg shoulder of pork	500 ml brown stock
100 ml oil	1 bunch watercress
500 g sage and onion stuffing	300 ml Apple Sauce
salt	

1. Bone the joint and score the skin; remove surplus fat and gristle, add the stuffing, roll and tie.
2. Proceed as for Roast Leg of Pork and serve with the gravy and Apple Sauce separately in sauceboats.

Roast Loin of Pork with Apples

Rub a 2 kg scored loin of pork with a mixture of salt, pepper and flour and roast at 220°C for 1 hour. When almost cooked, drain off the fat, swill the pan with vinegar and 25 g sugar, then add 250 g peeled, cored and quartered apples sprinkled with sugar and continue cooking for a further 30 minutes. Swill the pan with 500 ml stock and add 200 ml cream to make the accompanying sauce. Carve the meat, allowing one thick or two thin slices per portion, together with a piece of crackling. Arrange overlapping on a dish, lightly coat with some of the sauce and serve garnished with the apples. Serve the remainder of the sauce in sauceboats.

SHALLOW FRYING

Pork Chop Charcutiere (Côte de Porc Charcutière)

10 × 200 g pork chops
100 g butter
200 ml dry white wine
500 ml jus lié or demi-glace

10 g English mustard
75 g gherkins
50 g butter

1. Heat a shallow pan and add the butter.
2. Season the chops, place in the pan and shallow fry. When coloured, turn them over and cook until well done but still moist.
3. Arrange neatly on an oval flat dish; drain the fat from the pan, add the white wine, boil and reduce by two-thirds.
4. Add the jus lié and simmer gently to a coating consistency.
5. Add the diluted mustard but do not boil, then add the gherkins cut into julienne and finish with knobs of butter.
6. Coat the chops with the sauce and serve.

Note
Other garnishes that go well with shallow-fried pork chops are:

Flamande, with quarters or slices of apple fried with the chops.
Milanaise, coated with egg and crumbed and served with spaghetti mixed with julienne of ham, oxtongue and mushrooms, tomato concassée and tomato sauce.
Provençale, marinated with sage, thyme, bayleaf, garlic and oil, shallow fried and coated with jus lié flavoured with anchovy essence, lemon juice and tomato concassée, served with stoned black olives.
Normande, garnished with glazed slices or quarters of apple and served coated with a sauce made from the cooking sediment, calvados, cream and lemon juice.

Fillets of pork can be prepared in the same ways as pork chops.

Goujons of Pork with Cumin
(Rojoes à Mode de Viana do Castelo)

Cut 1.25 kg of pork into 5 cm goujons and marinate in 50 ml white wine and white wine vinegar with 2 chopped cloves of garlic, 1 sprig thyme, 1 crushed bayleaf and 1 tsp each of cumin seeds and paprika, for 1 hour. Sauté the drained goujons in 50 ml garlic-flavoured oil, add 75 g lardons of bacon and cook until nicely coloured, then moisten with the marinating liquid, previously reduced, bring just to the boil and serve.

Pork Chops in Port and Rosemary Sauce
(Costeletas de Porco)

Season 10 × 200 g pork chops and sprinkle with 50 g chopped rosemary; sauté in 100 ml oil and when cooked remove from the pan and retain. Sauté 100 g chopped onion and 2 chopped cloves of garlic in the same pan, add 175 g diced tomato flesh, cook for 2 minutes, then moisten with 100 ml port and 200 ml brown stock and allow to reduce. Serve the chops coated with this sauce.

Sautéed Belly of Pork with Apples (Aebleflaesk)

Shallow crisp fry slices of lightly salted belly of pork, remove from the pan and retain. Shallow fry apple rings in the fat, sprinkle with sugar and allow to caramelise. Serve the slices of pork garnished with the apple rings.

STEWING

Pork and Prune Casserole

1.5 kg	fillet of pork, cut into 2 cm cubes	1 bottle	white wine
100 ml	oil	100 g	redcurrant jelly
50 g	butter	250 ml	jus lié
30 large	prunes	225 ml	cream
			salt, pepper

1. Soak the prunes for 12 hours in the wine, then remove the stones.
2. Heat the oil and butter and sauté the pork until golden brown. Place into a casserole and add the prunes.
3. Drain the fat from the pan, add the wine, redcurrant jelly and jus lié, season, bring to the boil and simmer for 10 minutes, then pour into the casserole.
4. Cover with a lid and cook in the oven at 180°C for 35 minutes.
5. Warm the cream, mix into the meat and serve.

Chilli con Carne (Carne con Chile Colorado) MEXICO

1.5 kg shoulder of pork, cut into 2.5 cm cubes	
400 g pinto or red kidney beans	
500 g boiled rice	
1.5 litres brown stock	
125 ml oil	
50 g flour	
salt and pepper	

6 fresh red chillies ⎫
12 g toasted cumin seeds ⎪
2 cloves of garlic ⎬ blended to a paste
1 tsp oregano ⎪
75 g paprika ⎪
1 tsp sugar ⎪
50 ml stock ⎭

1. Soak pinto or red kidney beans for 12 hours, drain, cover with cold water and cook until soft with two cloves of garlic and a bayleaf. Add salt and a little sugar when nearly cooked.
2. Season the pork and fry in the oil to a golden-brown colour on all sides. Drain in a colander and transfer to a saucepan.
3. Sprinkle with the flour and place in a hot oven until the flour is browned.
4. Add the stock and 500 ml of the bean cooking liquid, bring to the boil, skim and season and add the spice paste, cover with a lid and simmer for 1½ hours.
5. Serve accompanied by plain boiled or braised rice.

Pork Stew with Sauerkraut USA

Cut 1.5 kg pork into 2.5 cm cubes, then fry in 200 ml oil with 250 g chopped onion and 2 chopped cloves of garlic. Stir in 1 tsp caraway seeds, 200 g diced tomato flesh, 8 juniper berries and 1 tsp sugar. Moisten with 1 litre brown stock, add 500g sauerkraut, cover with a lid and cook in the oven at 180°C for 1 hour.

Jambalaya Louisianna Style USA

Fry 500 g chorizo sausages in 100 ml oil, add 4 chopped cloves of garlic, 250 g diced green pimento, 125 g tomato flesh, 2 tsp sugar, 1 tsp rubbed thyme, 1 tsp chilli powder and a pinch of cayenne, moisten with 250 ml chicken stock and simmer for 15 minutes. Slice the sausages and return to the pan, add 500 g long-grain rice, 100 g diced smoked ham and 750 ml chicken stock and simmer for 20 minutes until the rice is cooked, then add 200 g cooked prawns and some chopped parsley and heat through.

Sweet and Sour Pork (Gwoo Lo Yook) CHINA

1.5 kg pork cut into 2 cm cubes	1 clove garlic
100 g cornflour	500 ml water
2 eggs (eggwash)	125 ml vinegar

300 g breadcrumbs	75 g sugar
300 g celery ⎤	75 ml soy sauce
300 g carrot ⎦ cut into julienne	300 g crushed pineapple
2 lemons, zest only	500 g boiled rice
15 g ginger	salt, pepper

1. Roll the pork in cornflour, then in eggwash and finally coat with the breadcrumbs.
2. Deep fry the pork at 180°C for 4 minutes, remove and drain.
3. Bring the water to the boil, season and blanch the celery and carrots for 3 minutes, add the grated zest of lemon, chopped ginger, and garlic. Drain and reserve.
4. Reboil the cooking liquid with the vinegar, sugar, soy sauce and pineapple, then thicken it with the remainder of the cornflour.
5. Mix in the pork, reheat and serve with the boiled rice.

Bacon

QUALITY POINTS

Bacon should be clean looking, have a pleasant fresh odour and not have any stickiness. It should be stored at a temperature of 5–7°C.

MAIN JOINTS

Ham (6 kg) – Boiling and braising. This is the whole leg cut with a rounded end to the end of the back; saw the knuckle bone.

Gammon (5 kg) – Boiling and braising. This is the leg cut straight across from a side of bacon; saw off the knuckle bone 3 cm from the end. Can be cut into smaller joints.

Back (7 kg) – Grilling and shallow frying. Remove bones, tendons, gristle and skin and slice into rashers.

Streaky (3.5 kg) – Grilling and shallow frying. Remove bones, tendons, gristle and skin and slice into rashers.

Collar (3 kg) – Boiling. Bone, roll and tie.

Hock (3.5 kg) – Boiling. Bone, roll and tie.

SMALL CUTS

Gammon Rasher – Grilling and shallow frying. Remove the skin and bone from a whole gammon. Cut into even slices 1 cm thick. Cut nicks in the outer rim of fat to prevent curling during cooking.

BOILING

Boiled Gammon

Soak a 5 kg gammon in cold water for 12 hours. Pour off the water and wash the gammon in fresh cold water. Place in a deep pan, cover with cold water, bring to the boil and skim, then simmer gently for 4 hours. When cooked, remove the skin, trim off some of the fat and carve into thin slices. Serve moistened with a little of the cooking liquor and, by tradition, accompanied with pease pudding.

To test if the gammon is cooked the small mustard bone can be pulled out of the knuckle end and the meat can be easily pierced with a needle at its thickest point.

BRAISING

Braised Ham with Madeira Sauce (Jambon Braisé au Madère)

1.5 kg boiled ham
1 litre jus lié or demi-glace
200 ml Madeira
100 g sugar

1. Remove the skin and trim off some of the fat from the ham.
2. Place the ham in a deep pan just large enough to hold it.
3. Add the Madeira, cover with a lid and place into the oven at 180°C for 30 minutes, basting once or twice.
4. Remove the ham and place in a shallow dish. Sprinkle the surface with the sugar and glaze in the oven until the surface is caramelised.
5. Add the sauce to the cooking liquor, bring to the boil and skim. Pass through a conical strainer and reboil.
6. Carve the ham into thin slices and arrange overlapping on a flat dish; coat with the sauce and serve.

Braised Ham with Madeira Sauce and Spinach
(Jambon Braisé aux Epinards)

Proceed as for Braised Ham with Madeira Sauce and serve sliced, coated with the sauce and garnished with purée of spinach.

GRILLING

Grilled Bacon

Bacon may be grilled on an open grill but the usual procedure is to remove the rind and arrange the rashers slightly overlapping on a tray. They are cooked on both sides under a salamander grill until slightly crisp.

Grilled Gammon Rashers

10 × 175 g gammon rashers
    50 ml oil
    250 g Straw Potatoes
1 bunch watercress

1. Brush the grill bars with oil, place the gammon rashers on the hottest part of the grill so that a criss-cross effect is marked on both sides. Move to a heat zone that will continue to cook them for a total of 3 minutes on each side.
2. Remove and arrange on an oval dish and garnish with the Straw Potatoes and picked watercress.

Veal

QUALITY POINTS

The flesh should be white to very pale pink in colour and finely and evenly grained. The outer covering of fat should be thin and the configuration of bones large in relation to the size and amount of flesh muscle. The bones should be bluish white in colour.

MAIN JOINTS

Saddle (16 kg) – Roasting, pot-roasting, braising, and as cuts for grilling and shallow frying. Remove the hip bones and cut off the flanks in line with the joint.

Loin (6 kg) – Roasting, pot-roasting, grilling and in cuts for shallow frying. Remove the kidneys from the inside, remove the fillets from underneath. Divide the short saddle through the centre to make two loins, then bone out completely. Cut away the flank in line with the joint.

Best End (7 kg) – Roasting, grilling and shallow frying of small cuts. Remove the breasts, leaving the joint twice as long as the eye of the meat. Remove the sinew along the width from under the back. Remove the flesh and skin from the end of and between the bones; when divided into small cuts these are known as chops, rather than cutlets.

Neck (2.5kg) – Stewing. Bone out completely, remove any sinew and cut into 2.5 cm cubes.

Breast (10 kg) – Roasting and stewing. Bone out completely, remove outer skin, sinew and fat, then either roll into a joint, or stuff, roll and tie into a joint for roasting, or cut into 2.5 cm cubes for stewing.

Shoulder (13 kg) – Roasting, braising, stewing. Bone out completely, remove outer skin, sinew and fat, then either cut into joints and tie for roasting or braising, or cut into 2.5 cm cubes for stewing.

Leg (17 kg) – Roasting, pot-roasting, braising. Remove the pelvic bone, saw off the knuckle bone end and trim off surplus meat. Use the membranes to divide into the component joints of thick flank, cushion and under cushion.

Knuckle/Shin (3 kg) – Stewing. Remove from the leg by cutting through the joint and either saw into 4 cm pieces on the bone, or bone out, trim the outer skin and sinew, then cut into 2.5 cm cubes.

Cushion (3 kg), *Rump* (2.5 kg), *Thick Flank* (3 kg) and *Under Cushion* (2.5 kg) – Roasting, pot-roasting, braising. Trim carefully, cover with strips of fat bacon and tie into shape or cut into slices for escalopes and escalopines.

SMALL CUTS

Escalope (120 g) and *Escalopines* (2 × 75 g) – Shallow frying. Cut from under cushion or thick flank into 2 cm thick slices across the grain and flatten with a dampened cutlet bat.

Grenadin (2 × 60 g) – Shallow frying and braising. Cut into 1.5 cm thick slices, trim into small oval pieces and lard with thin strips of salt pork fat.

Veal Cutlet (250 g) – Grilling and shallow frying. Cut between the bones of the prepared best end and the loin. Lightly flatten and trim.

OFFALS

Liver – Grilling and shallow frying. Skin, remove gristle and cut into slices on the slant.

Sweetbread – Braising and shallow frying. Soak in cold water for 30 minutes, blanch and trim the gristle and membrane.

BAKING

Côte de Veau en Papillote

50 g butter	2 slices cooked ham
1 × 250 g veal cutlet	1 tbs oil
50 g duxelles of mushrooms	seasoning

1. Heat a shallow pan and add the butter. Season the cutlet, and shallow fry until coloured, then turn over and colour the other side.
2. Lay one slice of ham on an oiled heart-shaped piece of greaseproof paper, spread with half of the duxelles mixture, place the cutlet on top, spread with the remainder of the duxelles and cover with the other slice of ham.

3. Fold the paper over and pleat the edge tightly to seal.
4. Place on an oiled oval flat dish and bake in the oven at 180°C for 6 minutes, allowing the trapped steam to swell and the outside to colour; serve at once for the waiting staff to cut open the papillote in front of the customer.

BOILING

Blanquette of Veal (Blanquette de Veau)

1.5 kg shoulder or neck end of veal	75 g butter
2 litres white stock	75 g flour
1 whole carrot	200 ml cream
1 studded onion	$^1/_4$ juice of lemon
1 bouquet garni	salt and cayenne pepper

1. Place the meat into a saucepan, cover with cold water, bring to the boil and cook for 5 minutes. Place under hot running water to remove scum, then refresh under cold running water and drain in a colander.
2. Place the blanched meat into a saucepan, add the stock, bring to the boil and skim.
3. Add the onion, carrot, bouquet garni and seasoning. Allow to simmer gently for 1 hour until cooked.
4. Remove and discard the onion, carrot and bouquet garni.
5. Make a second stage roux with the butter and flour while the stew is cooking and allow to cool.
6. Make a velouté sauce from most of the strained cooking liquid, keeping the meat moist and hot in the remainder.
7. Allow the velouté to cook for 30 minutes. Strain through a fine strainer, add the cream, lemon juice and a pinch of cayenne, reboil.
8. Add the drained meat to the velouté, allow to simmer for a few minutes and serve sprinkled with chopped parsley.

Blanquette of Veal with Mushrooms and Onions (Blanquette de Veau à l'Ancienne)

Proceed as for Blanquette of Veal with the addition of 30 button mushrooms and 30 button onions cooked separately.

Veal Quenelles (Quenelles de Veau)

Proceed as for Chicken Quenelles (see page 225), using veal instead of chicken.

BRAISING

Braised Cushion of Veal (Noix de Veau Braisée)

200 g sliced carrot		1.5 kg larded cushion of veal
200 g sliced onion		75 g melted butter
150 g sliced celery		500 ml brown stock
1 bayleaf	bed of	50 g tomato purée
1 sprig thyme	roots	50 g arrowroot
few parsley stalks		seasoning
1 crushed clove of garlic		

1. Heat the butter in a shallow pan, season the joint and shallow fry until light brown on all sides.
2. Place the bed of roots in a braising pan and the joint on top.
3. Moisten with the stock, add the tomato purée, cover with a lid and place in the oven at 180°C for 1½ hours, basting from time to time.
4. When nearly cooked, remove the lid and allow the meat to colour, then remove from the pan and keep it warm on a tray.
5. Place the pan on top of the stove, slightly thicken the cooking liquid with the diluted arrowroot and simmer for a few minutes.
6. Strain through a fine conical strainer into a saucepan, reboil, skim all traces of fat and season to taste.
7. Arrange slices of the meat overlapping on an oval dish, coat with some of the sauce and serve with the remainder in sauceboats.

Braised Cushion of Veal with Noodles (Noix de Veau Braisée aux Nouilles)

Proceed as for Braised Cushion of Veal and serve garnished with 300 g buttered noodles.

Braised Grenadins of Veal (Grenadins de Veau Braisés)

Using 10 × 150 g prepared grenadins of veal, proceed as for Braised Cushion of Veal. A garnish such as braised celery, braised fennel or a jardinière of vegetables may be added.

Braised Nut of Veal with Vegetables (Noix de Veau Braisée aux Légumes)

Proceed as for Braised Cushion of Veal and serve garnished with 250 g cooked mixed vegetables cut paysanne shape.

Braised Veal Sweetbreads (Ris de Veau Braisé)

200 g sliced carrot		1.5 kg veal sweetbreads
200 g sliced onion		150 g melted butter
150 g sliced celery		1 litre white veal stock
1 bayleaf	bed of root	salt and pepper
1 sprig thyme	vegetables	
few parsley stalks		
1 crushed clove garlic		

1. Soak the sweetbreads for 1 hour in cold water.
2. Place into a saucepan, cover with cold water, bring to the boil and cook for 5 minutes. Place under hot water, then refresh under cold running water and drain in a colander.
3. Remove the nerves and gristle and place the sweetbreads in a damp cloth with a heavy chopping board and weight on top in order to slightly flatten them. Leave for 2 hours.
4. Butter a shallow pan, add the bed of roots and place the sweetbreads on top, season with salt and pepper, cover with a sheet of greaseproof paper, and a lid and cook in the oven at 180°C for 10 minutes.
5. Remove from the oven, add the stock, bring to the boil, cover and braise for 1 hour until cooked, basting occasionally.
6. Transfer the sweetbreads from the cooking liquid into a shallow dish. Reduce the liquid by half, strain over the sweetbreads and serve.

Note
To test if sweetbreads are cooked press between the fingers. They should feel firm, if they are springy it means they are not cooked sufficiently.

Braised Veal Sweetbreads with Vegetables (Ris de Veau Bonne Maman)

Proceed as for Braised Veal Sweetbreads. Cut 150 g each of carrots, leeks and celery into julienne and cook in some of the braising liquid. Reduce the remainder of the braising liquid by half, skim off any impurities and season to taste. Serve the sweetbreads in an entrée dish, cover with the cooked vegetables and coat with the reduced braising liquid.

Sweetbreads in Cream Sauce (Ris de Veau à la Crème)

Proceed as for Braised Veal Sweetbreads. Strain the cooking liquid, reduce by two-thirds and add to 600 ml cream sauce. Serve the sweetbreads coated with the sauce.

Sweetbreads with Asparagus (Ris de Veau Princesse)

Proceed as for Sweetbreads in Cream Sauce and serve garnished with sprue asparagus and slices of truffle.

Braised Stuffed Shoulder of Veal Hanover Style   GERMANY
(Kalbsschulter auf Hannoversche Art)

Stuff a boned shoulder of veal with either thyme and parsley stuffing or sausage meat; cover with thin strips of salt fat pork, tie and braise as for Braised Cushion of Veal. When cooked reduce the cooking liquid, add cream to give a sauce consistency and finish with chopped fillets of anchovy and chopped fresh herbs. Serve slices of the veal garnished with turned carrots and turnips, button onions and sections of celery, masked with the sauce.

GRILLING

Grilling is not a very suitable method for cooking veal because there is very little natural fat content in veal as compared to the other meats. The different degrees of doneness cannot be applied as underdone veal will not be acceptable to many customers and a very well-done veal chop would be dry and tasteless. Veal offals such as calf's liver, kidney and feet are suitable for grilling.

POT-ROASTING

Pot-Roasted Cushion of Veal (Noix de Veau Poêlée)

100 g melted butter	1.5 kg larded cushion of veal
200 g sliced carrot	500 ml jus lié
200 g sliced onion	seasoning
150 g sliced celery	
1 bayleaf	bed of roots
1 sprig thyme	
15 g parsley stalks	
1 crushed clove garlic	

1. Butter and season the bottom of a braising pan or other deep receptacle just large enough to hold the joint.
2. Place in the bed of root vegetables, then put the prepared joint on top, season and coat with the melted butter.
3. Cover with a lid and cook in the oven at 200°C for 1½ hours, basting at 30-minute intervals.
4. Test the joint for the desired degree of doneness. When nearly cooked, remove the lid and allow the meat to colour.

5. When cooked, remove from the pan, retain in a tray and keep it warm.
6. Place the pan on top of the stove, add the jus lié and simmer gently for a few minutes, allowing the flavours from the juices and butter to be absorbed.
7. Strain through a fine conical strainer into a saucepan. Reboil, skim and season. Adjust the consistency if necessary, so that it will lightly coat the meat.
8. Arrange slices of meat slightly overlapping on an oval dish, coat with some of the gravy and serve.
9. Serve the remainder of the gravy in sauceboats.

Note
Pot-Roasted Cushion of Veal may be served with a number of suitable garnishes such as celery, (Noix de Veau Poêlée aux Céleris), carrots, (Noix de Veau Poêlée aux Carottes) or artichoke bottoms filled with minted peas and Château Potatoes (Noix de Veau Poêlée Clamart).

ROASTING

Joints of veal should be covered with slices of spek or fat bacon tied into position, which should be removed for the final 10–15 minutes of cooking time. Thyme, parsley and lemon stuffing is traditionally served as an accompaniment and the roast gravy is lightly thickened.

Roast Cushion of Veal (Noix de Veau Rôtie)

1.5 kg barded cushion of veal	25 g arrowroot
100 g dripping	500 g Thyme, Parsley and
salt	Lemon Stuffing
500 ml brown stock	1 bunch watercress

1. Season the joint and place onto some veal bones or a trivet in a roasting tray. Coat with the dripping and place into the oven at 220°C. Reduce the temperature after 20 minutes to 180°C and continue cooking for a further 1½ hours, basting at regular intervals.
2. Cut the string and remove the fat covering during the last 15 minutes of roasting to permit the joint to colour slightly. Roll the stuffing sausage-shape in buttered greaseproof paper and cook with the meat for the last 20 minutes.
3. When cooked, remove from the roasting tray and retain, preferably standing on a wire grid; any juices collected should be used in the making of gravy.
4. Place the roasting tray on the stove and heat gently, allowing the sediment to settle.
5. Add the stock and simmer gently for a few minutes, then strain through a fine conical strainer into a saucepan. Reboil and skim, then thicken with the diluted arrowroot and simmer for a few minutes.

6. Carve the joint into 3 mm thick slices at an angle of 45° and arrange over-lapping on an oval flat dish. Coat with some of the gravy and garnish with slices of the stuffing and picked watercress.
7. Serve the remainder of the gravy in a sauceboat.

Roast Loin of Veal (Longe de Veau Rôtie)

Proceed as for Roast Cushion of Veal, omitting the stuffing and carving the meat into 1 cm slices.

Roast Best End of Veal (Carré de Veau Rôti)

Proceed as for Roast Cushion of Veal, omitting the stuffing and carving the meat between the bones.

Roast Stuffed Breast of Veal (Telyachya Grud)   RUSSIA

Stuff 1.5 kg breast of veal with 300 g cooked buckwheat mixed with 200 g sliced cooked mushrooms, 50 g butter and 100 ml soured cream. Proceed as for Roast Cushion of Veal and serve garnished with watercress and accom-panied by roast gravy.

SHALLOW FRYING

Calf's Liver and Bacon (Foie de Veau au Lard)

1.5 kg calf's liver
125 g butter
  10 rashers of bacon
300 ml jus lié
150 g butter

1. Cut the liver into 5 mm thick slices, pass through flour and shake off any surplus.
2. Heat the butter in a frying pan and shallow fry quickly on both sides, keeping slightly underdone. Grill or shallow fry the bacon rashers.
3. Arrange the liver on an oval flat dish with the rashers criss-cross fashion on top.
4. Surround with a thread of the jus lié, heat the butter until it turns nut brown, pour it over and serve.

Note
When traces of blood appear on the surface of the liver during cooking it is ready to be turned. When blood shows on the coloured surface it is suf-ficiently cooked.

Calf's Liver and Onions (Foie de Veau Lyonnaise)

Proceed as for Calf's Liver and Bacon, omitting the bacon. Serve in an earthenware dish coated with Lyonnaise Sauce.

Breaded Escalope of Veal (Escalope de Veau Panée)

10 × 125 g escalopes of veal	150 ml oil
flour	300 ml jus lié
eggwash } for	150 g butter
breadcrumbs } coating	

1. Season the escalopes and pass through flour, eggwash and breadcrumbs, then mark trellis-fashion.
2. Heat a pan and add the oil, place in the escalopes and shallow fry until golden brown, then turn and fry the other side.
3. Arrange the escalopes on a flat oval dish and surround with a thread of the jus lié. Heat the butter until it turns nut brown, pour over and serve the remainder of the jus lié separately.

Escalope de Veau Cordon Bleu

Sandwich two very thin veal escalopes with a thin slice each of ham and Gruyère cheese, seal firmly, then coat with flour, eggwash and breadcrumbs. Shallow fry and serve surrounded with a cordon of jus lié and covered with nut brown butter.

Escalope of Veal in Cream Sauce (Escalope de Veau à la Crème)

10 × 125 g veal escalopes	300 ml veal velouté
flour	200 ml cream
150 g butter	seasoning
200 ml sherry	

1. Heat a shallow pan and add the butter.
2. Place the seasoned and floured escalopes in the pan and shallow fry until light golden brown on both sides, then arrange on a flat oval dish.
3. Drain the fat from the pan, add the sherry, reduce by half, then add the velouté and the cream and reduce to a consistency that will coat the escalopes. Season and pass through a fine conical strainer into a clean saucepan. Reheat, pour over the escalopes and serve.

Veal Escalope in Cream Sauce with Mushrooms (Escalope de Veau à la Crème et Champignons)

Proceed as for Escalopes of Veal in Cream Sauce with the addition of 500 g sliced cooked button mushrooms to the sauce.

Veal Escalope in Madeira Sauce (Escalope de Veau au Madère)

Proceed as for Escalope of Veal in Cream Sauce until cooked. Drain the fat from the pan, add 200 ml Madeira and reduce by half, then add 300 ml jus lié and reduce to a consistency that will coat the escalopes. Season, pass through a fine conical strainer into a clean saucepan; reheat, pour over the escalopes and serve.

Veal Escalope in Marsala Sauce (Escalope de Veau au Marsala)

Proceed as for Escalope of Veal in Madeira Sauce, substituting Marsala for Madeira wine.

Veal Escalope with Marsala (Piccata di Vitello alla Marsala)

Marinate 20 small veal escalopes in 50 ml lemon juice for 1 hour, then proceed as for Escalope of Veal in Cream Sauce. When cooked, add the marinade and 200 ml Marsala to the pan, reduce slightly, then add 300 ml jus lié and reduce slightly. Serve the veal coated with the sauce.

Veal Escalope Milanaise (Escalope de Veau Milanaise)

Proceed as for Breaded Escalope of Veal and garnish with 500 g Spaghetti Milanaise.

Veal Escalope Napolitaine (Escalope de Veau Napolitaine)

Proceed as for Breaded Escalope of Veal and garnish with 500 g Spaghetti Napolitaine.

Veal Escalope Viennoise (Escalope de Veau Viennoise)

Proceed as for Breaded Escalope of Veal. Decorate the dish at both ends with alternate semi-circles of chopped parsley, sieved hard-boiled white and yolk of egg and strips of anchovy. Arrange the escalopes neatly on the dish and place on each a slice of peeled lemon with a ring of anchovy fillet laid in its centre with a stoned olive inside, the lemon surrounded with chopped parsley, sieved white and yolk of hard-boiled egg. Finish with a cordon of jus lié and nut-brown butter.

Veal Escalope with Prosciutto (Saltimbocca)

Marinate veal escalopes in 50 ml lemon juice, rubbed sage and seasoning. Attach a slice of prosciutto to each escalope with a cocktail stick then shallow fry in sage-flavoured butter. Swill the pan with 300 ml white wine, reduce and pour over the escalopes.

Veal Escalope with Ham, Cheese and Tomato
(Scaloppa alla Bolognese)

Cook as for Breaded Escalope of Veal. Sauté 100 g chopped onion and 3 chopped cloves of garlic in olive oil, then add 250 g diced tomato flesh and 12 g chopped basil, season and cook. Place a slice each of prosciutto and Gruyère cheese on each cooked escalope, gratinate under a salamander grill and serve covered with the tomato mixture.

Shallow-Fried Sweetbread with Asparagus
(Escalope de Ris de Veau Maréchale)

Proceed as for Breaded Escalope of Veal, using 150 g breadcrumbed sweetbreads. Serve garnished with bouquets of asparagus tips and slices of truffle.

Note
Sliced sweetbreads should not be coated with flour, eggwash and breadcrumbs too far in advance or the coating will become soggy. The two dishes above should therefore be cooked to order.

Veal Cutlet Shallow Fried in Butter (Côte de Veau Sautée)

10 × 250 g veal cutlets
   125 ml butter
   300 ml jus lié
    150 g butter

1. Heat the butter in a sauté pan, add the seasoned cutlets and shallow fry on both sides for 10 minutes.
2. Arrange on an oval flat dish and surround with a thread of jus lié; heat the butter until it turns nut brown, pour over and serve.

Veal Cutlet Bonne Femme (Côte de Veau Bonne Femme)

Shallow fry 10 × 250 g cutlets. Neatly arrange in a cocotte with 100 g fried lardons of bacon and 40 each of cocotte potatoes and brown glazed button onions. Add 300 ml jus lié, cover with a lid and place in an oven for 5 minutes. Serve in the cocotte on a flat dish lined with a dish paper.

Veal Cutlet Milanaise (Côte de Veau Milanaise)

Using 10 × 250 g veal cutlets proceed as for Lamb Cutlets Milanaise.

Veal Cutlet Napolitaine (Côte de Veau Napolitaine)

Using 10 × 250 g veal cutlets proceed as for Lamb Cutlets Napolitaine.

Veal Cutlet with Fontina Cheese (Costolettà alla Valdostana)

Cut pockets in 10×250 g veal cutlets and fill with slices of Fontina cheese, then pass through flour, eggwash and breadcrumbs and shallow fry in olive oil. Serve surrounded with a cordon of jus lié.

Calves' Kidney in Port (Rim Salteado com Porto)   PORTUGAL

Prepare and cut 5×250 g veal kidneys into pieces. Season and shallow fry quickly in olive oil, keeping them underdone; drain and retain in a warm place. Add 100 g chopped shallots to the pan, cook for 2 minutes, add 100 g chopped mushrooms, then moisten with 50 ml port and 250 ml jus lié. Add the drained kidneys, mix in and season to taste. Serve on fried bread croûtons, coated with the sauce.

Calf's Liver in Wine Sauce (Lebergeschnetzeltes)   GERMANY

Proceed as for Calf's Liver and Bacon, omitting the rashers of bacon. Fry 75 g lardons of bacon and 100 g chopped onion in the same pan, swill with 100 ml red wine and reduce; moisten with 300 ml jus lié, then add rubbed thyme and rosemary. Serve the liver coated with the sauce, accompanied by knödel dumplings.

Calf's Liver with Apple and Onion (Leber Berliner Art)   GERMANY

Proceed as for Calf's Liver and Bacon, omitting the bacon. Serve garnished with shallow-fried apple and onion rings and grilled tomatoes.

Pojarsky Cutlet (Pozharskie Kotlety)   RUSSIA

Combine 1 kg finely minced veal with 175 g white breadcrumbs previously soaked in milk and squeezed out, 75 ml cream, 1 beaten egg, 50 g chopped dill or parsley, and salt, pepper and nutmeg. Divide into 10 pieces, mould cutlet shape and pass through breadcrumbs. Golden shallow fry in oil and serve garnished with sprigs of dill, accompanied by mushroom sauce.

Sautéed Grenadin of Veal with Wild Mushrooms   SPAIN
(Fricando con Setas)

Cut 10×175 g grenadins of veal 1 cm thick and sauté in 75 ml olive oil, remove and retain. Add 225 g chopped Spanish onions, 2 chopped cloves of garlic and 225 g diced carrot to the pan and cook without colouring, then add 225 g tomato concassée. Moisten with 300 ml white wine, 600 ml brown stock, a bouquet garni with a sprig of oregano, and seasoning. Replace the grenadins and simmer for 10 minutes, then add 675 g wild mushrooms sautéed in olive oil and 75 g toasted nibbed almonds. Thicken the liquid with diluted cornflour to a coating consistency and season. Serve the grenadins coated with the sauce and sprinkled with chopped fresh herbs.

Schnitzel

Coat 5 mm thick veal escalopes with flour, eggwash and breadcrumbs, deep fry and serve with lemon wedges.

Veal Escalope Holstein (Holsteiner Schnitzel)

Sprinkle veal escalopes with lemon juice, coat with flour, eggwash and bread-crumbs, then proceed as for Breaded Escalope of Veal. Garnish with fried eggs each with two strips of anchovy fillets on top.

Veal Cutlet with Paprika
(Chuleta de Ternera al Ajo Cabañil)

Shallow fry 10 × 250 g veal cutlets, remove and retain. Add 3 chopped cloves of garlic and 2 tsp paprika to the pan, moisten with 50 ml vinegar and 300 ml veal stock, season and simmer to reduce, then pour over the cutlets.

Veal Cutlet with Soured Cream and Paprika
(Paprikaschnitzel)

Season 10 × 250 g veal cutlets with salt and paprika, then shallow fry in olive oil, remove and retain. Add 100 g strips of green pimento, 100 g sliced onion and 150 g diced tomato flesh to the pan and cook for 5 minutes. Moisten with 300 ml jus lié, finish with 80 ml soured cream and pour over the cutlets.

STEWING

Osso Bucco

20 × 4 cm pieces knuckle of veal	1 bouquet garni
100 ml oil	350 g diced tomato
25 g flour	25 g arrowroot
50 g tomato purée	2 chopped cloves of garlic
1 litre veal stock	1 grated peel of lemon } gremolata
100 g carrots	
50 g turnips	1 tbs chopped parsley
100 g onion } cut into brunoise	seasoning
75 g celery	
100 g leek	

1. Heat the oil in a frying pan.
2. Add the knuckles and fry until golden brown on both sides.
3. Drain and transfer to a saucepan.
4. Sprinkle with the flour, shake and place in the oven for 10 minutes.
5. Remove from the oven, stir in the tomato purée and add the stock.

6. Bring to the boil, skim and season. Add the chopped tomatoes, the diced vegetables and bouquet garni and cook for 1 hour, either in the oven at 180°C or on the stove.
7. When cooked, remove the veal, dress in an earthenware dish and keep hot. Discard the bouquet garni.
8. Boil the cooking liquid and thicken with the diluted arrowroot, then finish with the lemon peel, parsley and crushed garlic.
9. Coat the knuckles with the sauce and serve.

Notes

1. Polenta, braised rice or braised saffroned rice is usually served as an accompaniment to this dish.
2. When cooked the meat should come away from the centre bone under slight pressure.

Veal Fricassée (Fricassée de Veau)

1.5 kg stewing veal, cut into 2.5 cm cubes	200 ml cream ⎫ liaison
100 g butter	3 egg yolks ⎭
100 g flour	10 heart-shaped croûtons
2 litres veal stock	12 g chopped parsley
1 bouquet garni	seasoning

1. Melt the butter in a shallow pan. Add the seasoned meat, cover with a lid and allow to set without coloration.
2. Sprinkle with the flour and stir it in with a wooden spatule. Cook to a second stage roux and allow to cool.
3. Add the hot stock a little at a time, season, bring to the boil, skim, then add the bouquet garni. Cover with a lid and place in the oven at 180°C for 1 hour until cooked.
4. Remove the bouquet garni, place the meat in a clean saucepan and keep hot.
5. Whisk the sauce onto the liaison and heat until it thickens but do not allow to boil. Pour over the veal and mix in.
6. Serve in an entrée dish. Dip the tips of the croûtons in some of the sauce, then into chopped parsley, arrange around the dish and serve.

Note
Instead of using cream for the liaison, crème fraîche or plain yogurt may be used.

Fricassée of Veal with Vegetables (Fricassée de Veau aux Légumes)

Proceed as for Veal Fricassée, adding 250 g mixed vegetables cut into dice or jardinière.

Veal Goulash (Goulash de Veau Hongroise)

1.5 kg stewing veal, cut into 2.5 cm cubes	75 g diced tomatoes
	1 bouquet garni
100 g lard	¼ tsp caraway seed
500 g chopped onion	2 chopped cloves of garlic
75 g paprika	20 small plain boiled potatoes
25 g flour	chopped parsley
50 g tomato purée	seasoning
2 litres veal stock	

1. Heat the lard in a shallow pan, add the seasoned veal and fry until a light golden brown on all sides.
2. Add the onion and cook gently for a few minutes, then add the paprika and flour; stir with a wooden spatule and place into the oven at 200°C for 10 minutes until the flour and paprika have coloured.
3. Remove from the oven, stir in the tomato purée and the stock.
4. Bring to the boil, skim and season. Add the diced tomatoes, bouquet garni, caraway seeds, and garlic and return to the oven at 180°C for 1 hour.
5. Remove from the oven and discard the bouquet garni.
6. Skim off the fat and serve in an entrée dish with the meat neatly arranged dome-shape, garnished with the potatoes and sprinkled with the chopped parsley.

Note
Gnocchi Parisienne may be added as an additional garnish.

Veal Stew with Mushrooms (Sauté de Veau aux Champignons)

1.5 kg stewing veal, cut into 2.5 cm cubes	500 g button mushrooms
	1 bouquet garni
100 ml oil	chopped parsley
1.5 litres jus lié	seasoning

1. Season the meat and fry in the hot oil to a golden brown colour on all sides. Drain and transfer to a stewing pan.
2. Moisten with the jus lié, bring to the boil, skim, season and add the bouquet garni.
3. Cover with a lid and cook in the oven at 200°C for 1 hour, or simmer gently on top of the stove.
4. When cooked, transfer the meat to another saucepan and discard the bouquet garni. Strain the sauce through a conical strainer over the meat.
5. Bring to the boil and skim to remove all fat.
6. Add the mushrooms previously cooked in butter and serve sprinkled with chopped parsley.

Veal Stew Portuguese Style (Sauté de Veau à la Portugaise)

1.5 kg stewing veal, cut into 2.5 cm cubes
200 ml oil
200 g chopped onion
2 chopped cloves of garlic
200 ml white wine
600 g diced tomatoes
1.5 litres jus lié
1 bouquet garni
chopped parsley
seasoning

1. Season the meat and fry in the hot oil to a golden brown colour on all sides. Drain and transfer to a stewing pan.
2. Add the onion and garlic to the oil, colour lightly and add to the meat.
3. Add the wine, reduce by half, then add the diced tomatoes and jus lié, bring to the boil, skim, season and add the bouquet garni.
4. Cover with a tight-fitting lid and cook in the oven at 200°C for 1 hour, or simmer gently on top of the stove.
5. When cooked, transfer the meat to another saucepan and discard the bouquet garni. Strain the sauce through a conical strainer over the meat.
6. Bring to the boil, skim to remove all fat and serve in entrée dishes, sprinkled with the chopped parsley.

Veal Stew with Cherries (Khoreshe Albaloo)   MIDDLE EAST

Cut 1.5 kg shoulder of veal into 2.5 cm cubes and sauté with 100 g chopped onion in 50 ml oil. Stir in 1 tsp turmeric and ½ tsp ground cinnamon, moisten with 1 litre stock and stew for 1 hour until the meat is tender. Finish by adding 300 g pitted sour morello cherries, 50 ml lemon juice and a little brown sugar.

CHAPTER 8 # Poultry

QUALITY POINTS

Poultry should have flexible breast bones and plump white breasts. The skin should be unbroken and free from bruises, blemishes, feather tips and hairs. Birds should feel heavy for their size and the packet of giblets, where included, look and smell fresh. Corn-fed birds are pale yellow in colour.

TYPES OF POULTRY

Single Poussin (300–400 g) – Grilling, roasting, pot-roasting.
Double Poussin (500–750 g) – Grilling, roasting, pot-roasting.
Chicken, small (1.25–2 kg) – Grilling, pot-roasting, roasting, sautéeing, shallow frying, stewing, poaching.
Chicken, medium (2–2.5 kg) – Grilling, pot-roasting, roasting, sautéeing, shallow frying, stewing, poaching.
Chicken, large (2.5–3.5 kg) – Grilling, pot-roasting, roasting, sautéeing, shallow frying, stewing, poaching.
Boiling fowl (2.5–3 kg) – Boiling.
Duck (2.5–3 kg) – Roasting, pot-roasting, braising.
Duckling (2–2.5 kg) – Roasting, pot-roasting, braising.
Goose (4–6 kg) – Roasting.
Guinea fowl (1.25–1.75 kg) – Roasting.
Turkey, young (3–6 kg) – Roasting, poaching.
Turkey, large (7–12 kg) – Roasting, poaching.

TRUSSING

Poultry can be improved in shape by being trussed (tying with string) as follows:

1. Remove the wishbone; cut off the spur at the end of the winglets at the first joint, then fold the wings underneath.
2. Insert the trussing needle through the centre of the leg and out through the other side, then through the winglet and neck flap, keeping the needle in a straight line and tie the two ends of string securely.
3. Pass the needle through the bird, underneath the thigh, in a straight line through to the opposite side, then pass the needle back over the top of the drumstick but under the breast and tie firmly.

PREPARATION OF SUPREMES

1. Remove each leg by cutting around the skin to the ball and socket joint at the carcass bottom.

2. Open the leg to the ball joint, cutting between the leg and the joint so as to pull off the leg.
3. Expose the wishbone by cutting around the bone with a knife and remove it, taking care not to cut away the surrounding flesh.
4. Remove the winglets to leave 2–3 cm bare bone attached to the breast.
5. Cut along one side of the breastbone down through the wing joint. Remove the supreme by laying the carcass on its side and gently pulling the supreme free. Remove the skin. Repeat on the other side of the bird.
6. Remove the fillet from underneath each supreme and remove the tendon from each fillet.
7. Make an incision along the length of the back of the supreme and place the fillet inside. Trim to form a neat shape.

PREPARATION OF CHICKEN FOR SAUTÉ

1. Remove each leg by cutting around the skin to the ball and socket joint at the carcass bottom.
2. Open out the leg at the ball joint, cut through and pull off the leg.
3. Cut through the centre joint of the leg where the thigh bone and the drumstick meet, thus separating the leg into two pieces. Cut away the end bones on each joint.
4. Remove the winglets, taking care to leave 2–3 cm of bare bone attached to the breast. Cut off the winglets just before the first bone.
5. Cut along the length of the bird halfway down each side of the breast bone, leaving ample flesh on the breast bone to form another portion. Cut downwards in a straight line until the socket joint is reached; cut through and remove.
6. Chop the remaining carcass away, leaving the breast, and cut along the centre to divide it into two equal pieces.
7. The carcass may be divided into three equal pieces for cooking with the chicken pieces, which can then be arranged around the pieces of carcass.

Note
For all Asian dishes, discard the skin from the chicken while cutting it up.

PREPARATION OF CHICKEN FOR GRILLING

1. Pass a large knife through the vent end of the bird till the tip shows at the neck end.
2. Cut through on one side of the backbone.
3. Open the bird flat and chop off the backbone.
4. Make an incision through the skin close to each leg and tuck the end of the drumstick through in order to hold it in position.

5. Turn the bird over with the centre bones exposed and lightly nick the breast bone once or twice – this will help to retain the shape of the bird during cooking – then flatten it slightly.

To cut a small chicken or poussin into the spatchcock position for grilling, insert the ends of the legs into the body, then make a cut under the breast and above the legs into the neck, open it out and flatten with the aid of a cutlet bat.

CARVING POULTRY

Portioning Chicken, Duck and Guinea Fowl

Remove the legs and divide each into two and cut out the bones from the drumsticks and thighs. Remove the winglets; with a carving knife halfway up the side of the breast, carve downwards towards the wing and with the point of the knife cut through the wing joint and remove the portion. Repeat the process on the opposite side and trim neatly. Remove the remaining breast from the carcass by chopping it through, then divide into two lengthways and, if necessary, trim neatly.

To divide a double poussin into two portions, cut through the breast bone and the backbone. A single poussin is served whole, either plain or stuffed.

Portioning Turkey

Remove the legs, divide into two, as the thigh and drumstick, bone out, remove any tendons and carve into 3 mm thick slices. Carve the breast into 3 mm thick slices on the slant so they are not so long that they overlap the edge of the plate. Serve slices of breast meat on top of slices of leg.

BAKING

Breast of Chicken Wrapped in Puff Pastry

10 × 125 g supremes of chicken
200 g duxelles
1 kg puff pastry
2 eggs
seasoning

1. Stuff the supremes with the duxelles from the underside, season and reshape.
2. Roll out the pastry 80 cm × 15 cm and cut into 10 strips 1.5 cm wide; brush each piece with eggwash.

3. Wrap the supremes in the pastry, spiralling and just overlapping it from the pointed end to the bone.
4. Eggwash, then allow to rest for 1 hour.
5. Bake in the oven at 200°C for 10 minutes, then reduce to 150°C for another 15 minutes until cooked.
6. Serve on a flat oval dish with a dish paper, garnished with sprigs of parsley.

Note
50 g foie gras may be added to the duxelles.

Chicken and Mushroom Pie

3 × 1.5 kg chickens	few drops Worcester sauce
12 streaky bacon rashers	seasoning
250 g sliced button mushrooms	650 g puff pastry
150 g chopped onion	2 eggs
500 ml chicken stock	

1. Cut the chickens as for sauté and remove the skin and bones, season and wrap each piece in a half rasher of the stretched bacon.
2. Place into pie dishes, add the mushrooms and onion and the Worcester sauce mixed into the stock.
3. Line the edge of the pie dishes with a strip of puff pastry 3 mm in thickness and lightly eggwash.
4. Cover with a sheet of pastry 3 mm thick, seal firmly and crimp the edges.
5. Trim around the edges to remove excess pastry, holding the knife at an angle of 45° from underneath the dish. Decorate with leaves of pastry and make a small hole in the centre to allow steam to escape.
6. Allow to rest for 1 hour, then brush with eggwash.
7. Place into the oven on a baking sheet and bake at 200°C until light brown in colour. Reduce the temperature to 150°C and, if necessary, cover with kitchen foil to prevent burning. Bake for 1 hour.
8. Remove from the oven, clean around the edges of the pie dish, place on an underdish lined with a dish paper and put a pie collar around the pie.

Chicken Pie (Empadas de Calinha)   PORTUGAL

Sauté diced boneless chicken and bacon in oil, add chopped onion, parsley, seasoning and nutmeg; moisten with wine vinegar and white wine, then simmer, reducing the liquid by half. Fill patty tins lined with puff pastry with the mixture, cover with pastry lids and bake.

Chicken Pie in Filo Pastry (Kotopitta)   GREECE

Line a 32 cm × 16 cm shallow dish with filo pastry and brush with oil. Fill the dish with 800 g cooked chicken cut into short slices and 100 g grated Kefalotiri cheese gently mixed into 1 litre cold chicken velouté, together with salt, pepper and nutmeg. Cover with 2 layers of filo pastry, brush liberally with oil and bake in the oven at 200°C for 35 minutes.

Chicken Pot Pie   USA

Cook 250 g diced carrots and turnips, diamonds of beans and peas and 250 g diced potatoes in chicken stock. Combine 500 g sliced poached chicken, the drained vegetables, seasoning and 250 ml chicken velouté; flavour with ground mace and nutmeg and finish with 200 ml cream. Place into pie dishes, cover with short pastry then bake at 180°C for 35 minutes.

Chicken Supreme and Mushroom Filo Pastry   GREECE
Parcels (Kotopoulo)

Combine 500 g duxelles of mushrooms with 50 g white breadcrumbs, 2 chopped cloves of garlic and 10 g chopped fresh herbs. Enrobe 10 × 100 g supremes of chicken in the mixture and encase in filo pastry to form small parcels. Place on a baking sheet, brush with oil and bake in the oven at 200°C for 25 minutes until golden brown. Garnish with picked watercress.

Vermont Chicken Pie   USA

Combine 500 g sliced poached chicken and 250 ml chicken velouté, season then fill into pie dishes. Cover with overlapping 5 cm circles of puff pastry, then bake in the oven at 180°C for 35 minutes.

BRAISING

Braised Chicken with Mushrooms and Cheese
(Pollo alla Parmigiana)

Sauté chicken pieces with 3 chopped cloves of garlic in hot olive oil, add 250 g sliced mushrooms, 200 g diced green pimento, 150 g diced tomato and 2 tsp oregano. Transfer to a casserole, moisten with 200 ml white wine and 200 ml chicken stock, then braise in the oven at 180°C for 1 hour. Sprinkle with grated Parmesan cheese and serve.

Braised Duck with Green Peas (Canard Braisé aux Petits Pois)

2 × 2.5 kg ducks	16 button onions, shallow fried
500 ml brown stock	400 g peas
500 ml jus lié or demi-glace	seasoning
200 g lardons of streaky bacon	

1. Roast the ducks for 30 minutes, then place in a deep pan.
2. Add sufficient stock and sauce to two-thirds cover the ducks, bring to the boil, skim and cover with a lid.

3. Braise in the oven at 180°C until three-quarters cooked.
4. Add the rest of the ingredients and continue to cook for another 30 minutes, total cooking time 1½ hours.
5. Remove the ducks and retain in a warm place.
6. Boil the sauce and skim off any fat.
7. Cut the ducks into portions, place in an entrée dish and coat with the sauce and its garnish.

Casserole of Pigeon with Olives (Pigeon aux Olives)

Heat 50 ml of oil in a pan, add 10 seasoned pigeons and quickly fry on all sides to seal. Add 350 g chopped onion, 450 g lardons of belly of pork, 350 g diced carrot, 4 crushed cloves of garlic, thyme and bayleaf and fry until golden. Place into a casserole, moisten with 600 ml dry white wine and 600 ml chicken stock and cook in the oven at 200°C for 1½ hours. Transfer the pigeons, lardons and vegetables to a clean dish and add 30 button onions previously fried golden until cooked. Add 275 ml Madeira to the cooking liquor and reduce by half, lightly thicken with diluted cornflour, add 30 stoned, blanched green olives and serve.

Braised Duck and Cabbage (Ente in Wirsing)   GERMANY

Remove the legs from the ducks and reserve for other uses. Roast the rest of the carcasses until half-cooked, then braise with quarters of blanched cabbage and rashers of streaky bacon at 200°C for a further 30 minutes. Serve the ducks carved into portions, with the bacon and cabbage, coated with the reduced and thickened braising liquid.

Braised Duck with Olives (Pato a la Sevillana)   SPAIN

Place 100 g sliced onions and 2 crushed cloves of garlic inside a duck, roast until half-cooked, then braise in 150 ml each of white wine, dry sherry and brown stock with the addition of 100 g brunoise of carrot, 10 chopped green olives and seasoning. Carve the duck and serve with the carrots and olives on top, coated with the thickened cooking liquid.

Braised Pigeon (Tejfölös Galamb)   HUNGARY

Seal pigeons in hot oil, place in a braising pan and moisten with white wine and lemon juice, then braise for 1 hour. Finish by adding soured cream to the liquor to thicken it to a sauce consistency. Pour over the pigeons on serving.

Casserole of Pigeon (Pichones à la Toledana)   SPAIN

Heat 50 ml oil, add 10 seasoned pigeons and quickly fry on all sides to seal. Add 275 g chopped onion and 10 peeled cloves of garlic and fry until golden. Moisten with 600 ml dry sherry, 50 ml sherry vinegar and add 3 bayleaves and 2 tsp fresh or dried marjoram. Cover with the lid and cook in the oven at 200°C for 50 minutes, allowing the cooking liquor to reduce to a coating consistency. Serve the pigeons with the onion, garlic and herbs, coated with the sauce.

Chicken Casserole Portuguese Style (Frango na Púcara)
PORTUGAL

Braise a chicken in a casserole with button onions, diced tomato flesh, lardons of smoked ham, garlic, sultanas and chopped fresh herbs in brandy, Madeira and white wine. Serve as it is.

Chicken Casserole in Lemon Sauce (Csirke Citromos Màrtàsban)
HUNGARY

Braise chicken pieces in a casserole with lardons of bacon, chopped parsley, chicken stock and lemon juice. Reduce the braising liquor and add to a velouté, flavour with nutmeg and finish with a liaison of soured cream and lemon juice. Pour over the chicken pieces and serve.

Chicken Casserole with Rice (Arroz de Frango à Portuguesa)
PORTUGAL

Sauté chicken pieces in oil with sliced onion and place in a casserole; add sliced chorizo sausage and lardons of smoked bacon, moisten with white wine and stock, cover with a lid and cook.

Duck Casserole with Apples (Farshirovannaia Utka)
RUSSIA

Stuff a duck with diced apple, roast until half done, then finish cooking in a covered casserole with a little jus lié.

DEEP FRYING

Chicken à la Kiev (Kotlety Po-Kievski) (Suprême de Volaille à la Kiev)

10 × 125 g supremes of chicken	seasoning
200 g parsley butter	picked parsley ⎫
flour, eggwash	250 g Straw Potatoes ⎬ garnish
and breadcrumbs	

1. Remove the fillets from the skinless supremes and cut a long incision into the thickest part; lightly flatten with a dampened cutlet bat and season.

2. Place a 20 g baton of the chilled butter into each supreme and enclose it completely by rolling the flesh closely around it.
3. Coat with flour, eggwash and breadcrumbs, then repeat to give a second coating.
4. Place into a frying basket and immerse in hot fat at a temperature of 170°C. Fry for 5 minutes until crisp and golden, turning them during cooking to ensure even cooking and coloration.
5. Drain and serve on an oval dish garnished with Straw Potatoes and deep-fried sprigs of parsley.

Notes
1. The parsley butter may be lightly flavoured with chopped garlic.
2. Goose liver pâté may be used as a filling in place of butter.
3. Chicken Kiev may be accompanied by buckwheat kasha made by boiling buckwheat in salted water, finishing with a little butter.

Fried Chicken Japanese Style (Tatsuta Age)   JAPAN

Marinate 1.5 kg strips of chicken in 150 ml soy sauce, 75 ml mirin and 20 g grated ginger for 30 minutes. Coat with cornflour, then deep fry, drain and serve garnished with spring onion flowers.

GRILLING

Grilled Spring Chicken (Poussin Grillé)

10 × 400 g poussins prepared for grilling	250 g Straw Potatoes ⎫
100 ml oil	100 g parsley butter ⎬ garnish
seasoning	1 bunch picked watercress ⎭

1. Season and brush the opened and flattened poussins with oil.
2. Brush the grill bars with oil, place the poussins on the hottest part of the grill so that a criss-cross effect is marked on both sides, then move to a heat zone to cook for 15 minutes to the desired degree.
3. Serve arranged on an oval dish. Garnish with the Straw Potatoes and watercress and serve the parsley butter separately in a sauceboat on crushed ice.

Grilled Chicken with Devilled Sauce (Poulet Grillé Diablé)

Grill the seasoned chicken on both sides, remove and brush the breast side with English mustard made with the addition of cayenne pepper. Sprinkle well with white breadcrumbs, then with melted butter and colour under a salamander grill. Garnish with Straw Potatoes, and serve with Devilled Sauce.

Grilled Chicken American Style (Poulet Grillé Américaine)

Proceed as for Grilled Spring Chicken. Garnish with grilled tomatoes, streaky bacon rashers, mushrooms, Straw Potatoes, parsley butter and picked watercress. Serve a sauceboat of Devilled Sauce separately.

Grilled Skewered Chicken Livers (Brochette de Foies de Volaille)

1.25 kg chicken livers	20g chopped parsley
100 ml oil	seasoning
250 g streaky bacon	50ml melted butter
40 small open mushrooms	1 bunch picked watercress
75 g white breadcrumbs	

1. Heat the oil in a frying pan, lightly season and add the prepared liver pieces and shallow fry quickly, keeping them underdone, then drain.
2. Arrange the pieces of liver, 3 cm squares of bacon and cooked mushrooms on skewers in that order, filling each skewer to the hilt.
3. Grill on all sides for 10 minutes.
4. Coat the brochettes with breadcrumbs combined with chopped parsley and melted butter and place on a greased tray. Brush with melted butter and place under a salamander grill until the breadcrumbs are golden, turning them over.
5. Serve on a flat oval dish garnished with watercress.

Spatchcock (Poussin Grillé à la Crapaudine)

Tuck the legs into the skin and cut the poussins from the front under the breast back to the winglets. Open out and flatten with a cutlet bat. Season, brush with oil and grill for 8 minutes on each side. Remove the breast and rib bones, sprinkle the top surface well with white breadcrumbs, place on a greased tray, brush with melted butter and place under a salamander grill to colour. Serve garnished with Straw Potatoes and picked watercress and accompanied by Devilled Sauce. An optional decoration is two eyes made of the end slices of hard-boiled egg with a slice of truffle or of pimento-stuffed olive, placed at the end of the breast part to make it look like a toad.

Grilled Chicken Ohio Style   USA

Marinate a prepared chicken in a mixture of 100 g English mustard, 50 ml melted butter, 50 ml maple syrup, 10 ml chilli sauce, 25 ml tomato ketchup, 25 ml cider vinegar and salt, celery salt and cayenne. Proceed as for Grilled Spring Chicken and serve accompanied by the heated marinade.

Grilled Chicken Texas Style USA

Blend 3 cloves of garlic, ½ tsp chilli powder, ¼ tsp cayenne and 50 ml lemon juice to a paste. Marinate a prepared chicken in the paste, then proceed as for Grilled Spring Chicken.

Grilled Chicken Tikka (Murgh Tikka) INDIA

75 ml sesame oil		3 × 1.5 kg jointed chickens
3 juice of lemons		3 lemons
2 tsp ground turmeric		picked parsley
1 tsp grated root ginger		
75 g chopped onion	blended	
600 ml yogurt	to a	
25 g ground coriander	paste	
1 tsp chilli powder		
3 crushed cloves of garlic		
1 tsp salt		

1. Marinate the skinned and boned chicken pieces for 12 hours in the blended mixture. Arrange on 10 skewers.
2. Grill the chicken pieces for 15 minutes, basting with the marinade until cooked.
3. Serve garnished with segments of lemon and picked parsley.

Note
This recipe can be served with Sambals (see p. 186).

Tandoori Chicken (Murgh Tandoori) INDIA

6 crushed cloves of garlic		3 × 1.5 kg jointed chickens
20 g grated ginger	marinade	125 g ghee
225 g yogurt		3 lemons
150 g tandoori masala		
225 ml water		

1. Combine the ingredients of the marinade and immerse the skinned pieces of chicken in it for 4 hours.
2. Grill or roast for 15 minutes, using a tandoori oven and basting frequently with the marinade.
3. Serve garnished with segments of lemon accompanied with boiled rice and Nan Bread.

Note
This recipe can be served with Sambals (see p. 186).

POACHING

Poached Chicken (Poulet Poché)

3×1.5 kg chickens
    2 carrots
    2 onions
  2 sticks celery

1 leek
1 bouquet garni
salt

1. Place the chickens in a deep pan and cover with cold water. Bring to the boil and skim.
2. Add the vegetables, bouquet garni and salt.
3. Simmer for 40 minutes, skimming occasionally.
4. When cooked, remove, cut into portions and serve with some of the strained cooking liquid. If required cold, retain in the liquid until cool, remove and cover with a damp cloth.

Chicken à la King

1.5 kg poached chicken breast
  75 g butter
 250 g button mushrooms
 150 g red pimentos
500 ml Sauce Suprême

600 g savoury rice
150 ml sherry or whiskey
   3 yolks ⎱ liaison
100 ml cream ⎰
seasoning

1. Heat the butter in a shallow pan, add the sliced mushrooms and skinned and diced pimentos, season and toss over until cooked.
2. Cut the chicken breasts into 5 mm slices on the slant, add to the pan, toss to mix in and reheat.
3. Add the alcohol and reduce slightly, then the sauce, and finish with the liaison but do not allow to boil.
4. Serve in an entrée dish with a border of savoury rice.

Hot Chicken Mousse (Mousse de Volaille)

500 g raw chicken breast
200 g frangipane panada
  2 egg whites

300 ml double cream
    salt, pepper and nutmeg
300 ml Sauce Suprême

1. Mince the chicken finely and pass through a sieve into a basin.
2. Mix in the warm panada and egg whites one by one, using a wooden spatule and working it hard.
3. Allow the mixture to rest, standing the basin in ice for 30 minutes.
4. Gradually add the cream, working it in well with a spatule and season.
5. Fill a buttered soufflé dish or 10 dariole moulds and cook au bain-marie in the oven at 200°C for 15–20 minutes. When the surface begins to colour, cover with a piece of kitchen foil or greaseproof paper.

6. When cooked, allow to rest for a few moments, turn out into a dish and serve on an underdish with a dish paper, masked with Sauce Suprême.

Notes
1. When cooked, the mousse should be firm to the touch. Insert a skewer into the centre, if the mousse is cooked, the skewer should be clean and free from any traces of soft, uncooked mixture when removed.
2. If the raw mixture will not absorb the cream it is because the mixture is not fine enough.
3. If the mousse disintegrates during cooking it is because the mixture was not fine enough.

Chicken Mousselines (Mousselines de Volaille)

Proceed as for Chicken Mousse but instead of cooking in moulds, form the mixture with two serving spoons into elongated oval shapes and place them into a buttered shallow dish. To cook, pour in hot seasoned chicken stock to cover, bring to the boil slowly and simmer for 10 minutes until they have puffed up slightly and are springy to the touch. Remove and drain, place in a serving dish and coat with Sauce Suprême. Suitable garnishes include asparagus tips, braised rice, fennel, mushrooms and crayfish.

Chicken Quenelles (Quenelles de Volaille)

These are made using the same ingredients and method as Mousselines of Chicken, moulding the mixture into oval shapes using two serving spoons, cooking and serving in the same way. The same mixture may be piped out as small fancy shapes for garnishing consommés or moulded with coffee spoons or tea spoons for bouchée and vol-au-vent fillings.

Chicken Pancakes with Mornay Sauce (Crêpes de Volaille Mornay)

750 g poached chicken	50 g grated Parmesan cheese
500 ml Sauce Suprême	50 g butter
20 savoury pancakes	seasoning
500 ml Mornay Sauce	

1. Cut the chicken into 1 cm dice and combine with the Sauce Suprême. Heat but do not boil and season to taste.
2. Lay out the pancakes on a work surface, divide the chicken mixture evenly between the pancakes and roll them up, folding the ends underneath.
3. Place a little sauce on the bottom of an earthenware dish and arrange the pancakes neatly, folded side down.
4. Coat with the Mornay Sauce, sprinkle with grated cheese and melted butter and glaze in a hot oven until hot and golden.

Chicken Vol-au-Vents (Vol-au-Vent de Volaille)

10 × 7 cm vol-au-vent cases
500 ml Sauce Suprême
1 kg poached chicken
sprigs of parsley
seasoning

1. Cut the chicken into 1.5 cm dice or into small pieces on the slant.
2. Place them into a shallow pan and add the sauce, mix in carefully, then heat gently to boiling point and season.
3. Heat the vol-au-vents and place in an entrée dish.
4. Fill the cases to overflowing with the chicken mixture, replace the pastry lids and garnish with sprigs of parsley.

Chicken and Mushroom Vol-au-Vents (Vol-au-Vent de Volaille et Champignons)

Using 750 g chicken, proceed as for Chicken Vol-au-Vents, with the addition of 250 g cooked button mushrooms.

Vol-au-Vents Toulousaine

Using 350 g cooked chicken, proceed as for Chicken Vol-au-Vents with the addition of 250 g diced braised sweetbreads, 200 g cooked button mushrooms and 250 g poached chicken quenelles moulded with teaspoons.

Poached Chicken with Rice and Supreme Sauce (Poularde Poché au Riz, Sauce Suprême)

3 × 1.75 kg chickens
500 ml Sauce Suprême
100 ml cream
seasoning
600 g savoury rice

1. Simmer the chickens in seasoned chicken stock for 1½ hours.
2. When cooked, remove the string and dissect the chickens on the bone, discarding the skin. Arrange in a dish, cover and keep warm.
3. Reduce 400 ml of the cooking liquid by two-thirds, add the sauce and cream and cook to a coating consistency.
4. Strain the sauce, pour over the chicken and serve accompanied by the dish of rice.

Notes
1. The chicken may be served whole, in which case the string and skin are removed and the chicken coated with the sauce. The rice is served separately.
2. The chicken may be carved, arranged on the rice and coated with the sauce.

Poached Chicken with Walnut Sauce (Satsivi)   RUSSIA

Poach a trussed chicken in water with carrot, onion, celery, bayleaf and thyme until nearly cooked. Remove the chicken, rub with salt and roast until lightly golden. Make a velouté from the liquor, flavoured with cloves, cinnamon and turmeric, strain and add finely ground walnuts. Coat portions of the chicken with the sauce and serve slightly chilled.

Poached Duck with Orange (Pato com   PORTUGAL
Arroz e Laranja)

Poach a duck in duck stock with a piece each of smoked ham and bacon, lemon juice and cloves. Brush the duck with butter and crisp the skin under the grill. Serve on a bed of braised rice made with duck stock with slices of the smoked ham and bacon and of chorizo sausage. Garnish with segments of orange.

POT-ROASTING

Pot-Roasted Chicken (Poulet en Cocotte)

175 g	sliced carrot		
175 g	sliced onion		3 × 1.75 kg chickens
125 g	sliced celery		100 g butter
75 g	bacon trimmings	bed of	500 ml jus lié
1	bayleaf	root	10 g chopped parsley
1 sprig	thyme	vegetables	seasoning
few	parsley stalks		
1	crushed clove garlic		

1. Butter and season a deep pan sufficiently large to allow room for basting the chickens, with a lid that does not touch the chickens.
2. Place the bed of root vegetables in the bottom of the pan.
3. Season the chickens and place on top and coat with the melted butter.
4. Cover with a lid and pot-roast in the oven at 180°C for 1 hour, basting from time to time.
5. Remove the lid and allow the chickens to colour for a further 20 minutes, basting occasionally, then remove and place in cocottes, cover and keep warm.
6. Place the pan on top of the stove, letting the vegetables colour slightly, add the jus lié and simmer until the flavour from the juices and butter has been absorbed into the sauce.
7. Pass through a fine strainer, reboil and skim off the fat. Season to taste and correct the consistency so that it coats the chickens.
8. Coat the chickens with the sauce, sprinkle with chopped parsley; replace the lids and serve.

Note

The terms 'en cocotte' and 'en casserole' are used to denote that the poultry has been pot-roasted in an earthenware or metal casserole, in which it is served. There is no difference between the two terms. It is more practical to pot-roast chickens in a braising pan and to serve them whole or carved in the casserole.

Pot-Roasted Chicken Bonne Femme (Poulet en Cocotte Bonne Femme)

Proceed as for Pot-Roasted Chicken, with the addition of olivette potatoes, brown-glazed button onions and lightly fried lardons of bacon.

Pot-Roasted Chicken Champeaux (Poulet en Cocotte Champeaux)

Proceed as for Pot-Roasted Chicken. When making the gravy swill the pan with 200 ml dry white wine, reduce by two-thirds, then add the jus lié. Garnish with olivette potatoes and brown-glazed button onions.

Pot-Roasted Chicken Grand'Mère (Poulet Poêlé Grand'Mère)

Proceed as for Pot-Roasted Chicken, with the addition of sautéed, quartered button mushrooms and diced fried bread croûtons.

Casserole of Chicken with Vegetables (Poulet en Casserole Paysanne)

Proceed as for Pot-Roasted Chicken, with the addition of glazed mixed vegetables cut paysanne-shape.

Pot-Roasted Duckling with Cherries (Caneton Poêlé aux Cerises)

Proceed as for Pot-Roasted Chicken. When making the gravy swill the pan with 200 ml Madeira, reduce by two-thirds, then add 500 ml jus lié. Add stoned cherries to the sauce and pour over the ducks.

Pot-Roasted Duckling with Orange Sauce (Caneton Poêlé à l'Orange)

3 × 2 kg ducklings		100 g butter
175 g sliced carrot		1 litre jus lié
175 g sliced onion		20 ml vinegar
125 g sliced celery	bed of	50 g sugar
1 bayleaf	root	3 juice of oranges
1 sprig thyme	vegetables	½ juice of lemon
few parsley stalk		seasoning
1 crushed clove garlic		3 oranges

1. Butter and season a deep pan sufficiently large to afford room for basting and cover with a lid without touching the ducks.
2. Place the bed of root vegetables in the bottom of the pan.
3. Season the ducks and place on the vegetables. Coat with the melted butter.
4. Cover with a lid and pot-roast in the oven at 180°C for 1½ hours, basting from time to time.
5. Remove the lid and allow to colour for a further 15 minutes.
6. Remove and keep warm.
7. Place the pan on top of the stove, letting the vegetables colour slightly, add the jus lié and simmer until the flavour from the juices and butter has been absorbed into the sauce. Pass through a fine strainer, reboil and skim off the fat.
8. Place the sugar and a little water in a saucepan. Boil and cook to a light caramel, then add the vinegar to stop the caramel darkening. Reduce by half and add the orange and lemon juices.
9. Add to the sauce, simmer gently for 5 minutes and skim. Strain into a clean saucepan, season and add the blanched strips of orange peel and complete with knobs of butter.
10. Carve the ducks into portions and serve on an oval dish; coat with the sauce and garnish each portion with the warmed segments of orange.

Poussin Polonaise

Stuff poussins with a mixture of 100 g white breadcrumbs soaked in 200 ml milk and 500 g game liver farce and proceed as for Pot-Roasted Chicken. When serving, heat 250 g butter in a small frying pan, add 150 g white breadcrumbs and fry until golden, pour over the poussins and finish with the juice of lemon and chopped parsley.

Pot-Roasted Chicken Hamburg Style (Stubenküken)   GERMANY

Stuff chickens with chicken liver, mushroom and basil stuffing then proceed as for Pot-Roasted Chicken. Carve and serve with portions of the stuffing.

Pot-Roasted Chicken Stuffed with Spiced Rice   GREECE
and Pine-nuts (Tavuk Dolmasi)

Shallow fry 75 g chopped onion and 175 g diced chicken livers in 50 ml vegetable oil; add 75 g pine-nuts, 50 g currants and combine with 1 kg boiled long grain rice. Season with 1 tsp ground cinnamon, ½ tsp allspice, salt and pepper. Fill into the cavity of the chicken, sprinkle with lemon juice, oil and marjoram and proceed as for Pot-Roasted Chicken.

Pot-Roasted Duck with Morello Cherries   GERMANY
(Ente Mit Sauerkirschen)

Proceed as for Pot-Roasted Duckling. Reduce 100 ml Madeira by half and add to the cooking liquor. Add 500 g stoned morello cherries, cook for 5 minutes, then finish with 50 ml kirsch. Serve the duck masked with the sauce and cherries.

ROASTING

Roast Chicken (Poulet Rôti)

3 × 1.5 kg chickens
salt
100 ml dripping
500 ml brown stock

1 bunch watercress
150 g Game Chips
200 ml Bread Sauce

1. Season the chickens inside and out.
2. Select a roasting tray large enough to allow the birds to be moved around around during cooking. Lay them on their sides, pour over the melted dripping and place in the oven at 200°C.
3. After 15 minutes, turn the birds onto the other side for a similar period, basting from time to time, then lay them on their backs with the breasts uppermost and continue to roast for a further 15 minutes.
4. For the last 15 minutes of roasting, stack the birds on the neck ends against the bottom of the roasting tray with the breasts downwards to allow the juices to lubricate the flesh.
5. When cooked, remove from the roasting tray and stack in a tray. Any juices should be used for making the gravy.
6. Drain off all fat and allow the sediment to remain in the roasting tray.
7. Add the stock and simmer gently for a few minutes.
8. Strain into a saucepan, reboil, skim off the fat and season to taste.
9. Remove the strings from the chickens and serve on an oval flat dish with a little of the gravy. Garnish with picked watercress and Game Chips, accompanied by sauceboats of roast gravy and Bread Sauce.

Notes
1. To test if cooked, hold the chicken over a dish and allow the juice to flow into it which should be quite clear.
2. Chicken may be carved into portions for service.

Roast Chicken Stuffed with Chicken Livers
(Pollo Ripieno al Forno)

Sauté 500 g chopped chicken livers, combine with 500 g fried breadcrumbs, 3 beaten eggs, 50 ml milk, 25 ml cream, 80 g grated Pecorino cheese and seasoning. Enrobe 10 hard-boiled eggs with this stuffing, place inside the birds and proceed as for Roast Chicken.

Roast Chicken Stuffed with Ham (Pollo allo Spiedo)

Combine 500 g chopped ham, 4 cloves of chopped garlic, 20 g sage, 20 g rosemary and 400 g breadcrumbs. Stuff the birds with it, brush with olive oil, sprinkle with sage and rosemary and leave for 1 hour. Bard the chicken with thin slices of smoked ham and proceed as for Roast Chicken.

Roast Chicken with Bacon (Poulet Rôti au Lard)

Proceed as for Roast Chicken and serve garnished with grilled rashers of bacon.

Roast Chicken with Thyme and Parsley Stuffing (Poulet Rôti à l'Anglaise)

Stuff each chicken with 175 g thyme and parsley stuffing and proceed as for Roast Chicken.

Roast Duckling with Orange Salad (Caneton Rôti, Salade d'Orange)

Proceed as for Roast Chicken and serve garnished with warm segments of orange and blanched julienne of orange zest, accompanied with a salad of lettuce leaves, orange segments and a sauceboat of acidulated cream dressing.

Roast Stuffed Duck (Canard Rôti à l'Anglaise)

Stuff a 2.5 kg duck with Sage and Onion Stuffing, truss and roast at 200°C first on one side, then on the other and finally on its back to colour, cooking evenly for a total of 2¼ hours. Decant the fat from the roasting tray, deglaze with brown duck stock to make the gravy and serve with the duck cut into slices or portions with the stuffing, accompanied with Apple Sauce.

Roast Guinea Fowl (Pintade Rôti)

Prepare, cook and serve as for Roast Chicken.

Roast Stuffed Goose (Oie Rôtie à l'Anglaise)

Prepare, cook and serve as for Roast Stuffed Duck.

Roast Whole Turkey

1. Allowing 225 g turkey raw weight per portion, place the turkey on one side in a roasting tray and baste with melted dripping and roast as for Roast Chicken. It may be stuffed at the neck end with an appropriate stuffing.
2. To test if a turkey is cooked, pierce the thigh with a trussing needle and press the flesh to extract some of the juice. If clear, the turkey is cooked. The best way to check is to use a probe, inserted at a point 2.5 cm from

the wing joint, which must show a final internal temperature of 80°. The traditional way of calculating cooking time was to allow 20 minutes per 500 g, but though this works for a smallish bird a 10 kg one works out at 6½ hours, which is obviously far too long nowadays when turkeys are battery-reared.

3. Turkey may be served with any of the following: watercress, Bread Sauce, Cranberry Sauce, braised chestnuts, grilled chipolata sausages, grilled bacon, slices of ham, and game chips.
4. The gravy should be made from brown stock derived from the giblets and bones. It may be thickened with arrowroot and is best if cooked for at least 30 minutes; the sediment from the roasting tray should be used in the gravy.

Roast Stuffed Turkey (Dindonneau Rôti à l'Anglaise)

1 × 5 kg turkey	brown turkey stock
salt	2 bunches watercress
100 ml dripping	500 ml Cranberry Sauce
1 kg Thyme and Parsley Stuffing	

1. Remove each leg by cutting around the skin to the ball and socket joint at the bottom of the carcass. Fold back at the joint, cut through and take off the leg. Repeat for the other leg.
2. Bone out the legs, removing all sinews.
3. Lay each leg out on foil with the skin side down and overlap the flesh where necessary to form a continuous length.
4. Season with salt and place a 5 cm thick roll of the stuffing along the length of each leg. Roll up in the foil and twist at each end of the roll to prevent the stuffing seeping out during cooking.
5. Place into a roasting tray, not allowing the legs to touch one another. Add a little water and cook in the oven at 180°C for 1 hour.
6. Place the trunk into a separate roasting tray, season with salt inside and outside, coat with the melted dripping and place in the oven to roast at 180°C for 1½ hours. Baste occasionally during cooking.
7. When cooked, remove from the roasting tray and retain, preferably standing on a wire grid. Any juices collected may be used to make the gravy.
8. Place the roasting tray on the stove and gently heat, allowing the sediment to settle. Drain off the fat and allow the sediment to remain in the tray.
9. Add the thickened brown stock and allow to simmer for 30 minutes. Strain through a fine conical strainer into a saucepan. Reboil, skim all traces of fat and season to taste.
10. Carve the turkey into thin slices and serve a slice each of breast and leg including the stuffing. Moisten with a little of the gravy. Additional garnishes can include chipolatas, bacon rolls, chipolatas rolled in bacon, braised chestnuts and Bread Sauce.

Note
The 5 kg turkey in this recipe should yield 20 portions.

Peking Duck (Peh-ching K'ao Ya)

3 × 2 kg ducks	500 ml Plum Sauce
100 g honey	30 Mandarin Pancakes
75 ml water	10 spring onions
1 tsp salt	225 g cucumber

1. Plunge the trussed ducks into boiling water for a few moments, then drain and hang to dry in a cool place for 12 hours.
2. Three hours before roasting the ducks, brush them with a solution of the honey, water and salt and hang again to dry.
3. Roast the ducks in the oven at 200°C for 1½ hours until well cooked and the skin very crisp.
4. Serve the crisp skin and flesh both cut into small pieces, accompanied by mandarin pancakes (see below), Plum Sauce, strips of spring onions and strips of cucumber.

Mandarin Pancakes

Beat 225 ml boiling water onto 500 g sifted plain flour and knead well to a smooth dough. Allow to rest, then divide into 20 pieces and roll out to 8 cm in diameter. Brush one circle lightly with sesame oil, place another circle on top and roll flat until 17 cm in diameter. Cook on a non-greased griddle plate until cooked on both sides and a few golden bubbles appear. Remove from the griddle plate, gently peel each pancake apart into two and retain. Continue to brush, roll out and cook the other rounds of dough. Place the pancakes on a clean cloth and reheat in a steamer.

Serve with Peking Duck.

Roast Chicken Stuffed with Rice (Amich)

Combine boiled rice with soaked and chopped apricots, soaked raisins, chopped almonds, hazelnuts and basil. Season with ground cloves and cinnamon, then stuff the chicken with the mixture and roast in the usual way, allowing additional time to cook the stuffing.

Roast Chicken Stuffed with Rice and Pine-nuts (Ornitha Kokkinisti)

Fill the cavity of a chicken with 500 g braised rice mixed with pine-nuts, then proceed as for Roast Chicken. Swill the roasting tray with 500 ml chicken stock, add 50 g tomato purée and 3 crushed cloves of garlic, then strain and serve as the gravy.

Roast Chicken with Orange Sauce (Pollo Asado con Salsa de Naranja)   SPAIN

Proceed as for Roast Chicken. Pour off the fat and swill with 150 ml each of chicken stock and jus lié. Boil 200 g sugar and a little water until it begins to caramelise, then add a little vinegar and 100 ml orange juice, add to the gravy and simmer for a few minutes, then strain. Serve the chicken cut into portions, coated with the sauce and accompanied by Orange Salad.

Roast Goose with Apples and Prunes (Stekt Gas)   SCANDINAVIA

Stuff a goose with poached and stoned prunes mixed with lightly sautéed sliced apple, then roast. Swill the roasting pan with the liquor from cooking the prunes and red wine and reduce by half; add jus lié and finish with pieces of butter.

Roast Goose with Walnut, Ginger and Onion Stuffing   USA

Stuff a goose with 500 g walnut, ginger and onion stuffing; rub over with a lemon then proceed as for Roast Duck. Swill the pan with 25 ml brandy, add 500 ml jus lié and finish with pieces of butter.

SHALLOW FRYING

Breaded chicken dishes

Breaded Supreme of Chicken (Suprême de Volaille Panée et Sautée)

10 supremes of chicken	200 ml butter or oil
flour ⎫	300 ml jus lié
eggwash ⎬ for	150 g nut-brown butter
breadcrumbs ⎭ coating	

1. Season the supremes and pass through flour, eggwash and breadcrumbs, then mark trellis-fashion.
2. Heat the butter or oil or a mixture of each in a plat à sauter.
3. Place the supremes in the fat, presentation side downwards, and shallow fry until golden. Turn and fry on the other side.
4. Arrange the supremes on a flat dish, and surround with a thread of the jus lié. Finish with the nut-brown butter and serve the remainder of the jus lié separately.

Chicken Maryland

Proceed as for Breaded Supremes of Chicken and garnish with 10 grilled small tomatoes, 10 grilled rashers of bacon, 10 breadcrumbed and deep-fried halves of banana, and 10 small sweetcorn galettes. Serve Horseradish Sauce separately.

Supreme of Chicken Doria (Suprême de Volaille Doria)

Proceed as for Breaded Supremes of Chicken and garnish with 500 g cucumber cut into small diamond-shaped pieces, cooked in butter for a few moments.

Supreme of Chicken Maréchale (Suprême de Volaille Maréchale)

Proceed as for Breaded Supremes of Chicken and garnish each portion with three asparagus tips and a slice of truffle.

Supreme of Chicken with Cream Cheese and Parma Ham (Pollo alla Valdostano)

Spread flattened boneless supremes of chicken with cream cheese mixed with grated Parmesan cheese and chopped chives. Place a slice of Parma ham on top of each and fold over, pass through flour, eggwash and breadcrumbs, then proceed as for Breaded Supremes of Chicken. Serve surrounded with a thread of jus lié.

Supreme of Chicken with Smoked Ham (Pollo alla Bolognese)

Sauté floured supremes in butter, then place a slice of smoked ham on top of each, sprinkle with grated Parmesan cheese and cook under a salamander grill until the cheese melts.

Supreme of Chicken Viennese Style (Wiener Backhendl)

GERMANY

Marinate boned supremes of chicken in 100 ml lemon juice seasoned with paprika, then proceed as for Breaded Supremes of Chicken.

STIR-FRYING

Stir-Fried Chicken with Almonds (Sien Gu Lu To Yan)

CHINA

Pass 1.5 kg strips of chicken through a mixture of cornflour, five-spice powder and soft brown sugar, then marinate in 20 ml each of light and dark soy sauces and saké. Heat 50 ml sesame oil in a wok, golden fry 75 g skinned almonds, remove and retain. Add the strips of chicken to the wok and stir-fry for 5 minutes, remove and retain. Add 20 g grated ginger, 75 g strips of green pepper, 50 g strips of leek and 200 g beansprouts to the wok and stir-fry for 2 minutes. Replace the chicken, moisten with the marinade, season, cook for 2 minutes and serve sprinkled with the almonds.

SAUTÉEING

Chicken Sauté Champeaux

3 × 1.5 kg chickens	5 g chopped parsley
100 g butter	50 g butter
150 g chopped shallots	20 brown-glazed
200 ml dry white wine	button onions ⎫ garnish
500 ml jus lié	30 pieces cocotte potatoes ⎭

1. Heat the butter in a thick-bottomed shallow pan.
2. Season and add the chicken pieces and shallow fry until golden on all sides. Cover with a lid and allow to finish cooking slowly for 20 minutes.
3. Remove and place in an earthenware dish to keep warm.
4. Add the shallots to the pan and sauté for a few moments, then drain off the fat.
5. Add the wine, boil and reduce by half. Add the jus lié and simmer gently until the sauce has a light coating consistency. Finish with chopped parsley and knobs of butter and season to taste.
6. Add the glazed onions and cocotte potatoes to the chicken, coat with the sauce and serve.

Notes
1. Where large numbers of portions are cooked it will be advantageous to cook the legs and thighs in one pan and the wings, winglets and breasts in another. Keeping the white and dark pieces separate helps in the serving as each portion consists of one piece of white and one of dark flesh.
2. When the chicken is cooked it may be covered with a lid and kept warm in the oven at a moderate temperature.
3. It is general trade practice to make the sauce separately from the chicken, bringing them together at the time of service.
4. Some chefs pass the chicken through flour before sautéeing, to give it a better colour. This, of course, thickens the finished sauce so a thin jus lié should be used to reduce with the wine. If it is too thin a little diluted arrowroot may be added.
5. The chicken carcass should be used in making the jus lié, or it may be sautéed at the same time as the pieces, which can be built up around it in the serving dish.
6. To test if cooked, remove a piece each of leg and breast and test by finger pressure – the thigh and drumstick should yield until the bone is felt and the breast be firm and resilient to the touch.

Poulet Sauté Bercy

Proceed as for Chicken Sauté Champeaux and garnish with 20 grilled small chipolata sausages and 30 button mushrooms cooked in lemon juice.

Poulet Sauté Bonne Femme

Proceed as for Chicken Sauté Champeaux and garnish with 20 brown-glazed button onions, 250 g fried lardons of bacon and 30 pieces of cocotte potatoes.

Poulet Sauté Bourguignonne

Proceed as for Chicken Sauté Champeaux, substituting red wine for white wine. Garnish with 20 brown-glazed button onions, 250 g fried lardons of bacon, 30 button mushrooms cooked in lemon juice and 10 heart-shaped croûtons.

Poulet Sauté aux Champignons

Proceed as for Chicken Sauté Champeaux, adding 500 g sliced button mushrooms just before the shallots.

Chicken Sauté Chasseur (Poulet Sauté Chasseur)

3 × 1.5 kg chickens	10 g chopped tarragon
150 g butter	500 ml jus lié
250 g sliced button mushrooms	5 g chopped parsley
150 g chopped shallots	50 g butter
250 g tomato concassée	seasoning
200 ml white wine	

1. Heat the butter in a thick-bottomed shallow pan.
2. Season the chicken pieces and shallow fry until golden on all sides. Cover with a lid and allow to finish cooking slowly for 20 minutes.
3. Remove the chicken and place in an earthenware dish to keep warm.
4. Drain off the fat, then add the mushrooms, sauté quickly, then add the shallot and cook for a few moments.
5. Add the tomato concassée, the wine, and the tarragon, boil and reduce by half.
6. Add the jus lié and simmer gently until the sauce has a light coating consistency.
7. Finish with chopped parsley and knobs of butter and season to taste. Pour over the chicken, sprinkle with chopped tarragon and serve.

Note
Poulet Sauté Cacciatore is the name given to the Italian version of this dish, which is virtually the same.

Poulet Sauté Hongroise

3 × 1.5 kg chickens	750 ml white stock
150 g butter	200 g diced tomatoes
500 g chopped onion	200 ml cream

50 g paprika	500 g savoury rice ⎱ mixed
25 g flour	150 g tomato concassée ⎰ together
25 g tomato purée	seasoning

1. Heat the butter in a thick-bottomed shallow pan.
2. Season the chicken pieces and shallow fry without coloration. Cover with a lid and allow to finish cooking slowly for 20 minutes.
3. Remove and place in an earthenware dish to keep warm.
4. Add the onion to the pan and cook for a few moments without colouring.
5. Add the paprika, flour and tomato purée, stirring with a wooden spatule. Add the stock and allow to simmer for 10 minutes. Add the diced tomato, boil, then simmer gently until the sauce is of a light coating consistency.
6. Add the cream, season to taste, and place the chicken in the sauce.
7. Serve in a dish surrounded with a border of the savoury rice previously mixed with the cooked tomato concassée.

Poulet Sauté Madras

Sauté chicken pieces in hot ghee and arrange in an earthenware dish. Cover with Curry Sauce and serve accompanied with boiled rice and a selection of sambals such as chutney, sliced banana, stem ginger, lime, grated coconut and the traditional accompaniments of poppadums and Bombay ducks.

Supreme of Chicken with Mushrooms in Cream Sauce
(Suprême de Volaille à la Crème et Champignons)

10 × 125 g supremes of chicken	600 ml chicken velouté
100 g melted butter	200 ml cream
250 g button mushrooms	seasoning
200 ml dry sherry	

1. Heat the butter in a thick-bottomed pan.
2. Place in the seasoned supremes and shallow fry until light golden on both sides for a total time of 8 minutes, then neatly arrange them on an oval dish.
3. Add the mushrooms to the pan and cook quickly.
4. Add the sherry, boil and reduce by half. Add the velouté and the cream and reduce to a consistency that will coat the supremes.
5. Season to taste, pour over the supremes and serve.

Ballotines

A ballotine of chicken is a leg of chicken with the bone removed, stuffed with Chicken Forcemeat and tied. They may be cooked in the same way as any of the sautéed chicken dishes above, e.g. Ballotine of Chicken Bonne Femme, Ballotine of Chicken Chasseur.

Sautéed Chicken Livers with Savoury Rice
(Pilaff de Foies de Volaille)

```
  1 kg  chicken livers
 50 ml  oil
500 ml  Madeira Sauce
500 g   savoury rice
        seasoning
```

1. Heat the oil in a thick-bottomed shallow-sided pan.
2. Season and add the prepared liver pieces. Quickly shallow fry, keeping them slightly underdone, then drain off the fat.
3. Add the sauce to the livers and season to taste, reheat but do not boil.
4. Place the savoury rice in a dish, slightly dome-shape, make an indentation in the centre. Fill with the livers and sauce and pour a thread of sauce around the outer edge of the rice.

Note

A savarin ring can be used to mould the rice in a round dish and the centre filled with the livers and sauce. Alternatively, a basin may be used by lining it with the rice, filling with the livers and sauce and sealing with more rice. Turn out onto the dish and surround with a thread of Madeira Sauce.

Chicken and Oyster Gumbo   USA

Sauté chicken pieces quickly; remove and place in a dish. Cook 100 g chopped onion, 2 chopped cloves of garlic and 100 g each of diced celery and green pimento in the same pan. Moisten with 500 ml jus lié, add 10 g flaked dried red chillies, 1 bayleaf, 1 sprig of thyme, salt, ground cloves and allspice. Add the chicken pieces to the sauce with 10 lightly poached oysters, 10 g chopped parsley, 50 g sliced spring onions and a little Worcester sauce. Serve accompanied by boiled rice. If desired 200 g cooked okra may be added when the chicken is placed in the sauce.

Chicken Vindaloo (Kholee Vindaloo)   INDIA

```
  3     green chillies           ⎫        3 × 1.5 kg  jointed chickens
  3     dried red chillies       ⎪         75 ml      oil
  8     cloves of garlic         ⎪        100 g       chopped onion
 10 g   coriander (ground)       ⎪        600 ml      chicken stock
 10 g   cumin (ground)           ⎪         75 g       garam masala
 25 g   turmeric ground)         ⎬ blended
 12     cloves (ground)          ⎪ to a
 25 g   fenugreek                ⎪ paste
 75 ml  lemon juice              ⎪
175 ml  vinegar                  ⎪
 12     peeled cardamom          ⎪
        seeds                    ⎪
  2     bayleaves                ⎭
```

1. Season the skinned chicken pieces and shallow fry in oil until golden brown on all sides. Cover with a lid and allow to cook very slowly for 30 minutes.
2. When nearly cooked, drain off the surplus oil, spread the paste over the chicken joints, replace the lid and continue to cook, together with the chopped onion.
3. Moisten with the stock and add the garam masala; simmer for another 5 minutes covered with a lid and serve accompanied by boiled rice.

Sauté of Chicken Hungarian Style (Csirke Paprika)   HUNGARY

Sauté chicken pieces, remove, then add chopped onion and garlic and fry; stir in paprika, diced tomato flesh and caraway seeds, then moisten with chicken stock and cook for 20 minutes. Strain and reduce the cooking liquor, garnish with cooked julienne of green pimento and finish with soured cream.

Sauté of Chicken Teriyaki (Tori No Teriyaki)   JAPAN

Sauté 3×1.5 kg chicken pieces in 50 ml oil, remove and retain. Drain off surplus oil from the pan, moisten with 125 ml Japanese soy sauce and 50 ml mirin, add 30 g sugar and cook until the sauce is almost completely reduced. Cut the chicken pieces into slices, coat with the reduced sauce and serve sprinkled with sansho pepper.

Sauté of Chicken with Dumplings   USA

Sauté chicken pieces, remove and place in a shallow dish to keep warm. Place 100 g each of cooked chopped onion and celery, including the leaves, in the pan; moisten with 200 ml dry white wine and 500 ml stock, season with salt, pepper and allspice and simmer for 5 minutes. Lightly thicken with 50 g diluted arrowroot and finish with 200 ml cream and 25 g chopped parsley. Coat the chicken pieces, then place circles of dumpling dough on top, cover with a lid and cook in an oven at 170°C until the dumplings are cooked.

Note
For dumplings rub 200 g butter into 450 g flour sifted with 25 g baking powder and a pinch each of salt and sugar. Add 100 ml milk and mix to a dough. Roll out 1 cm thick and cut out 20×6 cm rounds.

Sauté of Chicken Mole Style   USA

Sauté chicken pieces, remove and place in an earthenware dish. Add 100 g chopped onion to the pan, cook for a few minutes, then moisten with 200 ml red wine vinegar and a blended paste of 6 fresh green chillies, 3 cloves of garlic and 250 g tomato flesh. Moisten with 300 ml tomato juice, then add 125 g grated unsweetened chocolate; allow to simmer for 10 minutes and finish with chopped parsley. Coat the chicken pieces with the sauce and serve.

Sauté of Chicken in Sherry Sauce with Almonds (Pollo en Pepitoria)

SPAIN

Sauté chicken pieces, remove and place in an earthenware dish. Add 100 g chopped onion, 3 chopped cloves of garlic, 200 g small strips of jamón serrano and 20 g chopped parsley to the pan and cook until the onion is tender. Moisten with 100 ml sherry and 400 ml chicken stock, add a few strands of saffron and season with salt, pepper and nutmeg. Process blanched almonds in a blender with the cooking liquor and lightly thicken with 25 g diluted arrowroot. Pour over the chicken, sprinkle with sieved hard-boiled eggs and serve.

Chicken Sauté with Figs (Pollo con Higos)

SPAIN

Boil 500 ml water, 100 ml white wine vinegar, 100 g sugar, 1 lemon cut into slices and 1 cinnamon stick for 10 minutes; add 30 fresh figs and simmer for 10 minutes, then leave for several hours. Drain the figs and place in medium-sweet white wine with grated zest of lemon. Sauté chicken pieces, remove and place in an earthenware dish. Fry 150 g lardons of bacon in the pan, moisten with the wine from the figs and 300 ml chicken stock and boil to reduce to a light sauce. Pour over the chicken, garnish with the figs and serve.

Sauté of Chicken with Lemon (Ornitha Lemonáti)

GREECE

Marinate chicken pieces in 100 ml lemon juice and chopped parsley. Sauté in olive oil, remove and place in an earthenware dish. Add 100 g chopped onion and 3 chopped cloves of garlic to the pan, cook for a few minutes, then moisten with the marinade, 100 ml dry white wine and 400 ml chicken stock and add the grated zest of 3 lemons. Simmer, then thicken with 25 g diluted arrowroot. Pour over the chicken and serve.

Sautéed Chicken Livers with Mushrooms (Kyckling Lever med Svamp)

SCANDINAVIA

Sauté seasoned chicken livers and button mushrooms in oil, remove and retain. Swill the pan with sherry, then add cream. Replace the livers and mushrooms, reheat without boiling and serve.

Sautéed Goujons of Turkey with Lemon and Saffron (Pavo en Pepitoria)

SPAIN

Blend 500 g golden-fried breadcrumbs, 3 chopped cloves of garlic, 20 g parsley, the juice and grated zest of 2 lemons, a few strands of saffron, 2 crushed bayleaves and 500 ml chicken stock to a sauce consistency and season with cinnamon, cumin and paprika. Sauté goujons of turkey quickly in olive oil with 100 g chopped onion, then add to the hot sauce and serve.

STEWING

Chicken Fricassée (Fricassée de Volaille)

10 portions of chicken, cut for sautéeing	200 ml cream ⎱ liaison
100 g butter	3 egg yolks ⎰
100 g flour	10 heart-shaped croûtons
1.5 litres chicken stock	10 g chopped parsley
1 bouquet garni	seasoning

1. Melt the butter gently in a shallow pan. Season the chicken pieces, place in the butter and cover with a lid. Allow to set without coloration.
2. Sprinkle with the flour and stir it in gently with a wooden spatule to form a roux. Cook to a second stage and allow to cool slightly.
3. Add the hot stock a little at a time. Bring to the boil, skim, add the bouquet garni, cover with a lid and cook in the oven at 180°C for 40 minutes.
4. Remove the bouquet garni and place the chicken in a clean pan.
5. Whisk the liaison into the sauce and cook gently until it thickens but do not allow it to boil. Season to taste.
6. Serve the chicken neatly arranged in an entrée dish, coated with the sauce.
7. Dip the tips of the croûtons in some of the sauce, then into chopped parsley, arrange around the chicken and serve.

Chicken Fricassée with Vegetables (Fricassée de Poulet aux Légumes)

Proceed as for Chicken Fricassée. Garnish with 250 g mixed vegetables cut into dice or jardinière.

Brunswick Stew   USA

Cut poached chicken into 1 cm dice, place into a pan, barely cover with chicken stock, then add 350 g diced potatoes, 250 g diced tomato flesh, 200 g sweetcorn kernels and 200 g cooked lima beans and seasoning. Simmer until potatoes are cooked and serve sprinkled with chopped parsley.

CHAPTER 9 # Game

FEATHERED AND FURRED GAME

Game is a seasonal commodity that adds a lot of interest to menus from Autumn to Spring. There are 10 game birds that can be cooked in several different ways. Venison, either farmed or wild, is the meat from several kinds of deer. Hare, rabbit, wild boar, bison, goat and kangaroo also come under the heading of furred game. Ostrich meat is widely available and alligator and crocodile meat can add interest to a menu.

Quails are game birds which are bred in captivity and are thus available throughout the year.

ROASTING GAME BIRDS AND VENISON

Hanging grouse and pheasant for a short time helps to improve their flavour and tenderness. Game birds are trussed in the same way as chickens. To protect all game birds except wild duck from drying out during roasting they should be barded with rashers of streaky bacon or salt pork fat. It should be removed for the final minutes of cooking so as to colour the breast; it is served with the bird. Game birds are roasted at a temperature of 220°C. All garnishes, with the exception of the roast gravy which is prepared with

	No. of portions per bird	Cooking time	Degree of cooking	Internal temp
Feathered game				
Grouse	1	20 min	Rare or medium	65°C
Partridge	1	20 min	Just cooked	80°C
Pheasant	3–4	45 min	Just cooked	80°C
Plover	2 per portion	15 min	Just cooked	80°C
Quail	2 per portion	10 min	Just cooked	80°C
Snipe	1	10 min	Just cooked	80°C
Wild duck	2	25 min	Rare or just cooked	65°C
Woodcock	1	10 min	Just cooked	80°C
Furred Game				
Hare (Saddle)	1 × 500 g	20 min	Rare or slightly underdone	65°C
Venison (Saddle)	3 kg per 10 portions	2 hours	Rare or slightly underdone	65°C

juices from the roast, should be prepared while cooking the bird. This will ensure that the bird can be served immediately it is cooked. Venison is generally marinated before being cooked, after which it is placed on a trivet or on chopped bones, seasoned with salt and, if desired, pepper, and coated with dripping before being placed in a hot oven to roast. The other game birds are rarely available to order, e.g. blackcock and capercaillie; pigeons are classified as poultry. Game birds are not sold by weight but are priced by the brace.

SKINNING A HARE OR RABBIT

To remove the skin of a hare or rabbit: hold a hind leg, lift the skin and slit it to form an opening large enough to insert two fingers. Manipulate the fingers between the skin and the flesh to disconnect the connective tissue. Remove the skin from each leg through the incision and cut off the tail. Holding both hind legs in one hand, pull the skin gently towards the forelegs, removing it in the same way as for the hind legs and drawing the skin over the head to the ears. Cut off the ears, then remove the skin from the head, cutting the skin away from the mouth with a small knife.

BAKING

Game Pie (Pâté de Gibier)

4 breasts of pheasants	5 g chopped parsley
6 breasts of partridges	400 ml game stock
4 breasts of grouse	few drops Worcester sauce
350 g farce à gratin	650 g puff pastry
(made with livers)	eggwash
200 g streaky bacon	seasoning
50 g chopped onion	

1. Stretch the streaky rashers to double their length and line 2×22 cm pie dishes, leaving some overhanging around the edges.
2. Flatten the skinned breasts of game, season and arrange a layer in the pie dishes, then cover with a 1 cm layer of the game farce. Alternate them to fill the dishes dome-shape.
3. Turn back the overhanging rashers; season the stock, add the Worcester sauce and pour into the pie dishes.

4. Roll out the pastry 4 mm thick; cut 1.5 cm strips and lay on the dampened edges of the pie dishes. Brush with eggwash and cover with a sheet of pastry, sealing it firmly.
5. Cut off the surplus pastry, crimp the edges, brush with eggwash, and make a small hole in the centre; decorate with pastry leaves and brush with eggwash.
6. Refrigerate for 1 hour, then place in the oven at 220°C for 15 minutes, reduce the heat to 150°C and bake for another hour. Serve encircled with pie frills.

Note
Other kinds of pies, both hot and cold, can be made with all kinds of game birds and venison, alone or mixed or with ordinary meat, e.g. Grouse and Steak Pie made with Guinness Stout.

Rabbit and Mushroom Pie

Proceed as for Chicken and Mushroom Pie, substituting 1.5 kg jointed rabbit for the chicken.

BRAISING

Braised Partridge with Mushrooms
(Stekta Rapphöns med Champinjoner)

SCANDINAVIA

Seal old partridges in oil, moisten with Madeira and stock, add browned button onions and quartered button mushrooms, then braise at 180°C for 1 hour. Thicken the cooking liquor with arrowroot, finish with cream and pour over the partridges.

Braised Quail with Grapes
(Codornices Braseadas con Uvas)

SPAIN

Colour 20 quails in 50 ml hot olive oil together with 450 g sliced Spanish onions, 350 g mushrooms cut in quarters, 225 g diced carrot, 2 bayleaves and a sprig of thyme, then place in a braising pan. Liquidise 12 peppercorns, $1/2$ tsp grated nutmeg, 6 cloves of garlic, 450 g grapes, 150 ml Spanish brandy and 600 ml white wine in a blender. Add to the quails together with 450 g seedless grapes, cover and braise at 240°C for 20 minutes. When cooked, remove the bayleaves and thyme, reduce the cooking liquid by half and thicken slightly. Pour over the quails. Serve two per portion, coated with the sauce and its vegetables.

Braised Quail with Pimento

Sprinkle quails with salt and lemon juice, then seal in hot fat. Place on a bed of chopped spring onions, diced green, red and yellow pimento, garlic and rosemary. Moisten with red wine, jus lié and stock, braise for 15 minutes, then remove the lid to colour the quails for another 10 minutes. Serve coated with the cooking liquid and its contents.

Braised Venison Steaks

USA

Brown 10 × 150 g floured venison steaks in oil, then add 250 g chopped onion, 2 crushed cloves of garlic and 125 g squashed tomatoes. Moisten with 250 ml red wine and 750 ml brown game stock and braise for 40 minutes. Serve garnished with 500 g jardinière of vegetables, coated with the strained cooking liquid.

ROASTING

Roast game birds

Roast Pheasant (Faisan Rôti)

4 medium pheasants	75 g breadcrumbs
100 ml dripping	Game Chips
500 ml game stock	500 ml Bread Sauce
4 large croûtons	1 bunch watercress
100 g game liver farce	

1. Place the barded pheasants in a roasting tray on their sides, coat with the melted dripping and place in the oven to roast at a temperature of 220°C.
2. After 5 minutes turn the birds over onto the other side for a similar period, then lay on their backs with the breasts uppermost, basting occasionally.
3. After 40 minutes remove the bards and roast for a further 5 minutes to allow the breasts to colour.
4. Remove from the roasting pan and retain on a tray in a warm place, breasts downwards, to allow the juices to lubricate the flesh.
5. Drain the fat from the roasting tray, leaving the sediment, add the stock and simmer gently for a few minutes.
6. Strain through a conical strainer into a saucepan. Reboil, skim off all fat and season to taste. Retain for use.
7. Shallow fry the croûtons in the fat in which the pheasants were roasted, drain and spread with the game farce.
8. Remove the trussing strings and arrange the birds on the croûtons on an oval flat dish with a little of the gravy. Garnish with the picked watercress and Game Chips and serve accompanied by sauceboats of roast gravy, the breadcrumbs tossed in butter until golden, and bread sauce.

Note
1. Cut a groove the length of the croûton to prevent the bird from rolling off. When serving carved portions of pheasant the croûtons should be small oval or round shapes. They should be shallow fried to a golden colour in the strained fat from the roasted bird. The croûtons for serving whole cooked birds should be oblong in shape, with the corners removed, and of a size in relation to that of the bird.
2. All plucking and dressing is now done by the game dealer, unless the game is shot by the customer. Game birds are roasted in the same way as Roast Pheasant, timing them according to the chart at the beginning of the section. Roast snipe and woodcock are not eviscerated – only the gizzard is removed – because the cooked entrails are used on the accompanying croûton. These birds are trussed by threading their beaks through the entwined legs, without using string.

Pheasant with Celery (Faisan aux Céleris)

Truss and bard 4 pheasants and proceed as for Roast Pheasant. When cooked remove and retain. Drain off the fat from the roasting pan, add 500 ml veal velouté and 200 ml cream and allow to simmer for a few minutes, then pass through a conical strainer. Serve the carved pheasants garnished with braised celery and coated with the sauce.

Guinea Fowl with Celery (Pintade aux Céleris)

Prepare, cook and serve as for Pheasant with Celery.

Roast furred game

Roast Saddle of Hare (Râble de Lièvre Rôtie)

5 saddles of hare	1 bunch picked watercress
1 litre red wine marinade	200 ml redcurrant jelly
100 ml dripping	seasoning
500 ml brown game stock	

1. Marinate the larded saddles for 24 hours in a red wine marinade, drain and dry.
2. Season with salt and place in a roasting tray. Coat with the melted dripping and place in the oven at 220°C for 20 minutes to cook, basting occasionally.
3. When cooked, remove and retain for at least 5 minutes, preferably standing on a wire grid. Use any juices for making the gravy.
4. Add the stock to the roasting tray and allow to simmer for a few minutes. Strain through a conical strainer into a saucepan, reboil, skim off the fat and season to taste.

5. Bone the saddles lengthways, then carve the meat into very thin slices along the length. Place onto a serving dish, slightly overlapping or reform on the backbone and moisten with a little of the gravy.
6. Garnish with the watercress and serve the remainder of the gravy and the redcurrant jelly in sauceboats.

Roast Saddle of Venison (Selle de Chevreuil Rôtie)

Lard a 2.5 kg saddle of venison with strips of salt pork fat then marinate in red wine marinade for 24 hours. Roast at 210°C for 1¾ hours, basting occasionally. Serve carved into long or round slices with either cranberry sauce or redcurrant jelly.

Roast Saddle of Venison (Selle de Venaison Tourangelle)

Lard a 2.5 kg saddle of venison with strips of salt pork fat then marinate in red wine marinade for 24 hours. Roast at 210°C for 1¾ hours, basting occasionally. When cooked, flambé the pan with 25 ml brandy and moisten with the marinating liquid and 200 ml cream to make the sauce. Serve carved slices coated with the sauce, garnished with poached prunes filled with foie gras purée, and braised chestnuts.

Roast Haunch of Venison Poivrade (Cuissot de Venaison Poivrade)

Lard a 2.5 kg haunch of venison with strips of salt pork fat, then marinate in red wine marinade for 24 hours. Proceed as for Roast Saddle of Venison. When cooked, swill the pan with the marinating liquid, boil and reduce, then add to Sauce Poivrade. Carve into medium-thick slices, arrange on a dish, mask with the sauce and serve.

Game Liver Farce (Farce à Gratin)

Makes 800 g

125 ml fat	1 sprig thyme
200 g fat bacon scraps	1 bayleaf
100 g sliced onion	seasoning
500 g game livers	

1. Heat the fat from roasting the game in a frying pan, add the onion, followed by the bacon, and fry until both are light brown in colour.
2. Add the seasoned livers, thyme and bayleaf. Increase the heat and shallow fry very quickly, tossing frequently, keeping slightly underdone.
3. Place into a bowl with the fat and allow to cool.
4. Pass through a fine sieve or mincer, place into a clean basin and cover with clingfilm. Retain in a refrigerator for use as required.

5. To use, spread dome-shaped on the croûtons, sprinkle with game cooking fat or melted butter and heat in an oven.

Roast Marinated Rabbit (Arnhab Chermpoula)   MIDDLE EAST

Rub 1.5 kg saddles of rabbit with vinegar and leave for 2 hours. Blend 100 g onion, 3 cloves of garlic, 12 g coriander leaves, 3 fresh red chillies, 1 tsp paprika, a few strands of saffron and seasoning to a paste. Smear the rabbit with the paste, then proceed as for Roast Saddle of Hare. Serve accompanied with couscous or rice.

Roast Saddle of Hare in Cream Sauce   SCANDINAVIA
(Stekt Hare)

Marinate 1.5 kg larded saddles of hare in red wine, olive oil, roughly cut carrot, onion and celery, crushed garlic, allspice, crushed juniper berries and crushed peppercorns, thyme and bayleaves. Roast the saddles, swill the roasting pan with the marinade and brown stock and finish with cream and redcurrant jelly.

STEWING

Game Stew or Salmis of Pheasant (Salmis de Faisan)

10 portions cooked pheasant	20 glazed button onions
75 g butter	30 button mushrooms
50 ml brandy	10 heart-shaped croûtons
200 ml red wine	10 g chopped parsley
500 ml jus lié or demi-glace	seasoning
250 g lardons of bacon	

1. Heat the butter in a shallow pan, add the skinned pieces of pheasant, cover with greaseproof paper and a lid and reheat in the oven at 180°C for 10 minutes.
2. Boil the red wine in a pan until reduced by half. Add the brown sauce, simmer gently for 5 minutes, skim and pass through a conical strainer into a clean pan and retain.
3. Remove the pheasant from the oven, pour in the brandy and set it alight. Mix in the brown sauce, fried lardons of bacon, button onions and lightly sautéed mushrooms.
4. Dip the tips of the croûtons in the sauce then into the chopped parsley, place around the dish and serve.

Salmis de Pintade

Prepare, cook and serve in the same way as Salmis of Pheasant.

Jugged Hare (Civet de Lièvre)

Makes 8 portions

1 hare	200 g lardons of bacon
100 ml vinegar	16 glazed button onions
1 litre red wine marinade	24 cooked button mushrooms
100 g dripping	8 heart-shaped croûtons
50 g flour	15 g chopped parsley
50 g tomato purée	seasoning
1 litre brown stock	

1. Drain the blood from the hare into a basin, remove the liver and discard the gall bladder. Chop the heart, liver and lungs, place into the basin with the blood, mix in the vinegar and retain.
2. Cut the hare into 16 pieces, place into a basin, cover with the marinade and leave for 24 hours.
3. Remove the hare, and the vegetables from the marinade and retain the liquid. Heat the dripping in a frying pan.
4. Add the seasoned joints and fry until brown on all sides, then place in a braising pan.
5. Fry the vegetables in the same pan, drain and add to the hare.
6. Singe the hare and vegetables by sprinkling with the flour and placing in a hot oven until the flour takes on a brown colour.
7. Add the tomato purée and stir in the stock. Bring to the boil, skim and season.
8. Cover with a lid and cook in the oven at 180°C for 2 hours.
9. Transfer the hare to another saucepan and discard the vegetables. Strain the sauce through a conical strainer into a clean pan, reboil and skim to remove all traces of fat.
10. Whisk in the mixture of blood, liver and vinegar but do not allow to boil. Season to taste and pass through a conical strainer onto the cooked hare.
11. Serve in an entrée dish garnished with the fried lardons of bacon, button onions and mushrooms. Dip the tips of the croûtons in the sauce then into the chopped parsley, arrange around the dish and serve.

Rabbit Fricassée (Fricassée de Lapin)

Proceed as for Chicken Fricassée, substituting 1.5 kg jointed rabbit for chicken.

Rabbit Fricassée with Vegetables (Fricassée de Lapin aux Légumes)

Proceed as for Chicken Fricassée, substituting 1.5 kg jointed rabbit for chicken. Garnish with 250 g mixed vegetables cut into batons.

Braised Venison Burgundian Style (Civet de Chevreuil Bourguignonne)

Cut 1.5 kg venison into 2.5 cm cubes, marinate in red wine marinade for 5 hours, then proceed as for Brown Beef Stew. Just before serving add a garnish of 250 g fried lardons of bacon, 20 glazed button onions and 30 cooked button mushrooms.

Braised Venison with Vegetables (Civet de Chevreuil Jardinière)

Cut 1.5 kg venison into 2.5 cm cubes, marinate in red wine marinade for 5 hours, then proceed as for Brown Beef Stew. When serving garnish with 250 g jardinière of vegetables.

CHAPTER 10 # Vegetable and Potato Dishes

Vegetables

The vegetables and potatoes included in this chapter are those served with main dishes, though some, such as asparagus and globe artichoke, are served on their own as appetisers or as a vegetable dish, either cold or hot. Some of the recipes are also for use as garnishes to main dishes, particularly mixtures, button onions and mushrooms. Vegetables play a valuable part in other courses of the menu but these are not dealt with here.

Vegetables are no longer a minor accompanying item to a main dish but play an important part in a meal, often being served separately on a side plate as a selection to suit the main dish.

PREPARATION OF VEGETABLES

The correct preparation of vegetables is very important. If it is badly carried out, food costs will rise due to wastage. Further problems may be encountered at subsequent stages of cooking. For example, some vegetables may fall to pieces when they are to be served whole, whilst others may be completely inedible because the outer woodiness has not been removed by peeling, and the visual effect of the final result will be adversely affected. A controlled, systematic approach to this aspect is essential in order that high standards are maintained. When each kind of vegetable is introduced clear and precise instructions are given for its preparation.

VEGETABLE CUTS AND SHAPES

Batons or Jardinière de Légumes – cut 2 cm long × 5 mm square.

Rondelles – cut 1 cm in diameter × 2 cm thick, using either a mandolin or electric cutting machine.

Grooved slices – generally applied to carrots, lemon and cucumber; cut with a grooving knife (canneler knife).

Brunoise – very small dice, 4 mm square.

Diced, or Macédoine – cut either 0.5 cm × 0.5 cm or 1 cm × 1 cm.

Julienne – thin strips, 1 mm × 4 cm.

Paysanne – either triangles with 6 mm sides; squares of 1 cm × 1 cm; hexagons cut 1 cm across or rounds, 1 cm in diameter.

Mirepoix – roughly chopped mixed vegetables, for flavouring purposes only.

Turned barrel-shape – the size of these is dependent upon the use, e.g. as a vegetable 3.5–4 cm long × 2–3 cm. For a marmite-type soup 2 cm × 5 mm, for a bouquet of vegetables 4 cm × 1 cm, as an individual item 6 cm × 3 cm; parisienne or spoon cutters are numbered from 10 mm sized balls to 28 mm. Oval-shaped cutters are also used for cutting vegetables.

COOKING VEGETABLES

The introduction of high-speed steamers and combi ovens has rendered the traditional practice of cooking many vegetables in advance and reheating to order in a chaudfont out of date. Certainly, green vegetables ought to be cooked to order or to cover only a short length of time during the service period. They can then be buttered, creamed or sautéed to order. A microwave oven is useful for ensuring that vegetables, and other dishes, are served piping hot but not dried out, within a few seconds. The aim is to produce satisfactory results that suit customers' tastes, which means cooking vegetables for the minimum time so as to change them from the raw state to edible consistency without loosing their natural crispness and vitamin C content. It does not mean blanching vegetables for a few seconds and serving them almost raw and too hard to masticate.

Asparagus

Boiled Asparagus (Asperges à l'Anglaise)

    60 asparagus sticks
300 ml Hollandaise Sauce or hot
      melted butter

1. Cut off the spurs by shaving with the point of a knife and peel the ends with a vegetable peeler. Wash, place 6 heads together and tie into portions, cutting the ends straight.
2. Place the bundles into gently simmering salted water in a shallow pan and cook for 10 minutes.
3. When tender, remove from the water, lifting by the string with the point of a knife.
4. Serve on an asparagus dish with an inset drainer or on a folded table napkin.
5. Remove the string with a sharp knife, cutting away from the direction of the tips and serve with a sauceboat of one or both of the sauces.

Notes
1. Test if asparagus is cooked by pressing between the fingers just below the tip point – it should be firm yet yield to finger pressure.
2. For future use and for using cold, refresh in cold water. When cold, remove and place on a tray lined with a damp cloth. Cover with a cloth or cling film and store in a refrigerator.

Asparagus Sprue/Tips

These young shoots or thinnings of asparagus are particularly suitable for hors-d'oeuvre, canapés, garnishing fish, meat, poultry and other savoury dishes. They are usually cut 6 cm in length.

Snap off the fibrous ends at the base of the stalks, wash in cold water, then tie into manageable-sized bundles. Trim the stalk ends and place the bundles into gently simmering salted water in a shallow pan and cook for 8 minutes until tender. Remove from the water, lifting by the string with the point of a knife. Refresh and use as required.

Asparagus Milanese (Asperges Milanaise)

Arrange cooked asparagus in a buttered earthenware dish. Season, sprinkle with finely grated Parmesan cheese and melted butter and gratinate under a salamander grill. When lightly coloured, finish with nut-brown butter.

Beetroot

Buttered Beetroot (Betterave au Beurre)

Boil baby beetroots until tender, peel and trim, then roll in hot butter, seasoning with salt and pepper and a pinch of sugar. Serve sprinkled with chopped parsley.

Beetroot with Smetana (Svyokla so Smetanoi)   RUSSIA

Stew 1 kg grated raw beetroot in 50 ml oil and 25 ml lemon juice. Season and finish with 250 ml smetana.

Yale Beets   USA

Peel 20 medium-sized raw beetroots, cut into 3 mm thick slices, place in an oiled shallow dish and moisten with a mixture of 25 ml each of orange and lemon juices, 100 g sugar and 1 tsp salt with 25 g flour whisked in. Cover tightly with foil or oiled greaseproof paper and cook in the oven at 190°C for 1¼ hours until soft. Sprinkle with blanched, shredded orange and lemon peel on serving.

Broad Beans

Boiled Broad Beans (Fèves à l'Anglaise)

3 kg broad beans
20 g salt

1. Shell the beans and, if they are large, remove their outer skin. Wash in cold water.
2. Place into boiling salted water, bring back to the boil, skim and simmer until just tender.
3. Drain and serve dome-shape in a vegetable dish.

Broad Beans with Butter (Fèves au Beurre)

Proceed as for Boiled Broad Beans and serve tossed in 50 g melted butter.

Broad Beans in Cream Sauce (Fèves à la Crème)

Simmer cooked beans in 300 ml cream until the cream has reduced slightly, then season with salt and cayenne pepper.

Broad Beans with Mortadella (Fave Stufato)

Sweat 100 g chopped onion in 25 ml olive oil, then add 2 kg shelled broad beans, moisten with 300 ml stock and simmer for 10 minutes until almost cooked. Add 100 g diced mortadella and finish cooking, season and serve in vegetable dishes, garnished with fried bread croûtons.

Broad Beans in Cream Sauce (Favas com Molho Amarelo) PORTUGAL

Cook 1.5 kg broad beans in salted water flavoured with chopped savory and parsley. Drain and add to Cream Sauce finished with a liaison of egg yolks.

Broad Beans and Bacon in Cream Sauce (Dicke Bohnen in Specksobe) GERMANY

Prepare Broad Beans in Cream Sauce and mix with 150 g each of fried lardons of bacon and cooked shredded savoy cabbage.

Broad Beans with Bacon and Sausage (Favas à Moda de Lisboa) PORTUGAL

Sauté 75 g lardons of bacon and 75 g sliced chorizo sausage in lard with 100 g chopped onion and 10 g coriander leaves. Add 1.5 kg broad beans, moisten with stock, season with salt and simmer until cooked.

Broad Beans with Sherry and Lemon (Habas à la Rondeña) SPAIN

Top, tail and cut 2 kg young broad beans into even lengths in the pods. If very small, leave whole. Lightly fry 75 g chopped onion and 4 chopped cloves of garlic in 50 ml olive oil. Add the beans and moisten with 175 ml dry sherry and 600 ml stock; add a bouquet garni and 225 g fried lardons of bacon. Cover with a lid and simmer for 20 minutes. Remove the lid, discard the bouquet garni and allow the liquid to reduce to a glaze, then season with pepper and 2 tsp sugar. Stir in 75 g white breadcrumbs, 25 g chopped marjoram and the grated zest of 1 lemon. Lightly toss to ensure they are coated with the glazing liquid and serve dome-shape in a vegetable dish.

Broad Beans with Tomato (Koukia Yiachni) GREECE

Sweat 75 g chopped spring onions in 50 g olive oil and add 225 g tomato concassée, 25 g each of chopped dill, mint and parsley, 1 tsp sugar and seasoning. Moisten with 300 ml stock or water, add 1.25 kg shelled broad beans, simmer for 10 minutes and serve.

Broad Beans with Sesame Oil (Shengbian Candou) CHINA

Fry 1.25 kg broad beans in 25 ml sesame oil and season with salt and a little sugar. Moisten with 300 ml chicken stock and cook until the liquid is completely evaporated, then add 50 g chopped spring onions and 25 ml sesame oil. Serve dome-shape in a vegetable dish.

Broccoli

Boiled Broccoli Spears (Brocoli Nature)

Divide the head of broccoli into spears, cut off the stems close to the flowers, wash, drain and cook in boiling salted water for 4 minutes, keeping the broccoli firm. Drain and serve.

All the recipes for cauliflower are suitable for broccoli.

Broccoli with Garlic (Broccolo Strascinato)

Sauté florets of cooked broccoli in hot garlic-flavoured olive oil and serve arranged in a vegetable dish, sprinkled with chopped parsley.

Brussels Sprouts

Boiled Brussels Sprouts (Choux de Bruxelles Nature)

1 kg Brussels sprouts

1. Trim any discoloured or coarse outer leaves. Wash in cold salt water.
2. Place the sprouts into boiling salted water, skim and boil steadily for 8 minutes until tender but still fairly firm. Drain well.
3. Serve dome-shape in a vegetable dish.

Buttered Brussels Sprouts (Choux de Bruxelles au Beurre)

Proceed as for Boiled Brussels Sprouts, toss in hot butter and serve.

Sautéed Brussels Sprouts (Choux de Bruxelles Sautés)

Proceed as for Boiled Brussels Sprouts. Drain and toss in 75 g hot butter until slightly golden. Season with salt and milled pepper.

Brussels Sprouts with Chestnuts (Choux de Bruxelles Limousine)

Proceed as for Boiled Brussels Sprouts, then add an equal amount of braised chestnuts and toss in hot chicken fat.

Brussels Sprouts in Soured Cream (Kelbimbó)   HUNGARY

Cook 1.5 kg Brussels sprouts in salted water, drain and combine with 300 ml soured cream. Place into a shallow dish, sprinkle with 50 g white bread-crumbs and 50 ml melted butter and gratinate in the oven.

Brussels Sprouts with Garlic and Wine Vinegar   SPAIN
(Coles de Bruselas Salteados)

Heat 50 ml garlic-flavoured olive oil in a shallow pan, add cooked and drained Boiled Brussels Sprouts, sprinkle with 50 ml red wine vinegar, season with salt and pepper from the mill, toss over until the wine is reduced and serve.

Cabbage

Boiled Cabbage (Chou à l'Anglaise)

   2 kg cabbage

1. Discard any blemished leaves from the cabbage, cut into quarters, remove the centre stalk and separate the leaves. Cut off the thick centre vein of the leaves, then wash well in salted water.
2. Drain and place into boiling salted water, cover with a lid, bring back to the boil and remove the lid, skim and boil steadily for 10 minutes, leaving the cabbage slightly firm.
3. Drain in a colander.
4. Line soup plates with whole leaves, fill with the remainder and press with a plate to remove all water. Cut into sections and serve.

Note
Alternately, cabbage can be cooked in a small amount of boiling salted water, shredding it fairly finely in its raw state.

Boiled Cabbage with Apple and Cinnamon

Proceed as for Boiled Cabbage, shredding it first, then toss with 250 g sliced onion and 250 g diced apple shallow fried in butter; flavour with ground cinnamon and serve.

Buttered Cabbage (Chou au Beurre)

Proceed as for Boiled Cabbage and brush with 50g melted butter on serving.

Sweet and Sour Cabbage (Cavolo in Agrodolce)

Sweat 100 g chopped onion in 25 ml olive oil in a shallow pan, stir in 2 kg shredded cabbage, season with salt and pepper from the mill, cover with a lid and cook for a few minutes. Add 125 g diced tomato flesh, moisten with 125 ml white wine vinegar, add 25 g sugar, cover with a lid and cook for a further 10 minutes. Serve slightly dome-shape in a vegetable dish.

Baked Stuffed Cabbage   HUNGARY
(Erdélyi Tötött Tavaszi Kàposzta)

Form round parcels of 1.5 kg blanched cabbage leaves filled with a mixture of 250 g cooked rice, 75 g chopped onion and 150 g cooked minced pork and veal. Place into a shallow dish, moisten with 500 ml jus lié finished with lemon juice and soured cream and bake in the oven at 180°C for 45 minutes.

Cabbage with Spices (Gobi Foogath)   INDIA

1.5 kg shredded cabbage	10 g grated ginger
75 g chopped onion	1 tsp turmeric
3 dried, crushed chillies	25 g ghee
2 crushed cloves of garlic	salt

1. Golden fry the onion, chillies, garlic and ginger in ghee.
2. Stir in the turmeric, add the shredded cabbage, season and cover with a lid and cook for 10 minutes. Serve in a vegetable dish.

Savoy Cabbage and Potato with Caraway   HUNGARY
(Majorannàs Kelkàposzta-Fozelék)

Boil 1 kg shredded Savoy cabbage and 250 g diced potato in salted water with 1 tsp caraway seeds. Drain, then combine with 300 ml jus lié flavoured with marjoram.

Stir-fried Cabbage with Oyster Sauce   THAILAND
(Pak Bung Loy Fa)

Golden stir-fry 3 chopped cloves of garlic in 50 ml oil, then add 1 kg blanched shredded cabbage. Moisten with 300 ml stock, 25 ml each of Oyster Sauce and Yellow Bean Sauce and simmer for 2 minutes. Pour the cooking liquid into a vegetable dish, arrange the cabbage on top and serve.

Carrots

Boiled Carrots (Carottes à l'Anglaise)

1.5 kg carrots

1. Wash, peel, wash and cut the carrots into 3 cm sections and turn barrel-shape.
2. Place in a saucepan, barely cover with cold water, season with salt, cover with a lid and cook steadily for 10 minutes.
3. Drain in a colander and serve dome-shape in a vegetable dish.

Buttered Carrots (Carottes au Beurre)

Proceed as for Boiled Carrots and toss in 50 g melted butter.

Carrots in Cream Sauce (Carottes à la Crème)

Proceed as for Boiled Carrots, drain, add 300 ml cream and cook until slightly reduced. Season with salt and a touch of cayenne pepper.

Vichy Carrots (Carottes Vichy)

1 kg carrots
10 g sugar
50 g butter

1. Cut the peeled carrots into 2 mm slices. Place into a shallow pan and barely cover with cold water. Add salt, sugar and the butter.
2. Cover with a lid and allow to boil until almost cooked.
3. Remove the lid, continue to cook until the liquid has almost evaporated, leaving a syrupy glaze over the carrots.
4. Lightly toss to ensure that the carrots are coated with the glaze.
5. Serve dome-shape in a vegetable dish.

Glazed Carrots (Carottes Glacées)

Cut the carrots barrel-shape and proceed as for Vichy Carrots.

Carrot Fritters (Havuç Kizartmasi)   GREECE

Cut 1 kg carrots on the slant into 3 mm rondelles. Boil in salted water until just cooked. Drain well, then dry on a cloth. Pass the carrots through flour and yeast batter and deep fry until golden. Drain on kitchen paper, season with salt and serve accompanied by Yogurt Salcasi (yogurt with finely chopped garlic).

Glazed Carrots with Lemon (Havuç Plakisi)   GREECE

Sweat 100 g chopped onion in 125 ml olive oil, add 1 kg sliced carrots and cook for 5 minutes. Barely cover with water, add 25 ml lemon juice, 25 g chopped parsley and 1 tsp sugar, cover and cook until the liquid has almost evaporated. Toss to ensure that the carrots are coated with the glaze and serve dome-shape in a vegetable dish.

Cauliflower

Boiled Cauliflower (Chou-fleur à l'Anglaise/Nature)

1.5 kg cauliflower
   2 juice of lemons

1. Trim away the outer leaves, retaining some of the inner tender leaves; hollow out the stem to a depth of 2 cm, then wash in cold salted water.
2. Place into boiling salted water containing the lemon juice, reboil, skim and simmer for 8 minutes, keeping the cauliflower firm.
3. Drain well, serve neatly in a vegetable dish, either whole or cut into portions.

Buttered Cauliflower (Chou-fleur au Beurre)

Proceed as for Boiled Cauliflower and serve brushed with melted butter.

Cauliflower Hollandaise (Chou-fleur Hollandaise)

Proceed as for Boiled Cauliflower and serve accompanied with a sauceboat of Hollandaise Sauce.

Cauliflower Milanaise (Chou-fleur Milanaise)

Proceed as for Boiled Cauliflower; sprinkle with 50 g grated Parmesan cheese and 50 g melted butter and glaze under a salamander grill.

Cauliflower Mornay (Chou-fleur Mornay)

Proceed as for Boiled Cauliflower, coat with 800 ml Mornay Sauce, sprinkle with 75 g grated Parmesan cheese and 50 g melted butter and glaze under a salamander grill.

Cauliflower Polonaise (Chou-fleur Polonaise)

Proceed as for Boiled Cauliflower. Shallow fry 150 g white breadcrumbs in 200 g butter until golden, toss in 3 sieved hard-boiled eggs and chopped parsley and pour over the cauliflower when serving.

Cauliflower Sautéed in Butter (Chou-fleur Sauté au Beurre)

Proceed as for Boiled Cauliflower, cut in florets, then shallow fry in butter until light golden in colour, season with salt and milled pepper and serve.

Balti Cauliflower (Balti Gobi)
INDIA

1.5 kg cauliflower florets
25 ml oil
1 tsp sesame seeds
2 tsp mustard seeds
1 tsp turmeric

10 g grated ginger
75 g chopped onion
25 g chopped coriander leaves
few strands saffron
2 tsp Balti spice mix

1. Place the cauliflower florets into boiling salted water and simmer, keeping them on the firm side; remove with a spider and drain well.
2. Heat the oil in a balti pan, add the sesame and mustard seeds and stir-fry for a few moments, then add the turmeric, chopped onion and grated ginger.
3. Add the cauliflower florets and continue to stir-fry until lightly coloured.
4. Moisten with the saffron infused in 5ml water, cook for 2 minutes and serve sprinkled with the chopped coriander and the balti spice mix.

Cauliflower Bhajias (Gobhi Bhajias)
INDIA

Proceed as for Onion Bhajias (see page 288), substituting tiny cauliflower florets for the onion.

Cauliflower Florets with Creamed Coconut (Sayur Masak Lemak)
THAILAND

Grind 75 g shallots, 25 g blanched almonds, 2 tsp ground coriander, 1 tsp each of ground cumin, white pepper and turmeric, 125 ml peanut oil, 125 ml water and salt to a paste. Cook for 5 minutes, add 1 bayleaf, 100 g creamed coconut, 300 ml water, 700 g blanched cauliflower florets and 225 g sliced, cooked new potatoes and simmer for 5 minutes. Season and serve in a vegetable dish with some of the liquid, sprinkled with chopped chives.

Cauliflower Fritters (Karnibahar Kizartmasi)
GREECE

Cook 1 kg cauliflower florets in boiling salted water with lemon juice until nearly tender. Drain in a colander, then pass through eggwash and breadcrumbs and deep fry until golden. Drain on kitchen paper and lightly season with salt. Serve on a dish paper in a vegetable dish accompanied by Yogurt Salcasi (yogurt with finely chopped garlic).

Sautéed Cauliflower with Garlic (Coliflor Salteado)
SPAIN

Proceed as for Boiled Cauliflower, dividing it into florets while raw, then lightly sauté in 50 ml garlic-flavoured olive oil; season with salt and pepper from the mill and serve neatly arranged in a vegetable dish, sprinkled with chopped parsley.

Celeriac

Boiled Celeriac (Céleri-rave Nature)

1 kg celeriac
2.5 litres blanc preparation

1. Peel the celeriac thickly, wash, cut into 3 cm × 6 cm sections and turn barrel-shape, keeping them in acidulated water to prevent discoloration.
2. Place into simmering blanc, and cook gently for 6 minutes.
3. Drain well and serve in a vegetable dish.

Buttered Celeriac (Céleri-rave au Beurre)

Proceed as for Boiled Celeriac, then toss in 75 g butter and season with salt and milled pepper.

Buttered Celeriac with Fresh Herbs
(Céleri-rave aux Fines Herbes)

Proceed as for Buttered Celeriac, with the addition of freshly chopped tarragon, parsley, chives and chervil.

Baked Stuffed Celeriac (Töltött Zeller)   HUNGARY

Scoop out the centres of 5 boiled celeriacs and fill with 250 g duxelles of mushrooms combined with 150 g chopped celeriac and 50 g grated cheese. Sprinkle with 150 ml soured cream and 50 ml melted butter and bake in the oven at 180°C for 25 minutes.

Celery

Braised Celery (Céleris Braisés)

5 heads celery	1 bayleaf
25 g butter	2 cloves of garlic
100 g sliced carrot	1 litre white stock
100 g sliced onion	150 g bacon rind or trimmings
1 sprig of thyme	seasoning

1. Trim the roots to a point, cut to 16 cm in length and peel the outer stems with a peeler; wash well inside the stems.
2. Blanch for 10 minutes and refresh under cold water.
3. Butter and season a braising pan, place the sliced vegetables, thyme, bayleaf and garlic in the bottom and the celery on top; three-quarters cover with the stock and season.
4. Cover with the bacon, greaseproof paper and a lid, bring to the boil and braise in the oven at 175°C for 1½ hours.

5. Remove the celery; cut in halves lengthways and fold each piece over; place in a vegetable dish with a little of the strained cooking liquor.

Braised Celery in Gravy (Céleris Braisés au Jus)

Proceed as for Braised Celery. When serving coat with 200 ml jus lié.

Celery Milanaise (Céleris Milanaise)

Proceed as for Braised Celery, sprinkle with 50 g each of grated Parmesan cheese and melted butter and glaze under a salamander grill.

Chestnuts
Braised Chestnuts (Marrons Braisés)

    1.5 kg chestnuts
      50 g butter
    500 ml white stock
    1 stick celery
            salt and pepper

1. Slit the shells on both sides of the nuts and plunge into hot fat until the shells burst open, then remove the shells and inner skins. Alternatively, spread the nuts on a damp tray and place in a hot oven until they split.
2. Butter a shallow pan and add the chestnuts. Barely cover with the stock and add the celery and seasoning. Bring to the boil and cover with buttered greaseproof paper and a lid.
3. Braise at 175°C for 30 minutes.
4. Remove from the liquor and place on one side.
5. Boil and reduce the cooking liquor until it forms a syrupy glaze. Add the chestnuts and carefully incorporate them into the glaze. Use as soon as possible and handle carefully to avoid breaking them.

Chillies
Chillies

To deseed small fresh chillies, cut in half lengthways, cut out the veins, then scrape out the seeds. Large chillies with coarse skins may be placed over steam or under a salamander grill for a few moments to help rub off the skins. When skins have been removed, proceed as for small chillies.

Corn on the Cob
Boiled Corn on the Cob (Epis de Maïs)

      10 corn on the cob
    200 g melted butter

1. Remove the outer husk, wash and place the corns into boiling water and boil steadily for 20 minutes, according to size.
2. Remove with a spider, drain well and sprinkle with salt.
3. Serve on a folded table napkin, accompanied by a sauceboat of melted butter.
4. Instead of serving sweetcorn whole, the grains of corn may be scraped from the cob and reheated in hot butter or in cream, with the addition of a pinch of sugar.

Sweetcorn Cakes USA

250 g sweetcorn kernels, fresh, canned or frozen
2 beaten eggs
100 g flour
1 tsp baking powder
salt and pepper
200 ml oil

1. Mix the cooked sweetcorn, seasoning and eggs together. Add the sifted flour and baking powder and mix to a fairly stiff mixture.
2. Heat the oil in a shallow pan and fry 20 spoonfuls of the mixture in the form of small cakes until golden brown on each side.

Sweetcorn Fritters (Pergedel Jagung) THAILAND

Mix together 250 g drained sweetcorn kernels, 50 g chopped onion, 2 chopped cloves of garlic, 25 g chopped spring onions, 1 tsp ground coriander, 1/2 tsp chilli powder, 100 g rice flour, 1 tsp baking powder and 2 beaten eggs to form a dropping consistency. Fry spoonfuls of the mixture in oil until golden brown.

Eggplant

Deep-Fried Eggplant (Aubergine Frite)

1 kg eggplant
500 ml milk
150 g flour
salt

1. Peel the eggplant, cut into 4 cm rounds and soak in the milk; drain well and pass through flour, shake off the surplus and deep fry at 180°C until crisp and brown.
2. Drain on kitchen paper and lightly season with salt. Serve on a dish paper in a vegetable dish.

Eggplant and Tomato with Olives Caponata

Golden fry 2 kg peeled and sliced eggplant in 50 ml olive oil and retain. Sauté 80 g chopped onion in the oil, add 100 g diced blanched celery, 30 stoned olives and 100 g diced tomato flesh and cook for a few moments. Add a little sugar, 25 g capers and 50 ml vinegar, mix in the fried eggplant and allow to stew for 10 minutes. Serve in a vegetable dish, sprinkled with chopped parsley.

Ratatouille Niçoise

200 ml oil	500 g peeled, depipped and
750 g sliced onions	diced tomato
750 g eggplant	$^{1}/_{2}$ tsp coriander seeds
500 g red pimento	5 g chopped parsley
500 g courgette	5 g chopped basil
3 cloves garlic	seasoning

1. Heat the oil in a shallow pan, add the onions and cook without colouring.
2. Add the peeled eggplant and courgette, both cut into 1.5 cm dice, the skinned, deseeded pimento cut into 1 cm squares and the chopped garlic. Cover with a lid and allow to stew gently for 30 minutes.
3. Add the tomatoes, coriander seeds and seasoning.
4. Allow to stew gently for a further 10 minutes until all the vegetables are soft but not mushy.
5. Add the chopped parsley and basil and serve in a vegetable dish.

Stuffed Eggplant (Aubergine Farcie)

5 × 150 g eggplants	salt and pepper
100 ml oil	50 g white breadcrumbs
250 g duxelles	25 g melted butter
150 g tomato concassée	300 ml jus lié or demi-glace
5 g chopped parsley	

1. Cut off the stalks of the eggplants then cut them in half lengthways.
2. Place on an oiled tray, sprinkle with oil and cook in the oven until the centre of the vegetables is soft.
3. Remove the centre pulp from the eggplant with a spoon, place onto a cutting board and chop finely.
4. Add to the hot duxelles, followed by the tomato concassée, parsley and seasoning.
5. Fill the halves of eggplant with the stuffing, slightly dome-shape and mark trellis-fashion with the edge of a knife.
6. Place on the tray, sprinkle with breadcrumbs and melted butter and place in the oven to gratinate.
7. Serve in a vegetable dish, surrounded with either jus lié or demi-glace.

Vegetable Charlotte

3 eggplants	200 ml tomato coulis
50 ml oil	seasoning
125 g chopped onion	
3 cloves chopped garlic	
200 g courgettes	
150 g dried apricots ⎫ caponata	
50 g pine-nuts	
100 g red pimentos	
2 tbs honey	
100 ml white wine vinegar	

1. Line a 15 cm charlotte mould or 10 × 100 ml capacity ramekins with the blanched eggplant skins, leaving sufficient overhanging to enclose the moulds. Cut 10 × 5 mm slices of the eggplant and reserve.
2. Make the caponata. Heat the oil and shallow fry the onion and garlic, add the finely diced eggplant flesh, pimentos and courgette and cook until fairly soft. Add the diced, soaked apricots, pine-nuts, honey and vinegar and cook until fairly stiff; season to taste.
3. Fill into the prepared moulds, cover with the slices of eggplant, fold over the skins and bake at 180°C for 35 minutes for the charlotte mould or 25 minutes for the ramekins.
4. Turn out onto dishes spread with tomato coulis and serve as an appetiser or a vegetable dish.

Baked Eggplant and Banana   USA

Peel and slice 1 kg eggplant, lightly fry in 50 ml oil and drain. Arrange in an earthenware dish with 5 halved bananas, 275 g tomato concassée and seasoning. Sprinkle with 100 g breadcrumbs, the grated zest of 1 lemon and 25 ml oil and bake in the oven at 160°C for 30 minutes.

Deep-Fried Eggplant Turkish Style (Patlican Kizartmasi)   TURKEY

Cut 5 × 150 g peeled eggplant into 4 cm slices and place in a colander, sprinkle with a little salt and leave for 30 minutes. Drain, dry on kitchen paper, then pass through yeast batter and deep fry until golden brown. Serve on a dish paper, accompanied by chilled Yogurt Salcasi (yogurt with finely chopped garlic).

Eggplant in Sweet and Sour Sauce (Pacheri Terong)   THAILAND

Blend 1 tsp each of cumin, ground coriander and cinnamon, 4 crushed dried red chillies and 3 chopped cloves of garlic. Sauté 100 g chopped onion, 2 chopped cloves of garlic and 25 g grated ginger in 50 ml oil, then stir in the blended spices. Stir in 25 g paprika, moisten with 600 ml water and 2 tsp tamarind liquid, a little sugar and salt. Add 1 kg peeled and sliced eggplant, cover with a lid and allow to cook for 10 minutes. Serve in a vegetable dish.

Eggplant with Almonds and Cheese (Berengena con Queso)   SPAIN

Simmer 2 kg sliced eggplant and 100 g sliced onion in stock for 5 minutes. Drain in a colander, retaining some of the cooking liquid, and arrange the vegetables in a buttered and seasoned shallow dish. Blend 100 g of ground almonds with the cooking liquid and pour over the eggplant. Cover with 450 g sliced Munster cheese, sprinkle with 50 g grated Parmesan cheese, a pinch of nutmeg and 50 ml melted butter and gratinate in the oven until golden brown.

Purée of Eggplant (Rinjal Bartha)   INDIA

1 kg eggplant	½ tsp turmeric
250 g strips of tomato flesh	½ tsp chilli powder
75 g ghee	1 tsp garam masala
100 g chopped onion	1 tsp salt
10 g grated ginger	

1. Remove the stalk and green part and peel and cut the eggplant into dice.
2. Heat the ghee in a pan, add the chopped onion and fry until light brown and soft.
3. Add the ginger, turmeric, chilli powder, salt and garam masala and allow to cook for a few moments.
4. Add the eggplant and strips of tomato flesh, cover with a lid and stew until the vegetables are cooked to a purée and the liquid has almost evaporated.

Stuffed Eggplant with Yogurt (Baigan Dahi)   INDIA

Place 5 × 175 g halved eggplants on an oiled baking tray, sprinkle with oil and cook in the oven until the centre is soft. Remove the pulp from the eggplant with a spoon and chop finely. Golden fry 75 g chopped onion and 3 chopped cloves of garlic in 50 ml oil or ghee and add 2 tsp grated root ginger; stir in 2 tsp ground coriander, 1 tsp ground cumin, ¼ tsp turmeric, ¼ tsp chilli powder and salt. Add the eggplant flesh and ½ tsp garam masala and finish with 125 ml yogurt. Fill the halves of eggplant dome-shape with the filling and mark trellis-fashion with the edge of a knife. Place on the baking tray, sprinkle with oil or ghee and place in the oven to gratinate. Serve in a vegetable dish, garnished with sprigs of fresh coriander.

Endive

Braised Endive (Endive Belge Braisée)

10 × 100 g endives
    2 juice of lemons
  50 g butter
    salt and pepper

1. Remove any discoloured leaves and wash the endives.
2. Butter and season a shallow pan.
3. Place in the endives and sprinkle with the lemon juice.
4. Cover with buttered greaseproof paper and the lid.
5. Place in the oven at 175°C and braise for 30 minutes.
6. Remove from the liquid and place on a board. Cut in two lengthways and fold the top half underneath to form a triangular shape.
7. Arrange in a vegetable dish and coat with a little of the cooking liquid.

Braised Endive in Gravy (Endive Braisée au Jus)

Proceed as for Braised Endive and serve coated with jus lié instead of cooking liquid.

Endive Milanaise (Endive Milanaise)

Proceed as for Braised Endive and serve sprinkled with 50 g grated Parmesan cheese and 50 g melted butter glazed under the salamander grill.

Endive Mornay

Proceed as for Braised Endive and coat with 200 ml Cheese Sauce, sprinkle with grated cheese and melted butter and gratinate under a salamander grill.

Sautéed Endive (Endive Sautée au Beurre or Endive Meunière)

Proceed as for Braised Endive, drain and shallow fry in hot butter until lightly coloured. Arrange in a vegetable dish, squeeze a little lemon juice over, sprinkle with chopped parsley, then mask with 100 g nut-brown butter.

Braised Endive Wrapped in Ham   GERMANY
(Chicorée in Schinkenhemd)

Wrap each endive in a slice of ham, then place in an oiled shallow dish and proceed as for Braised Endive. When cooked, arrange in a vegetable dish, coat with Cheese Sauce, sprinkle with 50 g grated Emmenthal cheese and 50 ml butter and gratinate.

Fennel

Fennel is prepared by trimming the leaves and root end and washing in cold water. Large ones may be cut in half for serving.

Fennel (Fenouil)

Fennel is braised in the same way as celery, cooking large ones for the same length of time, serving them in the same way and with the same garnishes.

French Beans

Boiled French Beans (Haricots Verts à l'Anglaise)

 1 kg French beans

1. Top and tail the beans and pull off any hard strings around the edges; wash in cold water and drain.
2. Place into boiling salted water, bring back to the boil, skim and boil uncovered fairly rapidly for 4 minutes, keeping the beans crisp and green.
3. Drain and serve in a vegetable dish.

Buttered French Beans (Haricots Verts au Beurre)

Proceed as for Boiled French Beans, when serving, brush the surface with 50 g melted butter, seasoning with a little milled pepper.

Sautéed French Beans (Haricots Verts Sautés au Beurre)

Proceed as for Boiled French Beans, then toss in 75 g hot butter until lightly coloured; season with salt and milled pepper.

French Beans with Tomato (Fagiolini di Sant'Anna)

Sauté 3 chopped cloves of garlic in 50 ml olive oil, stir in 100 g diced tomato flesh and 1 kg raw French beans. Barely cover with water, season with salt and cook, reducing the liquor to a sauce consistency. Serve dome-shape in a vegetable dish.

French Beans in Sour Sauce (Sure Wälschbauna)   GERMANY

Proceed as for Boiled French Beans, then thicken 500 ml of the cooking liquor with 25 g arrowroot, add 25 ml vinegar and cook for 10 minutes to form a light coating sauce. Strain over the beans and serve.

French Beans with Cured Ham (Judías Verdes Bárcena)   SPAIN

Proceed as for Boiled French Beans. Sauté 100 g chopped onion and 2 chopped cloves of garlic in 75 g olive oil until lightly browned; add 100 g strips of cured ham, toss in the beans, cover with a lid and cook for a further 2 minutes.

French Beans with Almonds (Judías Verdes con Almendras)
SPAIN

Proceed as for Boiled French Beans. Golden fry 75 g flaked almonds in 50 g olive oil, toss in the cooked French beans, sprinkle with 50 ml lemon juice and season with salt and paprika.

French Beans with Chorizo Sausage and Eggs (Feijao Verde à Provinciana)
PORTUGAL

Sauté 100 g chopped onion and 2 cloves of chopped garlic in 50 g pork fat, stir in 250 g diced tomato flesh and 1 kg French beans, then barely cover with water. Add 250 g sliced chorizo sausage and 75 g fried lardons of bacon, season and cook. Serve with one poached egg per person, placed in a hollow in the beans.

Spiced French Beans (Tumis Pedas Kacang Panjang)
THAILAND

Blend to a paste 100 g chopped shallots, 3 cloves of garlic, 50 g grated root ginger, 1/2 tsp chilli powder, 2 tsp kapi, 50 ml lemon juice, 125 ml peanut oil and salt. Cook the paste for 5 minutes, add 300 ml water and 1 kg French beans. Season with salt, cover with a lid and cook for 10 minutes.

Stir-Fried French Beans (Chow Dau Kok)
CHINA

Stir-fry 1 kg whole French beans in 75 ml groundnut oil with 4 chopped cloves of garlic and 50 g grated ginger.

Globe Artichokes

Boiled Globe Artichoke (Artichaut Nature)

    10 globe artichokes
    2 lemons

1. Remove the stem either by twisting by hand or cutting with a knife. Cut one-third of the way down and trim the lower part with scissors. Rub the bottom with the lemon and tie a slice of lemon to the base.
2. Place into simmering salted water and cook for 15 minutes.
3. Remove with a spider, drain on a cloth and remove the string and lemon.
4. Pull out the central inner leaves in one piece.
5. Scrape out the choke from inside, using a small spoon or the end of a vegetable peeler and taking care not to damage or cut the base.
6. Replace the nicest centre leaves upside down and serve on a dish on a folded table napkin with a sprig of parsley in each artichoke.

Artichoke Hearts in Cider (Fonds d'Artichaut à la Bretonne)

Blanch 20 prepared artichokes, drain and cut into quarters. Sweat 100 g chopped onion in 50 ml oil, place into an earthenware dish, add the artichokes and 1 litre sweet cider, cover with a lid and cook in the oven at 200°C for 20 minutes. Remove the artichokes, reduce the liquor by half; add 25 ml lemon juice and reduce to a syrupy glaze, then incorporate 50 g butter and 5 g finely chopped parsley, tarragon, chervil and chives. Mask the artichokes with this sauce and serve.

Artichokes in Oil (Anginares ala Polita)   GREECE

Boil 10 shallots, 20 new potatoes and 20 whole new carrots for 5 minutes; add 50 ml olive oil, 10 prepared artichokes and salt and cover with grease-proof paper and a lid. Cook in the oven at 200°C for 10 minutes. When half-cooked, remove the chokes from the artichokes, replace and add 50 g chopped dill or fennel. When fully cooked, thicken the cooking liquor with 50 g diluted cornflour and serve the artichokes in a vegetable dish with the other vegetables, surrounded with the sauce.

Artichokes with Broad Beans (Anginares me Koukia)   GREECE

Sauté 550 g broad beans, 100 g chopped spring onions and 50 g chopped dill or fennel in 50 ml olive oil for 10 minutes. Add 10 small prepared artichokes, 50 ml lemon juice and salt, and barely cover with water; cover with a lid and cook in the oven at 200°C for 15 minutes. When cooked, remove the chokes and discard, replace the artichokes and allow to cool before serving.

Artichokes with Pine-nuts   SPAIN
(Alcachofas Estofadas con Pinones)

Blanch 10 globe artichokes in boiling salted water and lemon juice for 10 minutes. Drain and place in a casserole. Sauté 75 g chopped onion and 4 chopped cloves of garlic in 50 ml olive oil, add 20 ml each of dry white wine and water and pour over the artichokes. Cover with the lid and cook in the oven at 200°C for 20 minutes. Take out the artichokes, remove the chokes, reduce the cooking liquid by half and pour back over the artichokes in the casserole. Reheat, sprinkle with 50 g toasted pine-nuts and serve.

Artichoke Bottoms

Remove the stem either by twisting by hand or cutting with a knife and pick off the outer leaves. Scrape out the choke and trim the resultant hollow base using a stainless steel knife; rub the base with a cut lemon to avoid discoloration. Cook in a blanc until tender, rinse and use as required, or store in the blanc. Artichoke bottoms are mainly used as a garnish or appetiser rather than as a vegetable.

Stuffed Artichoke Bottoms (Cuori di Carciofi con Spinaci)

Sauté 50 g chopped onion and 2 crushed cloves of garlic in 50 ml olive oil, add 25 g chopped anchovy, 350 g finely chopped cooked spinach and 150 g breadcrumbs and seasoning. Fill the bottoms with the mixture, sprinkle with grated Parmesan cheese, melted butter and breadcrumbs and gratinate. Serve hot or cold.

Stuffed Artichoke Bottoms (Anginares Yemistes)   GREECE

Fill 20 cooked artichoke bottoms with 350 g cooked minced meat combined with grated 75 g Parmesan cheese. Mask with 300 ml Cream Sauce, sprinkle with breadcrumbs and oil and gratinate.

Jerusalem Artichokes
Boiled Jerusalem Artichokes (Topinambours Nature)

  1 kg Jerusalem artichokes
2.5 litres blanc preparation

1. Peel the artichokes and place immediately into acidulated water.
2. Cook for 8 minutes in the gently simmering blanc covered with a muslin, then drain and serve.

Buttered Jerusalem Artichokes (Topinambours au Beurre)

Proceed as for Boiled Jerusalem Artichokes and roll in 75 g melted butter.

Buttered Jerusalem Artichokes with Fresh Herbs
(Topinambours aux Fines Herbes)

Proceed as for Boiled Jerusalem Artichokes and lightly toss in 75 g butter with chopped fresh parsley, chervil and chives.

Leeks
Boiled Leeks (Poireaux à l'Anglaise)

10 × 125 g prepared leeks

1. Cut off the root and the top third of the green part, cut along the length from just above the root end and hold under the cold tap to wash inside and out.
2. Tie into two bundles, place in boiling salted water and simmer gently for 20 minutes.
3. Remove with a spider and drain, then remove the string.
4. Cut in two lengthways and fold the tops under in the form of triangles.
5. Serve arranged neatly in a vegetable dish.

Braised Leeks (Poireaux Braisés)

10 × 125 g leeks	2 cloves of garlic
25 g butter	1 litre white stock
1 sprig of thyme	150 g bacon rind or trimmings
1 bayleaf	5 g salt

1. Butter and season a braising pan and add the thyme, bayleaf and garlic. Arrange the leeks on top, season and three-quarters cover with the stock.
2. Cover with the bacon, greaseproof paper and a lid, bring to the boil and braise in the oven at 175°C for 45 minutes.
3. Serve folded in half in a vegetable dish with a little of the strained cooking liquor.

Buttered Leeks (Poireaux au Beurre)

Proceed as for Boiled Leeks, brush with 50 g melted butter and serve.

Braised Leeks in Gravy (Poireaux Braisés au Jus)

Proceed as for Braised Leeks and serve coated with 200 ml of jus lié.

Glazed Leeks with Rice (Prassorizo)   GREECE

Sweat 1.5 kg white of leek cut into 5 cm lengths in 300 ml olive oil; add 50 g tomato purée, 1 tsp sugar, $\frac{1}{4}$ tsp ground cinnamon and seasoning and barely cover with water. Boil and rain in 225 g rice, cover with greaseproof paper and a lid and cook until the leeks and rice are tender and the cooking liquor almost absorbed. Serve neatly arranged in vegetable dishes, coated with the reduced cooking liquid.

Lettuce

Braised Lettuce (Laitue Braisée)

10 cabbage lettuces	2 cloves of garlic
25 g butter	500 ml white stock
100 g sliced carrot	150 g bacon rind or trimmings
100 g sliced onion	10 heart-shaped croûtons
1 sprig of thyme	chopped parsley
1 bayleaf	seasoning

1. Remove any discoloured and coarse outer leaves and trim the root end. Wash in cold water, then blanch for 5 minutes, refresh and drain well.
2. Butter and season a braising pan, place in the sliced vegetables, thyme, bayleaf and garlic. Arrange the lettuce on top, season and three-quarters cover with the stock.

3. Cover with the bacon, greaseproof paper and a lid, bring to the boil and braise in the oven at 175°C for 40 minutes.
4. Remove, drain and cut in half and fold the top part underneath.
5. Arrange in a vegetable dish and moisten with some of the cooking liquid.
6. Dip the end of each croûton into the liquid, then into the chopped parsley, and place between each portion.

Braised Lettuce in Gravy (Laitue Braisée au Jus)

Proceed as for Braised Lettuce and serve coated with jus lié.

Lettuce with Ginger (Chow Sahng Choy)　　　　　　　CHINA

Cut 10 lettuces into small sections and stir-fry in 50 ml groundnut oil with 4 chopped cloves of garlic and 50 g grated ginger. Moisten with 300 ml stock, 2 tbs soy sauce, a little sugar and seasoning and cook for 2 minutes. Thicken the liquid with 25 g diluted cornflour to form a light sauce and serve.

Marrow and Courgette

Boiled Marrow (Courge à l'Anglaise)

1 kg marrow

1. Cut off the stalk, peel, cut in half lengthways and scoop out the seeds. Cut into 7 cm square pieces, trim the edges and wash in cold water.
2. Place into boiling salted water, bring back to the boil, skim and simmer gently for 5 minutes.
3. Remove from the water with a spider and drain on a cloth.
4. Serve in a vegetable dish.

Marrow Sautéed in Butter (Courge Sautée au Beurre)

Proceed as for Boiled Marrow, keeping underdone, then shallow fry in butter until golden brown. Season with salt and milled pepper and serve.

Marrow Milanaise (Courge Milanaise)

Proceed as for Boiled Marrow, sprinkle the surface with 50 g grated Parmesan cheese and 50 g melted butter, glaze under a salamander grill and serve.

Marrow Mornay (Courge Mornay)

Proceed as for Boiled Marrow, coat with 800 ml Mornay Sauce, sprinkle with 75 g grated Parmesan cheese and 50 g melted butter and glaze under a salamander grill.

Marrow Polonaise (Courge Polonaise)

Proceed as for Boiled Marrow. Shallow fry 150 g white breadcrumbs in 200 g butter until golden, toss in 3 sieved hard-boiled eggs and chopped parsley, pour over the marrow and serve.

Stuffed Marrow (Courge Farcie Braisée)

2 kg (2 large) marrow
          500 g rice pilaff
      500 ml thin jus lié or
               demi-glace
               seasoning

1. Peel, cut off the stalks and hollow out the marrows with a spoon and stuff with the rice pilaff.
2. Place into a pan and add the sauce.
3. Cover with buttered greaseproof paper and the lid and bring to the boil.
4. Braise in the oven at 175°C for 45 minutes, basting occasionally.
5. Remove the marrow from the liquid and allow to stand for 5 minutes before slicing.
6. Boil, skim and strain the cooking liquid and thicken with a few knobs of butter.
7. Cut the marrow into 2 cm slices and serve in a dish, slightly overlapping and surrounded with the sauce.

Notes
1. Instead of stuffing whole marrows they may be cut in half lengthways and filled with stuffing.
2. Additional ingredients such as sliced mushrooms and diced tomato flesh may be added to the rice.

Stuffed Courgettes (Zucchini Ripieni)

Cut 10 par-boiled courgettes in half lengthways and remove the centre seeds. Chop and combine with 250 g white breadcrumbs soaked in milk and squeezed dry, 2 tsp oregano, 75 g grated Parmesan cheese, 100 g diced prosciutto and 2 beaten eggs to bind. Stuff the courgettes with the mixture, sprinkle with 50 g grated cheese and 50 ml melted butter and gratinate.

Fried Baby Marrow (Courgette Frite)

   1 kg baby marrows
500 ml milk
 250 g flour
        salt

1. Dip the sliced baby marrows in milk, drain well and pass through flour. Shake off surplus flour and deep fry at 180°C for 3 minutes.
2. Drain on absorbent paper and lightly season with salt. Serve on a dish paper on a flat dish.

Baked Courgette (Tök au Gratin)   HUNGARY

Place 1.5 kg cooked courgettes into a shallow dish, cover with 300 ml soured cream mixed with 4 beaten egg yolks, sprinkle with 150 g white breadcrumbs mixed with chopped fresh herbs, dot with butter and gratinate in the oven at 180°C for 15 minutes.

Baked Courgettes with Coconut   THAILAND
(Urap Panggang Sayur)

Sauté 100 g chopped onion, 3 chopped cloves of garlic and 3 crushed dried red chillies in oil; stir in 2 tsp coriander powder, then add 50 g shrimp paste, 75 g desiccated coconut and 25 g tomato purée and moisten with 200 ml water; cook and reduce slightly. Place 2 kg sliced courgettes into a buttered and seasoned earthenware dish; add the sauce and bake at 180°C for 1 hour.

Courgettes with Tomato and Dill (Kolokythia Yiachni)   GREECE

Sweat 100 g chopped onion and 2 crushed cloves of garlic in 75 ml olive oil, add 225 g tomato concassée, 25 g chopped dill and 25 g chopped mint; season and cook for 5 minutes. Add 10 small courgettes cut into 0.5 cm slices and moisten with a little water, season with salt and simmer for 10 minutes. Allow to stand until cool then serve dome-shape in a vegetable dish. This dish may also be served warm.

Baked Sliced Courgette (Calabacín al Horno)   SPAIN

Place 2 kg sliced courgettes into a liberally oiled and seasoned earthenware dish. Season and bake in the oven at 180°C for 45 minutes. When almost cooked, cover with 100 g white breadcrumbs mixed with 4 chopped cloves of garlic and 25 g chopped parsley, sprinkle with 50 g melted butter and gratinate until golden brown.

Spiced Purée of Courgettes (Gooda Bartha)   INDIA

Proceed as for Boiled Marrow, using courgettes; drain well and pass through a sieve. Fry 1 tsp cumin seeds and 1 tsp mustard seeds in 25 ml oil or ghee until the seeds crackle. Add 75 g chopped onion and 3 sliced, fresh green chillies, the mashed courgette and 1/4 tsp chilli powder and cook until most of the moisture has evaporated. Serve in a vegetable dish, marked trellis-fashion.

Mixed Vegetables

Boiled Mixed Vegetables (Macédoine de Légumes)

400 g carrots	150 g peas
250 g turnips	50 g butter
200 g French beans	salt

1. Cut the peeled carrots and turnips into 8 mm dice and the beans into diamond-shapes.
2. Cook them and the peas separately in boiling salted water, drain in a colander and toss together in the hot butter; serve dome-shape in a vegetable dish.

Mixed Vegetables (Jardinière de Légumes)

Cut carrots and turnips into batons 3.5 cm × 4 mm × 4 mm and the beans into diamond-shapes and proceed as for Boiled Mixed Vegetables.

Glazed Mixed Vegetables (Macédoine de Légumes Glacée)

400 g carrots	100 g butter
250 g turnips	salt
200 g French beans	sugar
150 g peas	

1. Cut the peeled carrots and turnips into 8 mm dice and the beans into diamond-shapes.
2. Place the carrots into a shallow pan and barely cover with cold water. Add salt, sugar and 25 g of the butter, cover with a lid and boil for 3 minutes.
3. Add the turnips and continue to boil until both are cooked and the liquid has evaporated, leaving the vegetables glossy.
4. Boil and drain the beans and peas, add to the carrots and turnips and toss to mix. Serve dome-shape in a vegetable dish.

Blanquette of Vegetables (Blanquette de Légumes)

1.5 litres vegetable stock	75 g butter
150 g carrots	75 g flour
100 g swede	3 yolks of egg ⎫ liaison
150 g French beans	100 ml cream ⎭
100 g mangetout	10 heart-shaped croûtons
100 g broad beans	chopped parsley
100 g peas	seasoning
100 g asparagus tips	

1. Prepare all the vegetables, cutting the carrots and swedes into 2 cm dice and the French beans into 4 cm lengths.
2. Cook all the vegetables in the gently boiling vegetable stock, starting with the carrots, and adding the swede, French beans, mangetout, broad beans, peas and asparagus at 2-minute intervals, keeping them fairly firm.
3. Drain the vegetables, cover and keep them warm.
4. Melt the butter, add the flour and cook to a second stage roux, add the vegetable cooking liquid to make a velouté and cook gently for 30 minutes, then pass through a strainer. Finish with the liaison, then mix in the vegetables to reheat without boiling.
5. Serve sprinkled with chopped parsley and garnish with heart-shaped fried croûtons.

Vegetable Cutlets

350 g carrots	4 egg yolks
150 g turnips	flour
250 g celery	eggwash } for coating
250 g cabbage	breadcrumbs
100 g onion	500 ml Tomato Sauce
50 g butter	picked parsley
500 g dried mashed potatoes	seasoning

1. Melt the butter in a shallow pan, add the chopped onion and sauté without colouring.
2. Cut the vegetables into small dice, cook in boiling salted water for 3 minutes, then drain well.
3. Add the vegetables to the onions, add the mashed potato, yolks and seasoning, mix well over heat to a fairly firm consistency.
4. Allow to cool, divide into 70 g pieces and mould into a cutlet shape, using flour.
5. Pass through flour, eggwash and breadcrumbs, reshape and deep fry at 180°C until golden brown; drain on kitchen paper.
6. Arrange on dish papers, garnish with fried parsley and serve accompanied with the Tomato Sauce.

Stir-Fried Mixed Vegetables

100 ml sesame oil	150 g asparagus tips
2 cloves of garlic	150 bean sprouts
150 g spring onions	25 ml soy sauce
150 g carrot	50 ml vegetable stock
150 g water chestnuts	1 tsp cornflour
150 g button mushrooms	1 tsp five-spice powder
150 g mangetout, small	seasoning

1. Heat the oil in a wok, add the crushed garlic, stir-fry for 2 minutes, then discard.
2. Add the sliced spring onions, strips of carrot, sliced mushrooms, mange-tout, 3 cm lengths of asparagus and bean sprouts in that order, stirring continuously.
3. Sprinkle with the spice powder, salt and pepper, add the soy sauce and cornflour diluted in the cold stock.
4. Bring the boil, cook for 2 minutes and serve.

Note
Other vegetables which may be used are quartered artichoke bottoms, cauliflower florets, sections of French beans, sliced courgettes, shredded Chinese leaves, miniature corn on the cob.

Vegetable Pancakes (Crêpes Farcies)

20 savoury pancakes	150 g asparagus tips
50 g butter	250 g sweetcorn kernels
150 g red pimento	300 ml Cheese Sauce
300 g mushrooms	50 g grated Parmesan cheese

1. Melt the butter in a pan, add the diced pimento and cook for a few minutes, add the diced mushrooms and cook for a further 2 minutes. Add the sweetcorn and the cooked asparagus cut into 5 mm sections.
2. Season with salt and milled pepper, then bind with 100 ml of the sauce.
3. Lay out the pancakes on a work surface, divide the mixture evenly between the pancakes and roll up, folding the ends underneath.
4. Place a little sauce on the bottom of an earthenware dish and arrange the pancakes neatly, folded side down.
5. Coat with the Cheese Sauce, sprinkle with grated cheese and melted butter and glaze in a hot oven until hot and golden.

Mixed Vegetables in Yogurt (Aviyal) INDIA

Blend to a smooth paste 125 g desiccated coconut, 3 cloves garlic, 4 crushed dried green chillies, 1 tsp cumin seeds, 25 ml sesame oil and salt. Boil 1 kg diced mixed vegetables in a minimum amount of salted water and when half-cooked, cool, add the paste and 225 g diced mango, 6 curry leaves and 275 ml yogurt and simmer until cooked. Remove the curry leaves, season to taste and serve dome-shape in a vegetable dish.

Mixed Vegetables Tamil Style (Kuttu) INDIA

Boil 250 g red lentils in 1 litre water with 1 tsp turmeric until cooked. Fry 2 tsp cumin seeds and 50 g desiccated coconut in 100 ml oil or ghee, add 675 g diced mixed vegetables, 300 ml water and salt, cover with a lid and cook for 5 minutes, then add the drained lentils and cook for a further 5 minutes. Fry 1 tsp mustard seeds in 75 ml oil and when they begin to crackle add 1 tsp ground asafoetida, 2 crushed dried red chillies and 6 curry leaves. Add to the vegetables, cover with a lid to retain the flavours and simmer for 3 minutes. Remove the curry leaves and serve dome-shape in a vegetable dish.

Stir-Fried Mixed Vegetables with Oyster Sauce (Par Say Saw)
CHINA

Stir-fry 1 kg sliced mixed vegetables in 75 ml sesame oil with 4 chopped cloves of garlic and 75 g grated ginger for 2 minutes; moisten with 300 ml stock, 1 tbs light soy sauce and 2 tbs oyster sauce and simmer for 3 minutes. Lightly thicken the liquid with 25 g diluted cornflour to form a sauce and serve on a base of boiled rice.

Stir-Fried Mixed Green Vegetables (Pat Pak Ruam Mitr)
THAILAND

Lightly fry 4 sliced cloves of garlic and 50 g grated root ginger in 150 ml groundnut oil. Add and stir-fry 1 kg mixed green vegetables, e.g. French beans, broccoli and courgettes, 50 ml nam pla, 50 ml Oyster Sauce and seasoning. Serve dome-shape in a vegetable dish, garnished with 75 g chopped spring onions.

Stir-Fried Mixed Vegetables (Sabzi Bhaji)
INDIA

Lightly fry 1 tsp mustard seeds, 6 curry leaves and 3 chopped cloves of garlic in 50 ml oil or ghee. Stir in 2 tsp grated root ginger, 1 tsp turmeric, 2 sliced fresh chillies and salt. Add and stir-fry 225 g each of julienne of carrot, cauliflower florets, diamonds of French beans and shredded cabbage. Remove the curry leaves and serve dome-shape in a vegetable dish.

Mushrooms

Duxelles Mixture

750 g mushrooms
50 g butter
75 g finely chopped shallots
5 g chopped parsley
    salt and pepper

1. Melt the butter in a saucepan, add the chopped shallots and cook without colouring.
2. Add the finely chopped mushrooms and stew for 5 minutes, allowing the liquid from the mushrooms to reduce until they are fairly dry.
3. Add the chopped parsley and season with salt and pepper. If a firm mixture is required, mix in 100 g white breadcrumbs.

Grilled Mushrooms (Champignons Grillés)

        20 flat or field mushrooms
100 ml oil
        salt

1. Cut off the stalks level with the cup, wash and place on an oiled grilling tray, rounded side down; sprinkle with oil and season with salt.
2. Place under a salamander grill to cook for 5 minutes until soft. Serve as a vegetable or as a garnish with grilled meats.

Mushrooms with Marjoram (Funghi al Funghetto)

Sauté 3 chopped cloves of garlic in 50 ml garlic-flavoured oil, add 2 tsp chopped marjoram, 250 g sliced button mushrooms, 50 g tomato purée, salt and milled pepper and cook for 5 minutes.

Stuffed Mushrooms (Champignons Farcis)

        20 cup mushrooms
    500 g duxelles
     50 g white breadcrumbs
     50 g melted butter
          picked parsley

1. Grill the mushrooms until half cooked.
2. Place the duxelles mixture into a piping bag with a star tube and pipe into the centre of the mushrooms.
3. Sprinkle with breadcrumbs and melted butter and gratinate either in an oven at 200°C or under a salamander grill on a low shelf for 3 minutes.
4. Serve on a dish paper, garnished with picked parsley.

Turned Mushrooms

To decorate mushrooms for garnishing by turning, hold a firm cup mushroom by the stalk with the point of a small knife against the top. Turn mushroom and knife in opposite directions so as to cut a semi-circular groove, rotating around the mushroom, then cut through the base and stalk to remove the shreds of skin. Wash the mushrooms, rub with lemon and if they are required very white, cook for 5 minutes in a blanc.

Mushroom and Flageolet Cassoulet

50 ml oil	150 ml white wine	
200 g eggplant	200 g white breadcrumbs	
500 g mushrooms	100 g butter	
500 g flageolet beans	seasoning	
250 g tomato concassée		

1. Heat the oil in a shallow pan, add the peeled and diced eggplant and sauté until golden brown, then remove and reserve.
2. Add the quartered mushrooms to the pan and sauté quickly.
3. Mix the eggplant, mushrooms, cooked flageolets and tomato concassée, season and transfer to a shallow dish.
4. Moisten with the wine, sprinkle with the breadcrumbs and melted butter and bake in the oven at 180°C for 35 minutes.

Baked Oyster Mushrooms (Setas al Horno) SPAIN

Trim the stalks of 1 kg oyster mushrooms, place in an earthenware dish, season, sprinkle with 225 ml dry sherry and 225 ml olive oil and bake at 175°C for 5 minutes. Sprinkle the surface with breadcrumbs combined with 2 chopped cloves of garlic and 20 g chopped parsley; baste with a little of the cooking liquor and bake again at 175°C for a further 10 minutes to gratinate.

Breaded Chanterelle Mushrooms (Kirántott Vargánya) HUNGARY

Pass 1.5 kg mushrooms through flour, eggwash and breadcrumbs and deep fry.

Forest Mushrooms German Style (Steinpilze Försterinart) GERMANY

Golden fry 75 g chopped onion, 1 chopped clove of garlic and 275 g lardons of bacon in 25 ml oil. Add 1 kg sliced wild mushrooms and cook for 5 minutes, then add 20 g chopped parsley. Reduce the cooking liquid and finish with 300 ml cream, season and serve.

Glazed Mushrooms (Hung Shiu Doong Gwoo) CHINA

Stir-fry 75 g sliced, dried and reconstituted Chinese mushrooms in 50 ml sesame oil; moisten with the soaking liquid from the mushrooms and 2 tbs soy sauce, add a little sugar, cook until the liquid has reduced to a glaze and serve with boiled rice.

Mushrooms, Potatoes and Peas with Spices (Tazzi Khumben alu Mattarkari) INDIA

Lightly fry 75 g chopped onion in 50 ml oil or ghee, add 3 chopped cloves of garlic, 1 tsp grated root ginger and 25 g chopped coriander leaves, then stir in 1 tsp turmeric, 1/2 tsp chilli powder, 450 g quartered button mushrooms, 10 new potatoes, 225 g peas and 125 ml stock or water. Cover with the lid and cook for 10 minutes, then sprinkle with 1 tsp garam masala and continue to cook for a further 10 minutes. Season and serve in a vegetable dish.

Mushrooms with Smetana (Griby v Smetane)   RUSSIA

Remove the stalks from 1 kg ceps, cut into quarters and stew in 50 ml oil. Lightly fry 75 g chopped onion and the chopped cep stalks in 50 ml oil, add 50 g chopped dill and cook for 10 minutes. Add the ceps and 225 g smetana or yogurt and cook together for a further 5 minutes.

Stir-Fried Curried Mushrooms (Dhingri Kari)   INDIA

Lightly fry 100 g chopped spring onions, 3 chopped cloves of garlic, 1 tsp grated ginger and 6 curry leaves in 50 ml oil or ghee. Stir in 2 tsp curry powder, 1 kg button mushrooms, season with salt and toss over to cook. Sprinkle with 1 tsp garam masala, moisten with 225 ml coconut milk and cook for 5 minutes. Remove the curry leaves, finish with 25 ml lemon juice, season to taste and serve in a vegetable dish.

Stir-Fried Mushrooms, Bamboo Shoots and Sweetcorn   CHINA
(Hung Shiu Say Saw)

Stir-fry 1 kg soaked and sliced dried Chinese mushrooms in 50 ml groundnut oil, add 200 g bamboo shoots and 100 g baby sweetcorns, moisten with the soaking liquid of the mushrooms, 150 ml stock, 25 ml sesame oil, flavour with soy sauce and seasoning and simmer for 5 minutes; serve on a base of boiled rice.

Dried Mushrooms

These have to be soaked in warm water for 20 minutes, squeezed out and used whole or in slices. Keep the soaking liquid for adding its flavour to the dish at a later stage.

Okras

Stewed Okras

Wash and trim both ends of 1.5 kg small okras (ladies' fingers). Heat 100 g butter in a pan and sauté 200 g chopped onion without colour, add 250 g tomato concassée and the okras; season, cover and cook gently for 25 minutes. Serve sprinkled with chopped parsley.

Curried Okras (Bhendi Kari)   INDIA

1.5 kg okras	½ tsp turmeric
25 g ghee	½ tsp ground coriander
100 g sliced onion	½ tsp cumin
4 fresh green chillies	225 ml coconut milk
2 sliced cloves of garlic	salt
20 g grated ginger	

1. Trim the okras and wash in cold water.
2. Golden fry the onion, garlic, ginger and deseeded and sliced chillies in the ghee. Stir in the turmeric and continue to fry for a few moments.
3. Add the okras, coriander, cumin, coconut milk and salt and simmer uncovered for 10 minutes.

Spiced Okra (Bhendi Bhaji) INDIA

Lightly fry 1 tsp panch phora in 50 ml oil or ghee. Add and golden fry 75 g chopped onion, then add 1 tsp turmeric, ½ tsp chilli powder, ½ tsp garam masala and salt. Add 1 kg okras, cover with a lid and cook for 10 minutes. Season to taste and serve in a vegetable dish.

Onions

Braised Onions (Oignons Braisés)

10 × 125 g onions	150 g bacon rind or trimmings
25 g butter	70 g salt
1 litre white stock	200 ml jus lié or demi-glace

1. Peel the onions but do not cut the root ends too short.
2. Butter and season a braising pan, add the onions, season and three-quarters cover with the stock.
3. Cover with the bacon, greaseproof paper and a lid, bring to the boil and braise in the oven at 180°C for 1 hour.
4. Serve in a vegetable dish, coated with the brown sauce.

Brown-Glazed Button Onions (Petits Oignons Glacés à Brun)

800 g button onions
200 ml brown stock
50 g butter
10 g sugar
5 g salt

1. Melt the butter in a shallow pan, add the peeled onions and lightly colour golden brown.
2. Add the stock, salt and sugar. Cover with a lid and boil gently until cooked.
3. Remove the lid and continue cooking until the liquid has evaporated, leaving a syrupy glaze over the onions.
4. Lightly toss the onions to ensure that they are all coated with the glazing liquid.

Glazed Button Onions (Petits Oignons Glacés à Blanc)

800 g button onions
  5 g salt
250 ml water
  50 g butter

1. Place the peeled onions in a shallow pan, add the water, salt and butter. Cover with a lid and boil gently until cooked.
2. Remove the lid and continue cooking until all the liquid has evaporated, leaving a syrupy glaze.
3. Lightly toss the onions to ensure that all are coated with the glazing liquid.

French Fried Onions (Oignons Frits à la Française)

  1 kg onions
500 ml milk
250 g flour
      salt

1. Peel medium-sized onions, cut into 3 mm thick rings and separate the layers.
2. Dip in milk, drain well and pass through the flour. Place into a frying basket, shake off surplus flour and deep fry at 180°C.
3. When cooked and golden, drain thoroughly on kitchen paper and lightly season with salt. Serve on a dish paper in a dish.

Sautéed Onions (Oignons Lyonnaise)

  1 kg sliced onions
200 g butter
      salt

1. Heat the butter in a shallow pan, add the onions and season with salt.
2. Sauté the onions until cooked and a light golden brown in colour and serve in vegetable dishes.

Stuffed Onions (Cipolle Farcite)

Cook 10 × 125 g onions in boiling salted water for 30 minutes. Remove the centres from the onions, chop and combine with 100 g grated Parmesan cheese and 50 g butter. Fill the hollowed-out centres with the mixture, sprinkle with 50 g butter and a little brandy and gratinate until golden. Serve in a vegetable dish, garnished with sprigs of parsley.

Onion Bhajias

INDIA

175 g gram flour
1 tsp turmeric
1 tsp ground cumin
1 tsp garam masala

50 ml water
175 g finely sliced onion
1 tsp salt

1. Sift the gram flour, turmeric, cumin and garam masala into a basin, add the sliced onion and salt; moisten with the water and mix to a firm paste.
2. Drop tablespoonfuls of the mixture into hot corn oil and deep fry for 5 minutes until golden; drain and serve.

Stir-Fried Spiced Onions (Piaz Bhaji)

INDIA

Lightly fry 1 tsp cumin seeds in 50 ml oil or ghee and add 1 tsp turmeric, 1 tsp grated root ginger and 1 kg thickly sliced onion. Fry for 5 minutes, then sprinkle with 1 tsp garam masala, season with salt, cover with a lid and cook for a further 10 minutes; serve in a vegetable dish.

Parsley

Picked parsley

Wash in cold water, remove the sprigs from the stems and keep in iced water.

Chopped parsley

Wash in cold water. Remove the stalks and finely chop. Place into a cloth, squeeze out the liquid and place into a basin.

Parsnips

Boiled Parsnips (Panais à l'Anglaise)

1 kg parsnips

1. Place the peeled parsnips cut into 6 cm sections into a saucepan, cover with water, add salt, cover with a lid and boil steadily until cooked.
2. Drain the parsnips and serve in a vegetable dish.

Buttered Parsnips (Panais au Beurre)

Proceed as for Boiled Parsnips, then roll in 50 g melted butter.

Purée of Parsnips (Panais en Purée)

Proceed as for Boiled Parsnips, pass through a sieve or machine to make a purée, place 100 g butter into a saucepan, add the purée and heat, stirring with a wooden spoon. Season to taste and serve dome-shape in a vegetable dish, decorated with a scroll effect.

Peas

Boiled Peas with Mint (Petits Pois à la Menthe)

1 kg shelled peas
10 blanched mint leaves
    salt

1. Place the peas into boiling salted water, with a bundle of mint stalks; bring back to the boil and cook steadily for 4 minutes.
2. Discard the mint stalks, drain the peas and serve in a vegetable dish. Place the blanched mint leaves on top of the peas, each leaf denoting one portion.

Buttered Peas (Petits Pois au Beurre)

Proceed as for Boiled Peas with Mint, omitting the mint. Drain, toss in 50 g butter with a pinch of salt and serve.

Peas Flemish Style (Petits Pois à la Flamande)

Combine 500 g plain boiled peas with 500 g glazed carrots and serve.

Purée of Peas (Purée de Petits Pois)

Proceed as for Boiled Peas with Mint and pass through a sieve or machine to make a purée. Add 50 g butter, seasoning, mix together over heat and serve dome-shape in a vegetable dish, decorated with a scroll effect.

Peas in the French Style (Petits Pois à la Française)

1 kg peas
20 button onions
 1 cabbage lettuce
10 g sugar

250 ml white stock
50 g butter
  salt

1. Shred the lettuce coarsely, place with the other ingredients into a saucepan and bring to the boil.
2. Cover with buttered greaseproof paper and a lid and braise in the oven at 180°C for 30 minutes.
3. Lightly thicken the liquid by adding knobs of butter or beurre manié, removing the pan from the heat and shaking to mix in and serve.

Peas and Chorizo Sausage (Ervilhas à Portuguesa)   PORTUGAL

Sauté 100 g chopped onion and 2 cloves of chopped garlic in 50 ml oil; add 250 g diced tomato flesh, a sprig of thyme and chopped parsley. Serve 1.5 kg boiled and drained peas with fried eggs on top, garnish with sliced chorizo sausage and strips of smoked ham and surround with the tomato mixture.

Peas in Parsley Sauce   HUNGARY
(Petrezselymes Zöldborsófozelék)

Melt 50 g butter in a pan, add 25 g sugar and 1.5 kg cooked peas and chopped parsley. Moisten with 100 ml stock and simmer to reduce the liquor; finish with 225 ml soured cream.

Peas with Panir Cheese (Mattar Panir)   INDIA

Sauté 350 g cubes of Panir cheese in 100 ml oil or ghee until golden; drain and retain. Golden shallow fry 100 g chopped onion and 3 chopped cloves of garlic and stir in 2 tsp grated root ginger, 2 tsp ground coriander, 1 tsp ground cumin, 1 tsp turmeric, ¼ tsp chilli powder and salt. Add 75 g tomato concassée, 1 tsp garam masala and a little water, if necessary. Add 1 kg peas and simmer until half-cooked, then add the cheese, 25 g chopped mint, some chopped coriander leaves and salt. When cooked, serve in vegetable dishes, sprinkled with a little garam masala and with chopped mint and coriander leaves on top.

Pimentos (also called Capsicums or Sweet Peppers)
To Skin Pimentos

Peel the pimentos 1) using a potato peeler, 2) by immersing in hot deep fat for 1 minute, 3) by holding in a gas flame until the skin blisters and blackens, 4) by blanching in boiling water for 1 minute, enclosing tightly in a plastic bag for a little while, then opening and pulling the skin away. Cut off the top with the stalk and empty out the seeds.

Braised Stuffed Pimentos (Piments Farcis Braisés)

Prepare 10 × 100 g pimentos for stuffing and proceed as for Braised Stuffed Marrow.

Pimento and Tomato (Peperonata)

Sauté 100 g chopped onion and 3 cloves of chopped garlic in 50 ml olive oil; stir in 1 kg red pimento cut into strips, cover with a lid and cook for 20 minutes. Add 100 g diced tomato flesh, 25 g chopped basil and seasoning and finish cooking for another 5 minutes.

Baked Pimentos and Tomato (Asadillo) SPAIN

Place 250 g skinned sliced tomato and 1 kg of skinned pimentos in alternate layers in a buttered and seasoned earthenware dish; season with salt and milled pepper, sprinkle with 2 tsp chopped marjoram and 50 ml olive oil and bake in the oven at 180°C for 40 minutes.

Pipérade SPAIN

150 ml oil	350 g tomato concassée
200 g onion	20 eggs
1 clove garlic	seasoning
5 green pimentos	

1. Heat the oil in a shallow pan, add the chopped onion and garlic and cook until soft, without colour.
2. Add the finely diced pimentos and the tomato concassée and cook for a further 5 minutes.
3. Stir the beaten eggs into the vegetables until just set, season with salt and milled pepper and serve cut into wedges.

Red Cabbage

Braised Red Cabbage
(Chou-rouge Braisé or Chou-rouge Flamande)

1.5 kg red cabbage	200 ml vinegar
50 g butter	1 bouquet garni
100 g sliced onion	400 g bacon fat
1 muslin bag containing peppercorns, juniper berries, coriander seeds, cinnamon stick and cloves	250 g cooking apples
	10 g sugar
	20 g salt

1. Remove any discoloured leaves, cut the red cabbage into quarters and cut off the centre stalk. Wash and shred.
2. Place the butter in a braising pan, add the sliced onions and cook gently without colouring.
3. Season the finely shredded red cabbage and place in the pan. Add the vinegar, bouquet garni and the bag of herbs.
4. Cover with bacon fat, buttered greaseproof paper and a lid and braise at 180°C for 1¼ hours, then add the diced apple and sugar and cook for a further 30 minutes.
5. Remove and discard the bacon fat, bouquet garni and the bag of herbs and serve dome-shape in a vegetable dish.

Braised Red Cabbage with Stuffed Apples   GERMANY
(Rotkraut mit Speckäpfeln)

Sweat 1.5 kg shredded and seasoned red cabbage in 75 g oil or goose fat. Add 175 ml red wine, 50 g redcurrant jelly, 150 ml vinegar and a muslin bag containing cinnamon stick, cloves, coriander seeds, peppercorns and juniper berries. Cover with bacon fat, greaseproof paper and a lid and braise at 180°C for 1 hour. Golden fry 75 g chopped onion and 275 g lardons of bacon, then add 125 g diced ham and fill into the centres of 10 hollowed-out apples, place on top of the braised cabbage and continue braising for a further 20 minutes. Remove the bag of flavourings and the bacon fat and serve.

Runner Beans
Boiled Runner Beans (Haricots d'Espagne à l'Anglaise)

Top and tail and cut away the hard outer edges of the beans. Lay on a cutting board and shred finely into 8cm lengths. Place into boiling salted water, cover with a lid, return to the boil, skim and cook uncovered quickly for 4 minutes. Drain and serve.

Note
Runner beans can be cooked in any of the ways applicable to French beans.

Runner Beans with Tomatoes (Fassolia Yiachni)   GREECE

Sweat 100 g chopped onion and 2 crushed cloves of garlic in 75 ml olive oil, add 225 g tomato concassée, season and allow to cook. Add 1 kg sliced runner beans, barely cover with water, season with salt and simmer for 20 minutes. Season to taste and serve warm or cold in a vegetable dish.

Salsify
Boiled Salsify (Salsifis à l'Anglaise)

 1.5 kg salsify
2 litres blanc preparation

1. Wash, peel thinly, cut into 8 cm lengths and place in acidulated water.
2. Make the blanc and when boiling, add the drained salsify and simmer for 15 minutes.
3. Drain and serve arranged in a vegetable dish.

Seakale
Boiled Seakale (Chou de Mer à l'Anglaise)

 1 kg seakale
 2 juice of lemons

1. Discard any damaged stems and the roots, wash in cold water, and tie the seakale into bundles.
2. Place into gently simmering, salted water with the addition of lemon juice, bring to the boil, skim and simmer for 15 minutes.
3. Lift carefully from the water and drain.
4. Place on an asparagus dish with a drainer or on a dish lined with a folded table napkin. Remove the strings and serve as they are or with a suitable sauce such as Hollandaise.

Note
Seakale may be served in any of the ways applicable to asparagus.

Sauerkraut

Braised Sauerkraut (Choucroute Garni)

1.5 kg sauerkraut	500 ml dry white wine
3 carrots	500 g streaky bacon
2 onions	300 g bacon fat
1 bouquet garni	500 g garlic sausage
1 muslin bag containing	20 Frankfurter sausages
peppercorns, juniper berries,	20 boiled potatoes
coriander seeds and cloves	

1. Place half the sauerkraut into a braising pan, add the whole vegetables, bouquet garni, bag of flavourings and streaky bacon then cover with the remainder of the sauerkraut.
2. Add the wine, place the slices of bacon fat on top, cover with buttered greaseproof paper and a lid and braise in the oven at 180°C for 1 hour.
3. Remove the streaky bacon and place the garlic sausage in with the sauerkraut. Continue to braise for another 1 hour.
4. Poach the Frankfurter sausages in water for 5 minutes and drain.
5. Serve the sauerkraut in an earthenware dish garnished with slices of the garlic sausage, carrots and bacon; the Frankfurter sausages and the boiled potatoes are served separately.

Sauerkraut GERMANY

Melt 100 g goose fat or lard in a pan, add 1.5 kg sauerkraut and stir over heat for 2–3 minutes. Cover with boiling water, add 675 g quartered apples and season with 1 tsp caraway seeds and coarsely ground black pepper. Cover with a lid and cook at 180°C for 1 hour.

Sauerkraut with Bacon (Szalonnàs Savanyú Kàposzta) HUNGARY

Place 1.5 kg sauerkraut in water with a 250 g piece of bacon and 1 tsp paprika and simmer for 45 minutes. Remove the bacon, combine the sauerkraut with

300 ml velouté made from the cooking liquor and finish with 225 ml soured cream. Serve the sauerkraut with slices of the bacon on top.

Spinach

Boiled Leaf Spinach (Epinards en Branches)

2 kg spinach

1. Place the picked and washed spinach in 500 ml boiling salted water, cover with a lid and boil for 5 minutes.
2. Drain well in a colander, squeeze out all moisture, season and reheat, then serve loosely arranged in a vegetable dish.

Note
Spinach may be cooked in advance, refreshed, squeezed into balls and kept refrigerated ready for further use.

Leaf Spinach in Butter (Epinards en Branches)

Proceed as for Boiled Spinach and toss in 75 g butter in a shallow pan using a fork, to separate the leaves. Season with salt and milled pepper and serve in a vegetable dish.

Spinach Purée (Purée d'Epinards)

Proceed as for Boiled Spinach and pass through a fine sieve. Heat 50 g butter in a shallow pan and add the purée, stirring with a wooden spatule until hot. Season with salt, pepper and nutmeg and serve dome-shape in a vegetable dish, scrolled with a palate knife.

Creamed Purée of Spinach (Purée d'Epinards à la Crème)

Proceed as for Spinach Purée, mixing in 200 ml cream or Cream Sauce. Serve scrolled and surrounded with a thin band of cream.

Purée of Spinach with Croûtons (Purée d'Epinards aux Croûtons)

Proceed as for Spinach Purée and garnish with small triangular bread croûtons fried in butter until golden.

Subrics of Spinach

1.5 kg spinach	4 egg yolks
50 g butter	½ tsp nutmeg
250 ml Béchamel Sauce	150 ml oil
100 ml cream	seasoning
2 eggs	

1. Wash the trimmed spinach, drain and cook in a minimum of boiling salted water for 5 minutes, refresh, drain and squeeze out some of the moisture and coarsely chop.
2. Heat the butter in a shallow pan, add the spinach and cook to dry it out completely.
3. Add the béchamel, cream, egg and egg yolks and season with salt, pepper and grated nutmeg; mix well.
4. Heat the oil in a shallow pan and fry tablespoonfuls of the spinach mixture until lightly coloured on both sides.
5. Drain the subrics and serve as an appetiser or vegetarian dish accompanied by cream or Egg Sauce.

Leaf Spinach with Spices (Palak Bhaji)　　　INDIA

Mix ½ tsp each of cumin powder, coriander powder and turmeric, ¼ tsp chilli powder and salt. Golden fry 100 g chopped onion in 50 ml oil or ghee, add 2 crushed cloves of garlic and 1 tsp grated root ginger, then stir in the mixed spices and cook for a few moments. Add 2 kg boiled spinach and 50 ml water, cover with lid and simmer for 5 minutes. Drain off the surplus liquid and serve.

Leaf Spinach with Almonds and Raisins　　　SPAIN
(Espinacas a la Catalana)

Proceed as for Boiled Spinach and drain. Soak 225 g seedless raisins in 50 ml orange juice. Golden fry 75 g slivered almonds in 50 ml olive oil, add ½ tsp grated nutmeg, ½ tsp ground cinnamon, the raisins and orange juice and the grated zest of 2 oranges. Fork in the spinach, season, sprinkle with 25 ml lemon juice and serve.

Leaf Spinach with Rice (Spanakorizo)　　　GREECE

Sweat 175 g chopped spring onions in 150 ml olive oil. Add 50 g chopped dill, 2 kg boiled spinach and salt, cover with a lid and cook for 5 minutes, then add 125 g short-grain rice. Pour in 150 ml boiling chicken stock, cover with a cloth and lid and simmer gently for 10 minutes. When cooked, the liquor should have been completely absorbed by the rice. Keep covered for 10 minutes before serving.

Purée of Spinach with Raisins　　　GERMANY
(Sauerampfer mit Rosinen)

Proceed as for Spinach Purée and mix in 175 g soaked and drained raisins and season with salt, pepper and nutmeg. Serve brushed with melted butter.

Spiced Spinach (Palak Bhaji)
INDIA

1.5 kg spinach
½ tsp cumin
½ tsp ground coriander
¼ tsp salt

50 g ghee
2 chopped cloves of garlic
2 tsp grated ginger

1. Mix together the cumin, ground coriander and salt.
2. Golden fry the garlic and grated ginger in the ghee, then stir in the mixed spices.
3. Add the picked spinach, moisten with a little water, cover with a lid and simmer for 5 minutes.

Spinach Galette (Spenótkrokett)
HUNGARY

Combine 1 kg stiff spinach purée with breadcrumbs and shape into small cakes. Pass through flour, eggwash and breadcrumbs and shallow fry until golden.

Spinach and Turnip (Sagg)
INDIA

1.5 kg spinach
225 g diced turnip
100 g chopped onion
1 tsp mustard seeds
25 g ghee
10 g grated ginger

¼ tsp chilli powder
½ tsp turmeric
¼ tsp garam masala
25 ml lemon juice
salt

1. Place the spinach in a deep pan, add a little water, season with salt, cover with a lid and boil for 5 minutes until tender. Drain well, coarsely chop and retain.
2. Boil the diced turnips in salted water until cooked.
3. Lightly fry the mustard seeds in ghee, then add the chopped onion, grated ginger, chilli powder and turmeric.
4. Add the chopped spinach and drained turnips and cook for a further 3–4 minutes.
5. Serve sprinkled with garam masala and the lemon juice.

Stir-Fried Spinach (Paag Boong Paad)
THAILAND

Golden fry 4 chopped cloves of garlic and 250 g cooked soya beans in 50 ml oil, then fork in 750 g boiled spinach; season with salt and milled pepper and serve in a vegetable dish garnished with sliced, fresh red chillies.

Sugar Peas

Boiled Sugar Peas (Mange-tout Nature)

> 1 kg sugar peas
> 100 g butter
> 100 ml water
> 5 g salt

1. Top and tail the sugar peas, wash and drain.
2. Melt the butter in a saucepan, add the peas, salt and water. Cover with a lid and stew for 5 minutes.
3. Drain and serve in a vegetable dish.

Note
Sugar peas are sometimes called snow peas.

Swedes

Boiled Swedes (Rutabagas à l'Anglaise)

Peel the swedes thickly; cut into sections and turn barrel-shape 4 cm in length, allowing 125 g per portion. Place in cold water, season with salt, bring to the boil, skim and cook for 8 minutes. Drain and serve.

Note
Swedes may also be prepared as glazed, in butter and as a purée incorporating one-third its volume of dry mashed potato.

Turnip

Boiled Turnips (Navets à l'Anglaise)

> 1 kg turnips

1. Peel the turnips thickly, wash and drain. Cut into 4 cm pieces and turn barrel-shape.
2. Place in a pan and barely cover with water; add the salt, bring to the boil, skim, cover with a lid and boil steadily for 5 minutes.
3. Drain in a colander and serve in a vegetable dish.

Buttered Turnips (Navets au Beurre)

Proceed as for Boiled Turnips, then roll in 50 g melted butter.

Purée of Turnips (Navets en Purée)

Proceed as for Boiled Turnips, then pass through a sieve or machine to make a purée; heat 100 g butter in a saucepan, add the purée together with 350 g dry mashed potato and stir with a wooden spoon. Season and serve dome-shape in a vegetable dish, decorated with a scroll effect.

Turnips in Cream Sauce (Navets à la Crème)

Proceed as for Boiled Turnips, then add to 300 ml cream and cook until reduced slightly. Season with salt and cayenne pepper and serve.

Tomatoes

Preparation of tomatoes

To skin tomatoes – Cut around the stalk and remove; place the tomatoes in a strainer or basket and dip into boiling water for 10 seconds. Drain and peel off the skins with a small knife. Hard or unripe tomatoes may need a few seconds longer; do not over-immerse.

To make tomato concassée – cut peeled tomatoes in halves through the middle, empty the centres using the fingers or a spoon and cut into 1 cm dice.

To make cooked tomato concassée – heat a little butter in a pan and cook some finely chopped onion and garlic without colouring; add raw diced tomato, a pinch of salt, pepper and sugar and cook slowly until the tomato is soft and no moisture is left.

For stuffed whole tomatoes – wash, remove the stalks and cut a slice off the tops, scoop out the inside and turn upside down to drain. For halves, cut in half through the middle and empty the insides.

Stuffed Tomatoes (Tomates Farcies)

450 g duxelles	10 × 75 g tomatoes
200 g white breadcrumbs ⎫ filling	30 g melted butter
100 ml jus lié	salt
5 g chopped parsley ⎭	picked parsley

1. Remove the eyes and cut off the tops of the tomatoes. Carefully remove the seeds using a small spoon.
2. Add the breadcrumbs, jus lié, salt and chopped parsley to the duxelles and mix to a fairly firm consistency.
3. Fill the tomatoes dome-shape and sprinkle with breadcrumbs and melted butter.
4. Place on a buttered tray, and place in the oven at 180°C for 5 minutes to cook the tomatoes and reheat the filling.
5. Serve in a vegetable dish, garnished with picked parsley.

Tomatoes Provencale Style (Tomates Farcies Provençale)

100 g butter	10 × 75 g tomatoes
150 g chopped onion	seasoning
1 clove chopped garlic } filling	picked parsley
500 g white breadcrumbs	
5 g chopped parsley	

1. Remove the eyes and cut off the tops of the tomatoes. Carefully remove the seeds using a small spoon.
2. Heat 75 g of the butter in a shallow pan, add the chopped onion and garlic and cook gently without colour.
3. Add the breadcrumbs and chopped parsley and season to taste.
4. Fill the tomatoes slightly dome-shape and cover with the tops.
5. Place on a buttered tray, sprinkle with the rest of the butter and place in the oven at 180°C for 5 minutes to cook the tomatoes and reheat the filling.
6. Serve in a vegetable dish, garnished with picked parsley.

Stuffed Tomato with Pine-nuts (Tomates Rellenos con Piñones)   SPAIN

Lightly fry 50 g pine-nuts in a little olive oil, add 100 g chopped onion, 2 cloves of chopped garlic, 100 g diced tomato flesh, 25 g chopped oregano and seasoning, then stir in 500 g breadcrumbs. Fill the centres of 10 × 75 g tomatoes, sprinkle with oil and bake in the oven at 180°C for 5 minutes.

Vine Leaves

Stuffed Vine Leaves (Dolmas)   GREECE

40 vine leaves	1 tsp ground cumin
75 g olive oil	2 egg yolks
100 g onion	2 egg yolks } liaison
300 g mushrooms	50 ml yogurt
100 g Kefalotiri cheese	250 ml vegetable stock
350 g cooked rice pilaff	25 ml lemon juice
100 g anchovy fillets	seasoning
1/2 tsp rosemary	

1. Blanch the vine leaves for 2 minutes, refresh and drain.
2. Heat the oil and sauté the chopped onion, add the chopped mushrooms and cook until the moisture has evaporated.
3. Add the grated cheese, rice, chopped anchovy fillets and chopped rosemary, cumin and seasoning. Add 2 egg yolks and cook until the mixture is firm.

4. Lay out the vine leaves, season and enclose 25 g of the filling in the centre of each leaf. Fold over into cylinder- or parcel-shapes and place close together in an oiled shallow pan.
5. Moisten with a little white stock, cover with buttered greaseproof paper, place a lid on top and cook at 180°C for 30 minutes.
6. Reduce the braising liquid by half, add the lemon juice and a liaison of 2 egg yolks and yogurt. Cook until thick, without boiling. Pour over the dolmas and serve hot or lukewarm.

Stuffed Vine Leaves (Koupepia) GREECE

Discard any blemished vine leaves, wash in cold water and drain, then blanch 30 leaves in boiling salted water for 5 minutes, remove and dry. Golden fry 100 g chopped onion in 25 ml olive oil. Add 600 g minced cooked lamb, 300 g minced cooked veal, 100 g cooked rice, 20 g chopped parsley and 2 tsp chopped mint and mix to cohere. Lay out the 30 leaves, sprinkle with salt and place 35 g of the filling in the centre of each leaf. Fold over into cylinder- or parcel-shapes and place close together in an oiled shallow pan. Moisten with a little white stock, cover with buttered greaseproof paper and a lid and cook at 180°C for 30 minutes. Serve accompanied by Lemon and Egg Sauce.

Note
Other fillings such as duxelles, rice pilaff or fish mixtures may be used to stuff vine leaves.

PULSE VEGETABLES

Pulse vegetables with an outer shell, such as haricot and kidney beans, require soaking in cold water for 12 hours before cooking. Those without a shell, such as yellow and green split peas, do not require soaking before cooking.

Boiled Haricot Beans (Haricots Blancs)

750 g haricot beans	150 g bacon trimmings or
2 carrots	ham bone
1 onion clouté	salt
1 bouquet garni	

1. Soak the beans in cold water for 12 hours, then drain and wash.
2. Place into a saucepan, cover with cold water, bring to the boil and skim.
3. Add the remainder of the ingredients and simmer gently for 40 minutes.
4. When cooked, remove and discard the carrots, onion, bacon and bouquet garni; drain and serve the beans in a vegetable dish.

Notes

1. Do not add salt to the beans until they are nearly cooked.
2. To test if cooked, remove a bean and press between the fingers – it should be soft.
3. Beans which are known to have been dried recently do not need soaking.

Haricot Beans with Cabbage (Fagioli con le Verze)

Cook 750 g haricot beans in water with 100 g chopped fennel, 50 g chopped onion, 200 g shredded cabbage and 50 g tomato purée. When cooked, finish by adding 75 g fried lardons of bacon, 2 chopped cloves of crushed garlic and seasoning.

Haricot Beans in Cream Sauce (Haricots Blancs à la Crème)

Proceed as for Boiled Haricot Beans, then add 275 g fried lardons of bacon. Reduce 300 ml boiling chicken stock and 25 ml lemon juice until syrupy, add 275 ml cream and 75 g butter and mix into the beans. Finish by adding 25 g mixed chopped parsley, chervil, tarragon and chives and serve.

Haricots Beans with Tomato Sauce

Proceed as for Boiled Haricot Beans and mix with 1 litre Tomato Sauce.

Pease Pudding

400 g yellow split peas	75 g bacon trimmings or
2 carrots	ham bone
1 onion clouté	seasoning
75 g butter	

1. Wash the split peas, place into a saucepan and cover with cold water; bring to the boil and skim.
2. Add the carrots, onion and bacon, cover with a lid and cook in the oven at 180°C for 1 hour.
3. Remove and discard the whole vegetables and bacon trimmings; pass the peas through a sieve, return to a clean pan, mix in the butter and season.
4. Serve dome-shape as a vegetable or as an accompaniment to a main item, decorated scroll-fashion with a palette knife.

Kidney Beans in Butter (Flageolets au Beurre)

Cook 750 g soaked kidney beans as for Boiled Haricot Beans; drain, toss gently in 50 g butter and serve.

Lentil and Fennel Cassoulet

75 ml oil	100 ml white wine
300 g onion	250 ml vegetable stock
4 cloves garlic	500 g brown lentils, soaked
150 g red pimentos	1 tsp fennel seeds
3 fennel bulbs	5 g coriander leaves
50 ml tomato purée	150 g eggplant
250 g tomatoes	salt, milled pepper

1. Heat the oil in a shallow pan, add the chopped onion and garlic and sauté without colour.
2. Add the peeled tomatoes, pimentos and fennel, all cut into 2 cm dice, and cook for a few minutes. Add the tomato purée, wine, stock, lentils, seasonings and herbs, mix and place into a shallow ovenproof dish. Layer the surface with 5 mm slices of the eggplant, neatly overlapping, cover with a lid and bake at 165°C for 1 hour.

Nut Roast

150 g textured vegetable protein	150 g breadcrumbs
300 g chickpeas	3 eggs
250 g hazel nuts	1 tbs yeast extract
250 g peanuts	300 ml tomato coulis
100 ml oil	seasoning
150 g onion	

1. Soak the textured vegetable protein in cold water for 1 hour, then drain in a colander.
2. Boil the soaked chickpeas until tender.
3. Blend the nuts to a powder.
4. Heat the oil in a shallow pan, add the finely chopped onion and cook until soft and slightly coloured.
5. Mix together the textured vegetable protein, chickpeas, nuts and onion, season with salt and milled pepper, then add the beaten eggs, yeast extract and breadcrumbs and bind to a fairly firm consistency.
6. Fill into greased loaf tins, cover with lids and bake at 180°C for 1 hour.
7. Serve cut into slices with hot tomato coulis.

Black Beans with Rice (Moros y Cristianos)   SPAIN

Soak 350 g black beans for 12 hours. Wash, cover with water, add 100 g lardons of bacon and a bayleaf and cook for 1 hour, adding 5 g salt towards the end. Mould 350 g hot Rice Pilaff mixed with nutmeg, grated zest of lemon and 100 g grated Parmesan cheese in a savarin mould. Turn onto a dish, fill the centre with the beans and mask them with Sofrito.

Note

For Sofrito, sweat 75 g chopped onion and 2 chopped cloves of garlic in 50 ml vegetable oil. Stir in 25 g paprika, add 225 g tomato concassée and 50 g chopped fresh herbs, season and cook gently for 10 minutes.

Blackeye Beans with Spinach (Salq bi Loubia)   MIDDLE EAST

Soak 675 g blackeye beans for 12 hours. Wash, cover with water and cook for 1 hour. Lightly fry 75 g chopped onion in 150 ml olive oil, add 1 kg shredded spinach and sweat until cooked. Combine with the drained beans, season and serve hot or chilled.

Haricot Beans with Black Pudding (Fabada Asturiana)   SPAIN

Soak 675 g haricot beans for 12 hours. Wash, cover with water, bring to the boil and skim. Add 100 g lardons of bacon, 2 crushed cloves of garlic, 12 crushed peppercorns, $^1/_4$ tsp saffron and 2 salted pig's trotters. Simmer for 2 hours, remove the trotters, cut into dice and return to the drained beans together with 275 g slices of shallow-fried black pudding.

Hopping John   USA

Soak 200 g blackeye beans for 12 hours. Wash, cover with water and simmer for $1^1/_2$ hours, then add a little salt. Lightly fry 150 g lardons of bacon in 50 ml oil, then add 50 g chopped onion. Stir in 150 g long-grain rice, add the beans and moisten with 600 ml of the cooking liquid. Cover with a lid and simmer for a further 20 minutes until the rice is cooked.

Lentils in Spiced Sauce (Parpu)   THAILAND

Simmer 750 g brown lentils in water with 1 tsp turmeric, 1 tsp cinnamon and 2 crushed dried red chillies. When almost cooked, add 250 g diced potato, 3 cloves of garlic cut into strips, 2 tsp grated ginger and salt. Finish with 300 ml thin coconut milk. Meanwhile, sauté 150 g sliced onion in oil until golden, add 1 tsp each of mustard and fennel seeds and 3 crushed dried red chillies. Add to the lentils and serve in a vegetable dish.

Pinto Beans with Green Chillies (Frijoles Charros)   MEXICO

Soak 675 g pinto beans for 12 hours. Wash, cover with water and simmer for 1 hour. Fry 275 g lardons of bacon and 3 chopped fresh chillies in 50 ml oil, then toss in 275 g tomato flesh and 50 g chopped coriander leaves. Mix into the drained beans, season and serve.

Red Lentils with Spinach (Palak Dal) INDIA

450 g spinach
450 g red lentils
75 g sliced onion
2 sliced cloves of garlic
1 tsp ground ginger
¼ tsp chilli powder
salt
225 ml yogurt

1. Boil the prepared spinach in a small amount of salted water for 5 minutes; drain well, coarsely chop and reserve.
2. Place the lentils into a deep pan, cover with water, bring to the boil and skim.
3. Add the onion, garlic, ginger, chilli powder and salt and simmer until cooked to a purée.
4. Mix in the chopped spinach and the yogurt and serve.

Succotash USA

Simmer 500 g each of drained cooked or canned lima beans and sweetcorn kernels in 275 ml Béchamel Sauce and 25 ml cream for a few minutes.

Sweet and Sour Kidney Beans SCANDINAVIA
(Söt Sur Bruna Bönar)

Soak 450 g kidney beans for 12 hours. Cook for 1 hour in the soaking liquid with the addition of 2 whole carrots and onions, 225 g bacon trimmings and a bouquet garni. When cooked, remove and discard the bouquet garni, vegetables and bacon trimmings, then add 50 ml vinegar and 50 g brown sugar, boil and thicken the cooking liquid with 25 g diluted arrowroot.

Potato Dishes

VARIETIES OF POTATOES

Many different varieties of potatoes are grown in this country and imported from around the world. The main crop varieties are Desirée, King Edwards and Maris Piper; Pentland Crown, Pentland Dell, Pentland Hawk, Pentland Ivory and Pentland Squire are not nationally available.

Potatoes are available to the caterer in a variety of forms including powdered, dehydrated, canned, frozen, pre-peeled, and in their skins, washed and graded according to type and size.

Most new potatoes are waxy in texture, but none of the main British crop are, so it is necessary to purchase Dutch Bintjes potatoes for such uses as Pommes Macaire.

There are many varieties of sweet potatoes which are popular in Africa, the Caribbean, North and South America and parts of Russia. Sweet potatoes are peeled in the same way as for ordinary potatoes. They may be boiled, puréed, baked in their skins, roasted, deep and shallow fried.

STORAGE OF POTATOES

New potatoes should be purchased for immediate use and not kept in store for longer than forty-eight hours because, being freshly dug, they dry out quickly and will not then scrape easily. Old potatoes must be stored in a cool, dark, dry place in their bags, on wooden slats. If they become warm they begin to sprout, and, if kept in the light, they go green and cannot be used. Potatoes pick up other smells easily, so should be kept away from strong smelling materials and commodities. They bruise easily, even in their bags and should therefore be handled with care.

PREPARATION OF POTATOES

Loss in peeling varies significantly from 15 to 30 per cent, depending upon the type of potato and method of preparation. It is advisable to grade potatoes according to size before peeling: if they are to be turned barrel-shape, select ones that are the right size – any trimmings may be used for soup or incorporated into a Boulangère-type potato dish. In no circumstances should trimmings be used for mashed or purée potato dishes as they will become dark in colour and gluey in texture.

Wash the potatoes and peel using a potato peeler. Cut off any blemishes or green parts with a small knife. Rewash the potatoes, place them into a container and cover with cold water. The time it takes to peel by machine depends upon the abrasive material incorporated into the equipment. Do not overfill the machine or leave the potatoes in it too long, just long enough to remove the peel without any wastage. Cut off any blemishes and green parts with a small knife. Place into a container and cover with cold water. If peeled potatoes are to be stored overnight, they should be kept in a refrigerator at a temperature of 8°C. There are various ways of preparing and boiling new potatoes:

1. Wash the potatoes and cook them in their skins, peel them while still very hot and place into a pan of hot salted water.
2. Wash and scrape, place in a pan, cover with hot water, add salt and boil until tender.

BAKED POTATOES

1. Baked potatoes may be served plain, in the skin.
2. The pulp may be removed, mixed with other ingredients and replaced in the skin.

3. The pulp may be removed, mixed with other ingredients and either moulded into potato cakes and shallow fried or baked in moulds.

Baked Jacket Potatoes (Pommes au Four)

10 × 200 g potatoes
        sprigs of picked parsley
  10 × 25 g knobs of butter
        (optional)

1. Wash the potatoes to remove all traces of dirt.
2. Make an incision around the sides with the point of a small knife to a depth of 0.5 cm.
3. Place on a baking sheet on a bed of coarse salt, or wrap each one in foil, in which case it is not necessary to put them on a tray.
4. Place in the oven to bake at 220°C for 1 hour until cooked.
5. Remove the foil if used, cut a cross in the centre and press the skin to expose the inside.
6. Serve garnished with sprigs of parsley. If desired, a knob of butter may be placed in the centre of each potato.

Pommes Arlie

10 × 200 g baked jacket potatoes   100 ml cream
      100 g butter   salt, pepper and nutmeg
       25 g chives   75 g grated Parmesan cheese

1. Cut a slice from the tops of the potatoes lengthways. Carefully remove the pulp from the skins, using a spoon, and place in a basin.
2. Crush the potato with a fork, then add the butter, chopped chives, cream, salt, pepper and nutmeg, mixing with a wooden spatula.
3. Fill the skins dome-shape with the mixture.
4. Sprinkle with grated Parmesan cheese and melted butter and colour either in an oven or under a salamander grill.

Pommes Macaire

10 × 200 g baked jacket potatoes
     100 g butter
        salt, pepper and nutmeg
     25 g melted butter

1. Cut the potatoes in half lengthways, remove the pulp with a spoon, and place it in a basin.
2. Crush with a fork, then add the butter, salt, pepper and nutmeg and mix with a wooden spatula.

3. Heat an omelette pan, cover the base with some of the butter and allow to get hot.
4. Add the potato mixture to a depth of 3 cm, flatten it and sprinkle with melted butter.
5. Cook in the oven at 220°C for 30 minutes until golden brown on all sides.
6. Turn out onto a hot round dish, cut into segments and brush with melted butter before serving.

Pommes Byron

Proceed as for Pommes Macaire. When turned out of the pan, make a depression in the centre, fill with cream and sprinkle with grated cheese and melted butter and either serve as it is or put into an oven or under a salamander grill until the surface is golden. Alternatively, the mixture can be moulded into 4 cm diameter cakes, marked trellis-fashion, shallow fried in clarified butter and oil, then finished with cream and cheese.

Baked Sweet Potatoes with Chestnuts   PORTUGAL
(Batata Doce Recheada com Castanhas)

Bake 1.5 kg sweet potatoes in their jackets, scoop out the pulp, mash and combine with 250 g chestnut purée. Fill back into the skins, sprinkle with grated cheese and butter and gratinate.

POTATOES BAKED WITH STOCK

This method of cookery combines baking and stewing, the potatoes being cooked in dry heat with moisture coming from stock. When they are cooked, the liquid should be absorbed into the potatoes, so making them quite moist.

Boulangère Potatoes (Pommes Boulangère)

   1.5 kg peeled potatoes
   250 g sliced onions
600 ml white stock
   75 g melted butter
       salt and pepper

1. Slice the potatoes 3 mm thick into a basin, keeping sufficient to decorate the top. Add the onion, season and mix together.
2. Butter an earthenware dish and fill with the potatoes to a depth of 5 cm and arrange the reserved slices neatly overlapping to cover the surface.

3. Add the hot stock to come three-quarters of the way up the dish and brush the surface with melted butter.
4. Place in the oven at 200°C to cook, pressing from time to time to prevent the surface from becoming dry. After 20 minutes, reduce the temperature to 175°C and cook for a further 40 minutes.
5. When cooked, remove from the oven, clean the edge of the dish with a damp cloth and sprinkle with chopped parsley.

Pommes Savoyarde

These are prepared as for Boulangère Potatoes with the addition of 150 g crisply fried lardons of bacon. Sprinkle the surface with grated cheese and melted butter, then cook in the oven.

Fondant Potatoes (Pommes Fondantes)

1.5 kg potatoes, turned 6 cm
      barrel-shape
1 litre white stock
  50 g melted butter
      salt

1. Place a layer of the potatoes in a 5 cm deep dish.
2. Moisten with hot stock to come three-quarters of the way up, season and bring to the boil on top of the stove.
3. Brush the potatoes with melted butter and place in the oven at 200°C for 45 minutes, basting regularly. They should be a light golden brown on top, with all the stock absorbed by the potatoes.
4. Brush with melted butter and serve.

Note
When cooked the potatoes should be soft to the touch; to test, pierce with the point of a knife, which should enter without pressure.

Pommes Cretan

Proceed as for Fondant Potatoes, adding some powdered thyme to the stock. Serve sprinkled with a mixture of chopped parsley and fresh thyme.

Baked Potatoes and Rice   ISRAEL

Place 50 g chopped onion and 75 g short-grain rice in a baking dish with 2 kg barrel-shaped potatoes. Moisten with 300 ml white stock, brush with oil, then bake at 200°C until the cooking liquor has evaporated and the potatoes and rice are coloured golden brown and cooked.

Sweet Potato Glazed with Rum
CARIBBEAN

Peel and slice 1 kg sweet potatoes, cook in cold salted water for 15 minutes, then drain. Oil and season an earthenware dish and arrange the potato in layers, neatly overlapping. Sprinkle with 50 ml oil, 75 ml white rum and 20 g demerara sugar and glaze in the oven at 200°C for 15 minutes to finish cooking and colour.

POTATOES BAKED IN MOULDS

Pommes Anna

1.5 kg peeled potatoes
200 ml oil
75 g butter
    salt and pepper

1. Trim the potatoes into 4 cm cylinder shapes, then cut into 1 mm slices. Keep enough to line the bottoms of the moulds, wash and dry them twice. Place the remainder in a basin and season with salt and pepper.
2. Heat the oil in Anna moulds on top of the stove, sufficient to grease the bottom and sides. Arrange the washed and dried slices neatly overlapping on the bottom of the mould, allowing to fry gently, then fill the moulds to the top with the seasoned slices.
3. Brush the surface with melted butter and allow the moulds to become very hot as the potatoes begin to fry, cover with the lids, then place onto a baking tray and bake at 220°C for 1 hour. While cooking, press down firmly and brush frequently with melted butter; remove the lids towards the end.
4. When cooked, remove from the oven and place on the top of the stove for a few moments, away from direct heat. Make sure that the potatoes are not stuck to the side of the mould; if so, release by running a palette knife around the sides.
5. To turn out, give the potatoes a final press down, place a lid over the top and turn it upside down. Slide onto a flat serving dish if to be served whole, or onto a board for cutting into wedges. Brush with melted butter just before serving.

Note
To prevent sticking, clean the moulds thoroughly by heating a little salt in them, then wiping out with a cloth. It is advisable not to wash the moulds after use so as to build up a patina of fat.

Pommes Dauphin

Cut raw potatoes into julienne strips, season, fill the moulds and proceed as for Pommes Anna.

Pommes Mireille

Proceed as for Pommes Anna with the addition of slices of cooked artichoke bottoms and short julienne of truffle, mixing them into the potatoes before filling into the moulds.

Pommes Voisin

Proceed as for Pommes Anna, adding 50 g grated Parmesan cheese to the sliced potatoes, together with the seasoning.

BOILED AND STEAMED POTATOES

Boiled Potatoes (Pommes Nature)

1.5 kg potatoes
1 tbs salt

1. Place the prepared potatoes in a saucepan, cover with cold water, add the salt and bring gently to the boil.
2. When boiling, skim and reduce the heat so the potatoes simmer gently for 20–25 minutes until cooked. Drain and serve in a vegetable dish.

Notes
1. This applies to main crop potatoes prepared barrel-shaped 5 cm long or trimmed to the size and shape of a medium-sized potato.
2. If boiled too rapidly certain varieties of potato will break up.
3. To test if cooked, remove one potato with a perforated spoon and pierce it with a knife. If it is cooked the point will enter without resistance, alternatively, apply gentle pressure to the potato with the fingers – the potato will yield if cooked.

Boiled New Potatoes (Pommes Nouvelles Nature)

Wash and scrape 1 kg new potatoes, rewash, place into a pan of boiling salted water, reboil and skim. Boil steadily for 10 minutes or until soft when pierced with the point of a knife. Drain and serve in a vegetable dish.

Note
Instead of scraping off the skins, new potatoes can be boiled as they are, then peeled while still hot, replacing them in a pan of hot water as done.

New Minted Potatoes (Pommes à la Menthe)

Proceed as for Boiled New Potatoes, adding a bunch of mint stalks tied with string. Serve brushed with melted butter and place one blanched mint leaf on each portion.

Parsley Potatoes (Pommes Persillées)

Proceed as for Boiled New Potatoes. When cooked, brush with melted butter and sprinkle with chopped parsley. Alternatively, melt some butter in a shallow pan, mix in some chopped parsley and gently roll the drained potatoes in it until evenly coated.

Steamed Potatoes (Pommes Vapeur)

Place the prepared even-sized potatoes in a steamer tray lined with a damp cloth. Season with salt and steam until cooked. Serve quite plain in a vegetable dish.

Pommes à la Crème

Boil potatoes in their skins until two-thirds cooked. Peel and cut into 4 mm thick slices. Place into a pan, barely cover with milk, season and finish cooking. Add a little cream to the potatoes at the point of service.

Pommes Maître d'Hôtel

Proceed as for Pommes à la Crème with the addition of chopped parsley.

Mashed Potatoes (Pommes Purée)

```
 1.5 kg  peeled old potatoes
   75 g  butter
100 ml   milk
   1 tbs salt
         salt and pepper
```

1. Place the potatoes in cold salted water, bring to the boil, skim and cook for 20–25 minutes.
2. Drain and replace on the stove to dry out.
3. Pass through a sieve and place in a clean saucepan.
4. Add the butter, hot milk and pepper, plus a pinch of nutmeg if desired, and stir with a wooden spatula until the mixture is of a creamy consistency but do not overmix.
5. Serve dome-shape in a vegetable dish, decorated scroll-fashion with a palette knife.

Creamed Potatoes (Pommes Mousseline)

Proceed as for Mashed Potatoes but substitute cream for the milk.

Pommes Biarritz

Proceed as for Mashed Potatoes, then add 100 g each of finely chopped ham and red pimento and 10 g parsley.

Pommes Purée au Gratin

Proceed as for Mashed Potatoes; sprinkle the surface with grated cheese and melted butter and place under a salamander grill until evenly coloured golden brown.

Boiled New Potatoes with Spices   CARIBBEAN

Cook 1 kg new potatoes in their skins in salted water, drain, cool and cut into 5 mm slices. Lightly fry 3 chopped cloves of garlic and 25 g grated root ginger in 150 ml corn oil, add the potato slices and sauté until golden brown, then season with 2 tsp ground cinnamon, 2 tsp caraway seeds, salt and cayenne pepper. Sauté for a further 2 minutes and serve sprinkled with 50 g chopped coriander leaves.

Potatoes Cakes German Style (Kartoffelkroketten)   GERMANY

Cook 1 kg potatoes in salted water, drain, mash and combine with 25 g butter, 1 egg, 100 g flour, salt, pepper and nutmeg. Mould into 30 small oval cakes, mark trellis-fashion and shallow fry in oil until light golden on both sides.

Savoury Potatoes with Tomatoes (Alu Tariwale)   INDIA

Boil 1 kg potatoes in their skins until half cooked; skin and cut into 5 mm slices. Fry 2 tsp each of cumin seeds and mustard seeds in 175 ml oil or ghee until they burst, then add 1 tsp each of coriander seeds, ground turmeric and chilli powder. Add 450 g tomato concassée and 150 ml water, simmer for 5 minutes, then add the sliced potatoes. Season with salt and simmer until cooked and all the liquid has evaporated. Serve sprinkled with chopped onion.

Spiced Mashed Potatoes (Alu Bartha)   INDIA

Boil 2 kg potatoes in their skins in salted water, then peel and mash them. Fry 1 tsp mustard seed in 25 ml oil or ghee, add 2 sliced, fresh green chillies, 100 g chopped onion, 1 tsp turmeric, 10 g garam masala, 10 g salt, $^1/_4$ tsp chilli powder and 80 ml lemon juice. Mix into the mashed potato and serve sprinkled with chopped coriander leaves.

DUCHESSE POTATO MIXTURES

Duchesse Potato Mixture (Pommes Duchesse)

1 kg potatoes
75 g butter
3 egg yolks
salt and pepper
50 g melted butter

1. Boil the potatoes in salted water for 20–25 minutes until cooked.
2. Drain and place the pan on the stove to dry out any surplus water.
3. Pass the potatoes through a sieve and return to a clean saucepan. Add the butter, egg yolks and seasoning and stir with a wooden spatule over heat until the potato mixture is well bound but not overmixed. Use according to the following named recipes.

Note
If the mixture is to be piped through a piping tube it needs to be a little softer than for its other use; to soften it a little more butter should be used. Hand-moulded Duchesse Mixture needs to be on the firm side as there is a tendency for the moulded potato to disintegrate when fried. To adjust it potato flour or powder may be added as necessary.

Duchesse Potatoes (Pommes Duchesse)

1 kg Duchesse Potato Mixture
2 eggs (eggwash)

1. Place the mixture into a piping bag with a star tube.
2. Pipe onto a greased baking sheet in a spiral shape with a base of 2 cm to a height of 2.5 cm, allowing 2 pieces per portion.
3. Sprinkle the surface of the potatoes with eggwash.
4. Place in the oven at 200°C until the outer surface turns a light golden colour and the inside is hot.

Pommes Marquise

Pipe 20 nests with Pommes Duchesse Mixture onto a greased baking sheet using a star tube, then fill the centres with cooked tomato concassée. Sprinkle with eggwash and place in the oven until the outer surface turns a light golden colour and the inside is hot.

Galette Potatoes

Mould Duchesse Potato Mixture into the shape of small cakes 6 cm × 1.5 cm, using potato flour. Mark trellis-fashion and golden shallow fry in a minimum amount of hot butter and oil.

Note

Use a minimum amount of oil and butter for frying the galettes; for preference use a non-stick frying pan.

Croquette Potatoes (Pommes Croquettes)

Mould Duchesse Potato Mixture into 30×30 g cylindrical pieces 5 cm $\times$ 1.5 cm. Pass through flour, eggwash and breadcrumbs, remould and place on a tray. Place in a frying basket and deep fry at 190°C until crisp and golden. Drain on kitchen paper and serve garnished with sprigs of fried or fresh picked parsley.

Pommes Amandines

Proceed as for Croquette Potatoes but substitute finely chopped almonds for the breadcrumbs.

Pommes Florentine

Proceed as for Croquette Potatoes, adding some finely chopped ham to the mixture and substituting finely broken vermicelli for the breadcrumbs.

Dauphine Potato Mixture

This is made by mixing one and a half parts of Duchesse Potato Mixture into one part of unsweetened choux paste. The addition of choux paste gives the potato mixture extra lightness which can make handling a little difficult, particularly when moulding into the various named potato dishes. Egg-shaped Dauphine potatoes are moulded with two tablespoons which have to be dipped into hot water or warm oil to prevent sticking.

Pommes Dauphine

600 g Duchesse Potato Mixture
300 g unsweetened choux paste
  flour
  picked parsley

1. Mix the warm Duchesse Potato Mixture into the freshly made choux paste, using a wooden spatule.
2. Mould into 30×30 g round, oval, cork- or egg-shaped pieces, using flour to prevent sticking. Place them onto small squares of greaseproof paper large enough for two portions.
3. Place the papers into the fryer at 175°C, using a frying basket. During cooking the paper will separate and float to the surface, making it easy to remove with a spider. Carefully turn the potatoes whilst cooking to ensure even coloration.

4. When cooked, drain on kitchen paper and serve garnished with deep fried or fresh picked parsley.

Pommes Elizabeth

Enclose a little ball of chopped cooked spinach in each moulded round of the mixture and proceed as for Pommes Dauphine.

Pommes Lorette

Add 75 g grated Parmesan cheese to the Dauphine Potato Mixture. Mould into cigar-shapes and proceed as for Pommes Dauphine.

DEEP-FRIED POTATOES

Chip Potatoes (Pommes Frites)

Trim 2 kg potatoes oblong shape and cut into 6–8 cm × 1 cm baton-shaped pieces. Wash in cold water to remove the surface starch, drain and dry very well. Place into a frying basket and deep fry in hot fat at 170°C until cooked but not coloured. Drain well and retain on a tray on kitchen paper. When required for service, place the requisite amount of the blanched chips into a frying basket, plunge into hot fat at 190°C and fry until crisp and golden. Drain on kitchen paper and season with salt. Serve on a dish paper on a flat dish.

Game Chips (Pommes Chips)

Trim potatoes into 4 cm cylinder-shapes and cut on a mandolin into 1 mm slices. Proceed as for Straw Potatoes.

Straw Potatoes (Pommes Pailles)

Trim the potatoes oblong-shape and cut into 6 cm julienne. Wash in cold water to remove surface starch, drain and dry very well. Place into a frying basket and plunge into hot fat at 190°C, continuously shake the basket until the oil subsides, then tip the potatoes into the fat. Move them about with a spider and fry until light golden brown. Drain well on kitchen paper and serve as a garnish for grilled and fried meat dishes.

Matchstick Potatoes (Pommes Allumette)

Cut potatoes into thin strips 4 cm × 0.5 cm, or cut on a mandolin, using the special blade provided, and proceed as for Chip Potatoes. These are served mainly as a garnish for grilled and fried meat dishes.

Pommes Pont-neuf

Cut potatoes into 6 cm long × 2 cm pieces and proceed as for Chip Potatoes.

Wafer Potatoes (Pommes Gaufrettes)

Trim potatoes into 6 cm cylinder-shapes and cut on a mandolin, using the grooved blade, into 1 mm trellis slices, giving a half turn to the potato between each slicing movement. Proceed as for Straw Potatoes.

Fried New Potatoes with Almonds (Alu Badam)   INDIA

Wash, scrape and dry 1.5 kg new potatoes and deep fry until cooked, golden brown and crisp on the outside. Drain, combine with 175 g toasted flaked almonds, season with salt and 2 tsp garam masala and serve.

Sweet Potato Fritters   CARIBBEAN

Peel and cut 1 kg sweet potatoes into 1 cm thick slices, soak in cold salted water for 15 minutes, drain and dry. Pass through yeast batter and golden deep fry in groundnut oil; drain, season and serve.

Spiced Matchstick Potatoes (Alu Lachche)   INDIA

Cut peeled potatoes into matchstick shapes, 4 cm × 2 mm × 2 mm. Golden deep fry, drain and season with a mixture of equal quantities of salt, chilli powder, ground cumin and garam masala.

SHALLOW-FRIED AND SAUTÉ POTATOES

Sauté Potatoes (Pommes Sautées)

   2 kg even-sized potatoes
250 ml oil
  75 g butter
      salt
      chopped parsley

1. Boil the unpeeled potatoes for 15 minutes, keeping slightly underdone.
2. Peel, cool and cut into 0.5 cm slices.
3. Heat sufficient of the oil to cover the bottom of a heavy frying pan, add a layer of the potatoes, allow to colour underneath, then toss over to colour the other side. Toss again, but not unnecessarily. Clean the pan before sautéeing the next batch.
4. When all are coloured and fully cooked, toss in the butter in a clean frying pan and season with salt.
5. Serve in a vegetable dish and sprinkle with chopped parsley.

Lyonnaise Potatoes (Pommes Lyonnaise)

Proceed as for Sauté Potatoes and add one-third of the quantity of fried sliced onions, mixing them together.

Pommes Provençale

Proceed as for Sauté Potatoes, frying a few finely chopped cloves of garlic in the butter.

Pommes Sautées à Cru

Cut new potatoes into 0.5 cm slices, sauté in oil until an even golden colour, then drain. Replace them in the frying pan in hot butter, toss gently and season with salt.

Pommes Columbine

Proceed as for Pommes Sautées à Cru with the addition of strips of cooked red pimento.

Pommes Nouvelles Rissolées

Shallow fry new potatoes until cooked and coloured, then drain and roll them in melted butter. Alternatively, they may be boiled in the skins, peeled and shallow fried.

Pommes Parmentier

Cut potatoes into 1.5 cm dice, wash, dry and sauté in oil to an even golden brown colour. Drain, then replace in the frying pan in hot butter and season with salt.

Pommes Sablées

Proceed as for Pommes Parmentier, adding white breadcrumbs during the last few moments of cooking, tossing them over with the potatoes to a golden brown colour.

Pommes Cocotte

Cut potatoes into small barrel-shapes 1.5 cm in length. Sauté in oil to an even golden colour, then drain. Replace in the cleaned pan in hot butter, toss gently and season with salt.

Pommes Noisette

Cut potatoes into balls using a 25 mm Parisienne scoop. Sauté in oil to an even golden colour, then drain. Replace in the cleaned pan with hot butter, toss gently and season with salt.

Pommes Parisienne

Cut potatoes into balls using a 28 mm Parisienne scoop. Sauté in oil to an even golden colour, then drain and roll in melted meat glaze.

Note
Another way to cook Cocotte, Noisette and Parisienne Potatoes is to blanch them for 3 minutes in boiling water, drain, colour in hot oil in a frying pan and finish cooking in the oven. Drain off the oil, add 75 g butter per 10 portions and roll to coat. For Pommes Parisienne omit the butter and add melted meat glaze.

Potato Latkes   ISRAEL

Finely grate 2 kg raw potatoes and leave to drain on a sieve for 10 minutes. Combine with 4 beaten eggs, 225 g flour sifted with 10 g baking powder, salt and pepper. Shape into small cakes or spoon mould and golden shallow fry in oil for 7 minutes; drain and serve.

Potato Pancakes   GERMANY
(Grundrezept Für Kartoffelpfannkuchen)

Finely grate 2 kg raw potatoes and leave to drain on a sieve for 10 minutes. Combine with 175 g finely chopped onion, 3 beaten eggs, 75 g flour and seasoning. Shallow fry 40 g spoonfuls in a pancake pan until golden brown on both sides.

Potato Cakes with Bacon (Döbbekoche)   GERMANY

Finely grate 2 kg raw potatoes and leave to drain on a sieve for 10 minutes. Combine with 225 g finely chopped onion, 2 beaten eggs, 350 g fried lardons of smoked bacon, salt, pepper and nutmeg. Heat sufficient oil in Anna moulds, fill with the mixture, brush with oil, cover and bake at 220°C for 45 minutes until golden brown in colour and crisp. Turn out and cut into portions. Serve with plum sauce, plum jelly or a fruit compote.

Potato Puris (Alu Puri)   INDIA

Cook 600 g floury potatoes in salted water, drain, dry, mash and allow to cool. Combine with 600 g flour and knead for 5 minutes to form a firm dough, then allow to rest for 1 hour. Divide into 40 small pieces and mould

6 cm in diameter. Golden shallow fry on each side in oil or ghee, drain and serve.

Potato and Burghul Cakes with Cinnamon (Kibbet Batata Bi Sanieh)
MIDDLE EAST

Cook 1 kg unpeeled potatoes in salted water, drain, peel and mash. Rinse 350 g fine burghul under cold running water for a few minutes, drain on a sieve, place into a basin and stand for 15 minutes. Combine the burghul, mashed potatoes, 100 g finely chopped onion, 25 g chopped parsley, 10 g chopped mint, 1 tsp ground cinnamon, salt and pepper. Knead the mixture until firm, place in an oiled dish and spread evenly to a thickness of 1 cm then cool in a refrigerator. Turn out, cut into round or diamond shapes and shallow fry until light golden brown on both sides.

Rösti Potatoes (Rösti)
SWITZERLAND

Finely grate 2 kg potatoes. Heat 25 ml oil in a frying pan and lightly fry 175 g lardons of bacon, combine with the grated potato and season. Spread over the base of a hot buttered frying pan and cook for 10–15 minutes, occasionally stirring, then press flat and allow to colour underneath. Turn out and serve cut into wedges.

Savoury Potatoes with Spinach and Ginger (Palak Alu)
INDIA

Boil 2 kg potatoes in their skins until half-cooked; skin and cut into 1 cm cubes. Fry 4 dried, crushed red chillies and 2 tsp black mustard seeds in 175 ml oil or ghee until the seeds burst. Add the potatoes and fry until golden brown. Stir-fry 50 g grated ginger in 50 ml oil or ghee, add 1 kg shredded cooked spinach, stir in 225 ml natural yogurt, cook for 5 minutes, then add the cooked potatoes and seasoning. Serve sprinkled with chopped coriander leaves.

ROAST POTATOES

Roast Potatoes (Pommes Rôties)

  1.5 kg even-sized potatoes
100 ml dripping or oil
  50 g melted butter
      salt

1. Heat the fat in a thick-bottomed roasting tray on the stove.
2. Add the dried, trimmed potatoes and roll them over heat until lightly coloured.

3. Season with salt and place into the oven to roast at 220°C for 30–40 minutes. To test if the potatoes are cooked, press gently with the fingers.
4. When golden brown and cooked, drain off the fat and serve the potatoes in a vegetable dish.

Chateau Potatoes (Pommes Château)

Turn 2 kg potatoes into 6 cm barrel-shapes and proceed as for Roast Potatoes.

CHAPTER 11 Sweets and Bakery Items

Pastry Goods

BASIC PASTES

Pastry mixtures are made from approximately four parts of flour, two parts or more of fat and one part of liquid. There are several different kinds of pastry including short pastry, sweet pastry, puff pastry, suet pastry and choux paste, each having its particular uses. Some pastries are made to hold fillings and should therefore be sufficiently robust to hold them while at the same time being crisp on the outside, soft inside and pleasing to the taste. The type of fat used has an effect upon the taste and texture of the pastry and there are several kinds of margarines and shortenings purpose-made for each kind of pastry. Butter gives a good flavour but is more expensive and not necessarily better than margarine for making pastry. Soft flour gives the best result for short pastry and sweet pastry, whereas puff pastry needs strong flour. Self-raising flour is good for suet pastry and can also be used for short pastry but the result is spongy rather than short. General-purpose flour gives good results for all pastries except puff pastry. It is usual to use castor sugar rather than icing sugar. Care must be exercised when making pastry by machine as it quickly becomes overmixed, giving a tough result.

Short and Sweet Pastry

The difference between short pastry and sweet pastry is that sugar is used in the latter. Sweet pastry is used for fruit flans, etc. so egg is used as part of the mixing liquid rather than all water in order to give the special firmness required. Short pastry is usually made by rubbing the fat into the flour, whereas sweet pastry is made by creaming the fat with the sugar and egg, then incorporating the flour.

Short Pastry (Pâte à Foncer)

Makes 1 kg

  600 g soft flour
  1 tsp salt
  300 g margarine
150 ml water

1. Sift the flour and salt into a mixing bowl. Add the fat and rub together until it resembles breadcrumbs.
2. Make a bay in the centre, pour in the cold water and mix lightly until it binds into a paste.
3. Wrap in greaseproof paper and place in the refrigerator for at least 30 minutes before proceeding to roll it out.

Sweet Pastry (Pâte Sucrée)

Makes 1 kg

500 g soft flour
1 tsp salt
300 g margarine
125 g castor sugar
    2 eggs

1. Sift the flour and salt onto a working surface and make a bay in the centre.
2. Place the softened fat and the sugar into the bay and cream together.
3. Add the eggs one by one, mixing in well.
4. Incorporate the flour to form a paste.
5. Scrape twice with a palette knife and knead well together.
6. Wrap in greaseproof paper and place in the refrigerator for at least 30 minutes before proceeding to roll it out.

Filo Pastry

Makes 1 kg
Mix 400 ml warm water and 60 ml olive oil and add to 600 g strong flour sifted with 1 tsp salt, to form a dough. Allow to rest for 1 hour, then roll out very thinly indeed, ideally using a rolling machine.

Strudel Pastry

Makes 350 g
Mix together 30 ml olive oil, 125 ml tepid water, 50 g castor sugar and 1 yolk of egg. Sift 225 g strong flour into a mixing bowl, make a bay in the centre, pour in the liquid and mix to form a dough; knead until smooth and silky, then allow to rest for 30 minutes before rolling out.

Puff Pastry (Feuilletage)

Makes 1 kg

400 g strong flour
1 tsp salt
400 g butter
  $1/2$ juice of lemon
225 ml cold water

1. Sift the flour and salt into a basin and rub in a quarter of the butter.
2. Make a bay in the centre and add the water and lemon juice.
3. Mix to form a ball of smooth dough and knead lightly; cover and allow to relax for 30 minutes.

4. Cut a cross halfway through the ball of dough, then pull open from the centre to form a star. Lightly roll out the corners leaving the centre thicker than the sides.
5. Knead the remainder of the butter until it is soft and the same consistency as the dough and form into a block.
6. Place into the centre of the dough and fold over the four flaps to seal in the butter.
7. Roll out the pastry gently to a rectangle 80 cm × 20 cm, then give a double turn by folding the two ends to the centre, then in half again. Repeat this procedure three more times, allowing 30 minutes between each turn for the paste to relax.

Notes
1. Purpose-made fat gives a better result in volume but not such a good taste as butter.
2. In warm weather it is best to use iced water.
   The layers of fat and pastry in puff pastry are built up by the turns as follows:

Turn:	1st	2nd	3rd	4th
Number of layers:	12	48	192	768

3. The secrets of producing good results when making and using puff pastry are:
   (a) To get the consistency of the dough neither too hard nor too soft so that it rolls easily
   (b) To allow plenty of time between the turns and to leave the finished product time to relax before baking
   (c) To get the oven very hot so that the moisture trapped in the pastry quickly turns to steam to make it rise, then to lower the oven temperature slightly.

Suet Pastry

Makes 1 kg

500 g self-raising flour
1 tsp salt
250 g suet
250 ml water

1. Sift the flour and salt into a basin.
2. Add the suet, mix together and make a bay in the centre.
3. Mix in the water to form a fairly stiff dough without overmixing it.

Notes
1. Suet gives the pastry a short texture and subtle firmness and the use of self-raising flour gives it lightness. The chopped suet is held in pieces in the dough. During cooking the pastry absorbs the melted suet, leaving pockets of air, while the suet imparts its richness to the pastry.

2. General-purpose flour sifted with 15 g baking powder can be used instead of self-raising flour.

Choux Paste (Pâte à Choux)

Makes 650 g

250 ml water	100 g butter
pinch salt	125 g strong flour
pinch sugar	4 eggs

1. Place the water, salt, sugar and butter in a pan to boil.
2. When it boils and the butter has melted, remove from the heat and add the flour, mixing it in vigorously with a wooden spatule.
3. Return to the heat and mix until the mixture leaves the sides of the pan clean. Remove from the stove.
4. Allow the mixture to cool. Beat in the eggs one at a time until the mixture just drops from the spoon.

Note

Choux paste is softer than the other pastries and has to be piped out into the desired shape with a piping bag and tube. During baking the moistness turns to steam, which causes it to rise, leaving the centre hollow. Items of choux paste must be cooked until very crisp and golden brown, whether by baking or deep frying.

PUFF PASTRY GOODS

Bandes (Bands or Slices)

These are made by spreading lengths of puff pastry 15 cm wide with frangipane, then covering with fresh, poached or canned fruits and baking, or by covering baked lengths of puff pastry with fruit. They are finished with apricot glaze and served cut into 8 cm slices.

Apricot Slice (Bande aux Abricots)

350 g	puff pastry
500 ml	pastry cream
1	egg (eggwash)
400 g	apricot halves
100 ml	apricot glaze

1. Roll out the pastry 30 cm × 15 cm and cut off two 1.5 cm wide strips along the length.
2. Place the large strip on a damp baking sheet, brush the edges with eggwash and lay the thin strips one each side, pressing well onto the base.

3. Notch the edges with the back of a floured small knife, eggwash and prick the centre with a fork and allow to rest for 45 minutes.
4. Bake in the oven at 220°C for 15 minutes. Place on a wire cooling rack and allow to cool.
5. Spread the pastry cream along the centre, neatly arrange the halves of apricots and coat with apricot glaze.
6. Cut across the bande into 10 even portions.

Banbury Cakes

Makes 24

350 g currants		1 kg puff pastry
100 g brown sugar		2 egg whites
1 lemon juice and grated zest	filling	50 g castor sugar
100 g butter		
¼ tsp mixed spice		

1. Roll out the pastry 2.5 mm thick and cut out 24 × 10 cm rounds, turn over and brush with eggwash.
2. Place 20 g of the filling in each, fold over the edge, sealing in the filling.
3. Roll out oval-shape, brush with slightly beaten egg white, dip the top into the castor sugar and place on a damp baking sheet.
4. Make three incisions in the centre and allow to rest for 45 minutes.
5. Bake in the oven at 215–220°C for 15 minutes.

Cheese Straws (Paillettes au Parmesan)

Roll out 275 g puff pastry 60 cm × 30 cm; sprinkle with 50 g grated Parmesan cheese and a tiny pinch of cayenne and press in. Fold into three, roll out 3 mm thick, brush with eggwash and sprinkle with a further 25 g of grated Parmesan, rolling it in so as to make it stick. Cut into 15 cm lengths × 1 cm width, twist into spirals and press onto a damp baking sheet, also making a few 4 cm rings of the pastry. Allow to rest for 15 minutes, then bake in the oven at 220°C for 8 minutes then fill the rings with the straws to resemble sheaves.

Eccles Cakes

These are made in the same way as Banbury Cakes, using a filling of mincemeat and cake crumbs and making them round in shape.

Fleurons

Roll out puff pastry 3 mm thick and cut into crescent shapes with a 5 cm fluted cutter. Turn over, place on a damp baking sheet, eggwash and allow to rest for 45 minutes. Bake at 225°C for 10 minutes until golden.

Note

These are used to decorate many kinds of dishes e.g. Filets de Sole Vin Blanc where they add crispness to a smooth dish.

Pithivier

500 g puff pastry
50 g raspberry jam
200 g frangipane
1 egg (eggwash)
20 g icing sugar

1. Roll out the pastry 2.5 mm thick and cut out two circles, one 23 cm and the other 24 cm in diameter.
2. Lay the small round on a damp baking sheet, spread with jam and then with frangipane to within 1.5 cm of the edge. Eggwash the edges.
3. Cover with the other round of pastry, seal well together and notch the edge all round.
4. Eggwash and cut slits, scroll-fashion, starting at the centre and using the point of a small knife without penetrating deeply into the pastry. Allow to rest for 45 minutes.
5. Bake in the oven at 215°C for 30–35 minutes. Dust with the icing sugar and glaze either in the oven or under a salamander grill for a few moments.

Jalousie

500 g puff pastry
50 g raspberry jam
200 g frangipane
1 egg (eggwash)
20 g icing sugar

1. Roll out the pastry into an oblong shape 40 cm × 24 cm and cut in half lengthways.
2. Lay one half on a damp baking sheet, spread with jam and then with frangipane to within 1.5 cm of the edge. Eggwash the edges.
3. Fold the remaining piece of pastry in two lengthways and, using a sharp knife, cut incisions across the fold at 1 cm intervals.
4. Unfold and cover the base, seal well together and notch the edge. Allow to rest for 45 minutes.
5. Bake in the oven at 215°C for 30–35 minutes. Dust with the icing sugar and glaze either in the oven or under a salamander grill for a few moments.

Gâteau Millefeuille

Makes 1 × 20 cm round

600 g puff pastry
150 g raspberry jam
300 ml pastry cream

100 ml apricot glaze
500 g fondant
500 g toasted flaked almonds

1. Roll out the pastry 3 mm thick and cut into 3 × 20 cm diameter circles.
2. Lay on a damp baking sheet and prick all over with a fork. Allow to rest for 45 minutes.
3. Bake in the oven at 220°C for 15 minutes until golden and crisp. Place on a wire cooling rack and allow to cool.
4. Sandwich the three pieces of pastry with jam and pastry cream and lightly trim the edges.
5. Glaze the top layer with apricot glaze.
6. Melt the fondant in a pan to 37°C and coat the gateau, then pipe a spiral of chocolate-flavoured fondant from the centre to the edge.
7. Place the point of the back of a small knife at the centre of the gateau and make a feathering effect at 2 cm intervals around the entire surface.
8. Spread the sides with pastry cream and coat with flaked almonds. Serve on a doily on a flat round dish.

Mince Pies

Makes 24

1 kg puff pastry
350 g mincemeat
1 egg (eggwash)
15 g icing sugar

1. Roll out the pastry 2.5 mm thick and cut out 24 × 7 cm rounds and 24 × 8 cm rounds.
2. Place the small rounds on a dampened baking sheet and place about 15 g mincemeat in the centre of each.
3. Brush the edges with eggwash, cover with the larger rounds and press well together; allow to rest for 45 minutes.
4. Brush with eggwash and bake in the oven at 215°C for 15 minutes.
5. When cooked, remove from the oven, place onto a wire cooling rack and dredge liberally with the icing sugar; serve warm.

Palmiers

Makes 24

1 kg puff pastry
100 g castor sugar
100 g raspberry jam
200 ml whipped cream

1. Roll out the pastry 2.5 mm thick, using castor sugar instead of flour and forming a strip 36 cm × 24 cm.
2. Brush with water and sprinkle with sugar. Lightly mark the centre line and fold each side three times towards the line. Fold together to give a 6 cm strip.
3. Cut into strips 1 cm across and place on a greased baking sheet well spaced out. Open the folded ends outwards and allow to rest for 45 minutes. Bake at 225°C for 10 minutes until caramelised to a light golden brown, then turn them over with a palette knife and cook for another 3 minutes. Place onto a wire cooling rack and allow to cool.
4. Spread one piece with jam and cream and place another palmier on top to form a sandwich.

Note
Palmiers are usually made using puff pastry trimmings.

Sausage Rolls

Makes 24

650 g puff pastry
   1 egg (eggwash)
500 g sausage meat

1. Roll out the pastry 72 cm × 20 cm and cut into two lengthways.
2. Roll the sausage meat into 2 × 72 cm lengths, using a little flour to prevent sticking.
3. Place one roll of sausage meat onto each piece of pastry.
4. Brush the edges with eggwash, fold the pastry over the sausage meat and seal with a fork. Brush the top with eggwash.
5. Cut into 6 cm lengths at an angle of 45°. Place onto a dampened baking sheet and allow to rest for 45 minutes.
6. Bake at 220°C for 15–20 minutes.

Vol-au-Vent Cases

Makes 10

650 g puff pastry
   1 egg (eggwash)

1. Roll out the pastry 5 mm thick and cut out 10 rounds with an 8 cm pastry cutter; turn over and place on a damp baking sheet. Cut halfway through each piece with a second cutter 6 cm in diameter and allow to rest for 45 minutes.
2. Carefully eggwash and bake at 220°C for 20 minutes. Place onto a wire cooling rack and allow to cool.

3. Carefully remove and retain the centre pieces to replace when filled. Remove and discard any soft dough remaining inside and fill with an appropriate filling.

Note
Vol-au-Vents can also be made in large round or oval shapes for 2 portions.

Bouchées

These are smaller versions of vol-au-vents, cut with 4 cm and 3 cm cutters. They are mainly for use as a savoury item and served either hot or cold at cocktail parties.

CHOUX PASTRY GOODS

Chocolate Eclairs (Eclairs au Chocolat)

Makes 16

    650 g choux paste
      1 egg (eggwash)
    500 g fondant icing
      60 g plain chocolate
    600 ml whipped cream

1. Using a 1 cm plain tube pipe the paste onto a greased baking sheet in 10 cm lengths and brush with eggwash.
2. Bake at 220°C for 25 minutes, until very crisp.
3. When cooked, cool on a wire cooling rack.
4. Cut the éclairs open along one side and fill with the cream, using a plain tube. Ensure that none comes out when the éclairs are closed.
5. Melt the fondant in a shallow pan to 37°C, add the melted chocolate and mix together.
6. Dip the surface of each éclair into the fondant and smooth off any surplus. Keep the fondant well mixed, adding some lukewarm stock syrup as necessary to keep it from becoming too stiff.
7. Allow to set, then arrange the éclairs on a doily on a silver dish.

Note
Pastry Cream may be used in place of whipped cream.

Cream Buns (Choux à la Crème)

These are made by piping choux paste into 3 cm diameter balls which are baked at 220°C for 20 minutes and filled with whipped cream when cool. The cream is either piped through a hole in the bottom or a cut in the side. Dredge with icing sugar and serve.

Chocolate Profiteroles (Profiteroles au Chocolat)

These are made by piping choux paste into 1.5 cm balls which are baked at 220°C for 20 minutes, then filled with whipped cream through a hole in the bottom when cool. Arrange dome-shape in glass bowls, dredge with icing sugar and serve with cold chocolate sauce separately in a sauceboat, or the sauce can be poured over the undredged profiteroles.

FILO PASTRY ITEMS

Baklava
GREECE

Chop 450 g walnuts and 225 g almonds, add 50 g castor sugar and 1 tsp each of ground cinnamon and cloves. Line a 30 cm × 23 cm buttered tray with 10 sheets of filo pastry brushed with melted butter, spread with half the nut mixture, cover with 2 more sheets of buttered filo pastry, then with the rest of the nut mixture and finish with another 8 layers of buttered filo pastry. Brush with butter and sprinkle with water and bake at 160°C for 1 hour. Boil 600 ml water, 50 ml lemon juice, 350 g sugar, 50 g honey, 3 cloves and cinnamon to small thread stage (104°C); strain and cool. Cut the baklava into diamond-shapes and macerate with the syrup.

Batters

Beer Batter

Whisk together 450 g plain flour, 725 ml light ale, 1 tsp salt and 2 g saffron infused in 1 tbs water and allow to stand for 1 hour before using.

Pakora Batter
INDIA

175 g gram flour	1 tsp ajowan powder
1 tsp salt	1/4 tsp dried mint
1 tsp chilli powder	350 ml water
1 tsp garam masala	

1. Sift the flour into a basin, add the chilli powder, garam masala, ajowan powder and dried mint.
2. Whisk in the water to form a batter, then allow to rest for 30 minutes before using.

Tempura Batter
JAPAN

225 g plain flour
2 eggs
500 ml chilled water

1. Sift the flour into a basin.
2. Combine the eggs and chilled water and whisk into the flour to form a smooth batter, then strain and allow to rest for 30 minutes before using.

Yorkshire Pudding

225 g plain flour
¹/₂ tsp salt
2 eggs
400 ml milk
200 ml beef dripping

1. Sift the flour and salt into a basin.
2. Whisk together the eggs and milk.
3. Add the beaten eggs and milk to the flour and whisk to a smooth batter.
4. Strain through a conical strainer into a clean basin and allow the mixture to relax for about 1 hour.
5. Heat the dripping in 10 individual moulds or two 15 cm frying pans.
6. Pour in the batter mixture in equal amounts into the moulds and place into the oven at 220°C to bake for 30 minutes until it has risen, and is crisp and golden.

Yeast Batter

400 g strong flour
15 g yeast
600 ml milk at 37°C
1 tsp sugar
1 tsp salt

1. Sift the flour into a basin and make a hollow in the centre.
2. Dissolve the yeast in the milk with the sugar.
3. Pour into the hollow and whisk to a smooth batter.
4. Add the salt and allow the batter to stand in a warm place for 1 hour to prove before using.

FRITTERS

The three kinds of fritters are:

1. Those made with fresh or canned fruits such as apple, bananas and pineapple, dipped in batter.
2. Moulded rice and semolina mixtures, usually coated with egg and breadcrumbs.
3. Soufflé fritters made with choux paste without any outer coating.

Fruit fritters

Apple Fritters (Beignets de Pommes)

1 kg peeled and cored cooking apples	1 juice of lemon
50 g castor sugar	500 ml yeast batter
	icing sugar
5 g cinnamon	400 ml apricot sauce

1. Cut the prepared apples into rings 5 mm thick. Place in a tray, sprinkle with castor sugar, cinnamon and lemon juice and allow to stand for 30 minutes. If desired 50 ml calvados or rum may also be used.
2. Pass through flour, then the batter, removing any surplus and place into a deep fryer 180°C.
3. Fry for 5 minutes until crisp and golden, turning them with a spider during cooking to ensure even cooking and coloration.
4. Drain on absorbent kitchen paper, then place onto a tray, dust with icing sugar and place under a salamander grill to glaze.
5. Arrange on a dish lined with a dish paper and serve with the hot apricot sauce.

Banana Fritters (Beignets de Bananes)

Proceed as for Apple Fritters, using 10 bananas peeled and cut in two crossways. The bananas may first be coated with pastry cream and allowed to set before being fried. Serve with hot apricot sauce.

Pineapple Fritters (Beignets d'Ananas)

Proceed as for Apple Fritters, using 20 pineapple rings dipped into hot Pastry Cream and allowed to set, then coated with yeast batter. Serve accompanied by hot apricot sauce.

Banana Fritters (Pisang Goreng)   THAILAND

Combine 200 ml thin coconut milk, 300 ml thick coconut milk, 225 g rice flour and 50 ml melted butter to form a batter. Coat halves of banana with the batter and shallow fry in clarified butter, sprinkle with icing sugar and serve.

Caramelised Apple and Banana Fritters   CHINA
(Chah Ping Gwo, Chah Heung Jiu)

Deep golden fry yeast-battered apple rings and banana pieces, then dip them quickly into caramel, then immediately into iced water; drain and serve.

Note
For caramel boil 25 ml corn oil, 300 g sugar and 300 ml water to the crack stage of 150°C, then stir in a tablespoonful of sesame seeds and use immediately.

Combine 225 g chopped dates, 100 g chopped cashews, walnuts or almonds and grated zest and juice of 1 lemon. Fill into 40 wonton wrappers, twisting the ends to seal. Golden fry, drain, dust with icing sugar and glaze under a salamander grill.

Rice and semolina fritters

Rice Fritters

1 litre rice for Condé (without the cream)	500 ml yeast batter
	icing sugar
50 g flour	400 ml apricot sauce

1. When the rice is cooked spread in a 26 cm × 20 cm buttered tray to a depth of 1.5 cm. When cold, cut into 5 cm squares or rounds, pass through flour, then the batter. Drain off any surplus.
2. Place into the hot fat at 180°C and fry for 5 minutes until crisp and golden, turning the pieces during cooking to ensure even cooking and coloration.
3. Drain on absorbent kitchen paper, then place the fritters onto a tray, dredge with icing sugar and place under a salamander grill to glaze.
4. Arrange on a dish with a dish paper and serve with the hot apricot sauce.

Note
These fritters may also be made by coating them with breadcrumbs.

Semolina Fritters

Prepare and cook a Condé without cream using 200 g semolina in place of rice and spread in a 26 cm × 20 cm buttered tray to a depth of 1.5 cm. When cold, cut into 5 cm squares or rounds, pass through flour, then yeast batter. Drain off any surplus and deep fry in hot fat at 180°C until golden. Drain and dredge with icing sugar and glaze under a salamander grill. Serve accompanied by hot apricot sauce.

Soufflé fritters

Choux Paste Fritters (Beignets Soufflés)

650 g	choux paste
50 g	icing sugar
400 ml	apricot sauce

1. Take dessertspoons of choux paste, mould with another spoon and drop into hot deep fat at 155°C, allowing 40 pieces for 10 portions.

2. Fry for 5 minutes until crisp, hollow and golden brown, turning the pieces during cooking to ensure even coloration.
3. Drain on kitchen paper, then roll in icing sugar.
4. Arrange on a dish with a dish paper and serve with hot apricot sauce.

Beignets Soufflés Georgette

Proceed as for Choux Paste Fritters and fill with pastry cream containing chopped pineapple and kirsch. Serve accompanied by a sauceboat of apricot sauce, flavoured with kirsch.

PANCAKES

Pancakes are made from a batter the consistency of thin cream and are cooked in a 15 cm pancake pan. They should be thin and delicate and evenly cooked to a light golden colour on each side. They are featured mainly as a sweet item on a menu but may also be served with a savoury filling.

Lemon Pancakes (Crêpes au Citron)

Makes 30 × 15 cm

250 g flour	500 ml milk
1/2 tsp salt	50 g butter
25 g castor sugar	200 g lard
2 eggs	3 lemons

1. Sift the flour and salt into a basin.
2. Whisk the eggs, milk and sugar together.
3. Add to the flour and whisk until smooth. Strain through a conical strainer into a clean basin.
4. Heat the butter and whisk it into the batter, then allow to stand for one hour in a cool place in order to allow it to relax.
5. Heat some of the melted lard in a pancake pan until it is very hot and a light haze rises from it. Pour off any surplus fat, add 30 ml of the batter and allow to spread evenly in the pan.
6. Cook quickly until lightly golden brown on one side, then turn over with a palette knife or toss and continue cooking until coloured on both sides.
7. Turn out onto a plate and keep warm while continuing to make the others.
8. To serve, fold the pancakes into quarters, lightly sprinkle with lemon juice and castor sugar and garnish with lemon wedges.

Notes
1. If not for immediate use, cooked pancakes should be turned out onto a plate and allowed to cool completely, covered with clingfilm and retained in a refrigerator.

2. To reheat filled pancakes, cover with kitchen foil or greaseproof paper to prevent them drying out and place in an oven; unfilled pancakes may be reheated on a griddle top.

Apple Pancakes (Crêpes à la Marmalade de Pommes)

Spread the pancakes with lemon-flavoured apple purée and roll up. Arrange on a dish or plate with the joins underneath, sprinkle with castor sugar and serve.

Crêpes Suzette

Makes 4 portions

75 g butter	50 ml brandy
75 g castor sugar	12 pancakes
50 ml curaçao or Grand Marnier	100 ml brandy (or curaçao)

1. Melt the butter in a guéridon pan.
2. Add the castor sugar and cook until it begins to caramelise.
3. Pour in the curaçao or Grand Marnier and half the brandy and mix together with a spoon.
4. Dip each pancake into the mixture, fold into four and push to the side of the pan.
5. Sprinkle the pancakes with the remaining brandy or curaçao and tip the pan to one side so that it catches alight.
6. Sprinkle with a little sugar and serve just as the flames die down.

Note
This dish is usually prepared in front of the customer by a member of the waiting staff, using a table lamp fuelled by a gas cylinder or methylated sprit. Safety precautions need to be observed.

Jam Pancakes (Crêpes à la Confiture)

Spread pancakes with warm jam and roll up. Arrange on a dish or plate with the joins underneath, sprinkle with castor sugar, heat through in an oven and serve.

Pear Pancakes (Crêpes du Couvent)

Add 250 g diced poached pears to the pancake mixture and make slightly thicker than ordinary pancakes. Serve sprinkled with castor sugar.

American Pancakes   USA

Combine 3 beaten eggs with 350 ml milk and whisk onto 350 g flour sifted with 4 tsp baking powder, 3 tsp castor sugar and salt, to form a batter. Place tablespoonfuls of the batter into a pancake pan to form 7.5 cm pancakes. Coat with melted butter and maple syrup on serving.

Turkish Pancake Pie with Cream Cheese
(Rakott Turos Palacsinta)

Combine 450 g cream cheese, 25 g flour, 4 eggs, 25 ml oil and 150 g sugar. Line a greased baking tray with ordinary pancakes, spread with jam, then add the cheese mixture, making several layers and finishing with pancakes. Sprinkle with butter and bake in the oven at 175°C for 30 minutes. Decorate with meringue made with 3 whites of egg and 175 g castor sugar, dredge with icing sugar and glaze in the oven.

Blinis

Make a batter with 25 g yeast dissolved in 100 ml warm milk mixed with 50 g strong flour and allow to prove. Whisk 4 egg yolks with 300 ml warm milk, add to the yeast mixture together with 250 g strong flour and 1 tsp salt and mix to a batter. Prove, then fold in 4 stiffly beaten whites of egg. Make into 20×50 ml individual pancakes, using a 12 cm pan.

Note

Blinis can be made using buckwheat flour and are customarily served with caviar.

Sponges

Genoese Sponge

Makes 1×22 cm round

- 5 eggs
- 150 g castor sugar
- 150 g soft flour
- 75 g melted butter

1. Prepare the cake tin by lightly greasing with clarified margarine or softened white fat and coat with flour.
2. Place the eggs and sugar in the warmed mixing bowl of an electric mixer.
3. Whisk at high speed until the mixture is thick and creamy. It is ready when the drops falling from the raised whisk leave a mark on the surface.
4. Carefully fold in the flour using a metal spoon or a scraper, turning the mixing bowl at the same time.
5. Pour the cooled melted butter down the sides of the bowl, mixing gently. Do not overmix.
6. Pour into the tin and cook immediately at a temperature of 195°C for 25–30 minutes.
7. When cooked, remove from the baking tin at once onto a wire cooling rack.

Notes
1. If whisking by hand, stand the bowl in a pan of hot water, but do not allow the water to boil.
2. A few drops of glycerine may be added so that the sponge will keep longer without going stale.
3. Genoese should be cooked 12–24 hours before use in gateaux.
4. Genoese is a low fat, all-purpose sponge that is widely used to make a range of gateaux and individual sponge-based items. It is extremely light and well aerated and should not be confused with Victoria Sponge, which is made quite differently. The aeration of a Genoese Sponge comes only from the beaten eggs.

Chocolate Genoese Sponge

Proceed as for Genoese Sponge, replacing 30 g of the flour with 30 g of cocoa and sieving them together before folding in.

Genoese Sponge Gateau

1 × 22 cm Genoese Sponge
  75 ml stock syrup
  100 g raspberry jam
  500 g butter cream

nibbed or flaked, toasted almonds, or chocolate vermicelli

1. Slice through the sponge, making small incisions around it to act as a guide before cutting. The sponge may be divided into two or three layers, making certain that it is flat side uppermost and level.
2. Lay out the sections of sponge and sprinkle with the stock syrup.
3. Spread with the jam, then the butter cream, and reassemble the sponge.
4. Spread the top and sides with butter cream, making certain that the top is absolutely level by smoothing over the surface with a palette knife dipped in warm water.
5. Cover the sides with either toasted nibbed or flaked almonds or chocolate vermicelli.
6. Decorate the top with butter cream.

Swiss Roll

This is prepared in the same way as a Genoese Sponge, using 4 eggs and 125 g each of castor sugar and soft flour and omitting the butter. It is baked at 225°C for 8 minutes in a 32.5 cm × 23 cm Swiss roll tin, lined with greased greaseproof paper. It is turned out, spread with 200 g warmed raspberry jam and rolled up tightly as soon as possible. If desired, a few drops of glycerine can be added to improve the keeping quality. Other kinds of jam or buttercream may be used.

Chocolate Swiss Roll

Proceed as for Swiss Roll, replacing 25 g of the flour with 25 g of cocoa and sieving them together.

Victoria Sponge

Makes 2 × 18 cm

250 g butter	250 g soft flour ⎱ sieved
250 g castor sugar	10 g baking powder ⎰ together
3 eggs	25 g castor sugar
100 g raspberry jam	

1. Prepare the baking tins by lightly greasing with clarified margarine or softened white fat, and coat with flour.
2. Cream the butter and sugar with a wooden spatule until light, white and fluffy.
3. Gradually add the beaten eggs.
4. Fold in the flour and baking powder using a metal spoon; do not overmix.
5. Fill into the baking tins and cook in the oven at 180°C for 25 minutes.
6. When cooked turn out onto a cooling rack.
7. Spread one piece with the jam and place the other sponge on top. Dust with castor sugar and serve on a doily on a round flat dish.

Notes
1. Care must be taken not to curdle the mixture when adding the eggs; this can be avoided by adding 1 tbs of the flour each time.
2. Margarine may be substituted for butter.
3. When cooked, the sponge should be firm to the touch; when the pressure is released no marks remain.

Scones and Cakes

The cakes in this section are made from a soft mixture consisting of 2 parts flour to 1 of liquid.

Scones

Makes 12

125 g strong flour	50 g butter
125 g soft flour	25 g castor sugar
10 g baking powder	100 ml milk

1. Pass the two kinds of flour and baking powder through a sieve twice and place into a basin.
2. Rub in the butter until it resembles breadcrumbs.
3. Add the sugar and then the milk and mix quickly to a soft dough.
4. Dust with flour, roll out 2 cm thick and cut out with a 5 cm round plain cutter.
5. Place on a greased baking sheet and brush with milk.
6. Bake at 210°C for 15 minutes.

Note
The mixture can be moulded as an 18 cm round flat piece, placed on the baking tray and almost cut through into 8 wedges.

Sultana Scones

Proceed as for Scones, adding 75 g sultanas to the mixture.

Rock Cakes

Makes 10

125 g strong flour	100 ml milk
125 g soft flour	few drops lemon essence
10 g baking powder	60 g mixed fruit
125 g margarine or butter	eggwash
125 g castor sugar	25 g granulated sugar
1 egg	

1. Sift the flours and baking powder into a bowl.
2. Add the fat and rub in to a sandy texture.
3. Add the sugar, the egg beaten with the milk, the fruit and flavouring, and mix to a firm dough.
4. Divide into 10 roughly shaped pieces and place onto a greased baking sheet. Brush with eggwash, and sprinkle with granulated sugar.
5. Bake in the oven at 215°C for 15 minutes.

Note
Another way is to cream the fat and sugar, add the egg and continue to beat before folding in the sieved flour and baking powder, sugar, the milk and essence and finally the fruit.

Cherry Cakes

Prepare as for Rock Cakes omitting the mixed fruit, adding 75 g of chopped, washed and dried glacé cherries and a few drops of vanilla essence. Fill into greased bun tins and bake.

Coconut Cakes

Prepare as for Rock Cakes, adding 25 g desiccated coconut and a few drops of vanilla essence. Place into greased bun tins and bake.

Raspberry Buns

Prepare as for Rock Cakes without the dried mixed fruit and with a few drops of vanilla essence in place of the lemon essence. Mould into 10 balls and flatten with a palette knife, retaining a round shape. Eggwash and dip the tops into granulated sugar. Place onto a greased baking sheet, make a small hollow in the centre of each and fill with a little raspberry jam. Bake as for Rock Cakes.

Rice Buns

Prepare as for Raspberry Buns, dipping into sugar nibs and placing half a glacé cherry instead of jam, in the centre of each.

Basic Plain Cake

Makes 1×20 cm or 2×15 cm cake tins

250 g compound fat or cake margarine	5 eggs
250 g castor sugar	250 g flour, general purpose
	10 g baking powder

1. Beat the fat and sugar with a whisk or in a electric mixer on second speed until creamy.
2. Add the eggs one at a time, beating well.
3. Mix in the sieved flour and baking powder with a metal spoon or scraper, being careful not to overmix.
4. Fill the prepared cake tin(s) and bake in the oven at 165°C for 2–2½ hours.

Notes
1. If necessary, a little milk may be added with the flour to soften the mixture.
2. All large plain and fruit cakes are made by the creaming method. It is advisable to use cake margarine or shortening as they cream quickly. General-purpose flour sieved with baking powder gives the best result.
3. Rich fruit cakes that need a long baking time should be protected from burning by several thicknesses of paper underneath and on top.
4. The more cakes baked together at one time, the better the humidity of the oven. This is an important factor in achieving a thin top crust. A container of water at the bottom of the oven will supply moisture throughout the baking process, thereby keeping the top crust flat and giving better colour.

5. To test if the cake is cooked, check that it has been cooked for the prescribed time at the correct temperature. Insert a skewer into the centre of the cake and leave it for a few moments – when removed it should be clean. If it has some cake mixture stuck to it the cake needs further baking.

Cherry Cake

Proceed as for Plain Cake, adding 150 g whole glacé cherries to the cake mixture. Bake for 1¼ hours at 165°C.

Dundee Cake

Proceed as for Plain Cake, using brown sugar in place of castor sugar; add 600 g dried mixed fruit to the cake mixture and cover the surface with whole almonds in a neat pattern. Bake for 1¾ hours at 150°C.

Fruit Cake

Proceed as for Plain Cake, adding 150 g dried mixed fruit to the cake mixture. Bake for 1 hour at 160°C.

Madeira Cake

Proceed as for Plain Cake, placing a slice of candied citron peel on top. Bake for 1¼ hours at 165°C.

Rich Fruit Cake

Proceed as for Plain Cake, using brown sugar in place of castor sugar and butter in place of compound fat or cake margarine. Add 500 g dried mixed fruit, 5 g mixed spice and 50 g glacé cherries to the mixture. Bake for 3–3½ hours at a temperature of 150°C.

Egg Custard Puddings

Egg custard is a versatile basic mixture which has a number of different applications, including many hot and cold sweets and ice creams and sauces. In unsweetened form, it is the basis of a variety of savoury dishes such as quiches. Careful cooking is needed to produce perfect results.

Baked Egg Custard

6 eggs	1.5 litres milk
4 egg yolks	few drops vanilla essence
100 g castor sugar	grated nutmeg

1. Mix the eggs, yolks and sugar in a basin.
2. Warm the milk with the vanilla essence, add to the eggs and sugar and mix well without making it frothy.
3. Strain into pie dishes and sprinkle the surface with grated nutmeg.
4. Place the dishes into a tray half-filled with warm water and bake at 170°C for 45 minutes until set.
5. When cooked, clean the pie dishes and serve on a flat dish with pie collars around them.

Note
When cooked, the custard should be firm and slightly resistant to pressure. When a needle or the point of a small knife is inserted it should come out clean.

Bread and Butter Pudding

6 eggs	100 g sultanas, washed
4 egg yolks	5 thin slices of bread
100 g castor sugar	and butter
1.5 litres milk	25 g castor sugar
few drops vanilla essence	nutmeg

1. Mix the eggs, yolks and sugar in a basin.
2. Warm the milk with the vanilla essence, add to the eggs and sugar and mix well without making it frothy.
3. Strain the mixture through a conical strainer into a clean receptacle.
4. Sprinkle the sultanas over the bottom of pie dishes.
5. Remove the crusts, cut the bread into 4 neat triangles and arrange overlapping in the dishes.
6. Pour over the egg custard and sprinkle the surface with nutmeg and castor sugar.
7. Place into a tray half-filled with warm water and bake at 175°C for 40 minutes until set.
8. When cooked, clean the pie dishes and serve on a flat dish with pie collars around them.

Cabinet Pudding

5 eggs	50 g glacé cherries
3 egg yolks	50 g currants
100 g castor sugar	50 g sultanas
1 litre milk	25 g melted butter ⎱ for moulds
few drops vanilla essence	25 g castor sugar ⎰
300 g sponge cake	400 ml apricot sauce

1. Mix the eggs, yolks and sugar in a basin.
2. Warm the milk with the vanilla essence, add to the eggs and sugar and mix well without making it frothy.

3. Strain through a conical strainer into a clean receptacle.
4. Lightly mix the diced sponge, chopped glacé cherries, currants and sultanas together and fill into 10 previously buttered and sugared dariole moulds.
5. Pour in the egg custard to fill the moulds and allow to stand.
6. Place in a tray half-filled with warm water and bake at 175°C for 40 minutes until set.
7. Allow to stand for a few minutes, turn out onto flat dishes and serve accompanied by apricot sauce.

Notes
1. This pudding can be made in a large mould or basin for several portions, covered with a lid and cooked in a steamer.
2. It can be made as a cold sweet by lining a mould with sliced sponge cake or finger biscuits and fruits, and filling it with a cooked egg custard set with gelatine.
3. Bread without the crust can be used instead of sponge cake, increasing the sugar.

Diplomat Pudding

This is made in the same way as Cabinet Pudding but is served cold.

Crème Beau-Rivage

Butter 2 savarin rings and coat with powdered praline (crushed almond toffee). Fill with egg custard made with 1 litre hot milk, 8 eggs and 125 g sugar. Cook in a bain-marie at 160°C for 40 minutes. When cold, turn out onto serving dishes, fill the centres with whipped cream, place cornet-shape langues de chat filled with cream in the centre and decorate with crystallised violets.

Crème Brulée

4 eggs	500 ml cream
4 egg yolks	few drops vanilla essence
100 g castor sugar	30 ratafia biscuits
500 ml milk	

1. Mix the eggs, yolks and sugar in a basin.
2. Warm the milk and cream with the vanilla essence, add to the eggs and mix well without making it frothy.
3. Strain through a conical strainer into a clean receptacle.
4. Pour into 10 ramekins or individual pie dishes.
5. Place into a tray half-filled with warm water and bake in the oven at 175°C for 45 minutes.

6. Sprinkle the surface of each with icing sugar and place under a sala-mander grill to glaze. Serve on an underdish on a doily, accompanied by the biscuits.

Cream Caramel (Crème Caramel)

200 g castor sugar	caramel	100 g castor sugar	
150 ml water	mixture	1 litre milk	
6 eggs		few drops vanilla essence	
4 egg yolks			

1. Place the sugar and 100 ml water into a copper sugar boiler, bring to the boil and cook until the mixture turns a golden brown. Carefully add 50 ml cold water.
2. Pour the caramel mixture into the bottoms of 10 dariole moulds.
3. Mix the eggs, yolks and sugar in a basin.
4. Warm the milk with the vanilla essence, add to the eggs and sugar and mix well without making it frothy.
5. Strain the mixture through a conical strainer into the moulds.
6. Place into a tray half-filled with warm water and bake at 170°C for 40 minutes until set.
7. When cold, loosen around the top of the moulds, shake and turn out with the caramel, onto a flat dish.

Queen of Puddings

6 eggs	3 egg whites
4 egg yolks	175 g castor sugar
125 g castor sugar	pinch salt
1.25 litres milk	75 g raspberry glaze
few drops vanilla essence	75 g apricot glaze
250 g white breadcrumbs	

1. Mix the eggs, egg yolks and sugar in a basin.
2. Warm the milk with the vanilla essence, add to the eggs and sugar and mix well without making it frothy.
3. Strain the mixture through a conical strainer into a clean receptacle.
4. Place the breadcrumbs into lightly buttered pie dishes, then pour in the egg custard.
5. Place into a tray half-filled with warm water and cook in the oven at 170°C for 45 minutes until set.
6. Whisk the egg whites and salt in a clean bowl to a stiff peak, then whisk in half the sugar and fold in the remainder.
7. Place into a piping bag fitted with a 1 cm star tube and pipe the top trellis-fashion, then place in the oven for a few moments to colour the meringue.

8. Pipe the two glazes alternately in the spaces and serve the puddings on a flat dish with pie collars around them.

Zabaglione Gritti Palace

Whisk 12 egg yolks, 400 g sugar, and 300 ml marsala over heat until it becomes thick, light and aerated. Add 6 sheets of soaked and melted gelatine and whisk until cold. Fill into glasses and serve decorated with whipped cream.

Zabaglione with Marsala (Zabaglione alla Marsala)

Whisk 12 egg yolks, 400 g sugar and 300 ml marsala over hot water until thick and trebled in volume. Pour into glass goblets and serve warm, accompanied by lady finger biscuits.

Note
The grated zest and juice of 2 oranges may be substituted for the wine and the dish named Orange Zabaglione. It may also be served chilled.

Bread and Butter and Cherry Pudding   GERMANY
(Kirschenmichel)

Place 100 g stoned cherries into pie dishes. Remove the crusts from 5 slices of buttered bread, cut into triangles, then sprinkle with 200 ml rum and arrange over the cherries. Whisk 1.5 litres milk, 9 eggs, 175 g sugar and vanilla essence, pour into the pie dishes, sprinkle with castor sugar and bake in a bain-marie in the oven at 175°C for 35 minutes.

Coconut Custard (Vattalappam)   INDIA

Warm 850 ml coconut milk, 300 ml evaporated milk, 150 ml water, $\frac{1}{2}$ tsp ground cardamom, $\frac{1}{4}$ tsp ground mace, 3 cloves and 25 ml rose-water and whisk onto 9 beaten eggs and 100 g palm sugar. Strain into dariole moulds and cook standing in a tray of water in the oven at 165°C for 40 minutes. Chill, then turn out of the moulds and serve.

Milk Puddings

These are hot sweets made with milk and a cereal or pasta. They can be baked entirely in the oven or cooked on top of the stove, before being poured into pie dishes, sprinkled with castor sugar, then browned either in the oven or under a salamander grill.

Baked Rice Pudding

175 g short-grain rice
1.5 litres milk
175 g castor sugar
      grated nutmeg
50 g butter

1. Wash the rice, place into pie dishes and add the sugar and milk. Sprinkle the surface with grated nutmeg and distribute knobs of butter on top.
2. Place onto a baking sheet and bake in the oven at 150°C for 1½ hours until tender.
3. Remove from the oven and clean the edges of the dishes with a damp cloth.
4. Serve on a flat dish lined with a dish paper with a pie collar around each dish.

Boiled Rice Pudding

Using the same ingredients as for Baked Rice Pudding, cook the rice slowly in the milk with the sugar, stirring frequently. Fill into pie dishes, sprinkle with grated nutmeg, dot with knobs of butter and colour in a hot oven or under a salamander grill.

Rice Pudding French Style (Pouding au Riz à la Française)

175 g short-grain rice
1.5 litres milk
3 egg yolks ⎫
100 ml cream ⎭ mixed together

175 g castor sugar
few drops vanilla essence
      grated nutmeg
75 g butter

1. Place the milk and vanilla essence into a saucepan and bring to the boil. Rain in the washed rice, reboil and simmer gently for 45 minutes until cooked, stirring from time to time with a wooden spatule.
2. Remove from the heat and stir in the sugar and liaison of egg yolks and cream.
3. Pour the mixture into pie dishes and sprinkle the surface with a little nutmeg and knobs of butter.
4. Place into the oven or under a salamander grill until golden, then clean the edges of the dishes with a damp cloth.
5. Serve on a flat dish lined with a dish paper with a pie collar around each dish.

Rice For Condé (Riz Condé)

Simmer 90 g short-grain rice in 500 ml milk with 75 g sugar and a few drops of vanilla essence in the oven or on the stove until it is soft and thick. Add 2 yolks of egg and 25 g butter and, when cold, fold in 100 ml whipped cream.

Semolina Pudding

125 g semolina	175 g castor sugar
1.5 litres milk	3 egg yolks ⎫
few drops vanilla essence	75 g butter ⎬ mixed together

1. Place the milk, sugar and vanilla essence into a saucepan and bring to the boil. Rain in the semolina, reboil and simmer gently for 20 minutes until cooked, stirring from time to time with a wooden spatula.
2. Remove from the heat and stir in the egg yolks and butter.
3. Pour the mixture into buttered pie dishes and place into the oven or under a salamander grill until golden; clean the edges of the dishes with a damp cloth.
4. Serve on a flat dish lined with a dish paper with a pie collar around each.

Sago Pudding

Proceed as for Semolina Pudding, substituting 125 g sago for the semolina.

Macaroni Pudding

This is made in the same way as Boiled Rice Pudding, using 150 g short cut macaroni instead of rice.

Pineapple Creole

175 g short-grain rice	200 ml whipped cream
1 litre milk	20 pineapple slices
125 g castor sugar	100 ml apricot glaze
few drops vanilla essence	75 g angelica
20 g leaf gelatine	10 g currants

1. Place the milk and vanilla essence into a saucepan and bring to the boil. Rain in the washed rice, reboil and simmer gently for 45 minutes until cooked, stirring from time to time with a wooden spatula.
2. Mix in the sugar and add the soaked leaves of gelatine, stir and allow the gelatine to dissolve. Allow the mixture to cool, then fold in the whipped cream.
3. Mould the rice on a oval dish in the shape of a halved pineapple.
4. Sprinkle the surface with a little castor sugar and mark trellis-fashion with a red-hot poker.
5. Neatly arrange the slices of pineapple around the rice and brush them and the rice with hot apricot glaze.
6. Arrange the angelica at one end to resemble the leaves of the pineapple (alternatively, use the leaves of the fresh fruit). Dot with currants to give a realistic effect and serve cold.

Bread, Saffron and Nut Pudding (Shahi Tukra)   INDIA

Boil 1.5 litres milk to reduce by half, then add 425 ml milk and 8 cardamom pods, remove from the heat and add 75 g sugar and a few strands of saffron. Golden fry thirty 10 × 5 cm rectangles of bread in ghee, drain and arrange in pie dishes, pour in the saffron milk and stand for 5 minutes and cook in a tray of water in the oven at 175°C for 30 minutes. Serve chilled, sprinkled with pistachios and slivered almonds.

Carrot and Raisin Pudding (Gajar-Ka-Halva)   INDIA

Simmer 850 ml milk and 1 kg finely grated carrot with 2 cardamom pods until the liquid is completely reduced. Add 75 ml oil, continue cooking and, when reddish brown, add 75 g sugar. Lightly fry 450 g raisins and 450 g slivered almonds in oil and add to the mixture. Serve warm or chilled.

Indian Milk Pudding (Khir)   INDIA

Cook 150 g short-grain rice in 1.5 litres milk and a pinch of salt until nearly tender, then add 150 g ground almonds, 100 g desiccated coconut, 75 g chopped pistachios and 1 tsp each of cinnamon and orange-flower water and finish to cook. Stir in 200 g diced crystallised fruit, pour into coupes and chill. Serve with coconut cream.

Rice and Almond Pudding (Kheer)   INDIA

Boil 1 litre milk, add 175 g short-grain rice, 5 cardamom pods and simmer for 1 hour, then remove the pods. Add 125 g sugar, 75 g slivered almonds and 50 ml rose-water. Fill into dishes and serve sprinkled with ground cardamom or grated nutmeg.

Spiced Semolina Pie (Galatoboureko)   GREECE

Boil 1 litre milk with ¼ tsp salt, 175 g sugar, grated zest of 1 lemon, 50 g butter and a cinnamon stick. Remove the cinnamon and rain in 175 g fine semolina and cook for 5 minutes, stirring well. Cool, stir in 5 beaten eggs and a few drops of vanilla essence. Line a shallow dish with several sheets of filo pastry, pour in the semolina mixture, cover with more sheets of filo pastry, brush with butter, score and bake at 180°C for 45 minutes. Remove and cool. Boil 225 g sugar, 275 ml water, 50 ml lemon juice and a cinnamon stick to small thread stage (104°C). Strain the syrup, pour over the pie and serve chilled.

Steamed Puddings

Steamed puddings are made from either suet pastry or a Victoria Sponge mixture. Breadcrumbs may be added to a suet pudding mixture to give a lighter result.

Note

The times given for cooking steamed puddings should be checked in the equipment manual supplied by the manufacturer of the pressure cooker or combination oven being used.

STEAMED SUET PUDDINGS

Scottish Cloutie Dumpling

Mix together 175 g self-raising flour, 175 g brown breadcrumbs, 175 g chopped suet, 100 g soft brown sugar, 100 g currants, 175 g sultanas, 2 tsp mixed spice, 1 tsp bicarbonate of soda, 75 g treacle and 300 ml milk. Scald a pudding cloth in boiling water. Lay out and dust liberally with flour. Place the mixture onto the cloth, form into a large round dumpling shape and tie up. Place into simmering water and cook for 3 hours. When cooked, remove the cloth, transfer the pudding to a plate and allow the outer surface to dry off in the oven. Cut into slices and serve with Custard Sauce.

Spotted Dick

Sift together 500 g flour, 12 g baking powder and ¼ tsp salt, then mix in 300 g chopped beef suet, 150 g castor sugar and 100 g currants; moisten with 350 ml water to form a fairly firm paste. Divide into two, mould into rolls, then wrap in buttered greaseproof paper and tie in a pudding cloth, or place in greased pudding sleeves. Steam for 2 hours, then dredge with castor sugar and serve with Custard Sauce.

Steamed Apple Pudding

Makes 2 × 1-litre basins

850 g suet pastry	1 juice of lemon
2 kg peeled and cored	100 ml water
cooking apples	4 cloves
350 g castor sugar	

1. Divide the pastry in half, then take three-quarters of each piece, make a pocket in each and roll to fit into 2 × 1-litre greased basins.
2. Fill with the sliced apple and add the sugar, lemon juice, water and cloves.

3. Roll out the remainder of the pastry into two circular pieces to fit the tops of the basins.
4. Dampen the edges of the paste, place on the tops and seal. Cover with buttered greaseproof paper and a cloth and tie with string. Alternatively, cover with foil.
5. Steam for 2 hours.
6. Clean the basins and serve surrounded with a napkin on a dish covered with a doily, accompanied by Custard Sauce.

Note
Other fruits that may be used are rhubarb, plums, damsons and a combination of blackberries and apple.

Steamed Jam Roll

1 kg suet pastry
300 g jam

1. Roll out the pastry 30 cm × 35 cm and evenly spread with jam to within 1 cm of the edges.
2. Dampen the edges with water and roll up fairly loosely.
3. Cover with buttered greaseproof paper and either place into a pudding sleeve or tie in a pudding cloth.
4. Steam for 1½ hours and serve cut into slices accompanied by custard or Jam Sauce.

Reina Pudding

Makes 2 × 1-litre basins

225 g soft flour	250 g demerara sugar
10 g baking powder	250 g stoned raisins
200 g chopped suet	350 ml milk
150 g white breadcrumbs	10 g bicarbonate of soda

1. Sift the flour and baking powder together in a basin and mix in all the dry ingredients.
2. Dissolve the bicarbonate of soda in a little hot water and add to the milk.
3. Add the liquid to the dry ingredients and mix together.
4. Pour into buttered basins. Cover with buttered greaseproof paper and a cloth and tie with string, or cover with foil.
5. Steam for 4 hours. Allow to stand for 5 minutes, then turn onto a dish and serve accompanied by Custard Sauce.

Notes
1. Extensions may be made with the addition of glacé cherries, walnuts, currants and sultanas to a total quantity of 250 g.

2. Unlike most puddings of a similar type, the uncooked mixture is rather wet and loose.
3. When cooked it should be a rich brown colour and very light in texture.

Steamed Suet Pudding

350 g soft flour	250 g white breadcrumbs
10 g baking powder	150 g castor sugar
¼ tsp salt	3 eggs
250 g chopped suet	100 ml milk

1. Sift the flour, baking powder and salt into a basin. Add the breadcrumbs, sugar and suet and mix together.
2. Mix the eggs and milk together and add to the dry ingredients. Mix to a soft paste.
3. Divide into greased individual moulds. Cover with buttered greaseproof papers and foil and steam for 1½ hours.
4. Turn out of the moulds and serve with Custard Sauce.

Note
Extensions to this pudding may be made by putting jam, marmalade, syrup or fruit such as apple in the bottom of the moulds before the pudding mixture.

STEAMED SPONGE PUDDINGS

This hot sweet is made by the creaming sugar-batter method as for Victoria Sponge, which gives a lighter result than a suet pudding, very similar to that of a sponge cake. The puddings may be cooked in individual moulds, pudding basins, or pudding sleeves which must be coated with melted butter and castor sugar.

It is usual to serve a sauce reflecting the flavour of the pudding, e.g. Lemon Sauce with lemon sponge pudding, or Custard Sauce with all of them. They are made with many different flavourings, e.g. chocolate, jam and marmalade, lemon, orange and syrup.

Steamed Sponge Pudding

Makes 2 × 1-litre basins

150 g butter or margarine	225 g soft flour ⎱ sieved
150 g castor sugar	10 g baking powder ⎰ together
3 eggs	50 ml milk

1. Butter and sugar the pudding basins.
2. Cream the fat and sugar until light, white and fluffy.
3. Gradually add the beaten eggs.

4. Fold in the sifted flour and baking powder, using a metal spoon or scraper, but do not overmix; add a little milk if necessary.
5. Fill into the prepared basins. Cover with buttered greaseproof paper and a cloth and tie, or use foil.
6. Steam for $1\frac{1}{2}$ hours. Allow to stand for 5 minutes, then turn onto a dish and serve.

Steamed Chocolate Pudding

Proceed as for Steamed Sponge Pudding, reducing the flour content by 50 g and replacing it with cocoa powder sifted with the flour and baking powder. Serve accompanied by Chocolate Sauce.

Steamed Lemon Sponge Pudding

Proceed as for Steamed Sponge Pudding with the addition of the grated zest and juice of 3 lemons. Serve accompanied by Lemon Sauce.

Steamed Orange Sponge Pudding

Proceed as for Steamed Sponge Pudding with the addition of the grated zest and juice of 3 oranges. Serve accompanied by Orange Sauce.

Steamed Syrup Sponge Pudding (Golden Pudding)

Proceed as for Steamed Sponge Pudding. Place 100 g warm syrup in the bottom of the basins, followed by the sponge pudding mixture. Serve accompanied by Syrup Sauce.

Flans, Tartlets, Barquettes, Pies and Quiches

To line a flan ring

1. Grease a 20 cm ring and place it on a greased baking tray.
2. Mould 250 g pastry into a round flat shape on a floured work surface.
3. Dust the pastry with a little flour and roll out lightly, turning it so that it retains its round shape. It should be 2 mm thick and 2 cm larger than the ring to allow for lining the sides.
4. Roll around the rolling pin and unroll over the ring.
5. Press into the ring, using a spare piece of pastry dipped in flour to prevent sticking.
6. Bring up the edges on the inside of the ring and roll off any surplus paste.

7. Use the fingers to form a rim of pastry inwards above the edge and decorate with a pair of pastry tweezers or the back of a small knife, dipped in flour.

To line tartlet moulds

1. Grease the moulds and cut out rounds of pastry with a fancy cutter that is slightly larger than the moulds.
2. Turn the rounds of pastry over, lay in the moulds and press them down, using a piece of pastry, then bring the edges up over the edge of the moulds, bearing inwards.

To line barquette moulds

1. Grease the moulds and lay them closely together, roll out pastry and lay it across the top of them.
2. Press the pastry into each mould, using a spare piece of paste dipped in flour to prevent sticking.
3. Remove the surplus by rolling the pin across the top of the moulds.

Baking flans and tartlets blind

To prevent empty cases from distorting while cooking they should be filled with baking beans or, in the case of smaller items, rice. This is termed 'to bake blind'. To cook an empty flan, prick the bottom with a fork and fill it with baking beans resting on a round of greaseproof paper. Tartlets and barquettes should be pricked with a fork and filled with baking beans or, if very small, rice.

SWEET FLANS, TARTLETS AND BARQUETTES

Apple Flan (Flan aux Pommes)

Makes 1 × 20 cm

225 g sweet pastry
750 g cooking apples
125 g castor sugar
    1 juice of lemon
150 ml apricot glaze

1. Stand a 20 cm greased flan ring on a greased baking sheet and line with the pastry.
2. Make three-quarters of the apples into an apple marmalade by cooking the peeled, cored and quartered apples with very little water, the sugar

and lemon juice, on top of the stove, covered with a lid. When soft, lightly whisk and turn out into a tray to cool before use.
3. Fill the flan with the apple marmalade.
4. Arrange slices of the remaining apples neatly overlapping on top following the shape of the flan.
5. Bake at 215°C for 30 minutes, removing the flan ring when three-quarters cooked in order to colour and further cook the pale area previously covered by the ring.
6. Remove from the oven. Coat the surface of the flan with hot apricot glaze and serve on a board on a round flat dish lined with a doily.

Note
Flans may be filled with several kinds of purée or mixtures, baked, then covered with meringue and cooked at 230°C for a few minutes until lightly coloured. They may also be made with canned or poached fruit such as pears and peaches. Banana, raspberry and strawberry flans are baked blind, then filled with pastry cream and completed with the fruit and a jam glaze, according to kind.

Frangipane can also be used on top of fruit. When cooked it is then glazed with water icing.

Apple and Cheese Pie

Line a greased 20 cm flan ring with 200 g short pastry. Fill with 1 kg cooking apples which have been peeled, cored and sliced, 250 g grated Wensleydale cheese, 100 g sugar, 50 ml water and 2 cloves. Cover with a lid rolled from 100 g short pastry, seal well and bake for 40 minutes at 180°C.

Banana Flan (Flan aux Bananes)

Makes 1 × 20 cm

225 g sweet pastry
300 ml pastry cream
3 bananas
150 ml apricot glaze

1. Stand a 20 cm greased flan ring on a greased baking sheet and line with the pastry, then bake blind at 215°C for 30 minutes.
2. When cooked, fill three-quarters full with pastry cream.
3. Arrange slices of banana neatly overlapping on top, following the shape of the flan.
4. Coat the surface with the hot apricot glaze. Serve on a board on a round flat dish, lined with a doily.

Apricot Flan (Flan aux Abricots)

Proceed as for Banana Flan, using 400 g poached or canned and drained apricot halves and brushing with apricot glaze.

Cherry Flan (Flan aux Cerises)

Proceed as for Banana Flan, using 400 g stoned cherries, either poached or canned. Coat with raspberry glaze in place of apricot glaze.

Cherry Meringue Flan (Flan aux Cerises Meringuée)

Proceed as for Cherry Flan. When cooked decorate with meringue, dredge with icing sugar and colour and set in a hot oven at 200°C.

Pear Flan (Flan aux Poires)

Proceed as for Banana Flan, using 400 g drained halved pears, either poached or canned, and finish by brushing with hot apricot or cherry glaze.

Pineapple Flan (Flan aux Ananas)

Proceed as for Banana Flan, using 400 g small half rings of either fresh or canned drained pineapple and finish by brushing with hot apricot glaze.

Raspberry Tartlets (Tartelettes aux Framboises)

Line tartlet moulds with sweet pastry and bake blind at 210°C for 15 minutes and fill them with 200 g of washed and drained raspberries. Coat with raspberry glaze in place of apricot glaze.

Strawberry Barquettes (Barquettes aux Fraises)

Line barquette moulds with sweet pastry and bake blind. Fill with picked and washed strawberries and coat with raspberry glaze.

Lemon Meringue Pie

Makes 1 × 20 cm

225 g sweet pastry	30 g butter
400 ml water	3 egg yolks
85 g sugar	3 egg whites ⎫
2 lemons – zest and juice	150 g castor sugar ⎬ meringue
50 g cornflour	icing sugar ⎭

1. Stand a 20 cm greased flan ring on a greased baking sheet and line with the pastry. Bake blind at 215°C for 15 minutes.

2. Boil the water, sugar, lemon zest and juice and thicken with the diluted cornflour. Allow to cool for a few moments and add the butter and egg yolks, then fill into the flan.
3. Whisk the egg whites to a peak and fold in the castor sugar; cover and decorate the flan with the meringue, sprinkle with the icing sugar and place in the oven to lightly colour and set at a temperature of 210°C for 5 minutes.

Bakewell Tart

Makes 1×20 cm

225 g sweet pastry
75 g raspberry jam
600 g frangipane
150 ml apricot glaze
50 g melted fondant

1. Stand a 20 cm greased flan ring on a greased baking sheet and line with the pastry.
2. Spread with jam and three-quarters fill with the frangipane.
3. Bake in the oven at 215°C for 30 minutes.
4. When cooked, brush the surface with apricot glaze, then cover with the fondant or water icing.

Notes
1. Bakewell tart may be decorated with glacé cherries and diamonds of angelica.
2. When cooked, it may be sprinkled with icing sugar in place of apricot glaze and fondant.
3. The same ingredients may be used for making Bakewell Tartlets as afternoon tea pastries.

Chocolate and Orange Cheesecake (Cassata Italiana)

Beat together 1 kg ricotta cheese, 125 g castor sugar, vanilla essence and the grated zest of 2 oranges, then fold in 275 g chopped crystallised fruit and 100 g grated bitter chocolate. Line a 22 cm springform cake tin with sponge fingers and sprinkle them with 50 ml rum; fill with the cheese mixture, pressing it down firmly and place into the refrigerator. Demould and decorate with crystallised fruit, then dredge with icing sugar.

Apple Charlotte (Charlotte de Pommes)

800 g	peeled, cored and sliced cooking apples	1	juice of lemon
		1	loaf of bread
¼ tsp	cinnamon	250 g	butter
75 g	castor sugar	100 g	apricot jam

1. Cut 0.5cm slices of bread into 3 fingers, discarding the crust. Trim to the height of the charlotte moulds, then dip one side of each into melted butter. Arrange overlapping, buttered side outwards, around the sides of the two greased moulds.
2. Cut two rounds of bread to fit the bottom of the moulds, dip one side in butter, then place buttered side down in the moulds.
3. Place the prepared apples, sugar, lemon juice, powdered cinnamon and water in a saucepan. Cover with a lid and boil until the apples purée, then mix in the jam.
4. Fill the moulds with the apple and cover the top with buttered bread fingers. Bake at 210°C for 40 minutes. Allow to stand for 15 minutes, then turn out onto dishes and serve accompanied by hot Apricot Sauce.

Fruit Pies

Apple Pie

1 kg peeled, cored and sliced apples	6 cloves
150 g castor sugar	100 ml water
1 juice of lemon	750 g short pastry
	1 egg (eggwash)

1. Well fill 3 × 20 cm pie dishes dome-shape with the sliced apple and add the sugar, lemon juice, cloves and a little water.
2. Line the dampened edges of the pie dish with strips of pastry and lightly eggwash.
3. Cover the pie with a 3 mm thick sheet of pastry, seal firmly.
4. Trim around the edges to remove excess pastry, holding the knife at an angle of 45°, crimp the edges and make a small hole in the centre of the pie.
5. Brush the surface with water, sprinkle with castor sugar and place on a baking sheet. Bake at 180°C for 40 minutes. Serve with hot Custard Sauce.

Baked Apple Dumpling (Rabotte de Pommes)

1.5 kg short pastry	150 g demerara sugar
10 × 100 g medium-sized cooking apples	10 cloves
150 g currants	2 eggs (eggwash)
	20 g castor sugar

1. Roll out the pastry 5 mm thick, cut into 12 cm squares and wet the edges with water.
2. Place a peeled and cored apple in the centre of each piece of pastry and fill the centre with the mixed currants and demerara sugar and a clove.
3. Bring the edges of the pastry together to seal the apple inside.
4. Eggwash all over, place a small fancy round of pastry on top, make a small hole in the centre and eggwash again.

5. Place on a greased baking sheet and bake at 180°C for 25–30 minutes.
6. When cooked, sprinkle with castor sugar and serve hot with Custard Sauce.

Black Cherry Clafoutis (Clafoutis)

Line a buttered 25 cm flan ring with 200 g flan pastry, fill the bottom with stoned black cherries, then cover with a mixture made by whisking 2 eggs, 50 g castor sugar, 50 g ground almonds with 60 ml whipped cream and 25 g melted butter. Bake at 200°C for 25 minutes.

Tiramisu

Cream 2 yolks of egg and 30 g sugar until light, then mix in 225 g of mascarpone cheese and a few drops of vanilla essence. Whisk the 2 egg whites until stiff and fold into the cheese mixture. Dip 16 finger biscuits into 300 ml strong, sweet coffee laced with a little Tia Maria and arrange in layers in a 25 cm mould, alternating with the cheese mixture. Chill for several hours before serving, then dredge with two parts icing sugar to one part of cocoa.

Blueberry Pie   USA

Line a 23 cm shallow pie dish with sweet pastry, fill with 675 g blueberries combined with 75 g castor sugar, 50 g flour and 50 ml lemon juice, then sprinkle with melted butter. Cover the fruit with the same pastry and bake at 180°C for 40 minutes.

Cheesecake (Melopita)   GREECE

Line a 22 cm springform cake tin with pastry made with 175 g flour, salt, 125 g lard, 60 g sesame seeds and 2 eggs. Sieve 750 g cottage cheese, add 175 g honey, 4 eggs, 25 g toasted sesame seeds and 1 tsp cinnamon. Fill into the cake tin, sprinkle with sesame seeds and bake at 175°C for 45 minutes.

Key Lime Pie   USA

Line a 20 cm flan ring with 250 g sweet pastry and bake blind. Whisk 2 whole eggs and 3 yolks with 50 g sugar, the grated rind of 4 limes, 500 ml double cream and 50 ml condensed milk, pour into the flan and bake at 200°C for 20 minutes. Whisk the 3 egg whites with a pinch of salt until stiff, fold in 110 g castor sugar and pipe over the flan. Place in the oven at 250°C for 3 minutes to colour the meringue.

Pumpkin Pie   USA

Combine 450 g stiff purée of pumpkin with 75 g brown sugar, 50 ml melted butter, 3 eggs and ½ tsp mixed spice, then fold in 300 ml whipped double cream. Line a flan ring with sweet pastry and bake blind for 10 minutes, then fill with the pumpkin mixture and bake at 180°C for 30 minutes.

Sachertorte

GERMANY

Cream 150 g butter and 150 g icing sugar, add 6 egg yolks, then 150 g melted plain chocolate. Whisk 6 whites of egg with 40 g icing sugar to a peak and fold into the creamed mixture together with 150 g soft flour. Fill into a 23 cm sponge tin and bake at 180°C for 1 hour. Brush the top and sides with apricot glaze and coat with chocolate icing. Pipe the word 'Sacher' on top.

SAVOURY FLANS, TARTLETS AND BARQUETTES

Savoury flans and also tartlets and barquettes are made with short pastry with a filling consisting of a raw egg and milk mixture combined with precooked fillings such as mushrooms, bacon, onion, spinach and cheese. The filling is placed into the pastry case after it has been baked blind, and returned to the oven to complete the cooking.

Quiche Lorraine

225 g short pastry	3 eggs
75 g lardons of bacon (blanched and lightly fried)	2 egg yolks
50 g grated Gruyère cheese	300 ml milk
	salt and pepper

1. Mix the eggs, yolks and seasoning in a basin and add the hot milk, then strain through a conical strainer into a clean receptacle.
2. Stand the greased flan ring on a greased baking sheet, line with the pastry and bake blind at 215°C for 10 minutes.
3. Remove the beans, layer the bottom with the lardons of bacon and the cheese and fill the flan with the egg mixture.
4. Replace in the oven for 20 minutes until the custard is set and lightly coloured.
6. Serve hot on a flat dish.

Strudels

Apfel Strüdel

GERMANY, AUSTRIA

Stretch 450 g strudel pastry very thinly indeed to 45 cm square, brush with melted butter, then sprinkle with 100 g fried breadcrumbs and cover with 1.5 kg peeled, cored and sliced cooking apples, 150 g castor sugar, 175 g sultanas, 1 tsp ground cinnamon, 50 g slivered almonds and the zest and juice of 1 lemon. Sprinkle with butter, then fold in the sides and roll up lengthwise.

Brush with butter and bake at 190°C for 40 minutes, then dredge with icing sugar. Serve hot with Sauce Anglaise or chantilly cream. If a large baking tray is not available, this recipe can be used to make two half-sized strudles.

Cherry Strudel (Kirschen Strüdel)

This is made in the same way as Apfel Strudel, using poached halves of morello or black cherries, which are distributed, together with their sweetened and thickened cooking syrup and fried breadcrumbs across the rolled and pulled pastry.

Meringue

Meringue is a light confectionery item made from egg whites and castor sugar. The mixture can be used for spreading or piped into various shapes which may be filled with whipped cream or ice cream and decorated.

Meringue Shells

Makes 30

    10 egg whites
 pinch salt
 600 g castor sugar

1. Place the egg whites into a basin, copper bowl or the mixing bowl of an electric mixer. Add a pinch of salt.
2. Whisk to a stiff peak, using either a balloon whisk or the whisk of the mixer.
3. Whisk in half the sugar, then fold in the remainder, using a metal spoon or scraper.
4. Place the mixture into a piping bag fitted with a 1 cm plain tube.
5. Pipe onto silicone paper on a baking sheet.
6. Bake in the oven at 130°C without colouring until the shells are completely dry and crisp.

Notes
1. The use of an acid or alkali, such as cream of tartar, lemon juice or vinegar instead of salt helps the egg whites to peak and gives greater body and strength to the albumen; it also makes it easy to remove the meringues from the paper they were baked on. Shells that are baked until completely dry keep well in an air-tight tin and will remain firm and crisp.
2. Meringue for topping dishes such as lemon meringue pie must be lighter than that used for meringue shells; the amount of sugar must therefore be reduced to 50 g sugar per egg white.

Italian Meringue

Cook 500 g sugar with 250 ml water to 140°C, the soft crack stage and pour slowly onto 10 beaten egg whites. This kind of meringue is a good alternative to ordinary meringue.

Meringue with Vanilla Ice Cream (Meringue Glacée Vanille)

Sandwich two meringue shells with vanilla ice cream and serve decorated with whipped cream, on a doily on a silver dish.

Meringue Shell with Whipped Cream (Meringue Chantilly)

Sandwich two meringue shells with whipped cream, lay sideways, decorate with a rosette of whipped cream and sprinkle with grated chocolate, or decorate with a glacé cherry and angelica.

Snow Eggs (Oeufs à la Neige)

Take scoops of ordinary meringue and poach in milk at 180°C, turning them over carefully as they poach. Arrange in a dish on a bed of cold Egg Custard Sauce made from the poaching milk and decorate with flaked almonds.

Pavlova   NEW ZEALAND

Makes 2 gateaux

10 egg whites 600 g castor sugar } meringue mixture	500 g sliced kiwifruit and bananas, raspberries and strawberries
40 g cornflour	400 ml whipped cream
30 ml vinegar	

1. Make the meringue in the usual way, then fold in the last part of the sugar sieved with the cornflour and mix in the vinegar.
2. Fill 2 × 25 cm flan rings with the meringue mixture and pipe 4 single rings around the edge to form a deep nest.
3. Bake in the oven at 130°C without colouring until completely dry and crisp.
4. Fill with the prepared fruit and decorate with the cream.

Meringue Nests with Fruit (Vacharin aux Fraises)

10 egg whites \
600 g castor sugar } meringue mixture
250 g strawberries
200 ml Melba sauce
200 ml whipped cream

1. Make the meringue mixture as for meringue shells.
2. Place into a piping bag fitted with a 1 cm star tube and pipe 10 meringue nests 8 cm in diameter onto silicone paper on a baking sheet.
3. Bake in the oven at 130°C without colouring until the nests are completely dry and crisp.
4. To serve, fill the nests with the strawberries, coat with the sauce and decorate with whipped cream.

Bavarois

Vanilla Bavarois (Bavarois Vanille)

Makes 2 × 13 cm

4 egg yolks	few drops vanilla essence
125 g castor sugar	25 g gelatine
500 ml milk	500 ml lightly whipped cream

1. Mix the eggs and sugar in a basin.
2. Heat the milk with the vanilla essence to just below boiling point.
3. Add to the eggs and sugar and mix well but without making it frothy.
4. Place the mixture in a pan of hot water on top of the stove and stir occasionally with a wooden spatule until the mixture coats the back of the spatule.
5. Add the drained leaf or melted powdered gelatine and stir until completely dissolved.
6. Pass through a fine conical strainer into a clean bowl and stand it in a container of iced water, stirring continuously until the mixture is on the point of setting.
7. Fold in the lightly whipped cream.
8. Pour into 2 × 13 cm moulds and place in a refrigerator until set.
9. Shake the moulds to loosen the bavarois and turn out onto a dish. Serve decorated with whipped cream.

Coffee Bavarois (Bavarois au Café)

Proceed as for Vanilla Bavarois, using coffee extract to flavour and colour the bavarois in place of vanilla essence.

Chocolate Bavarois (Bavarois au Chocolat)

Proceed as for Vanilla Bavarois with the addition of 150 g grated chocolate melted in the milk.

Raspberry Bavarois (Bavarois aux Framboises)

Make an egg custard mixture with 250 ml milk, 3 egg yolks, 150 g sugar and 25 g melted gelatine. When cool, mix in 500 g raspberries passed through a sieve, then fold in 300 ml lightly whipped cream. Proceed as for Vanilla Bavarois.

Strawberry Bavarois (Bavarois aux Fraises)

Proceed as for Raspberry Bavarois, adding 500 g strawberry purée instead of raspberries to the cold mixture just before folding in the cream.

Charlottes

Peach Charlotte (Charlotte Montreuil)

Pour 100 ml orange jelly into the bottom of a charlotte mould and allow to set. Line the sides of the mould with finger biscuits and fill with Vanilla Bavarois mixed with 50 g peach purée and 75 g diced peaches soaked in kirsch. Allow to set, then turn out onto a flat dish and serve.

Charlotte Moscovite

Pour 100 ml melted raspberry jelly into the bottom of a charlotte mould and allow to set. Line the sides of the mould with finger biscuits. Fill with Vanilla Bavarois, and allow to set. Turn out onto a flat dish and serve.

Charlotte Royale

Pour 100 ml melted raspberry jelly into the bottom of a charlotte mould and allow to set. Line the sides of the mould with slices of small Swiss roll. Fill with Vanilla Bavarois, and allow to set. Turn out onto a flat dish and serve.

Sweet Soufflés

There are four kinds of sweet soufflé, the common factor between them being their lightness, which is attained by aerating the basic mixture with stiffly beaten egg whites.

- Cold soufflés are made from egg yolks and sugar whisked until thick and creamy, stiffened with gelatine, enriched with whipped cream and lightened with stiffly beaten egg whites. A wide range of flavours is possible using fresh fruit juice, essences, liqueurs and spirits. This kind is called a soufflé because the dish in which it is set is filled beyond the rim to give the effect that it has risen. In fact, apart from the lightly warmed egg yolks and sugar, this type of soufflé is not cooked at all and has to be kept in a refrigerator until set. It is recommended that pasteurised eggs are used for this dish.

- A sweet soufflé proper is cooked in a porcelain soufflé dish or mould and is served in the same dish without a sauce or garnish. The basic mix is a panada with egg yolks, lightened with whisked white of egg.
- The other kind of soufflé is known as a Soufflé en Surprise or Omelette Soufflé Surprise made with meringue mixture but is not a true soufflé. The domestic name for this sweet is Baked Alaska.
- Hot soufflé puddings are individual soufflé puddings made from a base of milk, sugar and flour boiled to a stiff consistency with added butter for richness. The egg yolks are added raw, stiffly beaten whites are folded in and the mixture is poured into moulds, leaving room for them to rise. They are then cooked in the oven au bain-marie and served with an appropriate sauce.

COLD SOUFFLÉS

Cold Lemon Soufflé (Soufflé Froid Milanaise)

9 egg yolks	5 egg whites
350 g castor sugar	100 g toasted nib almonds ⎫
4 lemons – juice and grated zest	200 ml whipped cream ⎬ decoration
25 g gelatine	25 g angelica
400 ml lightly whipped cream	25 g glacé cherries ⎭

1. Place the egg yolks, sugar, lemon juice and grated zest into a warmed mixing bowl standing in a container of hot water. Whisk until the mixture is thick and creamy and drops falling from the raised whisk leave a mark on the surface.
2. Remove from the heat, add the soaked or melted gelatine and continue beating until the mixture is cold.
3. When it is on the point of setting, fold in the lightly whipped cream, followed by the stiffly beaten egg whites, adding them in two or more stages.
4. Pour the mixture into the prepared soufflé moulds and place in a refrigerator until set.
5. To serve, remove the paper from the outside of the moulds and cover the exposed sides with nib almonds. Decorate the top with whipped cream, glacé cherries and angelica.

Note
To prepare the moulds line the outside with a circle of greaseproof paper to a height of 10 cm above the level of the mould.

Cold Orange Soufflé (Soufflé Froid à l'Orange)

Proceed as for Cold Lemon Soufflé, substituting orange zest and juice for lemons.

HOT SOUFFLÉS

These are very light hot soufflés cooked and served in multi-portioned soufflé dishes.

Vanilla Soufflé (Soufflé Vanille)

Makes 4 portions

40 g butter	few drops vanilla essence
60 g castor sugar	3 egg yolks
30 g flour	4 egg whites
100 ml milk	10 g icing sugar

1. Butter and sugar a 15 cm soufflé dish.
2. Mix the butter, sugar and flour together in a basin.
3. Heat the milk and vanilla essence and whisk onto the butter mixture, replace in the pan and boil until smooth and thick, stirring well, then allow to cool.
4. Mix in the egg yolks one at a time with a wooden spatula.
5. Fold in the stiffly beaten egg whites in two stages.
6. Two-thirds fill the prepared mould with the mixture.
7. Cook in the oven at 200°C for 35 minutes without opening the door.
8. When cooked, remove from the oven, dust with icing sugar and serve immediately.

Chocolate Soufflé (Soufflé au Chocolat)

Proceed as for Vanilla Soufflé, adding 50 g grated chocolate to the milk.

Lemon Soufflé (Soufflé au Citron)

Proceed as for Vanilla Soufflé, using the juice and grated zest of two lemons in place of vanilla essence.

SOUFFLÉ OMELETTES

These consist of a sponge base covered with ice cream and fruit then with meringue, baked in an oven for a few moments until lightly coloured. The French title is Omelette Soufflé en Surprise.

Omelette Soufflé Surprise (Omelette Soufflé Norvégienne)

250 g	Genoese Sponge	
200 ml	stock syrup	
500 ml	vanilla ice cream	
10	glacé cherries	

10 egg whites ⎱ meringue
600 g castor sugar ⎰
20 g angelica

1. Trim the sponge to the shape of the dish the sweet is to be served in.
2. Sprinkle with warm stock syrup and allow to cool.
3. Place 10 scoops of ice cream on the sponge base in the shape of a dome.
4. Cover with meringue and shape with a palette knife dipped in warm water. Decorate the omelette with the rest of the meringue, using a piping bag and star tube, then arrange glacé cherries and diamonds of angelica around it.
5. Place in the oven at a temperature of 200°C for 3 minutes to set and lightly colour pale golden brown. Serve immediately.

Omelette Soufflé with Pears (Omelette Soufflé Milord)

Proceed as for Omelette Soufflé Surprise with the addition of halves of poached pears. Serve Melba Sauce separately.

Omelette Soufflé with Peaches (Omelette Soufflé Milady)

Proceed as for Omelette Soufflé Surprise with the addition of halves of poached peaches. Serve Melba Sauce separately.

Orange and Almond Soufflé Pudding (Tortada de Naranja)   SPAIN

Whisk 6 egg yolks with 100 g sugar over a pan of hot water; when thick allow to cool slightly, then mix in 175 g ground almonds and whisk until cold. Fold in 6 stiffly beaten egg whites, pour into prepared soufflé moulds and cook in a tray of hot water in the oven at 200°C for 30 minutes. Thicken 225 ml orange juice heated with 100 g sugar with 10 g diluted arrowroot. Turn out the soufflés, decorate with warmed segments of oranges, then mask with the orange sauce.

HOT SOUFFLÉ PUDDINGS

Vanilla Soufflé Pudding (Pouding Soufflé Vanille or Pouding Soufflé Saxon)

150 g	butter	
150 g	castor sugar	
75 g	flour ⎱ sifted together	
75 g	cornflour ⎰	
500 ml	milk	

few drops vanilla essence
5 egg yolks
6 egg whites
10 g icing sugar
500 ml Egg Custard Sauce

1. Mix the butter, sugar, flour and cornflour together in a basin.
2. Heat the milk and vanilla essence and whisk onto the mixture until smooth and thick. Allow to cool.
3. Mix in the egg yolks one at a time with a wooden spatule.
4. Fold in the stiffly beaten egg whites in two stages until all is incorporated.
5. Two-thirds fill the prepared moulds and cook in the oven at 180°C for 20 minutes, standing in a tray of hot water.
6. When cooked, remove from the oven, allow to settle for a few moments, then turn out of the moulds onto a flat dish and serve accompanied by Egg Custard Sauce.

Note
To test if cooked, insert a fine skewer into the centre of the pudding and leave it for a few moments before withdrawing. If the skewer comes out clean with no trace of the mixture the pudding is cooked.

Lemon Soufflé Pudding (Pouding Soufflé au Citron)

Proceed as for Vanilla Soufflé Pudding, substituting the juice and grated zest of 3 lemons for the vanilla essence. Serve accompanied by Lemon Sauce.

Orange Soufflé Pudding (Pouding Soufflé à l'Orange)

Proceed as for Vanilla Soufflé Pudding, substituting the juice and grated zest of 3 oranges for the vanilla essence. Serve accompanied by Orange Sauce.

Mousses

These may be made with a variety of soft fruits such as fresh, frozen or canned loganberries, raspberries and strawberries made into a purée by passing through a fine sieve or food processor.

Strawberry Mousse (Mousse aux Fraises)

200 ml water	300 ml strawberry purée
250 g castor sugar	500 ml lightly whipped cream
1 juice of lemon	200 ml whipped cream
25 g gelatine	

1. Place the water, sugar and lemon juice into a saucepan and apply gentle heat until the sugar has dissolved.
2. Add the soaked gelatine and stir until it has dissolved.
3. Allow to cool slightly.
4. Add the strawberry purée and incorporate thoroughly.

5. Transfer to a basin and continue to stir until the mixture is on the point of setting, then fold in the lightly whipped cream.
6. Pour into moulds and place in a refrigerator until set.
7. Shake the moulds to loosen the mousse, turn out onto dishes and serve decorated with whipped cream.

Fruit based desserts

FRUIT FOOLS

These are made of equal quantities of sweetened purée of poached or raw fruit and whipped cream, served cold in coupes or Paris goblets, decorated with whipped cream and served with finger biscuits. They should be light and smooth in texture with a flavour which reflects the characteristics of the fruit used; it may be necessary to add a little food colouring to the mixture.

Gooseberry Fool

500 g	poached gooseberries
500 ml	whipped cream
200 ml	whipped cream for decorating
10	lady finger biscuits.

1. Pass the gooseberries through a fine sieve or purée in a food processor.
2. Place the whipped cream into a basin, fold in the puréed gooseberries and, if desired, adjust the colour.
3. Fill into serving dishes, smooth the surface and place in a refrigerator to set.
4. Decorate the top with a whirl of whipped cream and serve accompanied with the biscuits.

COMPOTES OF FRUIT

Preparation of fruit for poaching

Apples – Peel, cut in half or quarter, remove the core, wash and keep in acidulated water during preparation; small ones may be cooked whole.
Apricots – Remove the stalks, leave whole or cut in half and discard the stones.
Figs – Poach whole as they are.
Nectarines and peaches – Plunge into boiling water for 2–3 seconds, place in cold water and peel off the skin; leave whole or cut in half and discard the stones.

Pears – For serving whole, leave the stalk intact and peel; or cut in half and remove the cores.

Rhubarb – Remove the leaves and tough outer skin and cut into 6 cm lengths.

Blackberries – Remove any stalks and any hulls; wash and drain.

Blackcurrants – Remove the berries from the stalks with a fork, wash and drain.

Cherries – Remove the stalks and use a cherry stoner for the stones; wash and drain.

Gooseberries – Top and tail, wash and drain.

Greengages – These are prepared whole and need only be washed.

Loganberries – Prepare in the same way as strawberries.

Plums – Remove the stalks, leave whole or cut in half and discard the stones, wash and drain.

Raspberries – Prepare in the same way as strawberries.

Redcurrants – Prepare in the same way as blackcurrants.

Strawberries – Remove the hulls, discard any blemished fruit; wash and drain.

Dried fruit (including apricots, dates, figs, pears and prunes) Soak in cold water overnight, then drain and poach in a syrup containing lemon peel, a cinnamon stick or a vanilla pod.

Stewed Fruit (Compote de Fruit)

Make a sugar syrup, bringing 1 litre water, 750 g sugar and 50 ml lemon juice to the boil; for unripe and sour fruit, the sugar should be increased to 1 kg. To prevent the fruit from overcooking, it should be poached at below boiling point – preferably in the oven at 180°C. Cover all fruit with grease-proof paper or with a plate to keep it from floating to the top while cooking. Soft fruits do not require cooking and need only to be covered with the hot syrup. Stewed fruit served cold with liquid cream is suitable for serving at breakfast as well as a luncheon sweet.

Flambéd Bananas (Plátanos con Coñac) SPAIN

Poach bananas in a mixture of 450 g honey and 175 ml orange juice, remove, flambé with Spanish brandy and serve with some of the cooking liquid.

Fruit Salad au Gratin (Gratinado de Frutas) SPAIN

Whisk together 5 egg yolks and 175 g sugar then stir in 250 ml heated cream and cook to thicken slightly. Place fruit salad into a shallow pan, moisten with stock syrup and heat through. Pour the egg mixture over the fruit and gratinate under a salamander grill.

Hot Compote of Fruit (Arrope) SPAIN

Poach stoned quinces and plums in stock syrup until soft, then drain. Poach halves of peeled peaches, apples and pears in the liquid from the quinces, together with 300 ml fresh grape juice and sugar to sweeten. Place the fruits into dishes, reduce the liquor until it is fairly thick, pour over the fruit and serve.

Flambéd Fruit Salad

Caramelise 450 g sugar and 450 ml water, then add 150 ml orange juice and reboil. Place fruit salad into a shallow pan, moisten with the hot caramel liquid and heat through. Flambé it with brandy.

Oranges in Caramel (Aranci Caramellizzati)

Prepare caramel with 450 ml water and 450 g sugar and a stick of cinnamon, as the mixture begins to turn golden remove the cinnamon; add 150 ml water and reboil. Cook a julienne of orange zest in the caramel until candied, cool, then pour the sauce and zest over peeled and sliced oranges.

Pears Poached in Red Wine (Poires au Vin Rouge)

Poach peeled, whole pears in a syrup made with 750 ml red wine, 150 ml water, 175 g sugar and a cinnamon stick.

Summer Pudding

Lightly cook 450 g each of raspberries, redcurrants, blackcurrants and blackberries with 75 ml lemon juice and 450 g sugar. Line the bottom and sides of pudding basins with fingers of stale bread, fill the moulds with the fruit mixture and cover the tops with fingers of bread. Cover, press down under a weight and refrigerate. Turn out and serve accompanied by liquid cream.

BAKED FRUIT

Baked Apple (Pomme Bonne Femme)

10 × 200 g cooking apples
    100 g castor sugar
    100 g sultanas
    100 g butter
      10 cloves

1. Wash and core the apples and make a small incision around the centre of each with the point of a small knife.
2. Place the apples in a shallow baking tray, fill the centres with sugar, fruit and a clove and top with a knob of butter.

3. Cover the bottom of the tray with water and bake in the oven at 200°C for 30 minutes until the apples are soft and lightly coloured.
4. Serve on a dish with custard sauce.

Baked Apples (Bratäpfel)   GERMANY

Combine some marzipan, apricot liqueur and soft brown sugar and fill the centres of cored apples, sprinkle with white wine, dot with butter and bake at 175°C for 25 minutes.

FRESH FRUIT SALAD

Fresh Fruit Salad (Macédoine de Fruits)

Make a stock syrup by bringing 100 ml water, 75 g sugar and the juice of half a lemon to the boil. Allow it to get cold and drop the fruit into it as it is prepared. Peel, core and slice 3 dessert apples and 3 pears; skin, cut in half and depip 150 g grapes, or use small seedless grapes; stone 100 g cherries; cut segments from 3 oranges and 120 g pineapple, cut 3 bananas into slices and mix all together with a spoon. If desired, flavour with 25 ml kirsch or maraschino. Tip the salad into a serving dish and arrange a neat pattern on top, using slices of starfruit, kiwifruit, strawberries etc.

TRIFLE

English trifle consists of diced Genoese Sponge layered with raspberry jam or finger biscuits, sprinkled well with stock syrup or sweet sherry, covered with custard and decorated with whipped cream, and allowed to set. It is then decorated with whipped cream, glacé cherries and angelica. Trifles are generally made in glass bowls.

Sherry Trifle

250 g Genoese Sponge	100 ml sweet sherry
75 g raspberry jam	300 ml whipped cream
500 ml custard sauce	30 g glacé cherries
100 ml cream	30 g angelica

1. Cut the sponge through and sandwich with jam, cut into 1 cm cubes and place in a glass bowl.
2. Moisten with the sherry.
3. Cover with the cold custard combined with the cream.
4. Decorate with whipped cream, glacé cherries and diamonds of angelica, or sprinkle with toasted flaked almonds.
5. Serve on a round flat dish with a doily.

Frozen Desserts

ICE CREAM

Ice cream is a versatile commodity that can be served as a sweet in its own right and as an accompaniment to other dishes such as apple pie à la mode. There are many ways of making ice cream and hundreds of recipes for using it and for its combination with other items; it can even be served as a hot sweet.

As a basic cold sweet, ice cream is usually served in the form of balls moulded by means of a scoop of which there are several sizes. An average portion would be two No. 16 scoops which is equivalent to 110 g, served with wafers or small biscuits; cream may be piped on top.

Homemade ice cream must be produced and served in accordance with current legislation. Commercial ice cream is available in several qualities, many flavours and as ready-to-serve combinations. Ice cream powders may be used as an alternative to the following recipes.

Vanilla Ice Cream (Glace Vanille)

Makes 75 portions

2 litres milk
1 tbs vanilla essence
600 g castor sugar
16 egg yolks
600 ml cream

1. Place the milk and vanilla essence in a pan and bring to the boil.
2. Whisk the castor sugar and egg yolks together in a basin, add the milk, whisking continuously.
3. Return to the pan and cook gently, stirring with a wooden spoon until the mixture thickens sufficiently to coat the back of the spoon; do not let it boil.
4. Pass the custard through a fine strainer into a bowl and cool quickly, stirring occasionally.
5. Add the cream and whisk in thoroughly. Pour into the container of an ice cream machine and churn until frozen, then store in an ice cream conservator. During churning the amount will double in volume.

Strawberry Ice Cream (Glace aux Fraises)

Makes 60 portions

1 litre milk
600 g castor sugar
8 egg yolks

1 kg strawberries
few drops red colouring
600 ml cream

1. Place the milk in a pan and bring to the boil.
2. Whisk the castor sugar and egg yolks together in a basin, add the milk, whisking continuously.
3. Return the mixture to the pan and cook gently, stirring with a wooden spoon until the mixture thickens sufficiently to coat the back of the spoon; do not let it boil.
4. Pass the custard through a fine strainer into a bowl and cool quickly, stirring occasionally.
5. Hull and wash the strawberries and pass through a fine sieve or food processor. Add to the mixture with a few drops of red colouring if necessary.
6. Whisk in the cream thoroughly. Pour the mixture into the container of an ice cream machine and churn until frozen. Once frozen, store in an ice cream conservator.

Cassata Napolitana

Place a layer each of vanilla ice cream and strawberry ice cream in a bombe mould and chill. Boil 150 g sugar in 125 ml water to the soft ball stage (115°C), pour onto 3 stiffly beaten whites of egg and whisk until cool, then add 150 ml whipped cream and 225 g chopped glacé fruits. Fill into the mould, chill until set, then cover with a second layer each of strawberry ice cream and vanilla ice cream. Freeze until set, demould and serve cut into sections.

Chocolate Ice Cream (Glace au Chocolat)

Proceed as for Vanilla Ice Cream, adding 20 g of grated chocolate to the milk and vanilla essence when heating.

Coffee Ice Cream (Glace au Café)

Proceed as for Vanilla Ice Cream, using coffee extract instead of vanilla essence.

Raspberry Ice Cream (Glace aux Framboises)

Proceed as for Strawberry Ice Cream, using raspberries instead of strawberries.

WATER ICES

Apricot Water Ice (Glace à l'Abricot)

Makes 40 portions

1 litre water
600 g sugar
1.5 kg ripe apricots

1. Place the sugar and water into a pan and boil to a syrup which registers 32° on a sacrometer. Allow to cool completely.

2. Wash and remove the stones from the apricots. Pass the flesh through a sieve or food processor and add to the syrup. Mix together and adjust the colour if necessary.
3. Pour into the container of an ice cream machine and churn until frozen. Once frozen, store in an ice cream conservator.

Lemon Water Ice (Glace au Citron)

Makes 40 portions

2 litres water
  1 kg sugar
    10 juice of lemons
     4 grated zest of lemons

1. Boil the water, sugar, lemon juice and zest in a pan and reduce until the syrup registers 22° on a sacrometer.
2. Pass through a fine strainer and allow to cool completely.
3. Pour the mixture into the container of an ice cream machine and churn until frozen. Once frozen, store in an ice cream conservator.

Orange Water Ice (Glace à l'Orange)

Proceed as for Lemon Water Ice, using orange juice and zest instead of lemons. Colour the syrup a light orange.

Peach Water Ice (Glace aux Pêches)

Proceed as for Apricot Water Ice, using skinned and stoned peaches instead of apricots.

SORBET

A sorbet is a very light water ice with the addition of Italian meringue, usually served as a refresher between main meal meat courses in an extended dinner menu. It can also be served as a sweet in its own right and in various combinations.

It is best to make sorbet as required as the fluffy texture quickly deteriorates.

Lemon Sorbet (Sorbet au Citron)

Makes 30 portions

1 litre water
 700 g sugar
    6 juice of lemons
    2 grated zest of lemons
500 ml Italian meringue

1. Place the water, sugar, lemon juice and grated zest in a pan and bring to the boil. Reduce until it registers 17° on a sacrometer, pass through a fine strainer and allow to cool completely.
2. Pour the mixture into the container of an ice cream machine and as it begins to thicken, add the meringue and continue to freeze until light and fluffy.
3. Serve in frosted goblets or coupes on a doily on a plate.

Orange Sorbet (Sorbet à l'Orange)

Proceed as for Lemon Sorbet, using oranges instead of lemons and colouring the syrup a light orange.

COUPES

These consist of combinations of different flavoured ice creams, fruits and sauces served in well-chilled coupes, accompanied by a suitable wafer or biscuit. The range is extensive and the following examples are the most popular.

Coupe Alexandra

Place a little fruit salad flavoured with kirsch in the coupe, with a ball of Strawberry Ice Cream on top. Decorate with whipped cream and a strawberry.

Coupe Poire Belle Hélène

Place a ball of Vanilla Ice Cream in a coupe with a whole or half poached pear on top. Coat with hot Chocolate Sauce at the moment of service and decorate with whipped cream.

Coupe Edna May

Place stoned cherries in a coupe and a ball of Vanilla Ice Cream on top. Coat with Melba Sauce and decorate with whipped cream.

Coupe Jacques

Place a little fruit salad flavoured with maraschino in the coupe and a small ball each of Lemon Water Ice and Strawberry Ice Cream on top. Decorate with whipped cream.

Coupe Peach Melba

Place a ball of Vanilla Ice Cream in a coupe and place a half-skinned peach on top. Coat with Melba Sauce and decorate with whipped cream.

Raspberry Melba

Proceed as for Peach Melba, using raspberries instead of peaches.

Strawberry Melba

Proceed as for Peach Melba, using strawberries instead of peaches.

Creams, Butters and Fillings

Pastry Cream (Crème Pâtissière)

750 ml milk	110 g castor sugar
1 tsp vanilla essence	90 g flour
2 eggs	10 g butter
4 egg yolks	

1. Mix the eggs, egg yolks, sugar and vanilla in a basin, add the flour and mix in well.
2. Heat the milk with the butter to boiling point, pour onto the egg mixture, whisking vigorously.
3. Return to the saucepan, and cook, stirring all the time, until it boils. Pastry cream is used as a filling for éclairs and other pastry items.

Note
Pastry cream may be used immediately or retained in a basin with the surface either sprinkled with sugar or covered with buttered greaseproof paper to prevent a skin from forming.

Sweetened Whipped Cream (Crème Chantilly)

Place 1 litre of cream into a cold basin with 100 g castor sugar and 1 tsp vanilla essence, and whisk until it is sufficiently thick.

Note
Be careful not to overwhisk as this will cause the fat globules which are in suspension in the cream to combine. These larger particles then begin to separate out (this is the process by which butter is made). Slight over-whisking is not always apparent but when the cream is piped the pressure causes separation to take place and the cream weeps, thus reducing its life and spoiling the item with which it is used.

Buttercream (1)

200 ml milk
350 g castor sugar
4 eggs
850 g unsalted butter

1. Place the milk, sugar, eggs and 100 g of the butter in a saucepan and heat to boiling point.
2. Place into the bowl of a mixing machine with a spade attachment and mix on low speed until the mixture is cold.
3. Add the remainder of the butter, in two stages, increasing the speed as the mixture becomes creamy and light, flavour and colour as desired, e.g. chocolate with the addition of 150 g melted couverture; coffee with the addition of coffee extract.

Buttercream (2)

Using equal quantities of unsalted butter and icing sugar, soften the butter slightly and gradually whisk in the sieved icing sugar until light and fluffy.

Brandy Butter

Cream 125 g unsalted butter with 125 g castor sugar and slowly incorporate 50 ml brandy.

Frangipane

125 g butter
125 g castor sugar
2 eggs
30 g soft flour   ⎤ sieved
125 g ground almonds ⎦ together

1. Cream the butter and sugar until light and fluffy.
2. Gradually add the beaten eggs.
3. Fold in the flour and almonds, using a metal spoon or a scraper, but do not overmix.

Bread Doughs and Bread

A wide range of satisfying and interesting bread products can be produced from doughs made with yeast as the raising agent. These include bread, rolls, buns, baps, savarins and babas. In making bread dough, the protein in the flour is wetted and forms gluten and it is how gluten develops and is worked and moulded that determines the structure of the crumb inside and, to a certain extent, the final shape of the item.

There are several different kinds of dough. Plain dough is used for bread and rolls, sweet dough for buns and rich dough, containing extra butter, eggs and sugar for savarins.

Proving temperature and time plays an important part in the making of bread dough, which requires a warm, moist and draught-free atmosphere.

A 400 g loaf takes 35 minutes to bake at 200°C; a 800 g loaf takes 40 minutes at 225°C. The dough continues to rise in the oven until the yeast is killed at 57°C. The temperature inside the loaf rises to a maximum of 100°C, even though the air temperature in the oven is twice that.

White Bread

Makes 2 × 400 g loaves

550 g strong flour	25 g yeast
1 tsp salt	300 ml water at 40°C
10 g milk powder	10 g sugar
10 g lard	

1. Sift the flour, salt and milk powder into a warmed bowl and rub in the fat.
2. Dissolve the yeast and sugar in the water and mix into the flour to form a medium-soft dough.
3. Knead thoroughly, replace in the bowl, cover with a cloth and allow to prove in a warm place for 1 hour.
4. Knead the dough and divide into two equal pieces; mould and place into greased bread tins.
5. Allow to prove until double in size.
6. Bake at 200°C for 35 minutes.

Bridge Rolls

Makes 30
Proceed as for White Bread, adding 1 egg to the liquid. Divide into 30 equal pieces, mould into oval shapes and place onto a greased baking sheet. Allow to prove until double their size, then bake at 240°C for 10–15 minutes.

Dinner Rolls

Makes 20
Divide 800 g white bread dough into 20 equal pieces. Mould into round shapes and place onto a greased baking sheet. Allow to prove until double their size, then bake at 230°C for 15 minutes.

Wholemeal Bread

Proceed as for White Bread, using 450 g wholemeal flour and 50 g white strong flour instead of all white flour.

Baps

Makes 12
Make a soft dough, using 450 g strong flour, 2 tsp salt and 25 g yeast dissolved in 300 ml warm milk and water. Mould 12 round flattened pieces and allow to prove. Dust with flour and make a small indentation with the thumb, then bake at 220°C for 15 minutes.

Bagels

Makes 20
Sift 450 g strong flour with a pinch of salt and make a bay. Whisk 1 white of egg into 150 ml each of milk and water, add 15 g sugar and dissolve 20 g yeast in it. Add to the flour and mix to a soft dough. Knead well and prove until it doubles in size. Knock back, cut into 20 pieces, roll to form 10 cm knots or rings and poach in boiling water for 20 seconds. Drain, place on a greased baking tray, eggwash and bake at 220°C for 15 minutes.

Ciabatta

Makes 2 loaves
Pour 500 ml warm water into a bowl and dissolve 25 g yeast in it. Add 450 g strong flour and mix to a sticky dough. Oil a basin, put the dough in it, cover and prove for 4 hours in a cool place. Knock back, add 50 ml olive oil, 1 tsp salt and 285 g strong flour and mix to an elastic dough. Prove again for several hours. Cut into two pieces and press each piece into a greased shallow tin 20 cm in length. Cover and allow to prove, then place into an oven with a dish of boiling water in it at 250°C and bake for 25 minutes. Ciabatta should be a light and feathery loaf which sounds hollow when tapped.

Croissants

Make a dough with 450 g strong flour, 12 g salt, 25 g castor sugar and 25 g yeast dissolved in 300 ml warm milk. Roll out 50 cm square, spread with 250 g butter and fold the four corners to the centre to seal in the butter. Roll out 40 cm × 20 cm and fold in three, and give six similar turns, resting it between each turn. Roll out 4 mm thick and cut into triangles with 15 cm sides, form crescent shape, eggwash, prove in a cool place, then bake at 230°C for 15 minutes.

Focaccia

Makes 12

Sift 400 g strong flour with ½ tsp salt; add 25 g yeast dissolved in 250 ml warm water and 75 ml olive oil and mix to a smooth dough. Allow to prove, knock back, divide into 12 pieces, mould and roll out into 15 cm rounds. Place on a greased tray, allow to prove and bake at 200°C for 20 minutes. These are usually covered before baking with ingredients similar to pizzas or with sweet toppings. The dough may also be flavoured with herbs, cheese etc. They should be eaten as soon as they come out of the oven.

Chapatis   INDIA

Makes 24

Mix 250 g wholemeal flour sifted with 125 g strong white flour and 1 tsp salt with 250 ml warm water to make a soft, sticky dough. Allow to relax, then knead again and mould into 24 balls, lightly flatten and roll out to 20 cm in diameter, stretching well. Cook on a griddle until brown spots appear, turn and cook the other side.

Note
Chapati flour, which is finely milled wholemeal flour, may be used instead of ordinary wholemeal flour.

Nan   INDIA

Makes 40

Sift 450 g each of strong flour and self-raising flour. Dissolve 12 g yeast in 50 ml warm water and allow to ferment, then add to the flour together with 100 ml plain yogurt and 350 ml warm water to make a soft, pliable dough. Refrigerate for 12 hours, remove and prove, then knock back and divide into four pieces. Mould each into 10 tear-drop shapes, 6 mm thick. Prick all over, brush with oil and cook under the salamander grill for 1½–2 minutes, then turn over, sprinkle with sesame seeds and cook the second side, or bake in a tandoori oven.

Note
This is sometimes called tandoori bread because it is served with most tandoori dishes.

Paratha   INDIA

Makes 16

Sift 250 g wholemeal flour, 150 g strong white flour and 1 tsp salt, add 225 ml warm water mixed with 50 ml oil and knead well to a soft dough. Allow to relax for 30 minutes and knead once more, cut into 16 pieces, then roll into 15 cm thin discs. Brush with oil, then fold over or seal another disc on top and roll out and fold again. Repeat this several times, keeping them from getting dry and finishing with 20 cm circles or 15cm triangles. Cook on a hot griddle.

Phulka   INDIA

Makes 16
Sift 375 g wholemeal flour and 125 g strong white flour and mix in 250 ml warm water to make a fairly soft dough. Knead for 15 minutes, then leave to relax for 30 minutes. Knead again, mould into balls and flatten, then roll out into 15 cm rounds, stretching them well. Cook quickly on both sides on a hot griddle.

Pide   TURKEY

Makes 1 × 30 cm
Dissolve 25 g yeast and 1 tsp sugar in 250 ml warm water and separately melt 50 g butter in 175 ml warm milk. Sift 675 g strong flour with 1 tsp salt, add the two liquids and mix to a smooth dough. Allow to prove, knock back and mould to fit a 30 cm diameter greased tin. Brush with eggwash, sprinkle with sesame and fennel seeds, allow to prove, then bake at 195°C for 40 minutes.

Pitta Bread   MIDDLE EAST

Makes 10
Make a dough with 450 g strong flour, 1 tsp salt and 12 g yeast dissolved in 300 ml warm water with 3 tsp oil and 12 g malt extract. Mould 50 g round pieces and roll out into oval shapes 12.5 cm long. Dust with flour, prove for 10 minutes, then bake at 240°C for 8 minutes.

Poori or Puri (1)   INDIA

Makes 10 portions
Rub 50 g ghee into 225 g wholemeal flour and mix with 150 ml warm water. Knead well, relax for 15 minutes, mould into 20 balls, then roll out into 10 cm circles. Deep fry at 200°C until puffed up and golden.

Poori (2)

Makes 12
Mix 55 g each of chickpea flour, strong flour and wholemeal flour; add 125 ml water, 1 tbs oil and a pinch of salt and mix well for 5 minutes. Allow to rest for 1 hour, then divide into 12 pieces. Roll out into 12 cm circles and deep fry until puffy.

Poppadums INDIA

These are made by grinding white split gram beans to a paste, which is then made into a smooth dough with baking soda and seasoning. The paste is rolled out into paper-thin 17.5 cm circles and dried, ready to be deep fried at 180°C. Keep submerged under the fat to make them expand; alternatively, they may be cooked under a salamander grill.

Roti INDIA

Makes 16

Pour 125 ml cold water onto 450 g maize flour and mix to a fairly firm dough. Mould into 16 round pieces, then roll out to 12 cm in diameter. Dry fry on one side, remove and cook the other side under a salamander grill.

Tsoureki GREECE

Makes 2 loaves

Sift 450 g strong flour and 1 tsp salt into a basin. Mix 2 eggs with 150 ml warm milk, add 1 tsp sugar, 2 tsp water, 100 g melted butter and 15 g yeast also ½ tsp mastic, which is powdered resin. Add to the flour and mix to a dough. Allow to prove, divide into two, then mould each piece into 3 strands. Twist into plaited loaves, place on a greased tray, brush with eggwash and sprinkle with sesame seeds. Allow to prove, then bake at 180°C for 30 minutes.

Yeast Buns

Makes 25

550 g strong flour	150 ml water ⎫ (at 40°C)
1 tsp salt	125 ml milk ⎭
50 g butter	1 egg
50 g castor sugar	50 ml bun wash
40 g yeast	

1. Sift the flour and salt into a warmed bowl and rub in the butter.
2. Dissolve the yeast and sugar in the water and milk and add the beaten egg. Mix into the flour to form a medium dough.
3. Knead thoroughly, replace in the bowl, cover with a cloth and allow to prove in a warm place for 1 hour. This dough is now the basic one for all kinds of yeast buns.
4. Knead the dough, divide into 25 equal pieces and mould them round. Place on a greased baking sheet and allow to prove until double their size.
5. Bake at 230°C for 15 minutes.
6. Remove from the oven and brush immediately with bun wash.

Chelsea Buns

Makes 25

1 kg bun dough	100 g mixed dried fruit
50 g melted butter	25 g diced mixed peel
40 g castor sugar	50 ml bun wash
10 g cinnamon	25 g castor sugar

1. Roll out the dough 65 cm × 35 cm.
2. Brush with the melted butter, sprinkle with the sugar, cinnamon, fruit and peel.
3. Roll up like a Swiss Roll, keeping the length to 65 cm and seal the edges.
4. Cut into 25 × 2.5 cm pieces and arrange fairly close together in a greased baking tray with deep sides so that they become square as they expand with proving. Allow to prove until double in size.
5. Bake at 230°C for 15 minutes.
6. Remove from the oven, brush immediately with bun wash and sprinkle with castor sugar.

Hot Cross Buns

Makes 25

1 kg bun dough	100 g soft flour ⎫
1 tbs spice essence	25 g melted lard ⎬ batter
bun wash	pinch baking powder ⎪
	100 ml cold water ⎭

1. Add the spice essence while making the dough.
2. Divide into 25 equal pieces, mould them round and place on a greased tray, then pipe a cross on each with the batter.
3. Allow to prove until double their size, then bake at 230°C for 10–15 minutes.
4. Remove from the oven and brush immediately with bun wash.

Savarin Paste (Pâte à Savarin)

Makes 2 × 15 cm savarins

225 g strong flour	100 g melted butter
20 g yeast	25 g castor sugar
75 ml water	pinch salt
3 eggs	

1. Sift the warmed flour into a warm bowl.
2. Dissolve the yeast and sugar in the water, which has been heated to 35°C.

3. Make a well in the centre of the flour and add the dissolved yeast. Mix in just enough flour to make a light batter and dust a little of the flour over the top.
4. Cover with a cloth and allow to prove in a warm place until the ferment breaks through the flour
5. Break in the eggs and mix to a smooth dough. Add the salt, sugar and butter, then mix to a smooth and elastic dough.
6. Allow to prove covered with a cloth in a warm place until double its size.
7. Half-fill greased and floured savarin moulds and allow to prove again until it reaches the top of the moulds.
8. Bake in the oven at 235°C for 25–30 minutes until cooked. Remove from the moulds, place onto a cooling rack and allow to cool completely before using.

Fruit Savarin (Savarin aux Fruits)

1 × 15 cm savarin
  200 ml stock syrup
   50 ml apricot glaze
  300 g fruit salad (with kirsch)
  100 ml whipped cream

1. Soak the stale savarin in the hot syrup, remove carefully and allow to drain on a wire rack.
2. Brush the surface with hot apricot glaze and place on a round dish.
3. Drain the fruit salad and place in the centre.
4. Pipe rosettes of cream on top of the savarin.

Note
Savarins can also be filled with stoned cherries mixed with raspberry or cherry sauce, with halves of apricots mixed with apricot sauce, or with whipped cream only.

Marignans

Marignans are made from Savarin Paste baked in boat-shaped moulds, finished by soaking in stock syrup and glazing with apricot glaze. The recipe for Savarin Paste will make 10 Marignans.

Pomponettes

These are made from Savarin Paste baked in queen cake tins. The recipe for savarin paste will yield 10–12 pomponettes. They are soaked in hot stock syrup, drained and brushed with apricot glaze.

Rum Babas (Babas au Rhum)

These are made from Savarin Paste to which 50 g currants have been added. They are baked at 235°C for 15 minutes in dariole moulds, cooled and allowed to dry before being immersed in hot rum-flavoured stock syrup. Neat rum may be sprinkled over them before the babas are glazed with apricot glaze and decorated with chantilly cream.

Petits Fours and Biscuits

These are sweetmeats to round off a formal meal at dinner rather than lunch, usually while drinking coffee or a liqueur before the speeches and toasts begin. They consist of a colourful selection of small confections including cakes, biscuits, wafers, chocolates, nougats, marzipans, marshmallows, rum truffles and many more in all shapes but very small in size. Presentation can be in a casket made of pastillage, pulled sugar or praline with each petit four placed in a paper case. Petits fours are also known as Friandises, Mignardises, Frivolités and Délices des Dames.

Africaines

Cream 125 g each of butter and castor sugar, add 3 eggs one by one and fold in 125 g flour sifted with 50 g each of cornflour and desiccated coconut. Roll out 4 mm thick and cut into oblongs 5 cm × 3 cm. Brush with eggwash, sprinkle with desiccated coconut and bake at 180°C for 20 minutes.

Baisers Parisienne

Make 8 whites of egg into Italian meringue, divide it into four and flavour and colour one with pistachio and green, one strawberry and pink, one lemon and yellow and the other almond and left white. Pipe small balls onto greaseproof paper using a 1 cm plain tube. Sprinkle with granulated sugar and dry out at 110°C for 2½ hours. Sandwich two together, using the appropriately flavoured buttercream.

Battenburg Slices

Bake two Genoese Sponges, one coloured yellow and one chocolate, in square tins. Cut into 1.5 cm square lengths and stick together in pairs, 1 yellow and 1 chocolate, with hot apricot glaze. Then place two pairs together to give a chessboard pattern and place in the centre of a length of marzipan rolled 3 mm thick and 12 cm wide, previously spread with apricot glaze. Fold to enclose firmly, then cut into 1 cm slices and brush the surface with apricot glaze.

Biscuits Champagne

Whisk 4 whole eggs, 3 yolks of egg and 300 g castor sugar over heat until it reaches the ribbon stage. Remove from the heat and continue to whisk until it is cold, then gently fold in 300 g soft flour and a few drops of vanilla essence. Pipe the mixture into 2 cm diameter bulbs onto a greased and floured baking sheet and sprinkle them well with castor sugar. Shake off surplus sugar and leave in a warm place for 12 hours to form a crust before baking at 160°C, keeping them pale in colour.

Boules au Chocolat

Mix 125 g each of castor sugar and ground almonds with 25 g cocoa and 1 white of egg to form a stiff paste. Mould into 30 small balls and press a small toasted hazelnut in the centre of each. Pass each through lightly whisked white of egg then into granulated sugar. Place on a greased baking tray and bake at 200°C for 10 minutes.

Boulettes aux Marrons

Mix a 250 g tin of chestnut purée with 100 g castor sugar, 50 g ground almonds and 1 tsp vanilla essence to a stiff consistency. Mould in dessertspoonfuls and, when dried, coat with chocolate vermicelli.

Brandy Snaps

Makes 15

125 g butter	¹/₂ juice of lemon
125 g castor sugar	125 g soft flour
125 g golden syrup	¹/₂ tsp ground ginger

1. Melt the butter, sugar, syrup and lemon juice. Remove from the heat and beat in the sieved flour and ground ginger.
2. Deposit spoonfuls of the mixture onto a well-greased baking sheet, keeping them at least 7 cm apart.
3. Bake at 175°C for 10 minutes. Allow to rest for just a few seconds.
4. Mould each piece around the greased handle of a wooden spoon until set hard. Place onto a cooling rack and allow to cool and become crisp.

Carrot Sweetmeats

Sweat 450 g grated carrot in 50 ml oil or ghee, then boil to reduce any liquid. Prepare a syrup by gently boiling 150 ml water and 275 g sugar with 1 tsp ground cardamom and when the mixture reaches small thread stage (104°C) remove from the heat and add a few drops of rose-water. Pour the syrup onto the carrot, then stir in 300 ml cream, 100 g milk powder and 50 g chopped pistachio nuts. Spread the mixture in a dish 1 cm thick, place a weight on top and allow to cool. Cut into small diamonds or squares, garnish each piece with a pistachio nut and serve.

Cat's Tongue Biscuits (Langues de Chat)

Makes 20

125 g butter
125 g castor sugar
3 egg whites
125 g soft flour
$^{1}/_{2}$ tsp vanilla essence

1. Prepare a baking sheet by brushing with melted butter and sprinkling with flour.
2. Cream the butter and sugar together until light and fluffy.
3. Add the egg whites one at a time, beating thoroughly.
4. Mix in the sifted flour and flavour with vanilla essence.
5. Pipe the mixture onto the baking sheet in 7 cm lengths, using a 5 mm plain tube.
6. Bake at 215°C for 7–8 minutes until brown around the edges.
7. Remove from the baking sheet and place onto a wire cooling rack.

Chickpea and Almond Sweetmeats

Prepare a syrup by gently boiling 150 ml water and 75 g sugar with 1 tsp ground cardamom and when the mixture reaches small thread stage (104°C) remove from the heat and add a few drops of vanilla essence. Heat 100 g oil or ghee, then sprinkle in 50 g besan (chickpea flour) and cook for 5 minutes, pour in the syrup, continue cooking, then add 50 g oil or ghee and cook for a further 10 minutes. Spread in a shallow dish 2 cm thick and cool. Cut into diamonds or squares, garnish with slivered almonds and store in a dry place for a few hours to allow the sweetmeats to harden.

Chocolate Truffles

Melt 200 g grated plain chocolate, then beat in 175 g softened butter, 40 g icing sugar and 2 egg yolks. Allow to cool until slightly firm, then, using a 2 cm piping tube, pipe into 2 cm pieces on a tray dusted with cocoa. Shake to cover the truffles with the cocoa, mould them round and dredge again with cocoa.

Congress Tartlets

Line small tartlet moulds with sweet pastry cut with a fancy cutter and pipe a spot of raspberry jam in the bottom. Fill with a mixture made by mixing 250 g ground almonds and 500 g castor sugar with 5 whites of egg and a few drops of almond essence, place two thin strips of sweet pastry on top in the form of a cross and bake at 175°C for 15 minutes.

Cornets

Cream 100 g butter with 150 g icing sugar, add 4 egg whites, one at a time, adding a little of 100 g flour to prevent the mixture curdling. Mix in all the flour and pipe the mixture onto a greased baking sheet in 2.5 cm rounds, leaving room to spread. Bake at 230°C for 5 minutes until the edges only are slightly coloured. Remove the pieces one at a time and insert inside or outside a cornet mould until all are moulded and hard.

Crystallised Fruits

Prepare single green and black grapes with a piece of stalk attached, peeled segments of orange or tangerine with the membrane intact, barely ripe strawberries, cherries on the stalk etc. Dip into beaten white of egg, drain, then dip into castor sugar to cover completely. Allow to dry before serving.

Dames d'Honneur

Line small tartlet moulds with puff pastry trimmings and fill with a mixture made by mixing 100 g castor sugar, 50 g ground almonds and 15 g cornflour with 2 yolks of egg, 30 ml cream and a few drops of orange-flavoured water. Bake at 200°C for 15 minutes.

Dominoes

Cut a day-old sheet of Genoese Sponge into 6 cm × 3 cm oblongs. Brush with apricot glaze, then spread with royal icing. When set, decorate with dots of chocolate icing to resemble dominoes.

Duchesse

Cream 350 g butter with 250 g castor sugar, add 3 eggs, one at a time, then fold in 450 g flour, 30 g ground almonds, 1 tsp cinnamon and the grated zest of 1 lemon. Pipe three lines just touching one another along the length of a greased baking tray, using a 1 cm fancy tube. Bake at 160°C for 30 minutes, then coat with royal icing diluted with orange juice and bake for a further 10 minutes. Cut into 5 cm sections when cold.

Finger Biscuits (Biscuits à la Cuillère)

Makes 20

    4 eggs
100 g castor sugar
100 g soft flour
 15 g icing sugar

1. Prepare a baking sheet by brushing with melted butter and sprinkling with flour.
2. Place the egg yolks and sugar in a basin and whisk until firm and white.
3. Whisk the egg whites in a separate bowl until stiff.
4. Fold in half the quantity of egg whites into the creamed mixture, then carefully fold in the sifted flour and the remainder of the whites.
5. Pipe the mixture onto the baking sheet in 10 cm lengths, using a 1 cm plain tube.
6. Sprinkle with icing sugar, remove any excess and bake at 165°C for 15 minutes.
7. Allow to cool for 5 minutes, then remove from the baking sheet and place on a wire cooling rack.

Florentines

Melt 150 g butter in a pan with 150 ml golden syrup, 50 g each of chopped almonds, flour, glacé cherries and mixed peel, together with 2 tsp lemon juice. Drop teaspoonfuls on a greased baking tray, leaving space for them to spread. Bake at 180°C for 8 minutes, then allow to cool on a rack. Dip one side of each into 250 g melted plain chocolate and mark with a serrated scraper.

Fried Sweetmeats

Sift 250 g flour, 175 g milk powder and 1 tsp baking powder, then rub in 50 g butter and moisten with 275 ml milk to form an elastic dough. Divide and mould into 20 balls and golden shallow fry in oil or ghee. Prepare a syrup by gently boiling 600 ml water and 350 g sugar with a stick of cinnamon, when the mixture reaches small thread stage (104°C) remove the cinnamon, and add 50 ml rose-water. Place the fried sweetmeats into the syrup and allow to cool. The balls will become soft and spongy and should be served chilled.

Granville Tartlets

Cream 50 g butter with 90 g castor sugar, mix in 75 g cakecrumbs, 25 g ground almonds and 25 g each of currants and chopped mixed peel. Fill into small tartlets lined with puff pastry trimmings, bake at 180°C for 20 minutes and, when cold, coat the tops with lemon-flavoured water icing and sprinkle with desiccated coconut.

Japonaise

Whisk 6 whites of egg with a pinch of salt to a stiff peak, then fold in 150 g ground almonds sieved with 375 g castor sugar. Pipe out 5 cm circles on a silicone paper-lined baking sheet, using a 1 cm plain tube and bake at 150°C for 35–40 minutes. When cold, sandwich two together with coffee buttercream, spread the edges with the same cream and coat with ground almonds which have been lightly baked. The top may be coated with coffee-flavoured water icing with a roasted hazelnut in the centre.

Macaroons

Mix 250 g ground almonds with 400 g castor sugar and 30 g ground rice. Add 5 whites of egg and a few drops of almond essence to form a piping consistency. Pipe small 4 cm diameter balls onto a sheet of rice paper on a baking sheet, using a plain tube. Brush with water, place a split almond on each and bake at 180°C until pale golden in colour.

Marrons Glacés

Peel and skin good-sized chestnuts and simmer very gently in water until tender. Make a syrup with 350 ml water and 500 g each of sugar and gluc-ose, add the drained chestnuts and bring to the boil. Remove from the heat, cover with a lid and leave for 24 hours. Repeat this once more, this time flavouring the syrup with 1 tsp vanilla essence. After the second 24 hours, remove the chestnuts to a wire rack to drain, reforming any which have split. Allow to dry in a very low oven, then dip in a second syrup made of 500 g sugar cooked in 150 ml water.

Marshmallows

Soak 8 g agar-agar in 300 ml water for several hours, then warm until it is dissolved. Strain the liquid, add 500 g sugar, heat to dissolve and boil to 107°C. Add 250 g glucose and continue to boil to 118°C. Have 7 egg whites beaten stiffly and pour the syrup steadily into them, whisking all the time. Pipe into bulbs and allow to set, or fill into a tray dusted with cornflour, then cut into pieces and separate them using mixed icing sugar and cornflour.

Marzipan Fruits

These can be made by mixing 1 kg warmed marzipan with 125 ml glucose and 1 kg icing sugar with the flavour and colour of the intended fruits, e.g. apples, apricots, bananas, oranges, pears, strawberries etc. (Vegetables such as carrots, cauliflower, peas in a pod can also be made). Mould to shape, allow the outside to harden, then paint on the distinctive markings, using a brush or spray of edible colourings. It is also possible to use moulds to give the exact shape. Shelled nuts may be dipped in melted chocolate and added to the display.

Melting Moments

Cream 175 g butter with 75 g castor sugar, add 2 eggs, the grated zest of 1 lemon and fold in 225 g cornflour sieved with 1 tsp baking powder. Divide into small paper cake cases and bake at 180°C for 10 minutes.

Othellos

Whisk 6 yolks of egg with 25 g castor sugar, then fold in 100 g flour. Whisk 8 whites of egg to a peak and fold in 100 g each of castor sugar and flour. Fold the two mixes together and pipe 3 cm rings on a greased and floured baking tray. Bake at 220°C for 7 minutes.

Physalis

Turn back the leaves and hold them while dipping the fruit into plain or coloured and flavoured warm fondant. Allow to set and place in paper cases. Alternatively the fruit part may be egged and crumbed and deep fried, together with the leaves and served hot.

Petits Fours Gommés

Whisk 4 whites of egg, add 450 g each of ground almonds and castor sugar. Pipe 3 cm rounds onto silicone paper on a baking sheet, using a 5 mm fancy tube. Decorate with small pieces of glacé fruits, then allow to dry for several hours. Bake at 175°C for 12–15 minutes and brush with gum arabic jelly on removing from the oven.

Princesses

Cream 125 g butter with 250 g castor sugar, add 4 eggs one at a time, the juice of 1 lemon and fold in 250 g flour. Pipe 7 cm lengths on silicone paper on a baking sheet, using a 1 cm fancy tube. Bake at 180°C for 6 minutes, then glaze with water icing.

Puits d'Amour

Line small tartlet moulds with sweet pastry and bake blind. Fill with pastry cream and, when set, dribble some caramel on each.

Ratafias

Whisk 4 whites of egg to a foam and fold in 125 g ground almonds and 150 g castor sugar to form a paste. Pipe rounds onto a sheet of rice paper on a baking sheet, using a 1 cm plain tube. Dredge with icing sugar and bake at 200°C for 15 minutes.

Sablets

Cream 125 g each of butter and castor sugar, add 1 egg and the grated zest of 1 lemon and mix in 65 g each of sifted flour and cornflour. Roll out 4 mm thick and cut in various shapes, dredge with icing sugar and finely chopped almonds, place on a greased tray and bake at 180°C for 15 minutes.

Scotch Gingerbreads

Cream 250 g butter, then add 125 g fine oatmeal, 30 g ground ginger and 350 g flour. Now mix in 350 ml treacle or syrup and 125 g finely chopped candied peel. Pipe into greased madeleine moulds and bake at 190°C for 12 minutes.

Scotch Macaroons

Cut 5 cm rounds of puff pastry, prick and allow to rest for 30 minutes, then pipe with a ring made of 250 g ground almonds and 500 g castor sugar mixed with 5 whites of egg and a few drops of almond essence. Bake at 175°C for 12 minutes.

Shortbread Biscuits

Makes 20

  175 g soft flour
   25 g ground rice
  225 g butter
  110 g castor sugar

1. Sift the flour and ground rice into a basin.
2. Cream the butter and sugar in a bowl.
3. Add the flour and ground rice and press together to form a stiff paste.
4. Roll out 4 mm thick, dusting with ground rice or castor sugar and cut into desired shapes, e.g. circles, triangles, oblongs.
5. Place on a greased baking sheet and prick all over with a fork.
6. Bake at 220°C for 10 minutes without letting the biscuits colour. Allow to cool, then remove from the baking sheet and place on a cooling rack.

Souvaroffs

Cream 125 g butter with 55 g icing sugar, add 1 egg yolk and fold in 125 g flour. Roll out and cut into fancy oval shapes. Bake at 180°C for 10 minutes and, when cold, sandwich two together with apricot glaze and spread the top with kirsch-flavoured fondant.

Tulipes

Whisk 6 egg whites with 175 g castor sugar, then fold in 75 g flour and 60 g melted butter. Spread circles on a greased and floured baking sheet and bake at 200°C for 6 minutes. On taking from the oven, immediately press each piece on a greased orange or other round object to give a tulip shape.

Turkish Delight

Heat 500 ml water and 750 g sugar to 113°C (soft ball stage). Dilute 50 g cornflour in 75 ml grape juice, add to the syrup and mix in 1 tsp cream of tartar, 1 tablespoon rose-water and 50 g chopped pistachios. Cook until thick, divide into two and colour one part light pink. Pour each into an oiled shallow tray and leave to set. Cut into small squares and dust liberally with icing sugar.

Viennese Biscuits

Makes 20

    300 g butter
    100 g icing sugar
      2 eggs
    375 g soft flour
     15 g icing sugar

1. Prepare a baking sheet by brushing with melted butter and sprinkling with flour.
2. Cream the butter and sugar together until light and fluffy; add the eggs one at a time and continue beating.
3. Add the sifted flour and mix until smooth.
4. Using a large star tube pipe onto the baking sheet in shapes such as shells or rosettes.
5. Bake at 170° for 15 minutes until lightly coloured. Place onto a wire cooling rack and sprinkle with icing sugar.

Züicher Leckerli

Make a fairly stiff paste with 300 g ground almonds, 350 g icing sugar and 2 whites of egg. Roll out 7 mm thick, using icing sugar to prevent it sticking, and cut into 2.5 cm × 3.5 cm oblongs. Leave to dry out for 12 hours, then place on a greased tray and bake at 250°C for a few minutes. Glaze with gum arabic immediately they come from the oven.

Note
For gum arabic glaze place 20 g powdered gum arabic into 120 ml cold water and bring to the boil, stirring until dissolved.

CHAPTER 12 # Stocks and Sauces

Stocks

A stock is the liquid resulting from the cooking of bones, vegetables and herbs so as to extract their flavours, nutrients and salts. Stock is the foundation of many kitchen preparations including soups, sauces, stews and fish and rice dishes. The importance of good-quality stock cannot be underestimated, particularly in European traditional cookery. The two main kinds of stock are white stock and brown stock, the name being determined by the type of bones used, e.g. white veal stock made from veal bones for making a velouté and brown beef stock made from beef bones coloured in the oven for making a brown sauce. The vegetable flavourings used in the making of stocks and sauces can consist of large trimmings and end-pieces left from other uses.

White Chicken Stock (Fonds Blanc de Volaille)

Makes 10 litres

3.5 kg chicken bones	100 g mushroom trimmings	
10 litres water	1 sprig thyme	
250 g carrot ⎫	2 bayleaves ⎫	bouquet garni
250 g onion ⎪ roughly cut	parsley stalks ⎭	
150 g leek ⎪	10 peppercorns	
250 g celery ⎭		

1. Place the bones in a stockpot, cover with cold water and bring slowly to the boil.
2. Remove any scum that rises to the surface.
3. Add the vegetables, herbs and peppercorns.
4. Simmer gently for 2 hours, continuously removing all traces of scum and grease.
5. Pass through a conical strainer into a clean saucepan, reboil and use as required or cool as rapidly as possible and place in a refrigerator at 7°C until required.

Notes
1. To cool any kind of stock rapidly, place the pot on a stand in a sink of cold water.
2. The bones may be blanched first by covering with cold water, bringing to the boil and simmering for a few minutes, then draining and washing under hot water to remove all traces of fat and scum, then under cold water until any impurities are washed away.

Vegetable Stock

Makes 5 litres

250 g carrot		5 litres water	
250 g onion	roughly cut	400 g squashed tomatoes	
150 g leek		1 sprig thyme	bouquet garni
250 g celery		1 bayleaf	
100 g mushroom trimmings		parsley stalks	
50 ml oil		10 peppercorns	

1. Sweat the vegetables in the oil in a stockpot.
2. Add the water and bring gently to the boil, then add the mushrooms, tomatoes, herbs and peppercorns.
3. Simmer gently for 45 minutes, continuously removing any scum and fat.
4. Strain through a conical strainer into a clean saucepan, reboil and use as required or cool as rapidly as possible and place in a refrigerator at 7°C until required.

Brown Beef Stock (Fonds Brun or Estouffade)

Makes 10 litres

3.5 kg beef bones, chopped into small pieces any fat removed		10 litres water	
		100 g mushroom trimmings	
250 g carrot		1 sprig thyme	bouquet garni
250 g onion	roughly cut	2 bayleaves	
150 g leek		parsley stalks	
250 g celery		10 peppercorns	

1. Brown the bones in fat in the oven, then strain off all the fat.
2. Brown the vegetables in the same fat in a frying pan on top of the stove or in the oven, then strain.
3. Place the bones and vegetables in a stockpot, cover with the cold water and bring slowly to the boil.
4. Remove any scum that rises to the surface.
5. Add the bouquet garni and peppercorns.
6. Simmer gently for 3–4 hours, continuously removing all traces of scum and grease.
7. Strain through a conical strainer into a clean saucepan, reboil and use as required or cool as rapidly as possible and place in a refrigerator at 7°C until required.

Game Stock (Fonds de Gibier)

Proceed in the same way as for Brown Beef Stock, using game bones (hare, venison or pheasant) in place of beef bones and cook for 2 hours only.

Lamb or Mutton Stock (Fonds de Mouton)

Proceed in the same way as for White Chicken Stock, using lamb or mutton bones and cook for 1 hour only.

Veal Stock (Fonds de Veau)

Proceed in the same way as for White Chicken Stock, using veal bones and cook for 2 hours.

Fish Stock (Fumet de Poisson)

Makes 5 litres

50 g butter	1 bayleaf
2 kg white fish bones	a few parsley stalks
200 g sliced onion	5 peppercorns
1 juice of lemon	5 litres water

1. Melt the butter in a saucepan.
2. Add the washed fish bones, sliced onion, lemon juice and herbs.
3. Cover with greaseproof paper and a lid and sweat for 5 minutes without coloration in order to extract the juices from the bones.
4. Cover with cold water, bring to the boil and skim any impurities that rise to the surface, then simmer for 20 minutes.
5. Strain into a clean pan, reboil and use as required.

Japanese Soup Stock (Dashi)

Add 4 squares of kombu that have been thoroughly washed under cold water to 2 litres simmering water. Simmer for 2 minutes, then remove the kombu and add 450 g katsuobushi. Bring to the boil, stirring continuously, remove from the heat and allow the flakes to settle to the bottom of the pan; strain and use.

First Soup Stock

Place 2 litres cold water in a saucepan and add 2×10 cm squares of dried kelp with a 1 cm fringe, previously wiped with a damp cloth. Bring almost to the boil and remove the kelp, bring to boiling point, add 12 g bonito flakes and remove from the heat. Allow to stand for 3 minutes, strain and use as required. The kelp and bonito flakes should be kept for making Second Soup Stock.

Second Soup Stock

Place 1.5 litres cold water in a pan with the kelp and bonito flakes reserved from First Soup Stock and simmer for 5 minutes; strain and use.

Noodle Broth (Kakejiru)

Simmer 1 litre second soup stock, 50 ml dark and 50 ml light soy sauces, 125 ml mirin and season with salt and monosodium glutamate.

ASPIC JELLY

Aspic Jelly (Gelée Ordinaire)

Proceed as for Consommé, substituting veal stock for beef.

Add 25 g gelatine per 1 litre of consommé at the point where the consommé has been clarified completely and just before passing it through a muslin. It is advisable to test a small quantity in the refrigerator to see if it sets so that adjustments can be made as necessary.

Chicken Aspic Jelly (Gelée de Volaille)

This is made in the same way as Aspic Jelly, using chicken stock.

Fish Aspic Jelly (Gelée de Poisson)

This is made in the same way as Aspic Jelly, using fish stock.

Game Aspic Jelly (Gelée de Gibier)

This is made in the same way as Aspic Jelly, with the addition of 1 kg roasted game carcasses, bones and trimmings to the veal stock.

MEAT AND FISH GLAZES

A glaze is made by reducing a good-quality stock by continuous boiling until it becomes glutinous and highly concentrated in flavour. As it reduces in quantity the stock should be transferred to smaller pans. It should be cooled and stored in a refrigerator at 7°C in plastic or porcelain containers. Glazes are used for enhancing the flavour of sauces, stews and other dishes.

Sauces

Sauces are thickened liquids of varying consistencies, savoury or sweet, hot, warm or cold, according to type and purpose. They are served with a wide variety of dishes, either in contrast to or complementing the flavour and texture of the items with which they are served, at the same time aiding the digestion and enhancing the appearance of the dish. The range of flavours is considerable, from the most delicate to the very rich and distinctive, and can vary in cost from the inexpensive to the almost prohibitive. Their function and the importance attached to sauces should never be underestimated.

Thickening agents for sauces

The main thickening agents used for sauces are various kinds of fecule, dairy products, breadcrumbs and blood but the main one is a cooked mixture of flour and fat, known as a roux, of which there are three versions.

1. White roux, used for Béchamel Sauce, is known as a first stage roux; it consists of equal quantities of butter and flour, cooked for a few minutes to a sandy texture without coloration.
2. Fawn roux, used for Veloutés and Tomato Sauce, is known as a second stage roux; it consists of equal quantities of butter and flour, cooked for a few minutes to a sandy texture and a light fawn colour.
3. Brown roux, used for Espagnole, is known as third stage roux; it consists of a ratio of one-third dripping to two-thirds flour; cooked together until light brown in colour.
4. Fecules or starches, including cornflour and arrowroot, have to be diluted in cold water before being added to a sauce.
5. Beurre manié is made by mixing an equal quantity of raw flour and butter to a soft paste, adding a little at a time to an almost finished sauce.
6. Cream, crème fraîche, soured cream, natural yogurt.
7. Egg yolks either alone or mixed with cream to form a liaison.
8. Butter is usually added in small pieces to an almost finished sauce.
9. Blood is used to thicken jugged hare and entrées made with kidneys.

Sabayon

Whisk egg yolks and little water in a stainless steel or tin-lined copper pan. Place on the stove in a bain-marie of hot water and whisk continuously until the mixture reaches the consistency of double cream and clings to the whisk. Fold the sabayon into the prepared sauce using a ladle and taking care not to loose its aeration.

BÉCHAMEL AND EXTENSION SAUCES

Béchamel Sauce or White Sauce (Sauce Béchamel)

Makes 5 litres

450 g butter	1 small onion	
450 g flour	½ bayleaf	} studded onion
5 litres milk	1 clove	

1. Melt the butter in a deep saucepan, stir in the flour with a wooden spatule to form a roux and cook gently for a few minutes to a sandy texture, then allow to cool.
2. Bring the milk to the boil with the studded onion and allow to infuse for 8 minutes.
3. Remove the studded onion, add the milk gradually to the roux, stirring until it has all been completely absorbed. Beat out any lumps that may appear.
4. Cover with a lid and simmer gently for 20 minutes or place to cook in the oven at 175°C for 40 minutes, stirring occasionally.
5. Strain through a conical strainer into a clean receptacle and dot with small pieces of butter or cover with buttered greaseproof paper to prevent a skin from forming. Retain in a bain-marie.

Note
Béchamel is a foundation sauce and should not therefore be seasoned; its consistency should be that of double cream.

Extension sauces from Béchamel

All make 1 litre.

Anchovy Sauce (Sauce Anchois)

To 800 ml hot béchamel add 25 ml anchovy essence and finish with 50 g butter, 100 ml cream and salt and pepper.
    May be served with poached, boiled and grilled fish.

Cheese Sauce (Sauce Mornay)

To 800 ml béchamel add 75 g grated Parmesan cheese and finish with 50 g butter, 100 ml cream, salt and pepper and 2 yolks of sabayon.
    May be used for many pasta, fish and meat dishes, mainly those which are going to be coloured under a salamander grill or in the top of a hot oven.

Cream Sauce (Sauce Crème)

To 800 ml of hot béchamel add 50 g butter, 100 ml cream, and salt and pepper.
    May be served with pasta dishes, boiled fish and vegetables.

Egg Sauce (Sauce aux Oeufs)

To 800 ml hot béchamel add 3 diced hard-boiled eggs, salt and pepper and finish with 50 g butter and 100 ml cream.
    May be served with poached or boiled fish.

Mustard Sauce (Sauce Moutarde)

To 800 ml hot béchamel add 25 g diluted English mustard, salt and pepper and finish with 50 g butter and 100 ml cream.

May be served with grilled fish, herrings in particular.

Onion Sauce (Sauce aux Oignons)

To 800 ml hot béchamel add 100 g sliced onions cooked in 50 g butter without coloration and finish with 100 ml cream, salt and pepper.

May be served with roast mutton.

Parsley Sauce (Sauce Persil)

To 800 ml hot béchamel add 15 g chopped and blanched parsley and finish with 100 ml cream, salt and pepper.

May be served with boiled vegetables and boiled ham.

VELOUTÉ AND EXTENSION SAUCES

Velouté is made of a white stock mixed into a blond roux and cooked gently for 1 hour. It is the basis of many main dishes of fish, meat and poultry, soups, vegetables, hot and cold mousses, savoury soufflés, and several extension sauces, including chaudfroid. The main varieties are fish, chicken and veal.

Chicken Velouté (Velouté de Volaille)

Makes 5 litres

  450 g butter
  450 g flour
5 litres white chicken stock

1. Melt the butter in a deep saucepan, stir in the flour with a wooden spatule to form a roux and cook gently for a few minutes to a sandy texture and light fawn colour, then allow to cool.
2. Add the hot stock to the roux a little at a time until all the stock has been absorbed and allow to simmer gently for 1 hour on the stove or in the oven at 175°C for 30 minutes.
3. Strain through a conical strainer into a clean receptacle, dot with small pieces of butter or cover with buttered greaseproof paper to prevent a skin forming.
4. Retain in a bain-marie.

Notes
1. As a foundation sauce, velouté is not seasoned during its cooking.
2. Velouté should be the consistency of double cream, and be viscous and ivory in colour.

Fish Velouté (Velouté de Poisson)

Proceed as for Chicken Velouté, substituting fish stock for chicken stock.

Veal Velouté (Velouté de Veau)

Proceed as for Chicken Velouté, substituting white veal stock for chicken stock.

Extension sauces from velouté

Sauce Bercy

50 g butter	1 litre fish velouté
75 g finely chopped shallots	200 ml cream
300 ml fish stock	75 g butter (preferably unsalted)
300 ml dry white wine	

1. Lightly sweat the chopped shallots in the hot butter in a shallow pan.
2. Pour in the fish stock and white wine, boil and reduce by half.
3. Add the velouté and cream and simmer to the original velouté consistency, stirring frequently.
4. Finish by adding the chopped parsley and mixing in the 75 g butter, a little at a time, plus a point of cayenne.

Sauce Bercy is served with fish.

Sauce Chaudfroid Blanche

800 ml chicken velouté
400 ml aspic jelly
200 ml cream

1. Boil the velouté in a saucepan and gradually stir in the aspic jelly and cream.
2. Reduce by one-third, stirring frequently, then pass through a fine strainer.

Used in cold buffet work to coat various chicken dishes.

Sauce Suprême

Reduce 500 ml chicken stock by half, add 800 ml chicken velouté and 125 ml cream and reduce, stirring frequently until the original consistency of the velouté is achieved. Strain and mix in 100 g butter, little by little.
    May be served with poached chicken dishes.

White Wine Sauce (Sauce Vin Blanc)

300 ml fish stock	200 ml cream
300 ml dry white wine	75 g butter (preferably unsalted)
1 litre fish velouté	salt and cayenne pepper

1. Place the fish stock and wine into a shallow pan and reduce by half.
2. Add the velouté and cream and simmer to the original velouté consistency, stirring frequently.
3. Strain through a fine conical strainer, season with salt and a point of cayenne, then mix in the butter a little at a time.

Note
1. Should the sauce be required for glazing, add 2 eggs of sabayon at the final stage.
2. It is usual to add the strained cooking liquid in which the fish was poached to the reduction of fish stock and wine.

BASIC BROWN SAUCES AND EXTENSION SAUCES

Brown Sauce is a foundation sauce, rather than a sauce in its own right and can be made by either of these methods:

1. Add brown beef stock in stages to a mixture of dripping and flour made into a third stage roux; add fried vegetables, herbs and tomato purée and simmer for 6 hours.
2. Thicken brown beef stock with flour that has been coloured and dried brown on a hotplate at a low temperature; add fried vegetables and tomato purée and simmer for 6 hours.

Brown Sauce (Sauce Espagnole)

Makes 5 litres

300 g dripping	8 litres brown stock
350 g flour	200 g bacon trimmings
100 g tomato purée	400 g tomatoes
400 g carrot ⎤	400 g mushroom trimmings
400 g onion ⎥ roughly cut	parsley stalks
200 g leek ⎥	1 bayleaf
200 g celery ⎦	1 sprig thyme

1. Melt the dripping in a deep saucepan, stir in the flour with a wooden spatule and cook to a third stage roux, then allow to cool.
2. Add the tomato purée, then the brown stock, stirring well and bring to the boil.
3. Fry the bacon trimmings and vegetables in a little hot fat to a light brown colour, drain off the fat and add to the sauce.
4. Add the herbs, crushed tomatoes and mushroom trimmings.
5. Simmer gently for 6 hours, stirring occasionally and skimming as necessary.
6. Strain into a saucepan, reboil and retain for further use.

Sauce Demi-glace

Makes 1 litre

1 litre brown stock
1 litre brown sauce (Espagnole)

1. Place the stock and brown sauce together in a saucepan and bring to the boil.
2. Continue to boil and reduce until half its original quantity; skimming continuously.
3. Pass through a fine strainer; place knobs of butter on top to prevent a skin forming.

Notes
1. As well as being a basic sauce from which extension sauces are made, demi-glace is a sauce in its own right.
2. To make the sauce demi-glace mellow in flavour, knobs of butter are added.

Jus lié

Makes 5 litres

200 g dripping
400 g carrot ⎫
400 g onion ⎬ roughly cut
200 g leek ⎪
200 g celery ⎭
5 litres brown stock (usually a combination of veal, chicken and beef)
1 clove garlic

120 g arrowroot diluted with cold water
400 g tomatoes
400 g mushroom trimmings
100 g tomato purée
1 small sprig thyme
2 bayleaves
salt and pepper

1. Bring the brown stock to the boil and skim; thicken with the diluted arrowroot, reboil and allow to simmer.
2. Fry the vegetables in the hot dripping until brown, drain and add to the stock together with the tomato purée, squashed tomatoes, mushroom trimmings, herbs, salt and pepper.
3. Allow to simmer for 1 hour, skimming occasionally.
4. Pass through a fine strainer and correct the colour and consistency.

Note
This sauce can be used in some dishes such as chicken in place of demi-glace. It is transparent and less rich than demi-glace which is usually made in bulk and kept refrigerated for daily use whereas jus lié is usually made fresh daily.

Extension sauces from Brown Sauce

Bolognaise Sauce (Sauce Bolognaise)

500 g minced beef	50 g tomato purée
75 ml oil	400 ml jus lié or demi-glace
150 g chopped onion	200 ml red wine
1 clove crushed and chopped garlic	salt and pepper

1. Heat the oil in a saucepan, add the minced meat and fry until it is lightly coloured. Add the chopped onion and garlic and allow to cook until it all becomes soft, but not too brown.
2. Drain off surplus fat, add the wine, tomato purée and the chosen brown sauce. Bring to the boil, season and simmer gently for 40 minutes.
3. Serve on top of the cooked pasta, or separately in a sauceboat.

Bordelaise Sauce (Sauce Bordelaise)

50 g chopped shallots	200 ml red wine
10 crushed peppercorns	1 litre jus lié or demi-glace
1 bayleaf	25 g meat glaze
1 sprig thyme	50 g butter

1. Place the chopped shallots, crushed peppercorns, herbs and red wine in a shallow pan and reduce by two-thirds.
2. Add the brown sauce, simmer gently for a few minutes, then pass through a fine conical strainer.
3. Finish by adding the meat glaze and knobs of butter, then season to taste.

May be served with shallow-fried and grilled steaks.

Brown Onion Sauce (Sauce Lyonnaise)

Cook 500 g sliced onion in 100 g butter until lightly coloured, moisten with 100 ml vinegar and reduce by two-thirds. Add 600 ml jus lié or demi-glace and gently simmer for a few minutes, then season to taste.

   May be served with shallow-fried liver.

Chasseur Sauce (Sauce Chasseur)

50 g butter	600 ml jus lié or demi-glace
250 g sliced button mushrooms	5 g chopped tarragon
150 g chopped shallots	5 g chopped parsley
250 g tomato concassée	50 g butter
200 ml dry white wine	salt and pepper

1. Heat the butter in a saucepan, add the sliced mushrooms and cook for 3 minutes.

2. Add the chopped shallots and cook for a few moments, then add the tomato concassée and white wine, bring to the boil and reduce by half.
3. Add the brown sauce and the tarragon and parsley, season and simmer for a few moments. Finish with the butter.

Devilled Sauce (Sauce Diable)

50 g shallots	100 ml dry white wine
20 peppercorns	1 litre jus lié or demi-glace
1 bayleaf	50 g butter
1 sprig thyme	seasoning
100 ml vinegar	

1. Cook the chopped shallots, crushed peppercorns, the herbs, vinegar and the white wine in a shallow pan until reduced by two-thirds.
2. Add the brown sauce and simmer gently for 10 minutes, then pass through a fine conical strainer.
3. Finish by adding knobs of butter, then season, including a point of cayenne pepper.

May be served with grilled fish, meat or poultry.

Gratin Sauce (Sauce Gratin)

Cook 100 g chopped shallots in 50 g butter without colouring, add 450 g chopped mushrooms and continue to cook until the liquid has almost completely reduced. Add 600 ml jus lié or demi-glace and simmer gently for 20 minutes, then finish with 5 g chopped parsley.

May be served with grilled fish, meat or poultry.

Madeira Sauce (Sauce Madère)

Reduce 1 litre of jus lié or demi-glace until slightly thicker; thin with 100 ml Madeira and finish with 25 g butter.

May be served with sweetbreads, veal escalopes and ham.

Marsala Sauce (Sauce Marsala)

Reduce 1 litre of jus lié or demi-glace until slightly thicker; then thin with 100 ml Marsala and finish with 25 g butter.

May be served with veal escalopes, lamb noisettes, boiled ham and gammon rashers.

Sauce Robert

Cook 100 g chopped shallots in 50 g butter without colouring, add 200 ml dry white wine and reduce by half. Add 600 ml jus lié or demi-glace and simmer gently for a few moments. Complete with 5 g diluted English mustard and pass through a conical strainer.

May be served with grilled meat and poultry dishes and grilled fish.

Sauce Piquante

Reduce 100 ml each of white wine and vinegar with 100 g chopped shallots by two-thirds, add 1 litre jus lié or demi-glace and reduce to its original consistency. Add 50 g each of finely chopped capers and gherkins and 50 g chopped fines herbes.

May be served with grilled meats, especially pork and veal.

Sauce Poivrade

75 g butter or oil	100 ml red wine
100 g carrot ⎫	100 ml vinegar
100 g onion ⎬ chopped finely	1 litre jus lié or demi-glace
75 g celery ⎭	20 peppercorns
1 bayleaf	50 g butter
1 sprig thyme	salt and pepper

1. Heat the butter in a saucepan, add the vegetables and herbs and fry until brown in colour.
2. Add the red wine and vinegar, bring to the boil and reduce to a glaze.
3. Add the brown sauce and simmer gently for a few minutes, add the crushed peppercorns and continue to cook for a further 5 minutes and skim.
4. Strain through a conical strainer into a clean pan, reboil, skim and season to taste.
5. Complete the sauce at the moment of serving with knobs of the butter.

May be served with game animals such as hare and venison.

Reform Sauce (Sauce Réforme)

Reduce 600 ml Sauce Poivrade, 200 ml brown stock and 50 g redcurrant jelly by two-thirds. Pass through a conical strainer and garnish with 30 g each of the following, cut into julienne strips: truffle, ham, tongue, white of hard-boiled egg, gherkins, and button mushrooms cooked in lemon juice and water.

May be served with Breaded Lamb Cutlets in the Reform Style.

BUTTER SAUCES AND EXTENSION SAUCES

This kind of sauce is an emulsion of cooked egg yolks and butter, flavoured with vinegar, pepper and in some cases, fines herbes. Butter sauces require considerable skill in making at a fairly low temperature and must be kept at no more than 35°C; the use of pasteurised eggs is recommended. These sauces can discolour easily and a stainless steel or well-tinned copper sauteuse is recommended as being the most suitable pan to use.

Bearnaise Sauce (Sauce Béarnaise)

50 ml	vinegar	⎫		5	egg yolks
10	peppercorns	⎬ reduction		500 g	unsalted butter
25 g	shallots				
10 g	chervil and tarragon stalks	⎭			
10 g	chervil and tarragon leaves				

1. Place the vinegar, crushed peppercorns and the chopped shallots, chervil and tarragon stalks in a sauteuse and reduce until almost dry, then cool.
2. Add a little cold water to moisten the reduction, then add the egg yolks and whisk well, using a small balloon whisk.
3. Cook the yolks, whisking continuously until the mixture has the consistency of double cream and reaches the ribbon stage.
4. Allow to cool slightly, then add the warm melted butter a little at a time, whisking continuously over gentle heat until all is absorbed except the milky part of the butter.
5. Strain the sauce through a muslin or a very fine conical strainer.
6. Add the chopped chervil and tarragon and season with salt. Keep at 35°C.

Notes
1. This sauce is served with grilled fish and meats and is an obligatory accompaniment to Grilled Chateaubriand.
2. It should be similar to double cream in consistency and rather thick, egg-yolk yellow in colour, similar to mayonnaise and smooth in texture with absolutely no traces of coagulation or of curdling. It should have a distinct flavour of fresh tarragon.
3. A curdled sauce may be rectified by whisking it onto some uncurdled sauce. If the sauce has curdled because it is too hot it can be corrected by whisking it onto some cold water. If the sauce has curdled because it is too cold then whisk the sauce slowly onto some hot water.

Extension sauces from Béarnaise Sauce

Sauce Choron

Add 200 g purée of cooked tomato concassée to 500 ml Bearnaise Sauce.
May be served with grilled and sautéed meats.

Sauce Foyat (Sauce Valois)

Add 20 g meat glaze to 500 ml Béarnaise Sauce.
May be served with grilled and sautéed meats.

Sauce Paloise

Prepare in the same way as Béarnaise Sauce, substituting chopped mint stalks for the tarragon and adding 5 g chopped mint leaves at the final stage.
   May be served with roast and grilled lamb.

Hollandaise Sauce (Sauce Hollandaise)

5 egg yolks	500 g unsalted butter
50 ml vinegar ⎤	1 juice of lemon
10 white ⎬ reduction	seasoning of salt and
peppercorns ⎦	cayenne pepper

1. Place the vinegar and crushed peppercorns in a sauteuse and reduce until almost dry, then cool.
2. Add a little cold water to moisten the reduction, then add the egg yolks.
3. Cook the egg yolks, whisking continuously with a small balloon whisk until the mixture has the consistency of double cream and reaches the ribbon stage.
4. Allow to cool slightly, then add the warm melted butter steadily, whisking all the time over a gentle heat until all is absorbed except the milky part of the butter.
5. Strain the sauce through a muslin or a very fine conical strainer.
6. Finish with the lemon juice and season with salt. Keep at 35°C.

Note
Sauce Hollandaise can be added to any sauce in place of a sabayon.

Extension sauces from Hollandaise Sauce

Sauce Chantilly (Sauce Mousseline)

Add 100 ml lightly whipped cream to 500 ml Hollandaise Sauce.
   May be served with poached salmon and salmon trout and hot asparagus.

Sauce Maltaise

Add the juice of 1 blood orange plus its grated zest to 500 ml Hollandaise Sauce.
   May be served with hot asparagus.

Sauce Noisette

Add 50 g nut brown butter to 500 ml Hollandaise Sauce at the last moment.
   May be served with poached salmon, salmon trout and trout.

COLD SAUCES AND EXTENSION SAUCES

Mayonnaise may be served either as a sauce in its own right or as a basis for other sauces. It is an emulsification of egg yolks and oil, flavoured with vinegar and mustard. The type of oil used largely determines its flavour. It is used extensively in the making of hors-d'oeuvre variés, single hors-d'oeuvre, composite salads, fish and shellfish cocktails.

Mayonnaise is mainly served with cold foods but sauces derived from mayonnaise are suitable for hot fish dishes, e.g. Tartare Sauce is usually served with fish fried in breadcrumbs.

Mayonnaise Sauce

Makes 1 litre

25 ml malt vinegar
1 tsp dry English mustard
   6 egg yolks
1 litre oil, olive or salad
       salt and pepper

1. Place the vinegar, mustard, salt, pepper and egg yolks into a basin or the bowl of a mixing machine and begin whisking.
2. Incorporate the oil very slowly.

Notes
1. To make a light-coloured mayonnaise use lemon juice instead of vinegar.
2. 50 ml boiling water may be added at the end so as to stabilise the sauce.
3. Pasteurised egg yolks may be used in place of fresh ones.
4. The yolks and oil must be at room temperature.

Extension sauces from Mayonnaise Sauce

Mayonnaise with Soured Cream and Dill Sauce

Combine 500 ml mayonnaise with 500 ml soured cream, the juice of 2 lemons and 10 g chopped dill.

Cambridge Sauce

Blend 3 hard-boiled eggs, 50 g anchovy fillets, 25 g capers and 25 g chopped parsley, tarragon and chervil to a fine paste and combine with 1 litre of mayonnaise.

Cocktail Sauce

Add 100 ml tomato ketchup, 100 ml cream and a few drops of Worcester sauce to 800 ml mayonnaise.

Garlic Mayonnaise (Aioli)

Whisk 3 chopped cloves of garlic into 1 litre mayonnaise.

Sauce Remoulade

Prepare as for Tartare Sauce with the addition of anchovy essence.
   May be served with deep-fried fish in breadcrumbs.

Sauce Verte

Prepare by adding 200 g of a fine purée of picked, washed and blanched
spinach, tarragon, chives and watercress.
   May be served with cold trout, salmon and salmon trout.

Tartare Sauce (Sauce Tartare)

Prepare by adding the following chopped ingredients to 500 ml mayonnaise:
50 g each of capers and gherkins and 15 g chopped chives, tarragon, chervil
and parsley.
   May be served with deep-fried fish in breadcrumbs.

SHELLFISH SAUCES

Shellfish sauces are used with the actual shellfish which they were made
and with all kinds of other fish, to which they add a rich flavour and colour.
Any kind of crustacea can be used in making these sauces, lobster being the
most popular. Lobster Sauce can be made using whole live lobsters or from
crushed cooked shells.

Lobster Sauce (Sauce Homard) (1)

100 ml oil	50 ml brandy
100 g carrot ⎫	250 ml dry white wine
100 g onion ⎬ roughly cut	1 litre fish stock
50 g celery ⎭	450 g tomatoes
1 bayleaf	75 g tomato purée
1 sprig thyme	200 g butter
2 cloves crushed garlic	200 ml cream
2 kg crushed cooked lobster shells	seasoning

1. Heat the oil in a pan, add the vegetables, herbs and garlic and lightly
   colour.
2. Add the crushed lobster shells and cook for 5 minutes. Drain off the oil
   and flambé with the brandy.

3. Add the wine, stock, squashed tomatoes and tomato purée and seasoning.
4. Boil, skim and simmer gently for 1 hour.
5. Strain the liquid into a shallow pan and reduce by two-thirds.
6. Finish by thickening with small pieces of the butter, or lobster butter if available, shaking the pan away from the heat; finally, test for seasoning.

Note
This sauce may be finished with cream, which will lighten the colour, changing it from rich red to a more delicate shade and will enrich the taste.

Lobster Sauce (Sauce Homard) (2)

Proceed as for Lobster Sauce, add 1 litre fish velouté to the strained lobster liquid and reduce to sauce consistency.

MISCELLANEOUS SAUCES

Apple Sauce (Sauce Pommes)

800 g peeled, cored and quartered cooking apples	1 juice of lemon
	50 ml water
50 g sugar	15 g butter

1. Place the apples, sugar, lemon juice and water into a saucepan. Cover with a lid and boil until the apple is soft.
2. Pass through a sieve, replace in a clean pan and finish by mixing in the butter.

Bread Sauce

500 ml milk	150 g white breadcrumbs
1 small onion ⎤	50 g butter
bayleaf ⎬ studded onion	seasoning
clove ⎦	

1. Bring the milk to the boil with the studded onion and allow to stand over heat, without boiling, for 8 minutes.
2. Remove the onion, add the breadcrumbs and whisk until the sauce is fairly thick.
3. Add the butter and seasoning of salt, pepper and a pinch of ground mace.

May be served with roast chicken, turkey and game.

Cranberry Sauce

Cook 800 g washed cranberries in 500 ml water with 150 g sugar and the juice of half a lemon until the cranberries are soft.

This sauce may be served as it is or puréed, hot or cold, mainly as an accompaniment to roast turkey.

Horseradish Sauce (Sauce Raifort)

500 ml lightly whipped cream
150 g grated horseradish
150 g white breadcrumbs

300 ml milk
50 ml vinegar
seasoning

1. Add the grated horseradish to the cream.
2. Soak the breadcrumbs in the milk, squeeze out any excess and add them to the cream. Add the vinegar and season to taste.

May be served with hot or cold roast beef, smoked eel, smoked buckling and quail's eggs.

Horseradish and Apple Sauce (Apfelkren)   GERMANY

Combine 1 litre horseradish sauce with 250 g grated apple and the juice of 1 lemon.

Mint Sauce (Sauce Menthe)

125 g mint leaves
50 g castor sugar
30 ml water
300 ml vinegar

Chop the mint leaves finely with the sugar and place in a basin; add the hot water and allow to cool, then add the vinegar and mix to a fairly stiff consistency.

May be served with roast lamb.

Curry Sauce (Sauce Kari)

100 g butter
100 g finely chopped onions
1 clove garlic
30 g curry powder
30 g flour
50 g tomato purée

1 litre white stock
30 g chopped chutney
50 g tomato concassée
10 g desiccated coconut
50 ml cream (optional)

1. Melt the butter in a saucepan, add the chopped onions and garlic and lightly colour.
2. Add the curry powder and cook for a few minutes, then add the flour to make a second stage roux. Add the tomato purée and allow to cool slightly.

3. Add the stock, bring to the boil, skim, then add the remaining ingredients and allow to simmer gently for 45 minutes, skimming as necessary.
4. Season to taste and, if desired, complete with the cream at the last moment.

Pesto alla Genovese

Blend the following coarsely chopped ingredients to a fine paste: 175 g basil leaves, 225 g pine-nuts, 6 peeled cloves garlic and 2 tsp salt with 75 ml olive oil. Whisk in 600 ml olive oil gradually to form a liaison and finish with 450 g grated Parmesan or Caciocavallo cheese.

Tomato Sauce (Sauce Tomate)

350 g butter	400 g flour	
400 g carrot ⎫	500 g tomato purée	
400 g onion ⎬ roughly cut	5 litres white stock	
200 g celery ⎭	100 ml vinegar ⎫ reduction	
1 small sprig thyme	30 g sugar ⎭	
1 clove crushed garlic	salt and pepper	
200 g bacon trimmings		

1. Melt the butter in a saucepan.
2. Add the vegetables, herbs, garlic and bacon trimmings and fry to a light golden-brown colour.
3. Add the flour, stir with a wooden spatule and cook to a second stage roux.
4. Add the tomato purée, cool slightly and add the hot stock, mixing well. Season with salt and pepper.
5. Simmer gently for 1 hour, skimming as necessary.
6. Place the vinegar and sugar in a pan, reduce by half and add to the sauce in order to adjust the degree of tartness.
7. Pass through a conical strainer, reboil and use as required.

May be used as it is with fish, meat and vegetable dishes, and as a base for other sauces.

Yogurt, Lime and Dill Sauce

Combine 500 ml yogurt with the juice of 1 lime, 10 g chopped dill and seasoning.

Green Sauce (Salsa Verde) SPAIN

Blend to a paste a slice of bread soaked in the juice of 1 lemon and 100 ml vinegar, 5 g parsley, 30 g celery, 5 g chives, 5 spring onions and 2 crushed cloves of garlic, then gradually whisk in 300 ml olive oil and seasoning.

Lemon and Egg Sauce (Avgolémono Sàltsa) GREECE

Whisk 4 yolks of eggs until creamy, then gradually whisk in 150 ml lemon juice, followed by 500 ml hot stock. Pour into a saucepan and stir over heat until the sauce thickens but do not let it boil or it will curdle.

Note
This sauce can be served with fish, meat, vegetables and egg dishes and the stock should be appropriate to the dish with which the sauce is to be served. A lighter version is made using whole eggs.

Peanut Sauce (Sauskatyang) THAILAND

Heat a wok, add 50 ml coconut oil and stir-fry 6 crushed dried chillies, 75 g chopped onion and 4 chopped cloves of garlic. Stir in 2 tsp sambal trasi and 600 ml thin coconut milk; simmer for 2 minutes, then add 225 g peanut butter and 50 ml sweet soy sauce. When it thickens, add 25 ml lemon juice and seasoning.

Plum Sauce (Sumeizhi) CHINA

Place 75 ml lemon juice, 100 g chopped shallots or onions, 50 ml ginger syrup, 100 g sugar, 350 g purée of plums, 50 ml chilli oil, 50 ml light soy sauce, 125 ml dark soy sauce and 100 ml saké or dry sherry in a pan. Boil until reduced and thickened to a sauce consistency.

Tomato and Chilli Sauce (Salsa Rossa)

Sweat 50 g chopped onion in 50 ml olive oil, then mix in 225 ml cream, 50 ml brandy and 1 finely chopped fresh, red chilli. Bring to the boil, add 450 g chopped tomato flesh, season and cook for 30 minutes. Pass through a conical strainer, reboil, season to taste and use as required.

May be served with pastas and veal piccatas.

SWEET SAUCES

Apricot Sauce (Sauce Abricot)

> 250 g apricot jam
> 100 ml water
> 15 g cornflour
> few drops lemon juice

1. Boil the jam, sugar and water. Stir in the diluted cornflour, reboil and simmer for 5 minutes.
2. Strain through a conical strainer, then add the lemon juice.

Chocolate Sauce (Sauce au Chocolat)

500 ml milk
  60 g sugar
  50 g cocoa
  25 g cornflour

1. Mix the cocoa, sugar and cornflour in a little of the milk.
2. Boil the rest of the milk and whisk into the cocoa mixture.
3. Pour back into the saucepan and bring to the boil while stirring.

Rich Chocolate Sauce

250 g plain chocolate, grated
  50 g sugar
300 ml water
 75 ml cream
  15 g butter

1. Bring the chocolate, sugar and water to the boil and simmer gently for 25 minutes.
2. Add the cream, mix in and finish with the softened butter.

Custard Sauce

500 ml milk
  40 g custard powder
  75 g sugar

1. Place the custard powder and sugar in a basin and add sufficient of the cold milk to mix to a smooth paste.
2. Boil the remainder of the milk and whisk onto the diluted custard powder.
3. Return to the saucepan and bring back to the boil, stirring continuously until the mixture thickens. Sprinkle the surface with sugar to prevent a skin from forming.

Egg Custard Sauce (Sauce Anglaise)

    4 egg yolks
  60 g sugar
500 ml milk
  1 tsp vanilla essence

1. Mix the eggs and sugar in a basin.
2. Heat the milk with the vanilla essence to just below boiling point.
3. Add to the eggs and sugar and mix well but without making it frothy, then strain through a conical strainer into a clean pan.

4. Place in a container of hot water on the stove. Stir occasionally with a wooden spatule until the mixture coats the back of the spatule, then pass through a fine strainer. If the sauce is to be served with sweet dishes retain in a container of hot water which should not be permitted to boil.

Jam Sauce

Proceed as for Apricot Sauce, using any type of jam suitable for the pudding.

Lemon Sauce (Sauce Citron)

500 ml water
     3 lemons, juice and
         grated zest
150 g sugar
 25 g cornflour

1. Boil the water, lemon juice and zest and sugar.
2. Whisk in the diluted cornflour and allow to simmer for 5 minutes; strain if desired, to remove the grated zest.

Melba Sauce

450 g raspberries
200 g sugar
 75 ml water

1. Place all the ingredients into a saucepan, bring to the boil, cover with a lid and simmer for 20 minutes.
2. Strain through a conical strainer and, if necessary, adjust the colour with cochineal; stir occasionally until cold.

Orange Sauce (Sauce à l'Orange)

Proceed as for Lemon Sauce, using oranges instead of lemons.

Syrup Sauce

400 g golden syrup
 75 g sugar
175 ml water
 20 g cornflour
    1 juice of lemon

1. Boil the syrup, sugar and water, then whisk in the diluted cornflour, reboil and simmer for 5 minutes.
2. Add the lemon juice and, if necessary, adjust the colour.

COULIS

A coulis is the juice obtained by crushing a food, either raw or barely cooked, serving it cold as it is or heated as a sauce. The English form of the name is 'cullis', which means the essentials of the food when cooked to its most concentrated form in the form of say, a thick soup. Coulis can be made from vegetables, fruit and meats.

Tomato Coulis

Sweat 150 g mirepoix of vegetables, bacon and herbs in 25 g butter, add 1.5 kg chopped ripe tomatoes, salt, pepper, sugar and 15 g meat glaze, cover and cook for 30 minutes to a purée. Pass with pressure through a conical strainer or sieve to give a fairly thick, smooth sauce for serving with grilled fish and meat.

Pimento Coulis

Sweat 50 g chopped onion with 1 kg deseeded and chopped red peppers in 50 g butter. Add 100 ml white wine vinegar, 500 g tomato concassée, salt and pepper and cook for 30 minutes to a purée. Pass with pressure through a conical stainer or sieve to give a fairly thick, smooth sauce for serving with grilled fish and meat.

Coulis of Fruit

Prepare 1 kg of the selected ripe fruit or mixture of several fruits by removing hulls, stalks, stones etc. Wash, drain and make into a purée in a food processor or blender with 75 g or more of icing sugar and the juice of 1 lemon or lime; if necessary, pass through a fine sieve. The resultant sauce should be fairly thick, smooth, hold the colour of the fruit used and contain all its essentials. Serve cold with all kinds of cold desserts, ice cream sweets and pastries.

Savoury Butters

Lobster Butter (Beurre de Homard)

Mix together equal quantities of butter and raw lobster brain removed from the head. Use to thicken and enrich lobster dishes, bisque and sauce.

Parsley Butter (Beurre Maître d'Hôtel)

Mix together 500 g butter, 25 g chopped parsley, the juice of 1 lemon and a little cayenne pepper and mould into a cylinder shape 3 cm in diameter. Roll in greaseproof paper and store in a refrigerator until firm. Serve cut into 1 cm thick slices on or with fried and grilled fish and meat.

Shrimp Butter (Beurre de Crevettes)

Mix together equal quantities of fine purée of shrimps and butter and proceed as for Parsley Butter, adding a point of cayenne. Serve with shallow or deep fried fish, add to white sauce to give added flavour, and with grilled and poached fish.

Glazes

Apricot Glaze

500 g apricot jam
125 ml water

Place the jam and water into a pan and bring to the boil while stirring. Cook to the 130°C thread stage, and pass through a conical strainer. Use hot and if kept, reboil before using.

Raspberry Glaze

Proceed as for Apricot Glaze, using raspberry jam in place of apricot jam.

Syrups

Bun Wash

Boil 100 ml water with 100 g sugar until dissolved and use while still hot immediately the buns are removed from the oven

Stock Syrup

Boil 1 litre water with 750 g sugar and the juice of 2 lemons until the sugar is dissolved.

Basic Preparations

BREAD SIPPETS AND CROUTONS

Bread Sippets

Remove the four corner crusts cut along the length of a loaf of bread, then cut across into very thin triangular shapes approximately 2 mm thick. Arrange on a baking sheet, taking care not to overlap, and place in a hot cupboard or cool oven to dry out and colour slightly golden on each side. Alternatively, they may be toasted under a salamander grill set at moderate heat; this method requires constant attention.

Diced Fried Bread Croûtons

Remove the crusts from 1 cm thick slices of bread and cut into 1 cm dice. Shallow fry in melted butter until golden and drain off the fat as soon as they are coloured as they continue to cook and colour after being removed from the heat.

Heart-Shaped Croûtons

These are served with a number of preparations such as Fricassée of Chicken. They should be either shallow fried in melted butter or lightly soaked in melted butter, placed onto a tray and toasted under a salamander grill until golden on each side.

Browned Breadcrumbs

Fry 100 g white breadcrumbs in 200 ml melted butter until light golden brown in colour, turning and tossing to prevent them from burning.

BUTTER PREPARATIONS

Beurre Fondu (Beurre Blanc)

Whisk butter into a little warm water and lemon juice in order to melt the butter without separating the fat from non-fat constituents. This is usually served with poached salmon and trout.

Beurre Manié

This is made by mixing equal quantities of raw flour and butter to a soft paste and is added gradually to an almost finished sauce as a thickening agent.

Clarified Butter

Melt the butter in a saucepan standing in a bain-marie of hot water. When the surface is clear and sediment and impurities have sunk to the bottom, carefully drain off the clean oiled butter into a clean pan.

Nut-Brown Butter (Beurre Noisette)

Add the butter to a heated pan and shake continuously until it froths and turns light nut brown in colour. Pour over the food and serve immediately.

BLANC PREPARATION

Blanc Preparation

Place 50 g flour into a basin, whisk in 2.5 litres cold water, then strain into a deep pan, add the juice of 2 lemons and salt and bring to the boil. The food, e.g. calfs' feet, Jerusalem artichokes, is added covered with a muslin during cooking.

FRANGIPANE PANADA

Frangipane Panada

500 ml milk
150 g butter
8 egg yolks
250 g flour
salt, pepper and nutmeg

1. Mix the egg yolks in a basin with the flour.
2. Heat the milk and butter with the seasonings and pour onto the mixture, return to the saucepan and cook gently until the preparation loosens from the bottom of the pan.
3. Turn out onto a lightly greased tray, cover with a buttered paper and cool slightly before use.

Note
This preparation is used primarily to give binding power to fish and meat forcemeats and to lighten texture.

RED MEAT MARINADE

Red Wine Marinade

1 litre red wine	1 bayleaf
100 ml oil	1 sprig thyme
150 g carrot ⎤	15 g parsley stalks
150 g onion ⎬ roughly cut	2 cloves
150 g celery ⎦	20 peppercorns
1 crushed clove of garlic	

1. Place all the prepared ingredients into a basin.
2. Place in the prepared meat, cover with greaseproof paper and allow to marinate in a refrigerator for 12 hours.

Note
This marinade can be used for any type of red meat or game.

Stuffings

Chestnut Stuffing

Gently mix together 750 g pork sausage meat and 250 g braised chestnuts.

Sage and Onion Stuffing

150 g pork or duck dripping	5 g chopped parsley
100 g chopped onion	250 g breadcrumbs
10 g finely rubbed sage	salt and pepper

1. Heat the dripping in a shallow pan, add the onions and cook without coloration.
2. Add the sage, cook for a few minutes, then mix in the breadcrumbs, chopped parsley and seasoning.

Serve with roast duck, goose and pork.

Note
If this stuffing is to be cooked separately, moisten with extra dripping to bind or a little cold jus lié.

Sage, Thyme and Onion Stuffing

Proceed as for Sage and Onion Stuffing, using 5 g each of powdered sage and thyme.
    Serve with roast lamb, veal and poultry.

Thyme, Parsley and Lemon Stuffing

250 g white breadcrumbs	1 grated rind and juice
150 g chopped suet	of lemon
5 g chopped parsley	25 ml milk
10 g powdered thyme	nutmeg, salt and pepper
2 eggs	

1. Place all the dry ingredients into a bowl, mix in the beaten eggs and milk to a smooth consistency.
2. Roll into a cylinder 5 cm in diameter and wrap in buttered greaseproof paper.
3. Cook in a steamer for 20 minutes.

Serve with roast lamb, veal and poultry.

Apple and Chestnut Stuffing

Combine 200 g white breadcrumbs, 2 eggs, 100 g chopped cooked chestnuts, 50 g raisins marinated in 25 ml brandy, 350 g coarsely chopped unpeeled apple, 100 g sweated chopped onion, and seasoning.
    Serve with roast turkey or goose.

Basil, Lemon and Nutmeg Stuffing

Moisten 450 g breadcrmbs with water, squeeze out the excess moisture, then combine with 3 eggs, the grated zest and juice of 2 lemons, 50 g chopped parsley, 50 g chopped basil, salt, pepper, nutmeg and 100 g creamed butter.
Serve with roast lamb.

Chicken Liver, Mushroom and Basil Stuffing

Lightly fry 100 g chopped onion and 225 g chopped mushrooms in 75 ml oil; add 225 g chopped chicken livers and fry until firm, then cool. Combine with 75 ml cream, 50 g chopped basil, 100 g white breadcrumbs, 2 eggs and seasoning.
Serve with roast game birds.

Orange and Pork Stuffing

Finely mince and combine 225 g raw pork, 100 g bacon, 50 g chicken livers, 75 g onion, 2 cloves of garlic, 1 tsp oregano, grated zest and juice of 2 oranges, 50 g melted butter and seasoning.
Serve with roast pork.

Sage, Sultana and Apple Stuffing

Sweat 100 g chopped onion in 125 ml oil and add 2 tsp rubbed sage. Mix in 275 g white breadcrumbs, 50 g chopped parsley, 50 g lightly fried sultanas, 100 g lightly fried diced apple and seasoning.
Serve with roast duck and goose.

Sausage Meat Stuffing

Add 20 g chopped parsley to 1 kg pork sausage meat and mix together.
Serve with roast chicken and turkey.

Spiced Meat Stuffing

Golden fry 225 g chopped onion in 75 ml oil, add 350 g minced beef, 600 ml brown stock, seasoning, 1 tsp cinnamon and $\frac{1}{2}$ tsp allspice. Simmer until the liquid has evaporated. Skim off any fat and moisten with 225 ml pomegranate juice, 25 g sugar and 50 ml lemon juice.
Serve with roast pork or veal.

Walnut, Ginger, Sultana and Onion Stuffing

Combine 250 g white breadcrumbs, 275 g chopped onion, 8 chopped hard-boiled eggs, 275 g chopped walnuts, 50 g grated root ginger, 225 g sultanas and 4 chopped green fresh chillies.
Serve with roast poultry and roast pork.

APPENDIX 1 # Dish Assessment

What went wrong and why?

INTRODUCTION

Dish presentation as exemplified in present-day plate service, whether for a single customer or a banquet for 500 people ensures that the finishing artistic touches are visible to each guest. The customer's impression of a meal starts from its visual impact which should immediately stimulate the appetite.

Other factors which should be assessed are the size, shape and pattern of the plate; whether it should be very hot, cold or chilled according to the food; where the main item is placed, whether at the top or in the centre; how the garnish is arranged and the sauce or coulis distributed over or around the food to ensure that the colour scheme is attractive as well as being balanced and natural.

The texture and consistency of foods form an important part of the customer's meal experience: recognition and feeling of crispness and softness; the density of liquids, whether coarse or velvety, and the seasonings and flavourings they carry with them all contribute to the occasion. It is important to ensure the right amount of seasoning in the form of condiments suitable for the average customer, whether for a delicate or a highly spiced dish. Natural flavours of food need to be brought out during the cooking process and slightly enhanced by a judicious amount of seasoning. The caterer has to stipulate the size and weight of food portions at raw weight and show how correct preparation will show the item at its best.

The degree to which food is cooked must reconcile the distinctions between hygienic practices, customers' requests for very underdone meat, and portion sizes. This should be done without recourse to the probe of a thermometer or cutting into the item to view its degree of doneness. Overcooking results in substandard products shrunk to a fraction of their original size and undercooking results in inedible foods.

In the case of joints and whole birds, the thermocouple of a modern oven will cause the cessation of cooking as soon as they have reached their correct internal temperatures. Estimation without calculation of whether a joint is done is unscientific, though an experienced chef may become so adept as to know instinctively when an item is cooked, without having to look at the clock, or prodding it with a fork or needle.

No matter how clearly written a recipe is, to the consternation of people undergoing practical training many problems are encountered when preparing and cooking. Things that go wrong only come to light in a practical situation and in some instances they may require instant rectification if disaster is to be avoided. This section is not only important if food costs are to be controlled but is also an essential part of quality control. In many instances once the problem has occurred there is very little which can be done to rectify the situation other than to start again, which is both wasteful and time-consuming.

It is not possible to list every conceivable reason why a dish has failed to reach a certain standard. The causes given are the most common ones and the stages singled out for special attention are those most frequently encountered. In the following examples, reasons for problems are confined to the practical situation but problems may also arise as a result of a number of other factors, for example, poorly designed purchasing specifications, faulty storage or lax inspection on delivery.

BOILED ASPARAGUS WITH HOLLANDAISE SAUCE

Boiled Asparagus with Hollandaise Sauce should:

1. Look neat, with all spears the same size and length and properly trimmed of the small top spurs.
2. Have been cooked so as to keep, and enhance, the original colour, either vivid green or off-white.
3. Not be overcooked so that it is tasteless and so limp as to be difficult to eat with the fingers.
4. Be a standard portion of at least 6 spears.
5. Be correctly presented in an asparagus dish or on a folded table napkin; if cold to look fresh and moist, if hot be steaming and be hot to the touch.
6. Be accompanied with an adequate amount of sauce or melted butter.
7. The Hollandaise or other egg and butter sauce should be of the correct colour, taste and smooth thickness for dipping purposes, have the pronounced flavour of the vinegar reduction and lemon juice and be at ambient temperature.

What went wrong? – Boiled Asparagus with Hollandaise Sauce

Asparagus
1. Not properly washed; the small spurs not shaved off before tying and cooking
2. Poor colour and appearance:
   (a) not stored correctly either in raw or cooked form
   (b) overcooked
   (c) left too long in the cooking liquid after cooking or being reheating
   (d) not served immediately when cooked
3. Poor flavour:
   (a) insufficient salt in the cooking water
   (b) cooked for too long
   (c) when cooked, left too long in the cooking water

Hollandaise Sauce
1. Poor flavour:
   (a) inferior butter used
   (b) insufficient seasoning or lemon juice to give the required flavour
   (c) melted butter not skimmed and sediment used

2. Sauce is dark and has a greyish tint:
   (a) vinegar reduced too much, to correct add more butter to lighten the colour
   (b) was cooked in an aluminium saucepan

BROWN BEEF STEW

1. The stew should look appetising, sprinkled with chopped parsley in an entrée dish on an underdish with a dish paper, or on a plate, without any spillages.
2. It should be hot, moist and have the correct ratio of meat to sauce, evenly dispersed.
3. The meat should be tender and well-flavoured without any visible fat, sinew or gristle.
4. The sauce should be a deep, reddish brown in colour with a slight sheen to it, without any globules of fat and should be equal in quantity to the meat.
5. It should have a distinctive flavour and should not leave any coating of fat around the lips.
6. The standard weight of a 125 g portion should be served.

What went wrong? – Brown Beef Stew

1. The sauce is pale in colour:
   (a) meat was fried too slowly on a low flame, preventing it from colouring
   (b) too much meat was fried at one time. If the pan is overfilled it will not fry properly, and the juices will cause the meat to boil, so drain and dry it and begin the process again
   (c) meat not sufficiently singed with the flour
   (d) poor-quality brown stock
   (e) vegetables not fried until coloured
   (f) meat stirred continuously while frying
2. The sauce is too dark and bitter:
   (a) meat over-coloured during frying
   (b) stew cooked at too high a temperature for too long
   (c) poor-quality, overcooked stock
   (d) prolonged holding in a hot cupboard
3. The meat is overcooked, stringy and low in flavour:
   (a) poor-quality meat
   (b) stew cooked at too high a temperature for too long
   (c) stew was kept in a hot cupboard for too long at too high a temperature

CHICKEN SAUTÉ CHASSEUR

1. The dish should look appetising, with the portions of chicken arranged for ease of service. A piece each of leg and breast should be placed together, with the sauce coating all the chicken.
2. The chicken should be light golden brown on the outside and moist inside. It should be hot, flavourful and cooked to the correct degree. The chicken should be cut neatly into joints with no splintered bones and the ends of the winglets should have been removed.
3. The sauce should be reddish-brown in colour, taste of wine and tarragon and be sufficiently seasoned. The mushrooms should be neatly sliced and without stalks, the tomatoes free from pips, neatly diced and soft. The sauce should be transparent and lightly coat the chicken.
4. The correct standard quantity of chicken and sauce is sufficient for the number of portions.

What went wrong? – Chicken Sauté Chasseur

1. Problems associated with its preparation:
   (a) chicken not cut into even pieces
   (b) chicken not seasoned before cooking
   (c) inferior-quality fat used to sauté chicken
   (d) butter burnt during sautéeing
   (e) chicken not covered with a lid after sautéeing
2. Dryness, lack of flavour and discoloration of the chicken:
   (a) overcooked at the sautéeing stage
   (b) simmered and cooked in the sauce
   (c) completed dish retained in hot cupboard at too high a temperature and/or for prolonged period
3. Poor-quality Sauce Chasseur:
   (a) the base sauce, jus lié, of poor quality
   (b) the sauce lacks colour because of the poor colour of the base stock; base sauce was too light in colour
   (c) sauce is starchy and gluey because the base sauce was not sufficiently cooked
   (d) stale mushrooms used
   (e) insufficient tomato concassée used
   (f) poor-quality wine used
   (g) dried tarragon used

FRIED FILLET OF SOLE IN BATTER

1. The fish should be golden in colour, placed neatly on a dish paper free from traces of fat. The lemon wedges should be neatly cut, free from

excess pith, membrane and pips. The parsley sprigs should be crisp and look fresh.

2. The coating of batter should be hot, golden and crisp and the fish hot and cooked right through; the batter should not taste floury. The coating of batter should not be too thick.

3. The flavour should be a blend of the seasoned batter, the natural flavour of the seasoned fish and that of the fat.

4. The standard number and size of fillets per portion should be served according to specification.

What went wrong? – Fried Fillet of Sole in Batter

1. Pale-coloured batter:
   (a) fat was not hot enough or too many pieces of fish were fried at once
   (b) fat was not allowed to recover its heat between batches
   (c) incorrect type of flour used for the batter; i.e. strong flour should be used to make all batters

2. Soggy and messy results:
   (a) fat was not hot enough
   (b) too many pieces of fish fried at once
   (c) fish handled too much during frying
   (d) frying basket was used
   (e) fish too long for the pan
   (f) insufficient fat in fryer

3. Inner coating doughy:
   (a) batter too thick
   (b) surplus batter not removed before immersion in the fat

4. Over-coloured batter before the fish is cooked:
   (a) fat too hot
   (b) fish pieces too thick
   (c) wrong kind of batter used
   (d) fish not turned during frying

5. Lack of flavour:
   (a) poor purchasing, storage or production control
   (b) batter not seasoned
   (c) fish not marinated before coating with batter

IRISH STEW

1. The dish should look appetising in an entrée dish, on an underdish and a dish paper or in a clean soup plate.

2. Stew should be hot and moist, with most of the stock absorbed by the potatoes.

3. The meat should be whitish in colour, tender, moist and flavourful and free of excess fat, sinew and gristle.

4. It should have a distinctive flavour of lamb and not leave a film of fat around the lips.
5. The flavour of the vegetables should be evenly balanced with no one flavour predominating; attention given to seasoning.
6. The garnish should be not overcooked, the potatoes should be even in shape and size, the onions whole with no root ends. The parsley should be coarsely chopped.
7. Standard-sized portions should be served, according to specification.

What went wrong? – Irish Stew

1. Poor colour and with particles floating in it:
   (a) meat not blanched; scum and grease not skimmed off during cooking
   (b) vegetables not properly prepared; too much green of leeks and celery leaves used, but not enough potato
2. Stew is greasy:
   (a) meat not trimmed of excess fat
   (b) insufficient skimming
   (c) stew retained in hot cupboard or bain-marie for too long once cooked
3. Poor appearance:
   (a) the stew was overcooked
   (b) the contents were allowed to reduce considerably during cooking
   (c) stew retained in hot cupboard or bain-marie for too long once cooked
   (d) lack of care when serving the stew
   (e) button onions and potatoes not cooked separately

POACHED FILLET OF SOLE GLAZED IN WHITE WINE SAUCE

1. The fillets should be neatly folded and arranged to follow the contour of the serving dish, evenly coated with the sauce and with a light golden glaze on the surface.
2. The sauce should have a very light creamy colour and consistency so that it coats the fillets and the serving dish with sufficient for the number of portions. It should be correctly seasoned with an amalgam of the flavours of wine, fish stock, cream and butter with the fish predominating.
3. Once glazed the sauce should:
   (a) show no trace of curdling
   (b) show no trace of liquid seeping out because the fillets were not drained.
4. The standard number of 85 g fillets should be served according to specification.

What went wrong? – Poached Fillet of Sole Glazed in White Wine Sauce

1. Distorted shape of the fillets during cooking:
   (a) skin not removed
   (b) incisions not made on the skin-side
   (c) fillets not lightly flattened
   (d) fillets incorrectly folded
   (e) pan in which the fish was poached was overfilled
   (f) poached at too high a temperature and poached for too long
   (g) retained too long in a hot cupboard
2. Dryness of the cooked fillets:
   (a) the tray in which the fish was poached was not buttered and seasoned, consequently the fish stuck to the tray during cooking
   (b) fish not covered with a buttered greaseproof paper, causing the surface to become dry
   (c) insufficient stock and wine
   (d) overcooked
3. Liquid seeping from the fish around the edge of the completed dish:
   (a) fish not drained on a cloth before arranging in the serving dish
   (b) dish not wiped around before glazing
4. Poor glazing of the sauce:
   (a) velouté, if used, was undercooked
   (b) too much fat in the roux of the velouté
   (c) completed sauce either too thick or too thin
   (d) insufficient cream and/or sabayon
   (e) butter not added to the sauce away from the stove
   (f) completed sauce held at too high a temperature before use
   (g) temperature of the salamander grill too low
   (h) fish not drained properly before coating with the sauce
5. The sauce runs off the surface of the fish during glazing:
   (a) sauce too thin
   (b) temperature of the salamander too low
   (c) fish not drained properly before coating with the sauce
   (d) insufficient sauce used
   (e) sauce too hot
6. Sauce is too dark in colour:
   (a) aluminium saucepan used
   (b) velouté roux overcooked
   (c) fish stock was dark in colour
   (d) poor-quality white wine oxidised
   (e) single or insufficient cream used
7. Sauce is floury and gluey with a poor glazing quality:
   (a) velouté not cooked for correct length of time
   (b) too much flour in the roux

8. Sauce too salty:
   (a) cooking liquid over-reduced, it must all be used
   (b) salted butter used to finish the sauce
   (c) basic velouté and fish stock were seasoned
9. Poor-quality fleurons:
   (a) badly made or overstretched puff pastry
   (b) puff or flaky pastry not used
   (c) baked too soon after being cut out
   (d) not eggwashed

POT-ROASTED LOIN OF LAMB

1. The dish should look appetising, with overlapping slices of the lamb carved across the grain in even thicknesses, following the contour of the serving dish. The meat should be just sufficiently cooked and tender, coated with sufficient gravy to keep it moist, with the rest of the gravy in a sauceboat, on an underdish.
2. The gravy should be light red in colour, have the correct smooth consistency and be slightly transparent.
3. The number of standard weight 70 g portions should be correct.

What went wrong? – Pot-Roasted Loin of Lamb

1. Dryness and lack of flavour:
   (a) quality of the lamb below standard
   (b) joint not prepared correctly, too much fat removed from joint
   (c) joint cooked at too high a temperature
   (d) insufficient basting during cooking
   (e) overcooking of the joint
   (f) cooked without a lid
   (g) once cooked, long retention in hot cupboard either before or after carving
2. Poor yield:
   (a) joint badly prepared and tied incorrectly
   (b) joint cooked at too high a temperature and for too long, thus causing excessive shrinkage
   (c) joint not allowed to rest once cooked before carving
   (d) wrong knife used for carving, carving knife not sharp
3. Poor-quality sauce:
   (a) butter and vegetables burnt during cooking, making the gravy dark and bitter
   (b) poor-quality stock used, either lacking in flavour because poor-quality ingredients were used, or not being properly cooked out
   (c) traces of surface fat because the jus lié was not skimmed during cooking

(d) thickening agent not cooked out

(e) lack of seasoning

ROAST SIRLOIN OF BEEF

1. The dish should look appetising, with the sliced meat following the contour of the serving dish. The meat should be carved across the grain into slices of an even thickness, arranged overlapping and look moist under the clear gravy. The fresh watercress should be neatly placed to enhance the overall appearance and the serving dish or plate should be in pristine condition.
2. The meat should look freshly cooked and carved, be tender, hot and succulent, flavourful and cooked to the correct degree. It should be free from excess fat, sinew and gristle.
3. The roast gravy should taste of roasted beef, be seasoned to the correct degree, and be clear and amber in colour.
4. The number of standard 70 g portions should be served.

What went wrong? – Roast Sirloin of Beef

1. Joint looked dry and had no flavour:
   (a) quality of the joint was not good
   (b) joint not prepared correctly, too much fat covering removed, sinew and gristle not removed
   (c) joint not seasoned just before putting into the oven
   (d) joint not raised from the pan on a trivet or bones
   (e) joint not quickly coloured in the hot oven
   (f) joint put in roasting tray fat-side down
   (g) joint cooked at too high a temperature
   (h) lack of basting during cooking
   (i) joint overcooked, heat not reduced after initial 20 minutes
   (j) meat probe not used to check internal temperature of the meat
   (k) once cooked, long retention in hot cupboard before or during carving
   (l) joint not carved across the grain
   (m) insufficient gravy made
2. Poor yield and quality:
   (a) joint prepared and tied incorrectly
   (b) joint cooked at too high a temperature and for too long, causing excessive shrinkage
   (c) joint not allowed to rest once cooked before carving
   (d) wrong knife used for carving; carving knife not sharp
   (e) joint not carved properly by carving against rather than with the grain
3. Poor-quality roast gravy:
   (a) sediment in the bottom of the roasting tray burnt during cooking, thus making the gravy very dark in colour and bitter in flavour

(b) poor brown stock which is too dark in colour and bitter in flavour due to overcooking, or lacking in flavour due to poor-quality ingredients

(c) too much surface fat because it was not skimmed sufficiently during cooking

(d) fat not drained off from roasting tray

(e) gravy browning used, which should not be necessary

(f) lack of seasoning

ROAST POTATOES

1. The potatoes should look appetising and show evidence of care and attention to detail.
2. The potatoes should be of even size and shape.
3. The outer surface should be crisp, glistening and evenly coloured to a light golden brown. The inside should be fluffy, white and flavourful.
4. The standard number of 100 g portions should be served.

What went wrong? – Roast Potatoes

1. Dryness and lack of flavour:
   (a) poor-quality potatoes
   (b) wrong type of potato for roasting
   (c) potatoes not properly peeled, or peeled too far in advance
   (d) cooked for too long and at too high a temperature
   (e) long retention in a hot cupboard
   (f) lack of basting during cooking
   (g) potatoes not of even size
2. Lack of crispness and colour:
   (a) quality of potatoes below standard, or incorrect type used
   (b) potatoes were peeled too far in advance and became soggy in the water
   (c) fat not hot enough when potatoes put in the tray
   (d) potatoes not brought to high temperature on stove before placing in the oven
   (e) potatoes cooked at too low a temperature
   (f) long retention in hot cupboard
3. Dryness, lack of flavour with a shrivelled thick outer skin the inner pulp dehydrated and glutenous in texture:
   (a) cooked for too long and at too high a temperature
   (b) too long retention in a hot cupboard
4. Factors associated with poor yield:
   (a) selection of the wrong type of potatoes
   (b) overcooking and long retention in a hot cupboard

Types of potatoes best suited for roasting are Desiree, King Edward, Maris Piper, Maris Peer and Wilja.

VANILLA BAVAROIS

1. The bavarois should be well formed to the shape of the charlotte mould. It should be extremely smooth in texture and have a creamy white colour all through.
2. It should be smooth to the tongue and have a rich creamy taste, dissolve easily in the mouth and not be chewy in texture.
3. It should be served cold but not chilled.

What went wrong? – Vanilla Bavarois

1. Bavarois has not set properly:
   (a) gelatine was soaked in hot instead of cold water
   (b) full amount of gelatine not used
   (c) bavarois not kept in the refrigerator long enough
2. Bavarois is too firm in texture:
   (a) too many eggs used
   (b) too much gelatine used
   (c) mixture was still warm when the cream was added
3. Streaks of gelatine in the bavarois:
   (a) mixture was not warm enough when the soaked gelatine was added
4. Fluffy texture is over-aerated and has large holes:
   (a) too much cream used
   (b) cream was whipped too firmly
   (c) cream was whisked into the custard too vigorously
5. Lack of flavour:
   (a) full amount of sugar not used
   (b) full amount of cream not used
   (c) cream was whipped too firmly
   (d) full amount of vanilla essence not used

APPENDIX 2 # Cookery Methods and Techniques

INTRODUCTION

Heat is used to cook food so as to make it palatable and to bring out its flavour, colour and texture. Cooking is the transfer of heat, whether from coal, charcoal, electricity, gas, liquid petroleum gas or microwaves, by conduction, convection or radiation.

Conduction is where food is in direct contact with a utensil or other item of cooking equipment which spreads its heat evenly into the foodstuffs. Some metals are better conductors of heat than others, the best being copper, which heats very quickly and evenly. Aluminium utensils do not conduct so quickly and some stainless steel cooking utensils do not heat evenly. An oven has an insulating lining which stores its heat, so preventing it from passing rapidly through the ventilation system.

Convection is the transfer of heat by means of heated air or through a liquid or a fat. Water in a saucepan comes in contact with the base and sides where it is heated by conduction. This causes the water to expand and rise, allowing cool water to take its place and become hot. This continuous motion gives the convection currents which cook the food in the pan.

Radiation is infra-red waves bearing on food from a direct heat source such as a salamander grill, a bed of charcoal in an underfired grill, a toaster, or the electric bulbs over a servery counter which give out both heat and light.

Cookery methods fall into two categories, the moist method and the dry method. The first is where a food is cooked by contact with moisture in the form of a liquid, the other is where a food is cooked in a dry atmosphere or in contact with fat. There are thirteen methods of cookery that stem from these two categories. They are listed in alphabetical order and detailed in the following section.

Methods of Cookery

BAKING

Baking is a dry method of cookery, done in an oven by convection currents from the heat source which radiate as infra-red energy. The heat is conducted into the food being baked by conduction from the hot tray on which the foodstuff is placed or from the oven rack. There are many kinds of ovens – general-purpose; pastry; combination ovens, which incorporates steam or microwaves, and bakers' ovens with a steam injection system for yeast goods. Baking is usually done at a high temperature and is mainly used for pastry and confectionery dishes, some of the latter being cooked au bain-marie to prevent the food overcooking and curdling.

BOILING

In this moist method of cookery a food is immersed in water already at boiling point of 100°C, or is brought to that temperature from cool. The heat is conducted from the surface of the utensil in contact with the heat source. The water used for boiling must be drawn from the main supply and not from a storage tank. Green vegetables must be cooked in boiling water, which seals the exterior of foods, thus preventing break-up. Firm foods can be cooked from cold. Prolonged boiling causes disintegration and shrivelling. Food needing lengthy cooking becomes dry due to evaporation and the liquid needs to be replenished. A lid should be used when bringing foods to the boil rapidly; in the case of green vegetables the lid should be removed at boiling point, but for lengthy cooking processes it should be left on and the heat source reduced.

BRAISING

This is a moist method of cooking foods in a flavoured liquid in a braising pan or other suitable utensil with a tight-fitting lid. It is done by convected heat brought about by conducted heat from the pan and is ideal for tenderising and flavouring cuts and joints of meat, fish, poultry and vegetables of a coarse or tough nature by prolonged cooking. Root vegetables and herbs add their flavour to the food and to the cooking liquid, which is reduced or thickened to serve as an integral part of the dish. Foods to be served in front of customers may be glazed by constant basting under intense heat at the end of the cooking time. Items may be larded to make them more palatable and some are improved by prior marination; the marinade is then used as part of the cooking liquid.

In the brown braising method, the food is seared before braising. White braised foods are often blanched before sweating without colour.

Braising can be carried out in a casserole, thus giving this method the title 'casserole cookery'.

DEEP FRYING

This is termed a dry method of cookery and is done by immersing suitable items of food completely in hot fat. It is the quickest way of cooking foods because of the very high temperature that oil is capable of reaching. The convected currents of heat come from the heat source to reach as high as 195°C, though the ideal average cooking temperature is 180°C. Aerated foods such as choux pastry fritters and yeast goods are started at about 150°C to allow them to expand before increasing the heat.

The choice of frying equipment and the ideal frying medium combine to give good results. Moist foods need a protective coating to prevent them from breaking up and to ensure a pleasing golden brown appearance. The oil must be filtered regularly and discarded when it starts over-foaming or smoking and smells rancid. A thermostat control helps prolong the life of the frying medium. A pressure fryer prevents steam from the food escaping, speeds up cooking time and retains the moisture in the food but prevents it becoming too crisp.

GRILLING

This dry method is done by subjecting high-quality cuts of meat and whole cuts of fish to intense radiated heat which is rapidly absorbed by the food by conduction. Food should be of a uniform thickness of about 3 cm, be grilled so as to get branded by the bars and be basted with either oil or the marinade in which they were tenderised. True grilling is done over a charcoal, electric or gas-heated grill, but can be done under a salamander grill, on a griddle plate, or a cleaned stove top, or in a double contact electric grill by conducted heat. Terms such as saignant and très bien cuit are used to denote the degree of doneness. Fish are best grilled in a double fish grid. The foods being grilled, especially kebabs, should be turned or rotated to ensure even cooking, moving from the intense centre to the milder off-centre.

In the United States of America the word broiling is used to denote grilling.

Gratination is a form of grilling in which cooked foods are given a golden brown surface under a salamander grill. A blow torch can be used to colour the surface more rapidly.

POACHING

This is a moist method of cooking food in a liquid at just below boiling point. The heat source cooks the food by conduction and the amount and depth of liquid needed to cover the food determines whether it is shallow- or deep-poached. No special utensils are required; suitable cooking mediums include water, stock, milk, court-bouillon, stock syrup or wine.

Shallow poaching is done in a low-sided tray or pan with just enough liquid to come halfway up the items. It should be covered with greased paper or a lid, brought to the boil and allowed to barely simmer on top of a stove or in an oven set at Moderate.

Deep poaching is done in fish kettles of various sizes to hold the shapes and sizes of fish, in a saucepan, deep tray or boiling pan. Some foods are started in a cold cooking liquid, others in a boiling liquid but the heat must be reduced to 190°C immediately it boils and kept to a gentle movement of the liquid without any bubbles forming.

Foods cooked by poaching include eggs, fish, supremes of chicken, vegetables and fruits.

POT-ROASTING

The French word for this method of cookery is 'poêlé'. It refers to the cooking of good-quality meat, poultry or game in a tightly-lidded pan with its own juices and some butter. It is a moist method of cookery done in the oven at 200°C for 35 minutes per 500 g, removing the lid and basting the item during the last 20 minutes. As in the case of braising, a bed of roots may be used. The resultant juices are made into an accompanying sauce with the addition of veal stock, thickened with diluted arrowroot.

In effect, pot-roasting is a combination of braising and roasting and it is appropriate to serve the food with an elaborate garnish.

ROASTING

The main difference between this method of cookery and baking is that in real roasting, the item of meat, poultry, game, vegetables or fish must be placed on a trivet or bed of small chopped bones to take it off the base of the roasting pan. Both are dry methods of cookery.

Roasting derives from spit roasting in which foods were impaled on a rotating spit over or in front of an open fire; the juices and fat were caught in a gulley and used for basting. The modern rotisserie attachment in an oven or grill works in a similar fashion. Items should be seasoned just before being placed to roast, covered with a little clean fat and cooked at 220°C for 15 minutes before reducing the oven temperature to 175°C for an internal reading of 65°C for underdone beef. Foods being roasted should not be covered, even with foil, as this alters the resultant taste of a true roast. Only simple garnishes are used.

Roast foods are cooked by radiant infra-red heat which produces convection currents in the oven. It also gains some conducted heat from the trivet, around which the hot air circulates.

SHALLOW FRYING

This is a dry method of cookery carried out in a shallow pan with a small quantity of fat to act as a lubricant, or dry frying in a non-stick pan without any oil or fat. It can be done in a frying pan, omelette pan, sauté pan or oval fish pan in which it cooks the item quickly to seal and colour it, using butter, oil or fat, or a combination of fats. If the sediment and juices from the item are to be used for the accompanying sauce it is best to use a sauté pan and ordinary or clarified butter. It is advisable to heat the pan before adding the fat as this can prevent the food from sticking. The word 'meunière' or 'miller's style' is used to refer to a method of shallow frying fish or vegetables, serving them masked with foaming butter and lemon juice.

SAUTÉEING

This is akin to shallow frying with an emphasis on tossing items over and over in the pan to colour and cook them evenly in a short space of time.

The word 'sauté' is also given to small items or pieces of fish, meat and poultry being shallow fried to colour all over, then to make a sauce, with or without a quickly cooked garnish, in the same pan, cooking further to complete as a quickly done, short-liquid stew.

STIR-FRYING

This is a dry method of cooking, originating in China, whereby small pieces or items of food are rapidly cooked in a wok on the staggered system, the result being eaten by means of chopsticks. Its popularity is that the vitamin and mineral content of vegetables and other items is retained because the process is done so quickly over an intense convected heat. Unlike shallow frying, the food is stirred constantly while being fried; in some recipes rice wine or stock is added and thickened to add a sauce-effect.

STEAMING

In this moist method of cookery the food is surrounded by steam produced from heated water by conduction. The steam condenses as it touches the surface of the foodstuffs, giving off its heat as it turns to water. It is a quick method of cookery which allows foods to be cooked to order or in batches during the service period. Steam pressure is built up in the steamer to go above boiling point of 100°C and can reach a degree of heat six times that of boiling point. A low-pressure steamer will operate at 14 KPa and a high pressure one at 54 KPa. Steam pressure is measured in Kilopascals (KPa), 1 KPa being equal to 1 Kilonewton per metre square (Kn/m^2); 7 KPa is equal to the previous measurement of 1 pound weight per square inch (1 psi).

As a rule the food does not produce a liquid or stock of its own, because it is steamed in a perforated utensil.

STEWING

Stewing is a moist method of cooking done at a fairly low oven temperature of 165°C and for a long period of time so as to render the contents tender and succulent, the surrounding sauce being an essential part of the finished dish. The food should be cooked in a closely covered utensil in which heat is conducted to the surface of the food in contact with the interior of the pan and spreads throughout by conduction. Suitable containers are shallow sauce-pans, metal or earthenware casseroles, oven-to-table utensils and, for large-scale work, a bratt pan.

Suitable foods are small pieces of meat, poultry, and game and fish of a tough nature with some connective tissue. Stewing is best done in an oven. A brown stew is begun by frying the items to colour and adding brown stock. A white stew is started by blanching the items, then sweating them before immersing in a white stock. The liquid can be thickened by dusting the raw food with flour then singeing in a hot oven, or by adding diluted arrowroot or cornflour.

MICROWAVE COOKERY

Cooking by microwaves can be done by the dry or moist method, according to the kind of food being cooked or reheated. It works by electricity off a 13 amp plug, giving radiated energy which creates heat within the food. This causes the water molecules in the item to vibrate. Heat is thus conducted in the solid parts and convected in the liquid parts of each piece of food.

The heat is produced by a magnetron and is reflected around the oven, assisted by a fan and a rotating turntable. Food must be placed on non-metallic dishes, covered with clingfilm which is then pricked, and cooked by a timing device, and possibly a temperature probe. It is advantageous to stir the food or rearrange halfway through the cooking process and to leave for a few seconds after the time signal has gone off. It is good for some prime cooking, for defrosting and regenerating frozen foods and for à la carte service.

Cookery Techniques

The following information helps to explain the most commonly used techniques in the preparation, cooking and serving of meat dishes.

Basting – is the lubrication of foods being roasted, braised, grilled and barbecued to keep them moist and succulent. It should be done at regular intervals throughout the cooking process by spooning the fat and juices in the pan back over the item.

Barding – is done by covering the breasts of game and poultry and joints of meat (and fish) with thin slices of streaky bacon or salt pork fat to compensate for a lack of natural fat of the foodstuffs. The bards are tied on and removed towards the end of the cooking time so as to colour the item. The bards may be served.

Batting – is done with a cutlet bat or a heavy knife blade to even the thickness of small cuts of meat and poultry such as veal escalopes, chicken breasts, lamb noisettes. It is done by moistening the bat or placing the item between sheets of wax paper. It helps to make the portion look larger and to cook more quickly, keeping its shape.

Carving – should not be started as soon as the meat comes out of the oven; instead, meat should be left to stand for 20 minutes before being cut into slices against the grain, either thin or thick according to the kind of meat. It is in order to use a carving fork with a spring guard to keep the joint steady. Carving knives are made as 28 cm, 30 cm and 34 cm in length, some are plain, others serrated or scalloped at the edge, some have pointed ends, others rounded, each having a different use, e.g. carving ham, carving meat, slicing bread, etc. A sharpening steel or knife tuner is essential to keep a keen cutting edge. Carving can also be done with a food slicing machine.

Defrosting – of deep-frozen meat and poultry must be done to a formula as otherwise there is a risk of food poisoning. It must be done in a controlled environment in a refrigerator or defrosting cabinet. For example a 6.75 kg frozen turkey needs at least 24 hours to defrost in a refrigerator at 8°C; the wrapping can then be undone, the giblets removed and the bird kept at 5°C until being cooked.

Deglazing – is the melting of the sediment and juices in a pan after sautée-ing small cuts of meat, poultry or game, using the appropriate stock, wine, spirit or ready-made sauce. It should then be reduced or thickened with butter and served with the item. Deglazing is also done to roast and poêléed foods after excess fat has been drained off. Where a spirit is used for deglazing it can be set alight so as to concentrate its flavour.

Glazing – is done to give a shiny coat to a joint by continuously basting it with a sauce, under overhead heat at the top of an oven, or under a salamander grill. The term is also applicable to cold buffet work of coating with chaud-froid or aspic jelly.

Larding – is the sewing of an item of food with either small lardons of salt pork fat in a neat pattern on the upper surface, or straight through the centre of a joint that has no fat of its own. A larding needle is threaded with a strip of fat into the joint or cut of meat so that both ends are visible outside. The resultant pattern will show when the meat is sliced.

Marinating – is done to tenderise items and to give them extra flavour and colour. Marinades are slightly acidic from a wine, vinegar or citrus juice base and herbs, spices and sliced vegetables add their flavour. The length of time for which an item is marinated depends on its quality and size; oil and yogurt can assist in the process and the resultant liquid should be used to baste the item, or as part of the cooking medium. Marinated foods should be kept in a refrigerator and a marinade can be used over and over again. Marinades can be used cold or hot.

Paner à l'Anglaise – is the technical term for coating foods with flour, egg-wash and breadcrumbs so as to give a nicely coloured and crisp covering after deep or shallow frying. The kinds of foods done in this way include various kinds of mixtures shaped as croquettes and cutlets which are coated to stop them from breaking up and small cuts such as escalopes and supremes of chicken. In large-scale production the prepared items are seasoned where appropriate, dipped in flour, then into eggwash, the surplus being removed with the fingers, and finally covered completely with breadcrumbs. Surplus crumbs are shaken off and the item given a final moulding or flattened slightly and marked trellis-fashion with a knife. Eggwash is made by whisking five parts of whole egg with a tenth part each of oil and water. White breadcrumbs are made from the crumb part of one-day old loaves of bread, putting it through a food processing machine, then through a medium sieve. The crusts can be dried in a slow oven, then processed into crumbs for other uses.

Paner au Beurre – is the technical term for coating foods, mainly fillets of fish, with flour, melted butter and breadcrumbs. The items are then slightly flattened, marked trellis-fashion and placed on a greased tray, sprinkled with more melted butter and grilled under a salamander grill until golden brown.

Reheating – is done to help speed up the service of certain foods by immersing previously cooked and cooled items into a chaudfont, which is a pan of boiling salted water. Portions are reheated to order.

Rolling – is the rolling up of flat cuts of meat or poultry so as to form them into a neat round joint to be tied with string, or netted ready for cooking. The term also applies to the rumbling of items in a machine that will break down the texture so as to form them into neat joints, or fit them into plastic sleeves. This process can be finished with a flattened covering of suet or other fat and can assist in portion control and evenness of cooking.

Salting – is the curing or pickling of cuts or joints of meat by either the dry or wet method. The process helps to preserve and to modify the resultant colour and flavour. Salt, saltpetre with other seasonings, spice and herbs can be rubbed into the meat or injected by a syringe, or the joint can be immersed in a flavoured liquid in a previously sterilised container and kept under refrigeration until the process is completed.

Scoring – is done by cutting the exterior of items into a neat pattern, either in straight lines or as a trellis. It is done mainly to cuts of pork to make it easy to serve a piece of crackling with the slices of meat. It is also done to make incisions for inserting garlic, rosemary or thyme into a raw joint of lamb, or for rubbing herbs and spices into other cuts of meat. A half-cooked ham may be skinned and the fat scored diamond-fashion for glazing with sugar and Madeira during the rest of the cooking time.

Searing – is to colour a joint or cuts of meat or poultry in hot shallow fat prior to roasting, braising or pot-roasting.

Skimming – is to clear a liquid of any impurities or fat which rise to the surface to prevent them boiling back and so clouding the liquid. It may be necessary to do this continuously.

Stuffing – herbs or spices added to breadcrumbs, rice, mushroom, sausage-meat or forcemeat are used to add a contrast of flavour to a joint of meat or whole poultry. There are dozens of different stuffings, sweet as well as savoury, which may be enclosed in the main item or cooked separately.

Trimming – is done to give a good shape to an item or to remove unwanted fat, ventricles, sinews and blood spots. It helps give uniform shape, size and weight to items before they are cooked. The trimmings may be used for other dishes or added to a stockpot.

Trussing – is done to give a neat shape and conformity to meat, poultry and game with a view to making them easy to carve as well as giving greater eye-appeal. Meat is trussed with string or netting, birds with string on a trussing needle or they may be bought already trussed with a rubber band. Poultry and game birds are normally trussed with two strings, the first goes through the centre joint of the leg, out the other side then through the winglet, neck flap and second winglet and is tied tightly to give a good shape. The second string goes through the end of the thigh out and back over the top but not through the flesh; it is tied tightly. A whole rabbit can be trussed for roasting by means of metal skewers to lay the body out flat.

Food Presentation

The customer's first impression of the food that has been ordered is when the plate is put before him/her on the table. The food must have instant eye-appeal, i.e. it must be neatly arranged and consist of several colours; the plate should not be overloaded nor should the food be too sparsely laid out on an overlarge plate.

A customer's second impression is the bouquet or smell that assails the nostrils; if sight and smell are agreeable they will cause the gastric juices to flow and heighten the customer's appetite. The food on the plate must be in accordance with its name on the menu and with any classical nomen-clature. Ideally, there should be variety in consistency and texture, flavour and taste, just the right amount of seasoning and the dish should be nutri-tionally sound. It is important for all those engaged in food and beverage provision to have made a study of nutrition including daily allowances of calories, protein, carbohydrates, fat, vitamin and mineral salts content of all foodstuffs, vegetarian and vegan restrictions and so on. Portion sizes should be adequate and recipe formulas adhered to.

When serving customers who have a disability, such as a person who is visually impaired, it is advisable to keep to a plan such as placing the main item in the middle of the plate, the vegetables on the right and potatoes on the left, with a minimum of gravy or sauce. Adjuncts such as sprigs of parsley, slices of lemon, cocktail sticks or cutlet frills hold no eye-appeal for blind people and can be hazardous. Visually-impaired customers need fish and meat to be served off the bone – preferably free from skin and gristle, to make it easy to cut – or to be already cut into manageable sections. Soup should ideally be thick and without large pieces of vegetable; salad leaves are best torn into fragments or shredded; desserts are best served in bowls rather than on plates and cutlery must be strong to use as against thin plastic eating instruments.

Overcooking of food results in loss of portion size, colour, texture, the breakdown of sauces, poor appearance, flavour blur and off-putting smell. Timing devices on computer-controlled equipment and reliable experience help in preventing overcooking. A trained chef instinctively knows when an item has reached the ideal degree of doneness but this can be fallible and the word 'approximate' should not be part of the culinary vocabulary. It is far better to use equipment which is time-controlled and switches itself off at the right time. Cooking times are of great importance in à la carte catering because, apart from basic preparations (mise en place), no cooking is done until a customer has ordered. No matter the level of catering provision the food must be cooked and served so as to make the meal an experience rather than a means of providing sustenance – customers should leave the table feeling satisfied, uplifted and renewed.

Food Hygiene

Every head chef and each member of a kitchen brigade now has to bear the onus of ensuring that everything served is hygienically safe to eat. Food poisoning is classed as an acute illness brought about by a person eating contaminated and poisonous food. It is caused by bacteria or their toxins, viruses, mycotoxins, chemicals, and poisonous foodstuffs. These cause abdominal pain, diarrhoea, nausea and vomiting.

The hygiene regulations place the responsibility for supplying customers with safe food on caterers, who must ensure that these regulations are strictly adhered to. These measures are known as the Food Hazard requirements and entail 'risk assessment' to ensure that no risks are taken if there is any doubt about the freshness and quality of the food when first delivered, through storage and cooking and onto the customer's plate.

Infections can come from eggs, meat, milk and cream, poultry, seafoods and water; also from blown cans, pests such as flies, cockroaches, water supply, lack of personal hygiene, boils and cuts, pesticides, rodents, unpasteurised cheeses, and poor refrigeration facilities, all of which have to be given close attention so that the regulations are not flouted.

Culinary Glossary

HERBS

Basil – very highly scented, used to make pistou (q.v.) and as an ingredient of turtle herbs (q.v.); can also be used in soups, sauces and stews.

Bouquet garni – general-purpose seasoning mixture for inclusion in stock, sauces, soups and stews, usually made in the form of a faggot and of a size commensurate with the quantity of food to be flavoured. It consists of parsley stalks, celery, a sprig of thyme and bayleaves tied neatly together. Additional items can include crushed garlic and dried orange peel. Can be purchased ready-made in sachets.

Chervil – an essential ingredient of fines herbes (q.v.) and used chopped as a delicate flavouring ingredient in stuffings and salads. The whole leaves are known as pluches, and are used as a garnish in many soups.

Chives – thin green stems with a flavour of onion; always use freshly chopped, in salads and soups.

Coriander – herb of the parsley family, available fresh, dried or in seed form, the seeds being similar in shape to peppercorns but lighter in weight.

Dill – aniseed-flavoured plant much used in Russian and Scandinavian cookery and for pickling fish and gherkins.

Fennel – the bulb is cooked as a vegetable or sliced raw in salads and the frilly leaves can be used to garnish and flavour salads. It has the flavour of aniseed and is used for flavouring soups and enhancing stuffings.

Fenugreek – leguminous plant with aromatic seeds which are tangy in flavour; its fresh leaves are used in the making of salads in Indian cookery.

Fines herbes – this term means a mixture of finely chopped chervil, chives, tarragon and parsley in the proportions of three parts parsley to one part each of the other herbs. It has many uses such as omelettes, chicken dishes and sauces.

Lemon grass – this aromatic lemon-flavoured grass is used to flavour salads, soups, fish, meat and poultry dishes. It may be purchased in powdered form as Sareh Powder.

Marjoram – sweet marjoram has a mild, sweet and spicy flavour that blends well with meat and vegetable dishes; wild marjoram is known as oregano (q.v.).

Mint – mainly used as a seasoning for lamb in the form of mint sauce and for cooking with boiled new potatoes. It makes refreshing drinks and there are several varieties, not all of which are suitable for cookery.

Mustard – sold in powder and ready-mixed forms for eating with food as an aid to digestion. English mustard is quite strong and when made up from powder needs to be mixed with water, milk or cream, or with port or

Worcester sauce, then allowed to stand for 1 hour. French mustard is always sold ready-made and is available plain, with seeds, with white wine, pepper-corns, spices, herbs and vinegars. It is milder than English mustard. American mustard is mild and light in colour. German mustard is usually dark but mild, with a sour-sweet taste. Chinese mustard is very hot to the taste.

Oregano – wild marjoram, often used in dried form on pizzas.

Parsley – the best-known herb because of its fairly bland flavour and versatility of use. It is available as curled, dark green leaves and as flat-leaved or French parsley. It is used whole or chopped, to decorate dishes of food, especially for finishing them at the last moment. It is widely used in omelettes, fish, soufflés, quiches, sauces, soups and stews and can be deep fried for use as a garnish with deep-fried foods. Flat-leafed parsley has a subtle flavour though more pronounced than that of curly-leafed parsley, with a nice aroma in both the leaves and stalks. It is best added at the end of cooking a dish.

Rosemary – short, tough, pointed leaves with a very aromatic smell that blends well in the mixture of turtle herbs (q.v.) and is eminently suited to lamb and veal dishes.

Sage – greyish downy leaves with a very strong camphor-like smell, used in stuffings for duck and pork cooked in the English style, with veal in the Italian style and in eastern European cookery in conjunction with paprika.

Sweet basil – similar in appearance and flavour to European basil.

Turtle herbs – a mixture composed of three parts basil, two parts each of marjoram and thyme, one part each of fennel and chervil and half a part of rosemary; gives an exotic aroma and flavour to turtle soup and dishes cooked à la Tortue.

Tarragon – widely used herb with a distinctive flavour from its shiny, nar-row, dark green leaves which are useful whole for decorating dishes and chopped for inclusion in fines herbes, in chicken dishes and various cold sauces and salads.

NUTS

Almond – sweet almonds are available as whole, halves, chopped, slivers, flaked, nibbed, ground and as an essence and can play a large part in nearly every course of the menu. They are popular as salted almonds for recep-tions and buffets. Bitter almonds are used to make essence but can be used with a greater amount of sweet almonds to provide a slight bitterness.

Brazil – has a slightly oily texture and creamy taste.

Candlenut – also known as kemirinut. Hard oily nut used in Indonesian cookery to enhance flavour and to thicken curries.

Cashew – usually served salted at cocktail parties and receptions and on cakes.

Chestnut – sweet chestnuts can be used in sweet and savoury dishes and contain more starch than other nuts and much less oil. They are used in soups, stuffings, mixed with vegetables, in cakes and desserts and as petits fours. They are available in cans as purée and whole. Chestnuts can also be obtained in dried and frozen form.

Gingko nut – used in Japanese cookery, may be purchased in bottles and cans.

Hazel – similar to the cob nut and filbert which are small round nuts with a robust flavour; they are used whole and in ground form in many sweet dishes.

Kemiri nut – another name for candlenut (q.v.).

Macadamia nut or **Queensland nut** – grown in Australia and Hawaii, usually purchased shelled and roasted and mainly used roast and salted for receptions and cocktail parties.

Peanut – also known as groundnut. Used as whole roasted and as peanut butter, also in ground form to thicken soups and sauces. Peanuts may be purchased in nibbed form as a substitute for nibbed almonds.

Pecan – also known as hickory, similar in appearance to a walnut but more oval and with a smooth shell. Used, in ground form, in cakes and ice cream and whole at receptions.

Pine-nut – can be eaten raw or roasted and for cooking in sauces, soups and pesto; they are very small and white in colour.

Pistachio – a green-coloured nut in a purple-grey skin much used in stuffings, to decorate cakes and to make very delectable ice cream.

Walnut – unripe nuts can be pickled, fully ripe ones are served as part of desserts and to garnish cakes and ice cream.

SALAD GREENS

Belgian endive – often referred to as chicory, this salad ingredient is kept covered from the light so that it grows white, tinged with green at the tips. Its shape is an elongated oval and it has a slightly bitter taste.

Cabbage lettuce – the most popular kind of lettuce, which is the basis of most green salads. It is referred to as coeur de laitue when cut into quarters or wedges on the stem.

Corn salad – also known as lamb's lettuce or mâche, a delicate green, small leaf with no heart.

Cos lettuce – dark green, elongated lettuce, often called a romaine.

Dandelion – young leaves picked before the plant flowers can be blanched for use in a salad.

endive – known as frizzy or curly endive, batavia, escarole and chicory; lettuce-shaped with delicate curled leaves shading from white to pale green, bitter to the taste.

Iceberg lettuce – a crisp head lettuce that keeps fresh and crisp for a long time and has closely packed light green leaves.

Little gem lettuce – a small lettuce with a good heart, like a small version of a cabbage lettuce.

Lollo rosso – frizzy salad green with the ends of the green leaves tinged with red.

Mustard and cress – small grass-like sprouts more suitable as a garnish than a part of a salad.

Nasturtium – the leaves add a peppery taste to a salad and are a source of iron and vitamin C; the flowers can also be used in a salad.

Oakleaf – leaf or chicken lettuce, a less popular variety comprising a loose head of leaves.

Radicchio – small cabbage-type lettuce. The leaves are a distinctive colour of burgundy red with white veins. It is much favoured for its crispness and attractive appearance.

Rocket – a genus of garden herbs which grow wild but are now cultivated as a distinctive salad leaf.

Savory – long narrow leaves with a delicate spicy flavour and slightly bitter taste; can be used in stuffings and salads and is closely associated with the cooking of broad beans.

Watercress – pungent, peppery taste; dark green, roundish leaves.

Webb's wonder – a large-sized crisp and compact lettuce.

SEEDS

Caraway – narrow, black, curved seeds with a subtle taste of anise; used in Hungarian goulash, bread, cakes and in certain cheeses.

Celery – useful for adding to soups, marinades, fish dishes and dips.

Fenugreek – small flat brownish-coloured seeds used in making curries.

Lovage seeds – used in Asian cookery to impart their special flavour to food.

Poppy – very small black seeds used in Near Eastern countries in sweets, pastries, mousses, etc. and in Germanic countries. Often used to cover bread and rolls.

Sesame – used to make halva (q.v.), bread, pastry, hoummous (q.v.), as a condiment and for sprinkling on bread and rolls before baking.

Wild onion seeds – small black and irregularly shaped, used in Asian cookery to impart a sweet, nutty flavour to food.

SPICES

Allspice – so-called because it has the odour of cinnamon, cloves and nutmeg; it is the seed of the pimento tree of the Caribbean where it is called Jamaica pepper though it is not peppery. Available whole for use as a pickling spice and ground as a flavouring.

Aniseed or anise – pronounced flavouring used mainly in pastries and sweets and in the making of liqueurs and aperitifs (see also star anise).

Balti cooking spice mixture – a blend of the following dry stir-fried seeds and spices: coriander seeds, white cumin seeds, fennel seeds, cardamoms, cassia bark, ground mace, crushed fenugreek leaves, cloves, curry powder, garlic powder, chilli powder and mustard. This product may be purchased in packets or jars.

Cardamom – grows as green, black and white pods containing small seeds. Available in whole or ground form. Very aromatic and used as an ingredient in curry powder and as a flavouring in coffee. It is one of the most expensive spices.

Cassia – plant similar to cinnamon but without its subtle flavour; used in curry powder, for spicing meat and making pilaus.

Cayenne – a very pungent form of pepper used in minute amounts to bring out the full flavour of dishes; it is dull red in colour and not as intense as chilli pepper although it is made from chillies.

Chillies – very hot and spicy members of the pepper family. The small, dark, long ones are the hottest, the seeds being the hotter part. The jalapeño variety is usually available only in jars and cans and can be eaten whole, though very hot to the taste. Dried pods are stronger than fresh, and a crushed one is often part of pickling spices. Chilli powder is also very hot and should be added slowly, e.g. to a stew such as Chilli con Carne.

Cinnamon – available in the form of a stick which is the curled bark of a tree of the laurel family and is used in mulled wine, stock syrup and in pilaus and biriani. In powder form it is used in cakes, biscuits, Christmas pudding and mincemeat and is a component of mixed spice.

Cloves – available whole as hard, dried buds used to flavour certain sauces, pickles, marinades and syrups, and in powdered form as a component of mixed spice; cloves are highly flavoured and go well with cooked apples.

Coriander – aromatic seed with a faint smell of oranges, used in stock syrup, for pastry items and in a variety of savoury dishes; much used in dishes of North African and Asian origin.

Cumin – the hot and bitter dried fruit of a herb, used whole or ground as a spice.

Curry leaves – available fresh as shiny small leaves and in dried form; they do not taste of curry.

Fenugreek – an essential ingredient of curry powder.

Five spice powder – an essential seasoning condiment in Chinese cookery, comprising ground star anise, fennel seeds, cloves, cinnamon and Szechwan peppercorns.

Galingale – also spelt galangal, a reddish-coloured spice with a hot, strong flavour, used in exotic dishes. Available in root or powder form it has an aroma of cardamom and ginger and faintly of camphor.

Garlic – plant of the lily family with a pronounced flavour that needs to be used with discretion, when it will give a delicate result with no after effects. After parsley this is one of the most widely used flavourings and of much importance in Latin and oriental cookery. It grows as white bulbs consisting of numerous pods called cloves and can be eaten raw or cooked in stews, soups and vegetables. It is advisable to chop rather than squeeze garlic: lightly crush the cloves with the side of a knife to remove the skin, then remove the root and any green parts, flatten it and chop finely. It is available as a powder and a purée in tubes.

Ginger – available as fresh and dry roots, as a powder and in pickled and crystallised forms – sour and sweet. It has a biting taste and the best-quality roots come from India and Jamaica. It is widely used throughout the menu from melon with ginger to steamed puddings, and especially in the oriental cookery of India and China.

Horseradish – a very strongly flavoured root which can bring tears to the eyes while grating it, though it is usually only available in prepared form as horseradish sauce or cream and as a dried powder. Much used in German, Russian and Scandinavian cookery as an ingredient of dishes and as a dip.

Juniper berries – dried berries with a strong flavour and scent which go well with venison, in cooking sauerkraut, in sausages and with joints of mutton and pork. Also available in powder form.

Mace – the outer covering of the nutmeg sold as an orange-coloured powder and as blades for use in flavouring pâté, sausages, stuffings, biscuits and small cakes.

Nutmeg – dried seed of the fruit of a tree that grows in Southeast Asia and the Antilles with a pleasant flavour that makes it versatile in use in sauces, stuffings, potato dishes, vegetables, especially spinach, milk puddings in the English style and as an ingredient in mixed spice; it blends well with cooked cheese dishes and pastas.

Paprika – although often referred to as paprika pepper it is made from dried and ground sweet pimentos and should have a vivid red colour and soft pleasant aroma and flavour. It is widely used in Hungarian cookery where it is available in several qualities from sweet to strong; has many uses in sauces, stews, fish dishes, rice, in sausages and for decorative purposes.

Pepper – dried beans of the pepper vine which produce the most widely used spice. It has a very strong taste and smell that enhance the flavour of anything it is cooked with or sprinkled on, and it goes with all savoury dishes. Available as peppercorns for use whole and for grinding freshly, or in powdered form. There are a number of different varieties available:

Black peppercorns – unripe berries in their outer skin
Green peppercorns – unripe berries of the beans of the pepper vine
Mignonnette – name given to coarsely milled white peppercorns
Szechwan peppercorns – known as Chinese brown peppercorns; need to be dry-fried or roasted before grinding
White pepper – the strongest pepper, made from ripe peppercorns in powder form
White peppercorns – the best quality dried beans of the pepper vine.

Saffron – a pungent spice made from the stigma of the crocus, a native of Arabia but now grown in Spain, Italy, Iran, France, Latin America etc. It imparts a wonderful aroma, a golden yellow colour, and a delicate taste to many foods and is a feature of the cookery of many nations.

Seven-flavour spice or pepper – a seasoning comprised of ground chilli, black pepper, dried orange peel, sesame seeds, poppy seeds, nori seaweed and hemp seeds, ground into a powder.

Star anise – the fruit of a tree of the magnolia family, it grows in the form of a star and has the strong spicy taste and smell of anise. It is used in Chinese dishes and is very popular in Scandinavian cookery.

Tamarind – taken from the large pods of the tamarind tree which contain a red pulp and small seeds. It is usually sold as pulp or in dried form for making into juice by soaking in warm water, then discarding the pulp. It is used in making curry and chutney. Tamarind may also be purchased in concentrated liquid form.

Turmeric – the rhizomes of a plant of the lily family made into a powder to give a bright yellow colour and hot gingery taste to pilaus of rice, and to curry and mustard pickle. It is a substitute for saffron.

INGREDIENTS AND TERMS USED
IN THIS BOOK

Abalone – a mollusc sometimes called St Peter's ear, used extensively in Asian and American cookery; usually canned but may be purchased fresh.

Acidulated water – water, lemon juice and salt.

Ackee – fruit of West African origin used extensively in Caribbean cookery. It has a scarlet pod and shiny black seeds. The flesh is light cream in colour with a texture similar to scrambled eggs. May be purchased in cans.

Al dente – degree to which pasta should be cooked. Al dente pasta should be firm and have some 'bite' when eaten.

Angostura bitters – aromatic flavouring made from the bark of a tree grown in South America and various other aromatics.

Aromates – mixture of vegetables and herbs used to impart flavour to braised foods.

Asafoetida – dried resin extracted from *Ferula asafoetida*, a plant native to Asia. Purchased in powder form or in pieces, has a strong, acrid and bitter flavour, therefore only minute quantities are necessary.

Asam jawa – tamarind pulp, used to add a tart taste to many oriental dishes. Sold in packets. Needs to be softened in the proportion of 25 g in 150 ml warm water and squeezed to use the liquid only. Must be kept in a cool place.

Asam keping – dried tamarind slices soaked in warm water and the juice only used to add tartness to dishes.

Aspic – originally an entrée moulded in aspic but now used to refer to savoury jelly.

Assiette anglaise – selection of sliced cold meats.

Ata – wholemeal flour, also called chapati flour, used in the making of Indian-style bread.

Au bain-marie – (i) cooked in the oven in a shallow container of water to ensure an even temperature (ii) kept hot in a container of water.

Au beurre – cooked in butter or served with knobs of butter.

Azuki – small dark variety of mung bean, grown in the same way as all bean sprouts.

Baharat – ground spices including black peppercorns, paprika, cinnamon, cloves, cumin seeds, coriander seeds, nutmeg and cardamon seeds.

Balachan – paste made from fermented shrimps and salt for use as a flavouring ingredient in Thai cooking.

Balsamic vinegar – a rich, concentrated, sweet and sour vinegar with a slightly acid taste, made from the juice of Trebbiano grapes.

Balti – a Pakistani style of cookery associated with highly spiced curries, cooked and served in a balti pan.

Bamboo shoots – peeled pieces of bamboo spears usually sold cooked in cans; creamy-coloured and nutty in texture.

Barberries – rather sour berries which resemble currants in texture and colour.

Bard – to cover a joint of meat, fish, poultry and game with thin slices of salt pork fat.

Bean curd – ground soya beans made into a smooth curd, set with gypsum; has little flavour but is high in protein. Sold as fresh, also in dried sheet form and as dried pieces used for flavouring purposes.

Bean paste – soya beans made into a thick paste, used as a flavouring ingredient. Available as *Hot* – mixed with red chillies, *Sweet* – as a dip or sauce with added spices and garlic which give a dark red purée (also called Hoisin sauce) and as *Salted* – made as a yellow bean paste (also called Miso).

Bean sprouts – young sprouts of mung beans much used in oriental cooking as a stir-fry vegetable and a filling, e.g. in spring rolls or raw as a salad. Can be grown quickly indoors on damp cloth or cotton wool covered to exclude the light until ready to pick in 3–4 days.

Bed of root vegetables – sliced carrot, onion, celery, bayleaf and a sprig of thyme, used for braising meat and fish.

Besan – chickpea flour.

Beurre noir – black butter made by cooking it to a deep brown colour with the addition of a little vinegar and optional capers and chopped parsley.

Bhaji – a savoury fritter, also called a pakora.

Biriani – a genetic term for a highly spiced rice dish which is layered with curried beef, chicken, lamb, mutton or vegetables.

Blanc – water and lemon juice lightly thickened with flour used to boil certain vegetables to preserve their whiteness.

Blachan – made of small prawns fermented in salt until they form a paste by rotting away, then dried and packed. The strong odour disappears when cooked, to give a depth of flavour, and the cooking can be carried out by frying with other pounded ingredients, by grilling, or by holding a little on a piece of wire over a naked gas flame, without burning it.

Blanch – (i) to cover with cold water, bring to the boil and immediately refresh under cold water to remove bitterness or preserve colour and to make items more pliable so as to shape them; (ii) to deep fry potatoes until cooked and soft but not coloured.

Blinis – type of small pancake made from buckwheat flour; served with caviar.

Bombay duck – sun-dried fillet of Indian fish flavoured with asafoetida. Served grilled or baked for breaking up on top of a dish of any kind of curry.

Bonito flakes – dried flakes of fish used in Japanese cookery to flavour basic stocks and soups; bonito is a type of tuna fish.

Buckwheat – dried seeds of a grass made into groats (q.v.) then milled into flour that is grey/purple in colour.

Bulgar wheat or **bulghur** – the most ancient kind of cereal. It has to be soaked then cooked and dried before being milled and is an ingredient in couscous.

Bundnerfleisch – air-dried raw beef that is sliced very thinly and served as an hors-d'oeuvre.

Burdock – root of a plant of the aster family, crunchy in texture and rather neutral in flavour so it absorbs the flavours of other foods. The dock-like leaves are used as a salad.

Caciocavallo – an Italian hard cheese made from cow's milk matured for up to four months for ordinary eating or 12 months for grating and cooking; tastes somewhat similar to Gruyére.

Canapés – small pieces of fried or toasted bread covered with a variety of savoury items served at receptions and cocktail parties.

Cassareep – a thick black syrup made from the cassava root and used for colouring in Caribbean cookery.

Caviar – salted roe of the sturgeon, available in several qualities, Beluga being the finest.

Cellophane noodles – fine transparent noodles, also called gelatine noodles, made from starch extracted from green mung beans; used in Asian cookery.

Cep mushroom – fleshy, spongy-textured mushroom with a bulbous base to the stem.

Chanterelle mushroom – funnel-shaped mushroom that narrows into a short stalk; bright egg-yellow colour, apricot-like smell.

Chapatti – flat disc-shaped unleavened bread made from wholemeal or roti flour, ghee and water.

Chaudfont – pan of just boiling, salted water to reheat food to order.

Chayote – also called coo-coo or christophene. A tropical squash, extensively cultivated in the Caribbean and tropical regions. May be purchased fresh or canned.

Chickpeas – large-sized peas available whole or split and in ground form for use as the thickening agent known as gram. Chickpeas are the main ingredient of hoummus (q.v.) and are also known as garbanzos.

Cider vinegar – made from apples, yellowish in colour with a mellow flavour.

Chilli serrano – small green chilli grown in the Sierra mountain region of South America.

Chinese black beans – small black-skinned beans which are allowed to ferment with salt before use.

Chinese gooseberry – another name for the kiwi fruit.

Chinese mushroom – known as shiitake, a tree fungus having a distinctive flavour, available fresh or dried. The latter require to be soaked for approximately 30 minutes and the warm water in which they were soaked is used.

Chinese plum sauce – sauce made from plums, chillies and various spices; may be purchased in cans and in jars.

Chipotte sauce – hot Mexican sauce made from smoked-dried chilli jalapeño; purchased in bottles.

Ciseler – to make two or more very shallow incisions on each side of a fish, just penetrating the skin at the thickest part – this is to allow even cooking.

Chojang vinegar dipping sauce – condiment used as a dressing for a range of dishes in Korean cookery. It is made from cider vinegar, soy sauce, toasted sesame seeds, garlic, sugar and chilli powder.

Choke – fibrous centre of the globe artichoke which has to be removed before eating.

Chorizo – short fat sausage flavoured with paprika in sweetish or pungent versions made with pork and cayenne pepper; may be purchased either smoked or fresh.

Choux paste – light paste used for éclairs, fritters, etc.

Christophene – a tropical pear-shaped vegetable of the squash family, often with a prickly skin, whitish to pale green in colour. May be purchased in vacuum packs or pickled. Also known as chow chow or chayote.

Cilantro – Mexican parsley, an aromatic herb with a strong, distinctive flavour.

Citrus leaves – the leaves of the kaffir lime used to provide a distinctive flavour to some oriental dishes, particularly fish; they need to be torn into shreds for use.

Clam – bivalve shellfish much used in American cookery, e.g. in a clambake.

Clarified butter – butter melted and cleared of any particles and all sediment.

Clarify – to clear of impurities and sediment, making transparent, e.g. consommé or jelly.

Coconut milk – this is not the natural juice present in coconuts which is really only a refreshing drink; real coconut milk is purchased in packets, cans and as slabs. To make coconut milk blend 600 ml almost boiling water and 250 g desiccated coconut for 20 seconds, allow to cool then squeeze out the liquid.

Coconut cream – made commercially, is sold in block form which can be kept for several months and reconstituted by dissolving the required amount in hot water with a pinch of salt. It has a rich and quite sweet flavour. It can be made by soaking one part fresh coconut flesh in two parts water for 3 hours, then squeezing out the liquid through a muslin.

Cohere – (of ingredients) to stick or lightly bind together into a sauce.

Compote – fruit cooked and served in stock syrup.

Concassée – chopped or crushed items, e.g. pipped and diced tomatoes.

Cordon – line of sauce or gravy poured around an item of food once placed on the serving dish.

Coriander root – root of the coriander plant used in Asian cookery.

Coulis – essence made from shellfish used as a base for a sauce, or fresh fruits or vegetables made into a thin purée for use as a sauce.

Court-bouillon – cooking liquid used for boiling and poaching fish, meat and offal, made of water, wine, vegetables and herbs.

Crêpes – pancakes, usually small ones, for sweet and savoury uses.

Crème fraîche – slightly acidulated cream which gives a more pronounced flavour than ordinary cream when added to soups, stews and sauces.

Croûtons – small cubes and other shapes of fried or toasted bread used as an accompaniment, garnish or base for canapés.

Crushed garlic – cloves or sections of garlic made into a fine paste by removing the outer skin and crushing with the flat side of a knife, using a little salt as an abrasive.

Curaçao – liqueur made from the rinds of bitter oranges, used as a flavouring for desserts and pastry items.

Darne – fish steak cut across and through the bone of a large whole round fish.

Dasheen – also called eddo. A large tuber with a dark brown coarse skin used as a potato – though slightly bitter – varying in size from that of a small avocado to a large pineapple. The flesh may be white, pale yellow or pale grey in colour; it is used extensively in Caribbean cookery.

Dashi – the basic form of stock used in Japanese cookery, made of dried seaweed, which is called dashi kombu.

Decant – to pour off a liquid after allowing any sediment in it to settle in the same way as decanting a bottle of vintage port or a first-growth claret.

Deglaze – to add a liquid such as wine or stock to the sediment left in a pan after shallow frying.

Diablé – devilled, i.e. liberally seasoned with pepper and mustard and therefore hot to the tongue.

Duxelles – basic mushroom preparation made by cooking finely chopped onion and mushrooms in butter to a stiff consistency, often for use as a stuffing.

Daikon – elongated white radish used in Japanese cookery.

Daun pandan – also known as duan panduras leaf. Leaf of the screw pine tree used for flavouring certain sweet dishes and also in curries and pilaus.

Dhal – all the various kinds of lentils: brown, green, red and yellow. Sometimes spelt dal, the word also includes dried peas and beans.

Dim sum – an assortment of small snacks or titbits that can be eaten as a midday meal or as a prelude to a main meal. It is of Cantonese origin, consisting of a range of small delicacies, usually steamed or deep fried. Dumplings are served with fillings such as shrimps, shredded chicken, sesame seeds, mushrooms, coconut, lotus seeds, dates and red bean paste. Other steamed items can include meat balls, spare ribs, spring rolls, etc., some of which may be wrapped in lotus leaves. Fried items can include fish balls, batons of water chestnuts, tofu, yam fritters, and many others.

Dolmas – term used to denote a vegetable filled with a stuffing and baked or steamed, e.g. stuffed vine leaves and stuffed eggplant.

Doner kebab – spit-roasted boned lamb in the shape of a large joint from which slices can be shaved off.

Dried shrimp paste – a pungent paste made from fermented and salted shrimps.

Duan salan – an aromatic leaf similar to a curry leaf in flavour, used in Indonesian cookery.

Duan panduras leaf – also known as daun pandan. Leaf of the screw pine tree used for flavouring certain sweet dishes and in curries and pilaus.

Durum wheat – type of cereal coarsely milled into flour, mainly for use in making pastas.

Emmenthal – the most famous Swiss cheese from Berne, made as large cartwheels of up to 100 kg and with a fat content of 15–48%. Hard golden-yellow rind, fine aroma and flavour and lots of large holes. Copies are made in many other countries.

Empanadas – savoury turnovers made of rough puff pastry with a savoury minced meat filling, much eaten in Mexico.

Enchilada – another name for a tortilla, a Mexican cornmeal pancake with a bean, chicken or meat filling coated with chilli sauce and cheese.

Entrée – main dish of meat or poultry properly served before the roast and consisting of a lightly sauced item with a garnish.

Entremets – sweet dishes, the French name for the sweet course.

Epazote – dried, pungent-smelling herb used in Mexican cookery.

Escalope – thin round slice cut from fish, meat or poultry, usually flattened.

Extension dishes – dishes produced from a basic recipe with added ingredients, sauces and garnishes.

Farce – stuffing or forcemeat, either raw or cooked.

Fécule – general term for thickening agents including arrowroot, cornflour, rice flour and potato flour.

Felafel – small deep-fried balls of chickpea powder, matzo meal, eggs, cumin, coriander and garlic.

Féta – a famous Greek cheese made of sheep's milk or a mixture of sheep's milk and cow's milk, allowed to ripen in its own whey and brine which makes it quite salty to the taste. It has a piquant and slightly sour flavour. Very white in colour, made in a rectangular shape without a rind, and with a fat content of 45–60%. Also made in other countries.

Filo pastry – pastry made with a proportion of cornflour and with oil, widely used in Greece and countries in the Middle East; also spelt phyllo.

Fines herbs – mixture of chopped herbs, usually comprising chives, chervil, tarragon and parsley.

Fish sauce – there are several kinds of this oriental sauce sold in bottles as a strong fish flavouring made by macerating fish in salt over a period of months. Nuoc nam is the name for it in South East Asia and it is called nam pla in Thai cookery.

Flambé – to add a spirit such as rum and brandy to a dish for added flavour and set it alight to burn off the alcohol.

Fleurons – crescent-shaped items of puff pastry generally served with unglazed fish dishes. They add colour and crispness to what may otherwise be a completely white and soft-textured dish.

Floret – one of the small buds of cauliflower or broccoli.

Flower waters – these include orange-flower water, and rose-water, made from highly scented petals for use as delicate flavourings in icings and desserts.

Foie gras – the fattened liver from a force-fed goose or duck, a very expensive commodity used as an hors-d'oeuvre or main course.

Fortified wine – wine with the addition of brandy to increase its alcoholic strength, including Madeira, Marsala, port and sherry.

Frappé – chilled; foods set on crushed ice.

Friandises – alternative name for petits fours.

Friture – a deep-fat fryer, a frying kettle.

Fromage frais – very low fat, soft cheese with only 47 kcals per 100 g; white, tasteless, slightly grainy but fairly smooth consistency. Used mainly in cooking in place of cream. Also available in fruit-flavoured form.

Full gratination – cooking or heating an item in the oven in order to give the even coloration and slight crispness.

Garam masala – mixture of ground spices kept ready to flavour Indian and Pakistani curries and similar dishes. There is no set formula though it is available under brand names. It can include coriander, cinnamon, cumin, cardamom, cloves, chillies, ginger and nutmeg in various proportions, in powder form.

Gari – cassava meal, also called tapioca powder.

Ghee – clarified butter widely used in Indian cookery; can be heated to a higher temperature than ordinary butter.

Glaze – (i) to colour under a salamander grill; (ii) to cook vegetables in water and butter to give a sheen; (iii) a stock syrup with fruit purée or jam in various colours for finishing flans, bands and tartlets.

Glutinous rice – long-grain variety of rice which is gluten-free, frequently used for dessert dishes; when cooked it becomes very sticky.

Gnocchi – type of small dumpling made from semolina, potato or choux paste.

Goujons – small strips of fillets of fish or chicken used in stir-fry recipes. Goujonettes are smaller still.

Gram flour – flour made from dried split peas; may be replaced by wheat-flour or wholemeal flour.

Gratinate – to colour and give a crisp surface to foods by sprinkling it with grated cheese or breadcrumbs, oil or melted butter, then placing it under a salamander grill or in the top of an oven.

Gravlax – fillets of salmon cured with either whisky, gin or aquavit, sea salt, sugar, crushed peppercorns and dill for 2–3 days. Served uncooked, with lemon, brown bread and butter and dill and mustard sauce. Also called gravad lax.

Gruyère – popular cheese made in Switzerland, often compared with Emmenthal but more moist and highly flavoured; made in weights of 30–40 kg with small holes. It is excellent for the table and for cooking purposes.

Guacamole – dip or sauce made from purée of avocado, tomato, chillies, coriander, onion and lemon juice.

Guava – strong-smelling tropical fruit containing many seeds, round or pear-shaped and green to yellow in colour. Used to make jelly and ice cream.

Hachis – finely chopped cooked meat reheated in a suitable sauce.

Haute cuisine – finest type of high-class cookery.

Halal – the ritual method of slaughter for cattle, as practised by Moslems.

Halva – sweetmeat made with a syrup, fruit, lentil or chickpea paste, cooked with ghee and sometimes with added nuts and natural colouring.

Hoisin sauce – a thick, sweet, spicy, reddish-brown sauce made from soy beans, spices and garlic. May be purchased canned or bottled.

Hoummous – puréed chickpeas flavoured with garlic, lemon juice and olive oil; often served in a pitta or as a dip.

Infuse – to cover an ingredient with boiled water and let it stand for a while so as to extract the flavour and aroma.

Jalapeño chilli – a very hot variety of chilli, small, thin and green in colour, available fresh, canned or pickled.

Jalebi – batter made from flour, milk powder and yoghurt, piped in whirls, deep-fried and served as a sweet in heavy syrup.

Jamón serrano – a cured ham from Spain, carved thinly for eating as an appetiser or tapa.

Japanese artichoke – also called crosne or Chinese artichoke, similar to the Jerusalem artichoke but smaller.

Japanese mushroom – the shiitake mushroom, has a strong flavour whether fresh or dried.

Japanese noodles (harusame) – very fine noodles produced from bean starch; they become translucent when soaked and boiled. When deep fried they puff up and become opaque.

Japanese pepper (sansho) – used in Japanese cookery as a garnish. The ground leaf, called kona sansho, is used as a seasoning.

Jus – gravy, as in jus lié which means a thickened, light gravy, served as an accompanying sauce or used in the cooking of a meat dish.

Kaffta leaves – leaves of a citrus fruit grown in Asia; bayleaf may be used as a substitute.

Kapi – Thai name for dried shrimp paste which is usually purchased ready-made.

Kasha – roasted buckwheat grains used in Russian cookery; may be eaten with butter or formed into small balls with the addition of cottage cheese, sliced mushrooms, etc. and fried or baked. It can be served as an accompaniment to other dishes or with a sauce.

Katsuobushi – dried bonito flakes used in Japanese cookery for flavouring dashi, which is a Japanese stock, and for garnishing.

Kasseri – a Greek cheese of rubbery texture with good keeping qualities made by cutting Kefalotíri cheese (q.v.) into strips and immersing it in hot water to render it plasticised.

Kefalotíri – a hard cheese from goat's or sheep's milk, made in cylindrical shapes of 9–10 kg in weight; needs to be grated for use.

Kopanisti – a blue-veined cheese with a high salt content and peppery flavour; the mould which grows on the cheese is kneaded back into it and it is then ripened for up to two months.

Kelp kombu – brown seaweed much used in Japanese cookery.

Kencur powder – also known as galangale or aromatic ginger, used in Asian cookery.

Kimichi – fermented pickle used to accompany a range of Korean dishes; may be purchased in bottles.

Kiname – pepper leaf used as a garnish in Japanese cookery; not always readily available but can be replaced by kona sansho, which is ground pepper leaf.

Kirsch – spirit distilled from cherry stones, used to flavour sweet dishes, particularly fruit salads.

Kochujang – red pepper paste made from soy beans, glutinous rice flour and chilli powder, used extensively in Korean cookery.

Kombu – dried seaweed (kelp) used in Asian cookery, used for making dashi (Japanese stock) and sushi appetisers.

Kosher – food produced and prepared in accordance with strict Jewish religious laws.

Kvas – a fermented drink made from rye bread and yeast; may be flavoured with mint. Also spelt kvass.

Laos powder – woody roots of a tree of the ginger family that has a pine smell and flavour, available in powdered form as a spice.

Lardons of bacon – small batons of streaky bacon, usually blanched then shallow fried as part of a garnish for meat and vegetable dishes.

Laska noodles – Thai name for egg noodles.

Liaison – a mixture of egg yolks and cream, crème fraîche, yogurt or quark used as a thickening agent.

Lumpfish roe – salted roe of the lumpfish, available as black or orange-red from Iceland and Denmark, used as a substitute for caviar.

Maatjes herring – raw, boned herring cured in the Dutch way with vinegar, spices and sugar.

Macerate – to make a food soft by soaking it in wine or a liqueur so as to effect an exchange of flavours.

Madeleine mould – large or small scallop-shaped mould with a hinge.

Mandolin – hand tool for slicing vegetables into various thicknesses and shapes such as grooves, julienne and matchsticks.

Mango powder – made from sun-dried mangos, it has a distinctive and delicate, sour flavour.

Mangosteen – a dark-coloured, leathery-skinned fruit containing five delicately flavoured segments.

Maraschino – liqueur made from black Dalmatian cherries, used to flavour sweet dishes. Maraschino cherries are preserved stoned red cherries for use in cocktails.

Marinate – to tenderise and add flavour to foods by soaking in a liquid such as wine or vinegar with herbs, spices and vegetables. This liquid is known as the marinade.

Mascarpone – an Italian soft, fresh cream cheese with a delicious flavour which makes it ideal for use with desserts. It is the basis of tiramisu.

Matzo – unleavened bread made as flat, round or square biscuits, especially for eating during the Jewish Passover.

Matzo meal – meal of varying coarseness made from matzo.

Melon – used mainly as an appetiser either whole (if small), sliced, or as melon cocktail cut in small balls. Melon can also be used as a garnish with fish and white meat and as part of a fruit salad. The best-known varieties are cantaloupe, charentais, galia, honeydew, ogen and water melon.

Mirin – Japanese rice wine used only in cookery; dry sherry may be used as a substitute.

Miso – fermented soya bean paste made as dark red, brown and white.

Monosodium glutamate – white crystallised flavouring made by the hydrolisation of wheat or beet into glutamic acid, used extensively in Chinese and Asian cookery.

Moong dal – yellow split peas.

Mung beans – produce the Chinese bean sprout, a small green and white shoot that grows quickly. Also available as whole, split or skinless the beans can be ground into a flour used for making Chinese noodles called fen tian.

Nam pla – a fish sauce widely used in Thai cookery, it is the liquid obtained by letting fish ferment in salt for several months and is dark brown to golden in colour.

Nan bread – yeast dough moulded in the shape of a teardrop and baked in a tandoori oven.

Natives – name given to English oysters, particularly those from Whitstable.

Nuoc nam – fish sauce used in South-East Asian cookery.

Okra – also called ladies' finger or gumbo, a small green tapering pod vegetable with a glutinous quality. Young okra are used for preference for serving as a vegetable or in a soup or stew.

Oyster plant – name given to salsify, a long cylindrical vegetable. The black variety is known as scorzonera.

Oyster sauce – a flavouring ingredient and an accompaniment to various dishes, made as a thick brown essence from soya beans, oysters and starches.

Palm heart – the tender shoot of a palm tree, used as a vegetable.

Parmesan cheese – made in Italy, a full-cream cheese, salted for up to three weeks and cured for two or three years; after the first year it is coated with a mixture of earth and oil to give a solid crust. Very hard straw-coloured cheese, mainly for use grated in cookery and for sprinkling over pastas; spicy rather than sharp in flavour, it is made as *giovane* (young), *tipico* (4–5 years old) and *stravecchio* (very old).

Panada – preparation used to bind and thicken or extend forcemeats of fish and meat; made of flour, with eggs or breadcrumbs cooked in milk.

Pancetta – cured belly of pork, the Italian version of streaky bacon.

Panch phora – combination of 5 different whole seeds, consisting of black mustard, cumin, black cumin, fenugreek and fennel.

Panettone – sweet loaf made with yeast, eggs and dried fruit; a speciality of Milan and a traditional Italian Christmas treat.

Papain – tenderiser obtained from the papaya fruit (paw-paw).

Parma ham – good-quality cured raw ham from the town of that name in Italy, carved into wafer-thin slices and served as an appetiser.

Pastillage – gum paste, used in the making of ornamental items such as caskets and baskets used for the display and presentation of, for example, petits fours.

Passata – tomato sauce flavoured with oregano and basil.

Pâté de foie gras – pâté made from goose liver and often mixed with truffle as an appetiser or cold buffet item; sold in cans or jars.

Paw-paw – also called papaya fruit. Elongated oval, deep orange-coloured fruit which bruises easily. It is served cut in half, with the seeds removed as an appetiser or dessert. Papain is obtained from it.

Pecorino – a hard Italian cheese produced from ewe's milk. It is mainly used grated but may be served on a cheeseboard. Also made with peppercorns, when it is known as pecorino pepato.

Persillé – sprinkled with chopped parsley upon serving; containing a fair amount of parsley.

Petits fours – assortment of very small, fancy sweetmeats served at the end of a meal.

Piquante – sharp or spicy in flavour as in Sauce Piquante, which is made with a reduction of vinegar and dry white wine.

Plantain – looks like a giant banana but is peeled, sliced and sautéed as a vegetable or garnish.

Pluches – sprays of chervil or other fresh herbs, used as a garnish in clear soups.

Poeroet leaves – aromatic leaf used in Thai cooking, may be replaced with dried curry leaves.

Polonaise – cooked and sprinkled with shallow-fried breadcrumbs, chopped parsley and chopped hard-boiled yolk and white of eggs.

Pomodori secchi – Italian sun-dried tomatoes marinated in seasoned virgin olive oil.

Ponze – Japanese dressing of lime juice, rice vinegar, soy sauce, mirin, bonito flakes, kelp and tamarind.

Poppadum – thin wafer of lentil flour dough; grilled, baked or deep fried to accompany a curry.

Pourgouri – Greek name for cracked wheat (see bulgar wheat).

Prawn crackers (Chinese crackers) – a small, whitish, round crispy product made from a paste comprising prawn flesh, starch, salt and sugar which is then dried and deep fried.

Prawn powder – shredded dried prawns used in Chinese cookery.

Prosciutto crudo – cured raw ham from Italy, e.g. Parma ham cut into wafer-thin slices as an appetiser, with melon or pear; also used in cooking.

Purée – smooth thick pulp made from food passed through a sieve, blender or food processor.

Pumpkin – orange-coloured gourd; can be served as a vegetable, made into soup or pumpkin pie.

Quince – pear-shaped fruit which turns deep yellow when ripe. It has a very acid flavour and is usually cooked with apple in a tart or pie as on its own it forms a very stiff paste.

Quorma – also spelt korma, a very mild curry dish.

Quorn – artificial protein food which can replace meat in the diet while still giving its texture, taste and nutritional value. Grown from a tiny plant.

Rambutan – small, oval-shaped fruit which looks like a hedgehog, with a yellow to purple skin and translucent flesh.

Red spice paste – bean paste made from azuki beans, used in Japanese cookery; may be also be purchased in powder form.

Reduction – boiling a liquid so that it reduces in volume to concentrate the flavour or make it more pungent and noticeable.

Rice – grain grown as a grass in water-covered paddy fields, a staple food in the diet of many races. Available as unpolished, polished, brown, carolina or pudding, long-grain or patna, basmati, java, easy-cook and as ground rice and rice flour.

Roti flour – creamy in colour and granular in texture similar to wholemeal flour; used for making Indian bread.

Saké – Chinese and Japanese sweetish rice wine, much used in cooking and drunk warm from a cup.

Sambals – accompaniments served with curry dishes, a selection of items including banana, coconut, chutney, pimento, etc.

Sambal bajak – fresh red chillies, onion, garlic and trasi ground with a little water to a smooth paste. The mixture is fried in groundnut oil, grated kemiri nuts, laos powder, tamarind liquid and palm sugar are added, and it is then simmered until it is reddish-brown in colour and the oil shows signs of separating from the mixture. Used in Asian and, in particular, Indonesian cookery. May be purchased ready prepared.

Sambal trasi – a flavouring combination of red chillies, sea salt and trasi (dried shrimp paste). May be purchased in cans or as a cake.

Sambal ulek – dried red chillies, tamarind liquid and salt ground to a paste. Used in Indonesian cookery, it may be purchased ready prepared.

Samosas or **Samoosas** – deep-fried oval or triangular-shaped savoury-filled items served as part of a hot canapé selection or traditionally for afternoon tea. In the UK they are a very popular vegetarian dish, containing fillings such as rice and vegetables, curry-flavoured vegetables, potato and spinach, cottage cheese and tuna fish.

Samneh – clarified butter as used in Middle Eastern cookery.

Sareh powder – Indonesian name for an aromatic flavouring powder made from lemon grass.

Sashimi – a Japanese speciality consisting of small, thin slices of most kinds of fish, including squid, arranged on a serving dish with pieces of daikon, carrot, cucumber, celery and spring onions with several kinds of dipping sauce based on soy, ginger, horseradish or mustard.

Satay – an Asian dish of skewered spiced meat or chicken.

Sauerkraut or choucroute – shredded white cabbage fermented with salt, purchased in jars or cans ready for cooking as a main dish with frankfurters and bacon.

Savarin – a sweet item made from a light yeast sponge in the form of a ring mould.

Scorzonera – black-skinned salsify, prepared and served as for that vegetable.

Sesame paste – roasted and ground sesame seeds mixed to a paste with sesame oil. Sesame seeds become sweet and nutty when roasted or dry fried.

Shaohsing wine – fermented liquid made from glutinous rice and yeast, yellow in colour with a golden sheen, named after Shenyang, an eastern province of China. A medium-dry sherry may be used as a substitute.

Shichimi-togarashi – a mixture of spices, poppy and sesame seeds, kemp and rape, plus tangerine peel and pepper leaf.

Shiitake mushrooms – Japanese mushroom tasting slightly of garlic, with a long, hard stem and small cap; available dried and fresh.

Shoyu sauce – similar to soy sauce but less salty and lighter in colour, used in Japanese cookery.

Shrimp paste – a pungent-smelling and tasting paste made from dried shrimps with a distinctive flavour; may be purchased in jars and cans.

Smetana – soured cream, or equal quantities of natural yogurt and double cream, used extensively in Russian cookery.

Soya beans – the most nutritious of all beans because they contain all eight essential amino acids; they are small, oval-shaped and grow as black, green. red and yellow varieties. Can be cooked and eaten on their own or used to make tofu (q.v.), soy sauce, tamari sauce (q.v.), soya milk in powder or long-life form, soya oil and flour made of cooked beans, also as textured vegetable protein, a meat substitute (q.v.).

Soy sauce – made of salted soya beans, gives a meaty taste to dishes. Made as white sauce, which is thin, and black, which is thick. The name given to Japanese soy sauce is shoyu.

Speck – salted pork fat, used for larding and barding meat and fish which is devoid of natural fat, and in galantines.

Spring roll wrappers – also known as wonton or won ton wrappers. Thin white sheets of pastry used in Chinese cookery; they are fragile and need to be handled carefully. Usually purchased frozen; once thawed, separate and cover with a damp cloth to prevent drying.

Studded onion – an onion with a bayleaf and a clove inserted into it, used as a flavouring for sauces, soups, stocks and when cooking pulses.

Supreme – (i) fillet of large fish cut on the slant into portion-sized pieces; (ii) a chicken breast with the end of the wingbone attached.

Sweat – (i) to cook vegetables without colour in a covered saucepan with fat or oil; (ii) to cook vegetables without colour in their own juices in a covered saucepan.

Sweet potato – has white to orange-coloured flesh and a chestnut-like taste.

Tabasco – the proprietary brand name of a flavouring liquid made by macerating hot red pimentos and ageing them in salt and vinegar.

Tabbouleh – fine bulgar wheat soaked and squeezed, mixed with chopped parley, mint and tomato and a lemon and oil dressing. It is served as a salad on young vine leaves or cos lettuce. A Lebanese speciality.

Taco shells – these are deep-fried tortillas (q.v.) made horseshoe-shape by holding against the side of the fat fryer, served filled with a mixture of chicken, lettuce and guacamole

Tahina or **tahini paste** – an oily paste made from sesame seeds and lemon. May be purchased ready-made.

Tamara – salted roe of cod or mullet used in the making of the Greek hors-d'oeuvre taramasalata.

Tamari sauce – made from soya beans and sea salt only and used as an alternative to soy sauce.

Tamarind – an acid-tasting tropical fruit, similar to a large broad bean.

Tamarind liquid – liquid of the tamarind fruit. May be purchased in condensed form in jars or in dried form to be reconstituted by soaking in water.

Tandoori – Pakistani type of cooking using charcoal; meat is first marinated then cooked in a clay oven called a tandoori.

Tandoori Masala – an essential seasoning condiment in Indian cookery, comprising ground coriander, cumin, paprika, chilli powder, cinnamon, red food colouring and salt.

Tannias – similar to the dasheen or eddo but smaller in size and drier in texture. The flesh is either white, pale yellow, creamy or pale violet in colour. May be purchased in cans. Used as a vegetable.

Tapas – selection of titbits such as prawns, squid, chorizo sausage, chickpea purée, pieces of various flavoured omelettes with pine-nuts, olives, garlic, etc. Served as an appetiser in Spanish tapas bars.

Taro – starchy tuber also known as eddo and tannias; the flesh becomes slimy when boiled.

Tikki – brochettes of seafood, meat or chicken previously marinated before cooking in a tandoori oven.

Tiramisu – Genoese sponge flavoured with coffee, marsala, rum, brandy, etc. with mascarpone cheese, dusted with cocoa. May also be made with crème pâtissière and mascarpone.

Tofu – soya bean curd, much used by the Japanese and by vegetarians.

Tomato concassée – blanched, peeled, depipped and diced tomato.

Tomatillos – small, plum-sized, light green, tart-flavoured fruit used for many green-type sauces in Mexican cookery.

Tortilla – unleavened dough made of ground maize and hot water, pressed flat and cooked on a griddle plate.

Tourte – round, covered pie or tart.

Tronçon – section of fish cut on the bone from a large flat fish.

Truffle – a fungus that grows in clusters near the roots of young oak trees. There are two main varieties – black and white – and also a red-grained black truffle. All are rare, much in demand and very expensive.

Udon noodles – thickish noodles made from white wheatflour; tagliatelli may be used as a substitute.

Vert-pré – basic garnish for grilled meat and poultry, comprising straw potatoes, parsley butter and watercress.

Vésiga – dried spinal cord of the sturgeon, used mainly in the Russian dish Coulibiac.

Vindaloo – very hot Goanese curry originally of pork marinated in vinegar; also spelt vendaloo.

Wasabi powder – pungent green horseradish used in Japanese cookery to accompany raw fish dishes, may be purchased in cans.

Water chestnuts – tubers grown in water, an Asian delicacy used mainly in salads. Available fresh and may also be purchased in cans or jars.

Wonton wrappers – see Spring roll wrappers.

Yam – starchy tuber which quickly discolours when peeled; not the same as the sweet potato.

Yellow bean sauce – used extensively in Chinese cookery; made from fermented beans with the addition of various spices. May be purchased in cans and in jars.

Yogurt – produced from whole, partially skimmed or skimmed, dried or evaporated milk in many flavours. Made with a culture bacteria which is permitted to multiply at a controlled temperature. When made with cow's milk, yogurt curdles when heated, it therefore needs to be stabilised with cornflour or arrowroot, using 2 tsp to 600 ml of milk.

Yogurt salsa – Turkish dipping sauce made of yogurt, garlic and salt.

Yuzu citron – citrus fruit used mainly for the unique aromatic fragrance of its rind; lemon or lime may be substituted for it.

Zabaglione – sweet made from whisked eggs, sugar and wine or liqueur.

Zakuski – a pre-prandial selection of appetisers or hors-d'oeuvre similar to a smörgasbord but in bite-sized pieces, usually served with vodka; also spelt zakouski or zazuski.

Zest – thinly-peeled rind of citrus fruits such as oranges, lemons and limes.

EQUIPMENT AND UTENSILS

Avli – traditional Greek beehive-shaped oven used for baking, stewing and roasting, used extensively in Greek and Turkish cookery.

Bain-marie – (i) container of water for keeping food hot; (ii) a shallow container of water for cooking foods in the oven to ensure an even temperature.

Balti pan – versatile wok-shaped pan measuring 23–36 cm in diameter, made of cast iron, stainless steel, or tin-lined copper; used extensively in Northern India for cooking a variety of dishes in the balti style.

Fig. 1   Balti pan

Blini pan – small cast-iron or omelette type pan, 10 cm in diameter, used for making traditional Russian blinis or bliny.

Braisière – braising pan with a deep, close-fitting lid and usually two handles.

Brochette – skewer, whether an ornate one to put in front of customers, a plain stainless steel one or one made of bamboo.

Chinese wok cooker or **Chinese stove** – specially designed stove to accommodate the shape of a wok. Gas jets are set in the midst of a shallow water container used for reducing the high temperature required for stir-frying.

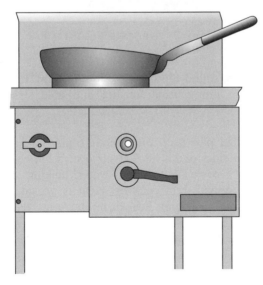

Fig. 2   Chinese wok cooker

Chinois – a fine mesh conical strainer for producing very smooth thickened liquids.

Chopsticks – made of plastic, wood or bamboo, lacquered or unlacquered or of ivory or metal, approximately 30 cm in length. Used for eating and for cooking foods instead of spoons, forks and even whisks.

Cocotte – shallow earthenware or porcelain dish with lid, made in several sizes, for oven-to-table use.

Couscous steamer – made in various sizes in the form of a double-lined saucepan for cooking couscous (q.v.).

Fig. 3 Couscous steamer

Dariole – small, deep, round mould with sloping sides, made of aluminium and copper with tin lining, used for hot and cold sweets and savoury mousses.

Degchi – two-handled pan used throughout India, made of brass or aluminium with straight sides and a lid that fits over a horizontal rim. The pan may be sealed with a paste of flour and water, making it a type of steam cooker for what is termed dum cooking. Heat is provided by placing hot coals onto the lid, thus providing heat from above as well as from below.

Dim sum or **dum steamer** – designed for cooking Chinese dumplings and snack items.

Gas-fired duck oven – oven specially designed for the traditional way of roasting Peking duck by hanging them on hooks at the top.

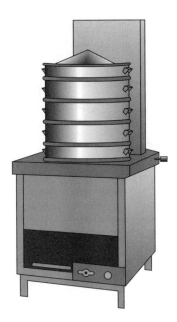

Fig. 4   Dim sum steamer

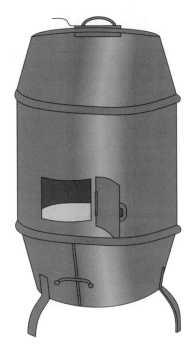

Fig. 5   Gas duck oven

Hashi – Japanese term for chopsticks (q.v.).

Jezve – long-handled coffee pot used for making Greek/Turkish coffee.

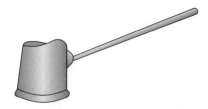

Fig. 6 Jezve

Karahi – another name for balti pan (q.v.).

Marmite – a lidded earthenware soup bowl made in individual and large sizes.

Mushiki – a stacking steamer of several sections made of bamboo or metal, used in Japanese cookery.

Paellera – special two-handled, shallow-sided pan, approximately 46 cm in diameter made especially for the cooking of paella, the traditional Spanish speciality.

Fig. 7 Paellera

Plat à sauter – round shallow pan for frying, made in several sizes in stainless steel and copper lined with tin.

Ramekin or **ramequin** – individual porcelain dish used for potted foods and egg dishes.

Ravier – an oval or oblong hors-d'oeuvre dish.

Rondeau – large, shallow, lidded pan used for making basic sauces in bulk.

Sacrometer – instrument used to measure the density of a syrup when making sorbets and fruit water ices.

Salamander grill – type of grill with an overhead source of heat, either electricity, gas or a combination of the two.

Sauteuse – shallow pan with sloping sides made in various sizes in stainless steel and copper lined with tin, used mainly for sauces and reductions.

Shin seol ro – name given to a Korean receptacle in which food is cooked and from which it is served at table. Ornate versions are generally made of brass or anodised aluminium. They are manufactured in different sizes with a central chimney for holding hot charcoal. Food is placed into a surrounding moat, moistened with stock and cooked to completion.

Fig. 8   Shin seol ro

Sushioke – shallow round bamboo dish for serving the traditional Japanese dish of sushi.

Tamago-yaki nabe – rectangular frying pan used to make traditional Japanese rolled omelettes.

Fig. 9   Tamago-yaki nabe

Tandoori oven or cooking pot – gas- or charcoal-heated oven pot made of clay, available in a range of sizes. Used extensively in Indian cookery for the slow cooking of bread, meat, fish and poultry dishes.

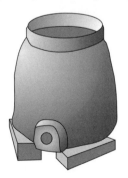

Fig. 10   Tandoori oven

Tannour – beehive-shaped clay oven used in Indian cookery.

Tempura pan – round iron pan with a built-in draining grid, used for deep-fried items in Japanese cookery.

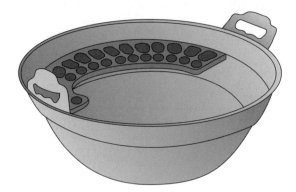

Fig. 11   Tempura pan

Terrine – earthenware dish, available in many shapes and sizes, for cooking and presenting pâté.

Timbale – deep round silver dish, the outer part holding crushed ice or hot water to keep food contained in the inner part chilled or hot.

Wok – metal pan with a curved base used extensively in Asian cookery; available in many sizes it may be made of stainless steel or iron and is designed to give the maximum heat contact necessary for stir-fry method of cookery.

Fig. 12   Wok

Weights, Measures and Conversions

Weights

	Metric grams	Imperial ounces	
	28.35	1	(16 drams)
	50	2	
	100	3½	
	125	4	(¼ lb)
	200	7	
(0.25 kg)	250	9	
	325	12	(¾ lb)
	454	16	(1 lb)
(0.5 kg)	500	18	

kilograms (kg)	lb	
0.9	2	
1.0	2⅕	(2lb 3oz)
1.33	3	
2	4¼	
2.5	5⅜	(5lb 6oz)
3.2	7	
6.3	14	
25.4	56	
50	112	(1 cwt)

Capacity

	millilitres (ml)	fluid ounces (fl oz)	
(1 dl)	100	3½	
	150	5	(¼ pt) (1 gill)
	300	10	(½ pt)
(approx 6 dl)	568	20	(1 pt) (4 gills)

litres (l)	pints (pt)	
1	1¾	(35 fl oz)
1.5	2½	
2	3½	
4	7	
4.8	8	(1 gal)
9	16	(2 gals)

millilitres (ml)	spoons
5	1 teaspoon (tsp)
15	1 tablespoon (tbs)

Length

	inches (in)	centimetres (cm)	
	2	5	
	6	15	
(1 foot)	12	30	
	18	45	
(1 yard)	36	90	
	39¼	100	(1 metre)
	72	1.8 m	

Oven temperatures

Gas Mark	°F	°C	Definition	Uses
Low	200	100	very cool	
1/4	225	110	very cool	estouffades
1/2	250	130	cool/slow	meringues
1	275	140	cool	milk puddings, egg custard
2	300	150	cool	pies with raw fillings
3	325	170	moderate	rich fruit cake, braised fish, shallow poached fish
4	350	180	moderate	braising, stewing, Genoese
5	375	190	moderate	shortbread, oven poaching
6	400	200	hot	roast meat, Swiss roll, baked potatoes, pot-roasting
7	425	220	quite hot	Yorkshire pudding, choux paste, scones, roast potatoes
8	450	230	very hot	⎫ yeast goods,
9	475	240	very hot	⎭ puff pastry
10	575	300	extremely hot	to glaze and gratinate

Sugar boiling temperatures – using a sugar boiling thermometer

Definition	°C	Uses
short thread	105	candied fruit
long thread	110	marrons glacé, crystallised fruits
soft ball	115	fondant, marzipan
medium ball	121	candy, fudge, nougat
hard ball	125	butterscotch, toffee, Italian meringue
soft crack	137	blown sugar fruits, pulled sugar
hard crack	155	spun, dipping, glazed fruits
caramel	182	toffees, crème caramel

American weights – dry and liquid

American	Metric	Imperial
1/4 cup liquid	60 ml	2 fl oz
1/3 cup liquid	80 ml	3 fl oz
1/2 cup liquid	125 ml	4 fl oz
1 cup liquid	250 ml	9 fl oz
2 cups (1 pint)	500 ml (approx)	16 fl oz
4 cups (1 quart)	1 litre (approx)	1 3/5 pints (32 fl oz)
1 cup butter – 1 stick	125 g	4 oz
1 cup flour, sifted	150 g	6 oz
1 cup sugar, castor	200 g	7 oz
1 cup breadcrumbs, fresh	100 g	3 1/2 oz
1 cup corn syrup	235 ml	11 fl oz
1 cup cream, milk	235 ml	8 fl oz
1 cup rice	200 g	7 oz
1 cup gelatine, powdered	15 g	1/2 oz

Australian weights are based on 1 oz equals 30 g.
In the UK most recipe books use the formula 1 oz equals 25 g.

Temperatures

°C (Celsius)	°F (Fahrenheit)
−17.8°	0°
−10°	14°
0°	32° freezing point
10°	50°
25°	72°
37°	98.4° = normal body temperature
40°	104°
50°	122°
75°	162°
100°	212° boiling point

To convert °C to °F multiply the Celsius number by 9, divide by 5 then add 32.
Degrees Celsius are the same as degrees Centigrade.

Measuring with an ice cream scoop

Scoop number	Weight in grams
6	170
8	120
10	90
12	75
16	55
20	40
30	28
60	15

Can sizes

Can size	Gross weight	Drained	Sample commodity
A10	3–3.5 kg	2.724–3.178 kg	apples, baked beans, vegetables
A6	2.7 kg	2.724 kg	tomato purée, solid pack apricots
A5	1–1.3 kg	1.136 ml	fruit juices
A2$\frac{1}{2}$	0.6–0.9 kg	704–908 g	fruits
A2	510–680 g	579–704 g	fruits and vegetables
A1	450–500 g	329–454 g	baked beans, fish, soup

Gastronorm container size

Module	Dimensions
full size	530 mm × 325 mm × 25 mm deep
double size	650 mm × 530 mm × 25 mm deep
half size	325 mm × 265 mm
quarter size	265 mm × 162 mm

These containers are available in various depths according to use: 40, 65, 100, 150 and 200 mm.

Sacrometer

A sacrometer is an instrument for measuring the sugar content of a liquid such as stock syrup. It is a hollow glass tube weighted with lead shot, which makes it stand upright in the liquid, and is calibrated in degrees Baumé or Brix. The floating ball indicates the density on a marked scale. A sacrometer is used in the making of sorbets, fruit ices, hot meringue and canning and bottling fruit. A stock syrup based on 1 kg is boiled until it reaches the required degree, as follows:

Water	Degrees	Uses
500 ml	14	Granités
900 ml	16	Sorbets
1 litre	18	Marquises
1.1 litres	20	Compotes
1.2 litres	28	Bombes

Small amounts

Coins of the realm may be used instead of very small weights which are easily mislaid.

Coin	Weight (g)
5 p	2.5
1 p	5
20 p	5
2 p	10
£1	10
50 p	15

A pinch of salt taken between normal fingers is approximately 10 g

Capacity

To calculate how much liquid a saucepan or stockpot will hold, measure the radius, double it, multiply by the depth and 3.142 (pi). The number of cubic centimetres (cm³) is the amount it will hold in millilitres. A straight-sided pan with a radius of 11 cm and a depth of 7 cm will hold 2 litres of liquid.

One kilogram is the weight of 1 litre of pure water at 4°C. One litre is equivalent to 1,000 millilitres, or 1,000 cubic centimetres.

Hygiene regulations for ice cream

The regulations which govern the production and sale of ice cream to the general public must be strictly adhered to and all establishments which make ice cream for sale must be licensed by the Environmental Health Officer.

The mixture must be pasteurised by heating to 65°C for 30 minutes, 71°C for 10 minutes. 80°C for 15 seconds or 140°C for 2 seconds. It must then be cooled to 71°C within $1\frac{1}{2}$ hours and kept at this temperature until it is frozen. It must be stored at a temperature not exceeding –2°C. The mixture must contain not less than 5% fat and 7% milk solids other than fat.

Index

Note: Recipes marked with an asterisk include full dish assessment together with an analysis of possible problems, causes and solutions.